T0294846

A Study of Income Distribution in China

Cai Fang, Zhang Juwei et al.

Translated by Wen Yayun

Paths International Ltd

中国社会科学出版社
CHINA SOCIAL SCIENCES PRESS

Contents

Chapter IV   Wage Changes and Wage Growth in China: Should Wage Grow? / 67

Chapter V   Tax System Reform and National Income Distribution / 93

Chapter VI   State-owned Enterprises and National Income Distribution / 121

Chapter VII　Economic Growth and Residents' Income Distribution--How to Achieve China's Residents' Income Growth / 155

Chapter VIII　Impact of Labor Market Changes on Income Distribution / 185

Chapter IX　Informal Employment and Income Gap between Urban Employees / 203

Chapter XIII　Conclusion and Suggestions　/ 331

References: / 357

Preface

ZHANG Juwei[1]

As the country with the fastest economic growth in the world, China is faced with the extremely complex income distribution showing both the commonalities of market economies with rapid development and the particularity of China's institutional mechanism. To study and understand income distribution, it is not only necessary to start with the general law of the development of market economy but with China's unique system and mechanism. Otherwise, it will be difficult to clearly depict the essence of China's income distribution.

World economic development shows that in the early rapid development of developed countries, there appeared the widening income gap, and then with the continuous improved systems and rules and improved economic development, the income gap began to decline when reaching a certain stage, forming the so-called Kuznets inverted "U" curve. However, strictly speaking, the inverted "U" curve of income distribution developed countries experienced is still a hypothesis, neither proved by strict economic theory nor confirmed by empirical research.

At present, China's income distribution seems to be partially interpreting the Kuznets curve, showing the trend of widening income gap with its rapid economic development. In this case, if the Kuznets hypothesis is correct, it is natural to think that the widening income gap will eventually narrow automatically with improved economic development and the income distribution can improve automatically through development. However, the evolution of

---

[1] ZHANG Juwei, Director of the Institute of Population and Labor Economics of the Chinese Academy of Social Sciences, Research Fellow, Doctoral Advisor.

income distribution in developed countries shows that the process of income gap widening and then narrowing is not entirely a matter of course but a matter of the continuous improved institutional rules. In this sense, the Kuznets curve changes not only with economic development but with the systems and rules to a greater extent. In fact, so far, no international experience has proven that the widening income gap will automatically narrow simply because of improved economic development. Therefore, income distribution studies should start not only with the relationship between economic development and income distribution from economic perspective but with the relationship between institutional rules and income distribution from an institutional perspective.

China's implementation of a socialist market economy determines that China's income distribution has its own unique law in marketization. China's basic economic system changes into public ownership as its main body with a variety of economic components developing together, requiring its income distribution to change into distribution according to both work and its production factors. Therefore, from the perspective of distribution system, China has both its commonalities and particularity compared with other market economies. Among them, distribution according to production factors reflects the distribution law of market economy and distribution according to work reflects the distribution characteristics of socialist public economy. Different distribution modes will inevitably result in different distribution. China's income distribution shares that of average market economy and particularity of its basic economic system. These two is intertwined and influence each other, thus leading to the complexity of China's income distribution.

With the transition from planned economy to market economy, China's basic economic system has changed from single public ownership to public ownership as the main body with a variety of economic components developing together and the distribution system has also changed from distribution according to work into distribution according to both work and various production factors. In this process, the relatively average income distribution pattern according to work formed under public ownership will be broken and the distribution mechanism of contribution according to production factors will be gradually formed with the income gap widening, giving rise to serious income distribution.

It should be said that China's current income distribution is deeply rooted in the reform of China's institutional mechanism and the change in distribution mode. As production determines distribution, income distribution is, to some extent, the embodiment of production in distribution. Over 6 decades since the founding of the people's Republic of China, China has experienced several changes in its ownership structure, bringing about changes in both production and distribution.

Between 1949 and 1956, the property of the Kuomintang government was owned by the people's government and the land of landlords confiscated belonged to the peasants, forming the ownership structure of the coexistence of various forms of ownership under the leadership of state-owned economy. This ownership structure has brought about great production vitality and rapid development of national economy, resulting in the first period of rapid development in the history of The Peoples's Republic of China. Between 1949 and 1956, the wage of workers in units owned by the whole people more than doubled with greatly improved living standards of the people. Meanwhile, income distribution remained within a reasonable limit. However, such rapid development did not last too long and the ownership structure went through another change.

After 1956, with the socialist transformation of private ownership of means of production, a single public ownership was formed, on the basis of which a socialist planned economy system was formed. The purpose of planned economy system based on single public ownership was to further speed up economic development only to result in economic stagnation and people's living difficulties. For example, in the 22 years between 1957 and 1978, the nominal wage of workers in units owned by the whole people grew by only 7 yuan (from 637 yuan to 644 yuan). Real wages in 1978 was only 85.2% of that in 1957, a decrease of 14.8% in 22 years (Zhao Dexin, 2000). In contrast to economic stagnation, the distribution pattern of income equalization was formed with the elimination of private ownership, the formation of a single public ownership and distribution according to work. Thus, China, a planned economy, became one of the world's poorest countries with the narrowest income gap in the world. It must be pointed out that such a poor but equalized society is an unfairly-distributed society since the distribution pattern of income equalization in its own way was achieved at the cost of economic efficiency, resulting from a distortion of factor allocation by subsidizing less contributors from greater contributors.

The evenly distributed poor society is not a socialist society. Since the reform and opening up in 1978, China has undergone another change in the ownership structure, which also marks a new historical period for China's development. During this period, Chinese Communist Party explored and formed the theory of the primary stage of socialism, perfected the basic socialist economic system, thus a socialist road with Chinese characteristics. In the primary stage of socialism, because of backward, low multi-level productivity, it is objectively required that other economic components other than the public economy be part of economic development, such as individual economy, private economy and foreign capital economy. Therefore, since the reform and opening up, China has vigorously encouraged and supported the development of non-public economic components. After more than three decades' of practice, Chinese society has gradually broke away from the fetters of a single public ownership structure on productive forces with public ownership as its main body, various forms of ownership coexisting, various economic components complementing each other and developing together. In the past 30 years, China's economy has grown at an average annual rate of about 10%, creating a miracle in the history of world economic development. At present, China's economy ranks second in the world with a GDP per capita of more than $8000, making it one of the middle-income countries. Of course, with the rapid economic development, China's highly equalized average income distribution in the past also changed fundamentally during this period with ever widening income gap, its Gini coefficient as high as 0.47, changing from the world's most equalized income country to a country with a serious income gap.

It should be said that the current income distribution is both completely out of proportion to and unsuitable for the basic socialist economic system. In theory, the social system with public ownership as its main body with various economic components developing together is conducive to not only economic development but also to the formation of a fair and reasonable income distribution pattern. In practice, various economic components have been part of China's market competition, a huge driving force of economic growth, a highly developed and competitive economy. In this regard, China's basic economic system has shown its advantages in promoting economic growth with its "institutional dividends", but fails to do so in income distribution. The income obtained by public ownership as the main economic component through participation in the market is supposed to be a natural barrier to the widening income gap, on the contrary, there has been a serious income distribution, the cause of which is the key to understanding China's income distribution.

China's current income distribution is characterized by the widening income gap and its inequality at the micro level and the imbalance of the basic income distribution pattern at the macro level: the low proportion of labor remuneration in initial distribution and the low proportion of residents' income in the national income. The seemingly different macro and micro situation is closely related. To a large extent, China's widening income gap and inequality are rooted in the imbalance of macro distribution pattern.

In the current income distribution pattern, the slow growth of labor remuneration and the rapid growth of capital income result in the ever declining labor share and the rapid growth of capital income share in initial distribution. According to the data of funds flow table by the National Bureau of Statistics, labor share decreased from 54.56% to 47.6% between 1992 and 2008 while the enterprise operating retained (profit) rose from 22.58% to 27.78% and the income of all capital factors rose from 30.93% to 36.4%. In national income distribution pattern, the increase in capital factor income share has different implications to personal income gap in different institutional societies. As the difference in individual possession of private capital is much higher than difference in labor factor under complete private ownership economic system, the increase of capital income will give rise to widening income gap. However, as capital income obtained by public economic component does not belong to individuals, the increase of its income will not directly lead to the income gap between individuals; on the contrary, fair distribution of its income will play a role in curbing the widening income gap. However, public economic component in China's basic economic system fails to do so.

Why is there still a widening income gap in China with public ownership as the main body of its basic economic system? There are two major causes here. The first cause, the major driving force of the income gap is that the increasing capital income is owned by individuals with the declining proportion of state-owned economy in China's economic component, the so-called "the decline of state-owned economy and the growth of private economy". After more than three decades of rapid economic development and support and encouragement of non-state-owned economy, the pattern of the dominant position of state-owned economic component has changed: from a functional perspective, public economic component still seems to dominate the lifeline of economic development, but from a structural perspective public economic component is on the decline. At the beginning of the reform and opening up in 1978, China's state-owned economy was in absolute dominant position, accounting for 99% of the gross national product with only 1% of the non-public economy. China's capital pattern has changed significantly which is mainly owned and used by the state and collective in that residents' capital has exceeded state-owned capital, even greater than the total amount of both state-owned capital and collective capital. Research shows that, among the total capital of RMB 28.7 trillion yuan in 2000, the state, collective, individual residents, Hong Kong, Macao and Taiwan and foreign capital accounts for 34%, 12%, 43%, and 11% respectively (Fan Gang, Yao Zhizhong, 2002). In recent years, the acceleration of "the decline of state-owned economy and the growth of private economy" has brought about the further decline in the proportion of public economic component in China's economic structure. Research shows that in 2008, the national capital assets totaled 14.4078 billion yuan, state-owned capital, collective capital, individual capital and foreign capital accounting for 10.50%, 2.76%, 79.92% and 6.82% respectively (Li Jiguang, 2011). Accordingly, this change in capital structure will inevitably lead to the change in income distribution pattern. The increasing share of non-state private capital in national income capital and huge differences in private capital share has become the major cause of widening income gap.

The second cause of the income gap is that without referring to the principle of distribution according to work, the income distribution of China's state-owned economic component is exclusively enjoyed by certain groups of people while all the other citizens, owners of rights and interests, do not get their due income so that the income of state-owned economic component which is supposed to narrow the income gap, to some extent, widens the income distribution gap, instead. The following aspects illustrate the point. First, employees' income of state-owned enterprises, state-owned monopoly enterprises in particular, are higher than the average income of the whole society, and enterprise executives are paid an amazingly high annual income, which widens the income gap among members of society. Second, profit of state-owned enterprises is mainly for the enterprise's internal circulation without benefiting owners of state-owned enterprises. In the past, state-owned enterprises did not pay dividends to the state for a long time. Although they have done so since 2007 with a low proportion, only 5% to 15% of the enterprise's profits, nearly 90% of the after-tax profits still belongs to the enterprise. Third, the distribution system of state-owned resource income and monopolistic income is not reasonable. The profits of industries including oil, coal, black and non-ferrous metal mining, banking, insurance, telecommunications, tobacco, etc. are one-fold or several times higher than that of average competitive industry, most of which is resource or monopolistic income and should be part of public finance for social welfare. But for a long time the profits of these industries are basically owned by enterprises. Despite the introduction of resource tax reform, its limited coverage and implementation cannot solve the income distribution problem.

To sum up, China's current income distribution has been caused by complicated factors, such as market mechanism itself, systems and rules, economic development stage itself. China's income distribution is characterized by the following aspects.

First, China's income distribution is characterized by the same widening income gap as in the rapidly developed market economies, a common problem in development. It's a distribution law that production factors obtain income according to their contribution and the means to realize effective resource allocation in market economy. China's economy has transformed from planned economy to market economy in which market mechanism plays an increasingly important role in determining income distribution. It is inevitable that there is a difference in the income of market subjects due to the difference in the quantity and quality of production factors. In initial distribution, the increasing difference in the quantity and quality difference of production factors among residents is the objective basis and basic driving force of the current widening income gap. From the point of view of labor factors, labor supply of simple work exceeds its demand while the supply of high-skilled workers is insufficient so that there is slow growth of labor remuneration of low-skilled workers and rapid income growth of high human capital endowment. Since there is still a capitalization trend of technology and management factors related to human capital, the remuneration of senior managers and senior professionals and technical personnel is more determined by their scarcity, resulting in a number of working "emperors" and high-paid strata, widening the income gap among laborers. From the perspective of capital factors, "the decline of state economy and the growth of private economy" in China's economic composition has enabled social assets and wealth to go to private sector and capital to go to few people of private sector so that the income of the private capital from the whole society goes to few people, thus further widening the income gap and the gap between rich and poor. From the perspective of redistribution, China's tax system is mainly indirect tax with only a small proportion of direct tax, which fails to regulate income distribution. Indirect tax-based tax systems have given rise to heavy taxes for average laborer and light taxes for high income groups. Therefore, China's current income distribution pattern is closely related to the basic structure and characteristics of its tax system to some extent. At the same time, China's social security system is not perfect enough with less protection for low-income groups, failing to narrow the income gap. The small proportion of transfer payment in China fails to have any redistribution effect. Therefore, the failure of China's redistribution system to regulate income distribution is also responsible for China's widening income gap. Thus it can be said that China's initial distribution is efficiency-oriented, resulting in a more serious income distribution issue, and that redistribution supposed to be fair fails to make up for the income gap, and that both initial distribution and redistribution is more efficiency-oriented without being fair.

Second, closely related to its basic economic system, China's income distribution has its own characteristics, unfairness. Specifically, unfairness is mainly reflected in the fact that the income of China's public economy is overused by certain groups of people without referring to the principle of distribution according to work. At the same time, wealth and assets supposed to belong to the whole people are taken as private property by few people through improper and illegal means, widening the income gap and the gap between rich and poor, the most serious income distribution problem in China and the biggest threat to social stability.

Third, China's income distribution is a problem in transitional period. At the current stage of rapid industrialization and modernization, economic development determines income distribution and higher capital income is brought about by investment-driven economic growth. At the same time, China transforms from dual economy to unitary economy in which rural labor force continues to migrate to cities and towns and unlimited labor supply has become limited and labor remuneration grows low and slow. As China transforms from planned economy to market economy, there are not only market forces but the influence of planned economy in income distribution. The rules of income distribution are not perfect, which widens the inequality of income distribution. The transitional characteristics of China's income distribution means that it is necessary to solve China's income distribution problem from the point of view of development so that any China's hasty practices may do harm to its economic and social development.

This book is the result of the major project of the National Social Science Fund. This project on China's income distribution, one of the four major issues when central government leaders came to the Chinese Academy of Social Sciences in spring festival of 2011, becomes the task of the Institute of Population and Labor Economics. According to the plan, the project will be aided by experts from other institutes of the Academy of Social Sciences and well-known experts from other institutions outside the Academy of Social Sciences. Professor Li Yang, then vice president of the Academy of Social Sciences, presided over a series of seminars, attended by both members of the research group of the Institute of Population and Labor Economics and Professor Zhu Ling and Professor Wei Zhong of the Institute of Economics of the Academy of Social Sciences and Professor Li Shi of Beijing Normal University. After clarifying many issues, the research team provided guidance and suggestions on how to do the research. This book, based on a study on China's income distribution conducted by the research team over the past few years, has fulfilled its goal as some of its published papers have become policy recommendations affirmed and instructed by central government leaders as internal reports. Finally, on the occasion of the publication of this book, I'd like to extend our gratitude to the leaders and experts who have provided help and support for this research, especially Professor Li Yang, Professor Zhu Ling, Professor Li Shi and Professor Wei Zhong who have participated in the discussion of this project.

Chapter I

China's Income Trap and Middle-Income Trap

CAI Fang, WANG Meiyan[1]

China will face a series of tough challenges on its way from a middle income country to a high income one in the face of economic slowdown. Only by narrowing the widening income gap can China have a common understanding of reform and development among its people, enhance social cohesion, and thus maintain sustained economic growth and social development. This chapter sheds light on the significance of deepening the reform in initial distribution and redistribution by discussing China's economic and social challenges, the relationship between income gap and the middle-income trap as well as China's current income distribution.

---

1   CAI Fang, Vice-President of the Chinese Academy of Social Sciences, Academician, Doctoral Advisor; WANG Meiyan, Research Fellow of the Institute of Population and Labor Economics, Doctoral Advisor

I. China's Middle-Income Trap

During its three decades of reform and opening up, China has achieved an average annual economic growth rate of 9.8%. It's predicted by both Chinese and foreign researchers that at that rate China will soon overtake the U.S. in terms of aggregate GDP, becoming the world's largest economy. According to IMF's forecast[1], China's aggregate GDP at purchasing power parity (PPP) will grow from $11.3 trillion in 2011 to $19 trillion in 2016, accounting for 18% of the world economy while the U.S.'s aggregate GDP will grow from $15.2 trillion to $18.8 trillion, accounting for only 17.7% of the world economy.

The IMF's forecast is justifiable as it is based on China's growth experience. According to the economies of scale in terms of exchange rates--the conventional statistics, China's aggregate GDP ranked 10th in 1990, 7th in 1995 by surpassing Canada, Spain and Brazil and 6th in 2000 by surpassing Italy. During the first decade of the 21st century, China surpassed France, Britain and Germany and finally Japan, thus becoming world's second largest economy after U.S. in 2010. In 2011, China's aggregate GDP reached $7298.15 billion, accounting for 48.4% of U.S.'s GDP and 10.5% of the world's GDP. However, China will still remain an upper-middle-income country for quite a long time. The biggest challenge for China now is how to develop from a middle income country to a high income one.

According to the target set by Chinese Communist Party's 18th National People's Congress, China's aggregate GDP will double between 2010 and 2020 at a growth rate slightly below an annual average of 7%. Given that the annual population growth rate for between 2010 and 2020 is only about 0.3% and that GDP grows by about 7.3% a year, GDP per capita will double from $4,382 in 2010 to $8,764 by 2020 at comparable prices. Even so, China will still be an upper-middle-income country. If there were a significant growth slowdown after 2020, China would remain a middle income country for quite a long time.

---

1 3 .http://www.imf.org/external/data.htm

In economic history, countries with a rapid economic growth tend to experience a significant decline in growth rate afterwards. According to Eichengreen et al. (2011) who analyzed long-term historical data of quite a large number of countries, when GDP per capita of a country reached $17,000 US calculated according to purchasing power parity of year 2005, its economic growth would slow down with the average annual growth rate declining from 6.8% to 3.3%, a decline rate as high as 51.5%. Both developed and middle-income countries will experience significant growth slowdowns. Middle-income countries with significant slowdowns will not be able to become high income countries at the same pace as they escaped the poverty trap. Once a country stays too long in the middle income stage, the threshold for entry into a high-income country, it can be said that this country has been caught in the middle-income trap.

During the reform and opening up, China with its superior population factor has achieved unprecedented rapid economic growth and outshone other countries in the world economy. But since 2011, the absolute decline in the working age population between 15 and 59, the reverse demographic structure and the vanishing demographic dividend have given rise to the inevitable sharp decline in the economic growth rate. That is, due to the adverse changes in both labor supply and capital accumulation, China's potential GDP growth rate will also decline even if the trend of productivity increase remains unchanged. China's potential growth rate between 1978 and 1994, between 1995 and 2010, the 12th Five-Year Plan and 13th Five-Year Plan was estimated at 9.66%, 10.34%, 7.55% and 6.2% respectively (Lu Yang & Cai Fang, 2013).

As an economy makes full use of the sources of growth in a specific development stage and enters a new economic development stage, the decline in the economic growth rate is an inevitable and acceptable result of economic law. But accompanied by a series of phenomena not conducive to tapping new sources of sustainable growth, the significant growth slowdown could turn into growth stagnation. A number of interrelated factors put China at real risk of getting caught in the middle-income trap.

China's demographic transition is characterized by the fact of "getting old before getting rich", that is, China with a low level of per capita income is aging more extensively and more rapidly. According to the data of the United Nations, China's population aged 60 and above as a developing country accounted for 12.3% of the total population in 2010, compared with an average of 7.5% for developing countries excluding China in the same period. Among other challenges, this aging challenge undoubtedly leads to China's premature growth slowdown. By the same caliber, China's GDP per capita is only equivalent to 67.5% of the international average deceleration point per capita income benchmark in 2010 taken as a turning point for China's growth slowdown. That is, premature aging gives rise to premature growth slowdown. More importantly, at the start of the slowdown in the middle-income stage, China is characterized by factors related to the middle-income trap, such as a widening income gap which has not improved significantly.

II. Income Distribution and Middle-Income Trap

The relationship between income distribution and middle income trap can be viewed from two aspects. On one hand, if rapid economic growth slows down or even stagnates, income growth slows down or stagnates accordingly. No empirical evidence shows that income distribution can improve in the event of economic slowdown. On the contrary, the income gap tends to widen due to stagnant economic growth and stagnant income growth. On the other hand, if reaching a certain limit and not curbed by effective policies and measures, the widening income gap accompanied by economic growth can result in social instability and reduced social cohesion without a consensus on reform direction and measures, which poses as an obstacle to economic growth and causes further slowdown or even stagnation.

Early middle-income countries such as Latin American and some Asian countries were never able to rank among high-income countries as their economic growth was slow or even stagnant. When the cake is unable to continue to grow, it's impossible to share economic growth. According to the logic of political economy, in the absence of good and effective system, the rich can have greater bargaining power to obtain a larger share of the cake, causing income and wealth accumulation of the Matthew Effect and thus widening income gap. Well-motivated or in-need-of-votes politicians often find it hard to keep their promises to improve income because of stagnant economic growth, only to be caught in a dilemma of politically populist policy (Dornbusch et al., 1989). The country is thus trapped in a middle-income trap characterized by frequent social unrest and political instability as a result of widening income gap.

The experience of countries in middle-income traps also suggests that serious inequalities in resource allocation and income distribution coexisting with stagnant economic growth result in vested interest groups making every effort to maintain this distribution pattern beneficial to themselves only, which, as a result, makes the accumulated disadvantages of the system too severe to overcome that are not conducive to escaping the middle-income trap. This system enables the vested interest groups to make corresponding economic and social policies, making economic growth stagnant, making it hard to change the system, and solidifying the system not conducive to economic growth. Accordingly, production factors are allocated in accordance with maximization principle of vested interest instead of principle of the highest productivity. Thus, any country in this situation will never be able to escape the middle income trap and may even fall back into the low income country.

So far, China's economic growth has been participatory on the whole. Although the widening income gap has caused widespread social concern and dissatisfaction of the middle-low income groups, each income group has more or less improved and the existing income gap is still bearable when the cake is still able to continue to grow. Although distribution changes among different income groups shows the widening gap, whether in terms of per capita disposable income of Chinese urban residents or in terms of per capita living consumption, there are no significant distribution changes. In other words, as the income gap widens, there has been increases in both income and consumption within each income group, which, however, tends to change when the cake is no longer able to grow. That is, when insufficient increment caused by economic slowdown makes it impossible to provide equal distribution, income share of the powerful groups is further expanded and income distribution of low-income groups will definitely deteriorate, inevitably causing widespread social discontent and typical Latin American dilemma.

On one hand, the improvement of income distribution must take economic growth as the premise. International experiences of both Latin America and developed countries show that economic growth and an overall increase in per capita income are conducive to the reduction of income inequality. For example, in the first decade of the 21st century, some Latin American countries, such as Brazil, has achieved better economic growth, and accordingly, their Gini coefficient has declined significantly. Since the 1970s, significant growth slowdown in the U. S. has brought about widening income gap, the largest in the developed countries. On the other hand, widening income gap can only be curbed and eventually narrowed by major reforms breaking the income distribution pattern of vested interests groups.

III. Debate over and Empirical Research on Income Distribution

According to official statistics, China's income gap is wide by international standards, but it has begun to narrow and the Gini coefficient has begun to get lower in recent years. The official Gini coefficient rose from 0.29 in 1985 to 0.42 in 1995 and to 0.49 in 2008 and declined to 0.47 in 2012. Some international research teams come to the same judgment through empirical research. However, studies suggest that China's Gini coefficient is much higher than that and that there is no significant sign for its getting lower. For example, Gan Li, with his team's unique research, calculated that China's Gini coefficient in 2010 was as high as 0.61 (Gan Li, 2012).

In addition, through investigation and estimation, Wang Xiaolu found that China's urban residents' hidden income reached 15.1 trillion yuan in 2011, which is not covered in regular statistics (Wang Xiaolu 2013b). According to him, the real per capita disposable income of urban residents in 2011 was twice that of official statistics and more than 70% of hidden income was owned by the top 20% of high-income residents. According to my surveys in 2005, 2008 and 2011, hidden income is expanding. Be this huge hidden income divided into different residents' income groups in extreme inequality, there will no doubt be greater income inequality.

Holders of different views on income distribution tend to reject the opposite conclusion (see Song Xiaowu et al. 2013). However, a conclusion of such a complex economic and social phenomenon as income distribution cannot be drawn with simple logic. In fact, both theoretically and empirically, seemingly opposing views should be taken into consideration so as to get more information. The data surveyed and published by the National Bureau of Statistics are accurate and authoritative in reflecting residents' regular income, labor income in particular, with an underestimation of property or asset income, especially gray income. So Wang Xiaolu's (2013a; 2013b) research data can serve as a supplement to that of the National Bureau of Statistics.

Wang Xiaolu's research estimates the per capita disposable urban residents' income in 2005 and 2008 by taking hidden income into account with grouping analysis. By taking hidden income into account with model analysis, Wang Xiaolu (2013b) estimates the per capita disposable urban residents' income in 2008 and in 2011 was 32,154 yuan and 43,663 yuan respectively, twice the per capita disposable urban residents' income published by the National Bureau of Statistics. Based on this, it can be estimated that the average urban residents' income in 2011 was 21,853 yuan and that the per capita urban residents' hidden income in 2009, 2010 and 2012 can be estimated with an an average annual growth rate of 10.1%.

According to Wang Xiaolu's grouping analysis (2013a) by taking hidden income into account, the per capita disposable urban residents' income in 2005 and in 2008 is 19,730 yuan and 35462 yuan respectively, 1.9 times and 2.2 times the per capita disposable urban residents' income published by the National Bureau of Statistics. According to the calculation, the per capita urban residents' hidden income in 2005 and in 2008 was 9,237 yuan and 19,681 yuan respectively. Based on the average annual growth rate of per capita urban residents' hidden income between 2005 and 2008 of 28.7%, the per capita urban residents' hidden income in 2006 and in 2007 can be estimated. Assuming that the per capita urban residents' income grows at the same rate between 1997 and 2004, the per capita urban residents' hidden income in these years can be estimated.

As a result, the per capita urban residents' hidden income between 1997 and 2012 can be estimated. Urban residents were divided into seven groups: lowest income (10%), lower income (10%), lower-middle income (20%), middle income (20%), upper middle income (20%), higher income (10%) and highest income (10%) by the National Bureau of Statistics according to the per capita disposable income. According to Wang Xiaolu (2013b)'s estimation of the distribution of hidden income in all income groups in 2008 and 2011, there isn't much distribution difference between these two years. Assume that the distribution of hidden income in 2010 and 2012 is the same as that in 2011 and that the distribution of hidden income in 2009 and before 2008 is the same as that in 2008, the hidden income of each income group over the years can be calculated. By adding hidden income to the per capita disposable urban residents' income published by the National Bureau of Statistics, the per capita disposable income (which is called the estimated per capita disposable income) of every income group including hidden income can be estimated.

According to the nature of the data, here's the inter-group ratio (see Chart 1-1) between the estimated per capita disposable income and the per capita disposable income published by the National Bureau of Statistics. First, it's quite natural to estimate the ratio of the top 10% income group to the lowest 10% income group, that is, to compare the income of the highest income group to the income of the lowest income group in order to observe the income gap. Second, the income ratio between the top 10% income group and the lowest 40% income group is estimated. Economist Parma found that in an era of globalization, the income gap is largely determined by the income of the rich, which affects all other income group, for example, to see whether middle-income earners can hold on to their income and whether low-income earners fall deeper into poverty in an unfavourable competitive environment (Palma, 2011). This income gap model can also well reflect the reality of China. Therefore, the ratio of the estimated income and published income will be estimated between the top 10% income group and the lowest 40% income group.

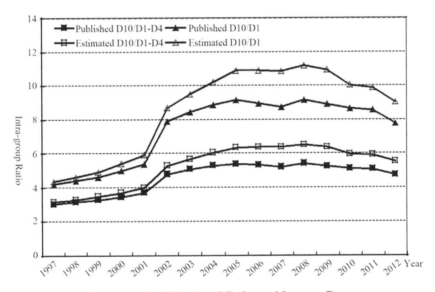

Chart 1-1 Published and Estimated Income Gap

Source: Published D10/D1-D4 and published D10/D1 is obtained according to the data of the National Bureau of Statistics. Estimated D10/D1-D4 and estimated D10/D1 is estimated by the author according to Wang Xiaolu (2013a; 2013b)'s data and *China Statistical Yearbook*.

Judging from the two ratios calculated, here are changes in China's income gap. First, the income gap measured by inter-group ratio has expanded over the years, consistent with most studies. Second, the widening trend of income gap has been more or less restrained and shown certain convergence meaning that the income gap began to narrow after the peak, which undoubtedly supports the judgment that Kuznets' turning point is coming empirically. Third, no matter what kind of inter-group ratio is adopted, income gap widens significantly after hidden income is added to each income group published by the Bureau of Statistics. It should be pointed out that Wang Xiaolu's hidden income data show that hidden income is underestimated (mainly as asset income), but it does not necessarily mean that his specific estimation of hidden income is accepted. Thus, the inter-group ratio with hidden income is not the actual income gap but is intended to reveal the consequences of widening income gap that may result from unfair and unequal allocation of resources in order to carry more targeted policy implications.

IV. Conclusion and Policy Implications

Only through reform can the middle-income trap be avoided and the income gap can be narrowed. Narrowing the income gap can be achieved by increasing the income of low-income groups and by expanding the size of the middle-income group (40% of the lowest income group), as well as by regulating excessive income (10% of the high-income group). In general, income distribution problems are usually formed and regulated in initial distribution and redistribution.

In initial distribution, a number of factors have widened the income gap for a long time. The first factor is long-standing surplus labor force as income distribution is oriented towards the more scarce capital factor. The second factor is that when production factor price is distorted and the relative price of capital factor is artificially lowered, the income distribution is also oriented to capital factor instead of labor factor, giving rise to widening income gap. The third factor is that there is injustice, unfairness and opacity in the allocation of resources and means of production. For example, someone who takes advantage of his special identity or by dishonest means obtains the exploitation right of land, minerals and other natural resources or the right of use and income of the original state-owned assets, inevitably giving rise to the unequal and unfair income distribution.

Therefore, to solve income distribution problem is to further initial distribution reform by taking advantage of Lewis turning point.

The widening income gap in initial distribution can be regulated through redistribution. In fact, the relatively harmonious income distribution pattern in the developed countries with seemingly narrow income gap is mainly formed after redistribution. Japan, for example, is not, as is commonly thought, a highly equalized country in terms of income. Since its income doubling program, Japan has increasingly invested and supported large-scale enterprises, as the main force to promote its heavy industry and chemical industry. Such economic growth pattern would inevitably give rise to widening income distribution gap. The impression of Japan's equal income distribution is because no one sees the income distribution before Japanese government redistributes. In fact, the Gini coefficient of initial distribution in Japan in 1967 was 0.375, which was reduced to 0.328 after redistribution, thus improving by 12.62%. The Gini coefficient of initial distribution in 2008 was 0.532 and was reduced to 0.376 after redistribution with an improvement of up to 29.3% (Sun Zhangwei 2013).

It's not a matter of course for redistribution to play its role in regulating income distribution. In fact, the distorted institutional arrangement and inappropriate policy orientation can not narrow the income gap in redistribution and may widen the existing gap. Public services, such as social security and social assistance of redistribution nature that are partial to certain enterprises, regions or special identities or even to the exclusion of certain groups are regressive, widening the gap in residents' quality of life. So, redistribution reform is the prerequisite for redistribution to give full play to its regulation function.

In initial distribution and redistribution, whether it is the income gap that has been formed or unfair resource allocation that has caused this income gap, or even redistribution policy not conducive to regulating income distribution, it may result in vested interests. These vested interest groups have consciously or unconsciously become a hindrance to deepening income distribution reform. Breaking institutional gridlock requires greater political courage and greater political wisdom so as to push the reform further.

Chapter II

Manifestation and Essence of China's Income Distribution Problem ----Factor Capitalization and Unfair Distribution

ZHANG Juwei, CHENG Jie[1]

The State Council has recently approved and transferred the National Development and Reform Commission's "*Opinions on Deepening the Reform in the Income Distribution System*" (hereinafter referred to as "Opinions") which fully analyzes the current income distribution and puts forward ideas and measures for it. "*Opinions*" will greatly accelerate the income distribution reform and lead to the establishment of a fair, reasonable and efficient distribution system. However, as is pointed out in the "*Opinions*", "Deepening the reform in the income distribution system, a very arduous, complex and systematic project, cannot be accomplished overnight. With the basic conditions, the development stage of China and the current situation in mind, we must further our reform by overcoming major

---

1 ZHANG Juwei, Director of the Institute of Population and Labor Economics of the Chinese Academy of Social Sciences, Research Fellow, Doctoral Advisor; CHENG Jie, Associate Research Fellow of the Institute of Population and Labor Economics of the Chinese Academy of Social Sciences.

difficulties in an orderly manner for long-term development." Therefore, the study of China's income distribution won't stop with the introduction of the *"Opinions"*. On the contrary, we must realize that "the reform in the income distribution system is arduous and complex." Only a conscious awareness and deep and full understanding of the essence and crux of China's income distribution problem now and in the future can we "forge the consensus of all parties so as to make a joint effort in this reform" which is of vital importance to average Chinese people.

China's current income distribution is characterized by the widening income gap and the serious social division at the micro level and by the unreasonable income distribution pattern and the low labor share and the low percentage of residents' income in national income revenue at the macro level. In terms of the distribution rules, the distribution is disorderly with private coffers, bonuses given out at will, and no equal pay for equal work. Income distribution problems at different levels are complex, interrelated and affect each other. Only with a full understanding of the essence and characteristics of income distribution problems can we find effective ways and methods to solve them. This chapter first analyses the differences between China's income distribution problems and those of other countries from the international perspective, then discusses what makes it difficult to narrow the income gap in China, characteristics and essence of the current income distribution problems and attempts to put forward the ideas and countermeasures to solve them.

I. China's Income Distribution

When a country's economy develops rapidly, its income gap tends to widen. Some countries' income gap will get narrower when the income gap reaches its peak while other countries' income gap remains wide for a long time. For example, the income gap in the United States reached its widest in the 1920s with its Gini coefficient exceeding 0.5, and then it began to decline; the Gini coefficient of the the United Kingdom also declined after reaching a peak of 0.54 to 0.55 in 1867. Japan's Gini coefficient reached 0.57 in 1937 but after World War II, its income gap began to narrow and gradually became the narrowest among developed countries (Atkinson & Bourguignon, 2000). Other developed countries' income gap has generally undergone similar changes.

(I) China's Income Gap From the International Perspective

At present, the income gap in developed countries are relatively narrow with a Gini coefficient at around 0.3. The Gini coefficient of the United States was the widest at 0.38; the Nordic countries had the narrowest one below 0.3; Japan, South Korea, France, Germany and the United Kingdom had a Gini coefficient of 0.32, 0.31, 0.28, 0.3, and 0.34 respectively. The OECD countries had an average Gini coefficient of 0.31(see Table 2-1). Low-income countries' Gini coefficient is generally stable at 0.3 to 0.4. Egypt, India, Pakistan, Bangladesh and Indonesia have a Gini coefficient of around 0.33. Middle-income countries with rapid economic growth tend to have the widest income gap: Gini coefficients of Thailand, Malaysia and the Philippines are above 0.4. Brazil has the world's widest income gap with a Gini coefficient close to 0.6. South Africa is similar to Brazil. At present, as a middle income country, China with its rapid economic growth has a relatively wide income gap in terms of per capita income from international perspective.

However, there is no consensus on China's income gap. In fact, for a long time in the past, research teams across China have had totally different research results in judging the current situation of China's income gap. Due to different data sources and research methods, some research believe that China's income gap is still widening with worsening income distribution problem (Zhao Renwei, 2007; Chen Guangjin, 2010; Li Shi & Luo Chu-liang, 2011; Knight, 2011; etc.) while others believe that the widening income gap in China has stabilized or even shown signs of convergence (Cai Fang & Du Yang, 2011; Richard, 2011; Gao Wenshu, et al., 2011; Lai Desheng & Chen Jianwei, 2012; etc.). After many years, the National Bureau of Statistics has published China's Gini coefficient since 2013, which provides a reference for a better understanding of China's income gap.

Table 2-1 Gini Coefficient of Initial Distribution and After Redistribution of Major Developed Countries in Recent Years

Country	Gini Coefficient of Initial Distribution	Gini Coefficient After Redistribution	Base Point of Change	Percentage Change (%)
Australia	0.47	0.34	0.13	-28.2
Austria	0.47	0.26	0.21	-44.7
Belgium	0.47	0.26	0.21	-44.8
Canada	0.44	0.32	0.12	-26.5
Chile	0.53	0.49	0.03	-6.1
Czech Republic	0.44	0.26	0.19	-42.3
Denmark	0.42	0.25	0.17	-40.4
Estonia	0.46	0.32	0.14	-31.2
Finland	0.47	0.26	0.21	-44.3
France	0.48	0.29	0.19	-39.3
Germany	0.50	0.30	0.21	-41.5
Greece	0.44	0.31	0.13	-29.6
Hungary	0.47	0.27	0.19	-41.6
Iceland	0.38	0.30	0.08	-21.2
Israel	0.50	0.37	0.13	-25.5
Italy	0.53	0.34	0.20	-36.9
Japan	0.46	0.33	0.13	-28.8
South Korea	0.34	0.32	0.03	-8.4
Luxembourg	0.48	0.29	0.19	-40.2
Mexico	0.49	0.48	0.02	-3.6
Netherlands	0.43	0.29	0.13	-31.0
New Zealand	0.46	0.33	0.13	-27.5
Norway	0.41	0.25	0.16	-39
Poland	0.47	0.31	0.17	-35.1
Portugal	0.52	0.35	0.17	-32.2
Slovakia	0.42	0.26	0.16	-38.2
Slovenia	0.42	0.24	0.19	-44.2
Spain	0.46	0.32	0.14	-31.2

contd.

Country	Gini Coefficient of Initial Distribution	Gini Coefficient After Redistribution	Base Point of Change	Percentage Change (%)
Sweden	0.43	0.26	0.17	-39.2
Switzerland	0.41	0.30	0.11	-25.9
Turkey	0.47	0.41	0.06	-13.0
the U. K.	0.46	0.35	0.11	-24.3
the U. S.	0.49	0.38	0.11	-22.2
OECD Average	0.46	0.31	0.14	-31.3

Source: calculated according to relevant data from OECD Bureau of Statistics with the latest year available mainly Year 2008-2010

According to the data published by the National Bureau of Statistics[1], the Gini coefficient of the national residents' income in 2003, 2004, 2005, 2006, 2007, and 2008 was 0.479, 0.473, 0.485, 0.487, 0.484, and 0.491 respectively, then it was gradually on the decline: 0.490 in 2009, 0.481 in 2010, 0.477 in 2011, 0.474 in 2012. But these Gini coefficients republished by the National Bureau of Statistics are not entirely consistent with the findings of researchers and the feelings of the general public. So China's income gap is still an open question. However, it is an indisputable fact that there is a widening income gap in China, from both international experience and from the experience of average Chinese people (see Chart 2-1).

Judging from the experience of developed countries, social system and rules conducive to a narrow income gap must improve before the income gap narrows, which isn't a matter of course. The income gap of the United States began to narrow mainly because of the Roosevelt New deal implemented in the 1930s by greatly improving the social welfare of low-income groups and raising their income. Japan's narrowing income gap after World War II was due not only to

---

1   The National Bureau of Statistics: " Ma Jiantang answered reporters' questions on the performance of the National economy in 2012"; http: / www.stats.gov.cn / tjdt/ gjtjdt/ t20130118 / t20130118. this is January 18, 2013.

its land reform, the dissolution of the plutocrats and the policy of prohibiting monopoly but to the strengthening of trade unions and the better protection of labor rights and interests. On the whole, developed countries' narrowing their income gaps is closely related to the establishment of fiscal and taxation policies to regulate income distribution, the establishment of social security system and the enhancement of workers' right to speak. Without these conditions, it remains a mystery whether the income gap in the developed world will narrow.

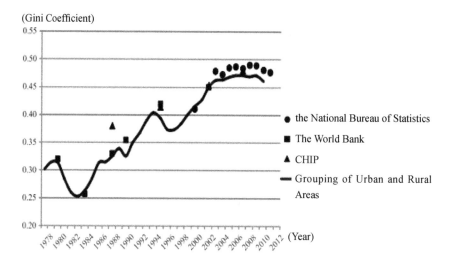

Chart 2-1   Gini Coefficient Variation in China: 1978-2012

Source: The National Gini coefficient for 2000 and 2003-2012 was published by the National Bureau of Statistics. The World Bank estimated the Gini coefficient for some years completed by Ravallion and Chen (2007) with household survey data from the National Bureau of Statistics. Li Shi (2011) and Gustafsson (2007) estimated the Gini coefficient in the survey year of CHIP, a Chinese household income survey based on the sample frame of the National Bureau of Statistics. Quite a number of researchers estimated National Gini coefficient by grouping residents' income of urban and rural areas across the nation. With the estimation of Chen Zongsheng et al. (2012) and Zhou Yun Bo (2010) for reference, Cheng Yonghong (2007), Xu Bing and Zhang Shangfeng (2010), Hu Zhijun et al. (2011), etc., estimated the Gini coefficients and found that, though with different methods, the trend of variation is basically the same.

The effect of redistribution in developed countries on the regulation of income gap can be explained by the differences in Gini coefficients after their initial distribution and after redistribution. Judging from initial distribution, the current income gap in developed countries is not narrow at all. The Gini coefficient after initial distribution is 0.49, 0.46, 0.50, 0.46 in the United States, the United Kingdom, Germany and Japan respectively. In general, the initial distribution of the Gini coefficient mainly reflects the income gap caused by market forces and can be regarded as the market Gini coefficient, which means that even in developed countries, the income gap caused by the market itself stays wide and that there is no significant difference compared with most developing countries. However, after redistribution, the income gap in developed countries has narrowed considerably. After redistribution, the Gini coefficient of the United States, Japan, Germany, France, the United Kingdom, OECD countries decreased from 0.49 to 0.38, 0.46 to 0.33, 0.50 to 0.30, 0.48 to 0.29, 0.46 to 0.35, and 0.46 to 0.31 respectively (see Table 2-1). On the whole, after redistribution, the Gini coefficient of developed countries will decline by more than 10 Gini points. Table 2-1 summarizes the changes of OECD countries in Gini coefficient of initial distribution and after redistribution in recent years.

However, due to the fact that there is no redistribution system to regulate income gap in developing countries, there isn't much changes between the income gap of initial distribution and the income gap after redistribution. After redistribution, developed countries have basically achieved a relatively equal income distribution while the income gap in developing countries after redistribution remains as wide as that after the initial distribution. Thus, the income gap in developing countries is a reflection of the direct result of market forces without too much intervention while the income gap in developed countries, to a large extent, is the result of the regulation of their government's redistribution policies. Therefore, whether redistribution policy can be adopted to achieve a reasonable income gap or not makes a lot difference in whether a country can become a developed one.

(II) Difficulty of Narrowing China's Income Gap

Like other developing countries, China's Gini coefficient mainly reflects the income gap of initial distribution because China's redistribution system can't regulate the income distribution. On the contrary, it has an "inverse regulation" to some extent. Some studies have pointed out that taking into account the cost of living, housing, social security and other factors, China's Gini coefficient may be 0.48 to 0.49, which means the income gap has not narrowed at all, but widened further (Li Shi & Luo Chuliang, 2011). Judging from the situation, China is undoubtedly one of the countries with a wide income gap in the world (see Chart 2-2) , wider than both developed countries and developing countries except South Africa, Brazil and Mexico.

(Gini Coefficient)

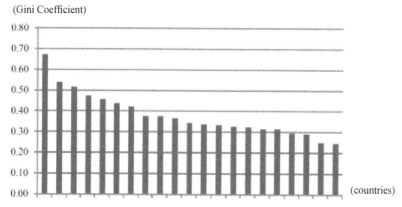

(Countries are from left to right: South Africa, Brazil, Mexico, China, Argentina, the Philippines, Russia, U.S., Vietnam, India, U.K., Italy, Australia, Japan, Canada, Spain, Korea, Germany, France, Norway, Denmark.)

Chart 2-2   Gini Coefficient After Redistribution in Major Developed and Developing Countries

Source: China's data is released by the National Bureau of Statistics in 2012; other countries' data are released by the OECD Bureau of Statistics and WDI (World Development Indicators) of the World Bank database with the latest year available, mainly year 2006-2010.

The main cause for China to fail to narrow its income gap is that its redistribution is not able to regulate income distribution. China's public finance, the major means of redistribution, can't play its role in regulating the income gap in both revenue and expenditure.

In terms of revenue, China's taxation system is mainly indirect with a very low percentage of direct tax (Li Zhuo, 2009). The personal income tax with a strong redistribution function accounts for less than 7% of revenue and less than 20% of salaried workers are taxpayers. The indirect taxation system, including value-added tax, business tax, domestic consumption tax, tariff, makes average worker pay a heavier tax while the high income groups pay a relatively low tax. Therefore, China's current income distribution pattern is, to some extent, closely related to the basic structure and characteristics of its taxation system. Developed countries have mainly adopted direct taxation system. The personal income tax in the United States and Japan is its largest source of revenue, ensuring that the income gap will be greatly regulated from the income distribution, the taxation system playing its role of "cutting the peak". China's taxation system fails to do so.

In terms of expenditure, a very low proportion of expenditure is spent on Chinese people's livelihood with almost no redistribution function. China's public expenditure on health care, education and housing is seriously inadequate; the social security system is not perfect with little protection of low-income group. Transfer payment of the central government is mostly project expenditure lacking the redistribution function of narrowing the income gap. Generally speaking, the expenditure on people's livelihood in developed countries is usually more than 50%, of which a large proportion is spent directly on the low-middle income groups. Expenditure of the United States accounts for 32% of its GDP, 8% of which is to narrow its income gap; the number with Japan is 12%, and the number with developed countries is generally above 10% with an average of 15%. The number with China is less than 1% so that public expenditure fails to fulfil its function of "filling the valley" in the income distribution.

In addition, China's social security system is still imperfect in that it does not regulate its income distribution so as to narrow the income gap. The basic institutional framework of social security has been established in China, among which the social insurance system of urban workers does not regulate income distribution. Due to the high contribution rate, so far only half of the total urban employees are well-protected by the social insurance system for urban workers while low-income groups are not. Instead of regulating income distribution, the social security system tends to have an inverse regulation (HE Li-xin & Hiroshi Sato , 2008).

To sum up, although China's widening income gap is no different from any country with a rapid economic development, the difference lies in that the developed countries effectively curb the widening income gap and regulate the gap reasonably with redistribution. Judging from the experience of developed countries, lack of the regulation function of redistribution is the main reason why it's difficult to narrow the widening income gap.

Objectively speaking, although the widening income gap is getting serious, China's current income gap is neither wider than the gap the developed countries once reached, nor wider than that of the developing countries. It is now basically the same as the current income gap after initial distribution in developed countries. All this is not to justify China's income distribution problems but to show that China's income gap is quite common when compared internationally. It reflects the general characteristics and laws of economic development. But why has China's income distribution problem caused such great dissatisfaction in society? There is more to it than the income gap itself .

II. "Crux" of China's Income Distribution: Unfair Distribution and Factor Capitalization

In market economy, the income gap is a common occurrence. And there is no telling to what extent a country can endure it. The U.S. once got the widest income gap in developed countries. But there isn't much complaints about it among American people. Generally speaking, if the widening income gap results from fair distribution in market economy, there won't be much social discontent. But if the income gap is caused by unfair distribution, there will be intense social discontent even if the income gap is not very serious. Judging from the income gap that countries in the world have reached, society can endure the income gap more than they do the unfair income distribution. The root cause of political instability in North African countries, to a large extent, is a matter of their endurance of unfair income distribution. The income gap of Egypt, whose Gini coefficient is 0.3 to 0.35, does not seem to be very large, but the unfair income distribution[1] brought about by the lack of job opportunities and excessive wealth concentration has given rise to social unrest and regime change.

(I) Cause of Current China's Income Distribution Problem: Unfair Distribution

The cause of China's income distribution problem is not simply the widening income gap itself. The widening income gap is largely caused by unfair distribution. Unfair income distribution, simply put, is that social wealth or income goes to the certain groups or individuals illegally, unreasonably or dishonestly excluding the groups or individuals who deserve the wealth or income. In other words, unfair income distribution actually means that those who don't deserve take the income while those who do do not.

China's current economy is growing rapidly, creating abundant social wealth, a considerable amount of which has been distributed unfairly. This not only widens the income gap as well as the gap between rich and poor, but is a critical root cause of social rift and the most dangerous threat to social stability. Therefore, China's income distribution problem cannot be solved without solving the unfair distribution even if the income gap can be narrowed.

Admittedly, China's current unfair income distribution, though prevailing, is more extensive, more serious and more harmful compared with other countries. China's unfair income distribution is different and complex mainly because China has to adapt its socialist basic economic system to a market mechanism.

In the marketization reform, China's basic economic system has changed from

---

1   The Mubarak family has a fortune of $70 billion, equivalent to a third of Egypt's GDP ($217 billion) of that year, according to estimates by the International Monetary Fund (IMF).

a single public ownership to a side-by-side development of different economic components with public ownership playing a dominant role. With the acceleration of marketization, economic components have to be part of the market competition and needs to be capitalized. State-owned economy and state-owned assets are in this, too. State-owned assets will be capitalized, a progress of marketization reform. In capitalization, however, income inequality has emerged considerably: certain groups and individuals take advantage of the institutional loopholes in social transformation to secretly acquire the social wealth for themselves only.

At this unique development stage of China, those who have obtained huge amounts of social wealth through unfair distribution have already become the super-rich or rich class with a considerable social impact, though not large in number, causing an intense social impact. The fact that social wealth belongs to a small number of people through unfair distribution makes the majority of people in society feel relatively deprived. Even the middle-high income earners often consider themselves to be the low income class or the weak group. This sense of relative deprivation is more likely to cause social discontent and conflict than income inequality and absolute poverty (Nagel,1974). China has become the second largest country with overnight billionaires around the world. The increasing number of rich people is inevitable in economic development, but the problem in China is that the wealth accumulation of the "rich class" is closely related to unfair distribution. China's "super-rich class" is characterized by its limited industries and its limited wealth accumulation channels. According to *The Global Wealth Report* released by Boston Consulting in 2007, about 41% of China's wealth is controlled by 0.1% of "super-rich families." The main channels for wealth accumulation of Super-rich class are the acquisition or merger of wholly-owned enterprises at a low price, the listing of money and access to real estate, minerals and other industries. According to the *2011 China Private Wealth Report* jointly investigated and released by China Merchants Bank and Bain Information, 27% of the rich people with 100 million yuan of investable assets have emigrated, and 47% are considering emigration, long-term investment, venture-oriented investment so as to evacuate overseas. This is clearly an extremely dangerous signal of China's economic development.

Compared with the widening income gap, unfair income distribution tends to be more threatening and more harmful to society. Generally speaking, unfair income distribution does not always come in the form of a widening income gap. During planned economy in China, despite the seemingly small income gap, there was seriously unfair income distribution with reasonable income gap being bridged by some people not getting their due income while others taking what they don't deserve. As a result, unfair income distribution leads to both economic and social stagnation. Of course, it's more dangerous for unfair income distribution to be both accompanied by and be the cause of a widening income gap. In fact, China is in this state now with the urgent need to improve income distribution in its current economic and social development.

(II) Main Cause of Unfair Distribution: Factor Capitalization

The basic economic system of Chinese socialism is the side-by-side development of different ownership economy with public ownership playing a dominant role. In the marketization reform, means of production of public ownership priced through market transactions will become factor capital in order to accomplish the separation and transfer of ownership and right of use with various forms of market transactions and free flow such as property rights contracts, financial instruments and negotiable securities so that means of production will realize its optimal factor allocation and wealth re-creation. In planned economy, means of production of public ownership in China were not priced "wealth" with a large amount of land, mineral resources, state-owned enterprises, public facilities and so on being merely "dead", unable to create new wealth through market transactions without any attributes of capital. Factor capitalization has changed the situation that China has abundant wealth without capital, turning a "lack-of-money" China into a country with abundant capital.

Factor capitalization, a symbol of the development and progress of market economy, is required by the reform and development of China's socialist market economy. Well-developed market economy is characterized by its a more-than-a-century capitalization, well-developed rules, accumulated wealth, and competitive advantages of the world market. China's economic development has to go through factor capitalization. The achievements of China's reform and opening up, especially the rapid economic growth in the past decade, benefit from factor capitalization. Although China's early marketization reform, making possible the free trade of various products, has shortened the distance between "wealth" and "money"(Chen Zhiwu, 2009), a large number of productive factors have not become capital that can create new wealth. Factor capitalization brought about by the deepening reform has transformed resource factor into capital, making resource allocation more efficient, faster and less costly, giving momentum to China's rapid economic growth.

China's factor capitalization, however, different from that of other market economies, is characterized by its peculiarity which is shown in the following two aspects. First, factor capitalization of average market economy is based on private property rights while China's is mainly based on public ownership requiring the separation of ownership and right of use, which is where the difficulty lies of theoretical innovation of socialist market economy with Chinese characteristics without any experience for reference. Second, any well-developed market economy is characterized by a hundred years' experience of capitalization, a well-developed market and perfect rules. China's newly-established market mechanism and imperfect market development with factor market lagging behind will add to the difficulty and complexity of factor capitalization. Developing side by side with marketization reform, China's factor capitalization of "exploring and pushing forward" will undoubtedly face more challenges.

(III) Main Manifestation of Unfair Distribution: No Reasonable Share of Public Assets Income in Factor Capitalization

The particularity of China's factor capitalization leads to unfair income distribution, the main source of income inequality in China. Although capitalization of such factors as land, mineral resources, state-owned enterprises, public goods have created abundant new wealth, the state and all the people, owners of resource factor, were not able to enjoy the benefits of capitalization fairly as a great deal of wealth is held by a small number of people who have the right to use or have actual control in factor capitalization. The related fields of factor capitalization have become the target of public discontent and social conflict, which can be summed up in the following four aspects.

First, income from land capitalization hasn't been fairly distributed. Income from land capitalization has been over-occupied by developers, local governments and interest groups with the interests of farmers and collectives eroded. Although land capitalization has provided an important source of capital for the construction of urbanization and accelerated the development of urbanization, the village collectives and villagers with land ownership who do not have enough control and income distribution right can not get their fair and reasonable income share. Collective land needs to be expropriated by local government to become state-owned before entering market transactions, during which there emerges illegal, unreasonable expropriation and occupation of land, and even violent demolition, seriously infringing on the rights and interests of farmers. For instance, the compensation price is far lower than the market price and the land expropriation compensation is often only 30,000 to 50,000 yuan per mu, but the actual market value of the land can be as high as several million yuan, which has seriously eroded the interests of farmers. The income distribution of land capitalization has been seriously imbalanced and unfair. Some studies have shown that[1] in the distribution of the value added income of collective land use transfer, the government, the village economic organizations and farmers gets 60%-70%, 25-30%, and 5-10% respectively. Land transfer funds have become an important source of local finance. In 2010, the total land transaction price (by statistical caliber of Ministry of Land and Resources) reached 2.9 trillion yuan, transfer

---

1 People's Website: "Introduction of Negotiation Mechanism to Solve Unfair Distribution of Farmland Compensation", http://house.people.com.cn/GB/11227826. html, March 26, 2010.

funds of Anhui, Shaanxi, Chongqing and other provinces (cities) accounting for more than 40% of the local revenue[1]. The unfair distribution of land capitalization has damaged the interests of the villagers and collective, has given rise to a group of overnight wealthy real estate owners and stimulated the "land finance", and is extremely likely to cause social conflict with frequent occurrences of such group incidents as petitions, self-immolation, explosions, attacks on local governments.

Second, capitalized income from mineral resources has been over-occupied by mining owners forming the super-rich group, damaging the interests of the state and the whole nation. Many mining rights of mineral resources are granted by way of administrative transfer and agreed pricing. However, the imperfect market trading system of "bidding and trading", low price transfer or even free plunder, low cost mining, extremely low tax on the use of mineral resources, local protection and rent seeking corruption, has enabled a small number of people to control mineral resources owned by the whole people, and to make high profits and even huge profits while the relevant management departments have also obtained grey income from it, seriously eroding the rights and interests of the owners of state-owned resources. Even in 2010, coal mines in Pinglu, Shanxi worth hundreds of millions was transferred for 10,000 yuan. The tax on mineral resources and the compensation for mineral resources are on the extremely low side. For example, the current coal resource tax is 0.3-5 yuan per ton, less than 2% of the market price; the natural gas resource tax is 7 to 15 yuan per thousand cubic meters, less than 3% of the price; the average oil resource tax is only 26 yuan per ton, less than 2% of the market price. Too low a resource use tax results in a too small proportion of the country's added value income and even less for its citizens. The unfair distribution of income from mineral resource capitalization has given rise to a group of super-rich coal boss, iron boss, copper boss and so on. According to *Research Report on Private Capital Investment in China* released

---

1 People's Website: "Adjustment of Land Grant Policy by Ministry of Land and Ministry of Finance", http://house.people.com.cn/GB/14893494.html, June 14, 2011.

jointly by the Ministry of Housing and Construction and Goldman Sachs in 2011, there are no fewer than 7,000 billionaires of coal bosses in Yulin, Shaanxi, known as "China's Kuwait," boasting of 1 billion yuan of wealth per square kilometres. In 2010, 90% of China's Land Rover cars in mainland China were bought by coal owners in Ordos where there are at least 100,000 people with assets of tens of millions of yuan. The sharp contrast between the luxury life of these super-rich group and the difficult life of low-income group has become the source of social discontent.

Third, capitalized income of state-owned enterprises hasn't been shared reasonably by the whole people. Capitalized income of the state-owned enterprises has been divided up by actual controllers, interest groups and internal workers instead of the state and the whole people who have to burden a large amount of subsidies. Although reform of and capitalization of state-owned enterprises have greatly promoted efficiency of enterprises with valued state-owned assets and with transformation from "burden" to "wealth", due to imperfect distribution mechanism, unfair income distribution has only benefited interest groups, damaging the interests of real owners of state-owned assets. Capitalization of state-owned enterprises, controlled by executives and insiders of enterprises, has resulted in embezzlement or sale of state-owned assets at a low price, and the fact that huge annual income of senior executives is inconsistent with their operating performance, and the fact that staff and workers of enterprises are well-paid with good welfare and monopoly income. In addition, state-owned enterprises enjoy resource factors, financing loans and other preferential treatments at the same time while the majority of corporate income is shared by only a small number of people. Between 2001 and 2009, the total profits of state-owned and state-owned holding industrial enterprises amounted to 5.8462 trillion yuan, only 6% of which is handed over to the state in 2009, and only 2.2% in 2010, with the rest of the profits distributed within the enterprises. As a result, the national dividend is also transferred mainly within the enterprise system, and the public finance basically does not get the income of the state-owned capital, let alone benefit the whole people. Moreover, state-owned enterprises also enjoy preferential treatment and financial subsidies from all citizens in terms of resource factors. From 2001 to 2009, state-owned and state-owned holding industrial enterprises should have paid a total of 2.5787 trillion yuan in government rent accounting for 64% of the total nominal net profit of state-owned and state-owned holding enterprises; rents for natural resources, such as oil, gas and coal, were underpaid by about 497.7 billion yuan. Between 2007 and 2009, state-owned and state-controlled industrial enterprises received financial subsidies of about 194.3 billion yuan. In addition, some state-owned enterprises have been heavily involved in the real estate industry. In 2009, more than 70% of the 136 state-owned enterprises involved in real estate business, creating state-owned enterprise "land kings" one after another. Some state-owned companies have used their policy and credit advantages to pump billions of dollars into non-major businesses such as stocks, housing, derivatives and commodities, fuelling asset bubbles and worsening residents' income distribution. In all, capitalization of state-owned enterprises lacks a perfect income distribution mechanism, leading to serious unfair distribution, and few interest groups have directly deprived the country or the whole people of their wealth, triggering increasingly intense public discontent.

Fourth, capitalization of public goods has damaged the public interest. Capitalization of public goods have enabled actual controlling organization and internal staff to get excess income while the public bears high costs, seriously infringing on the rights and interests of the public. Although capitalization of some public goods has accelerated the construction of infrastructure in China, broken the bottleneck of economic growth and promoted the rapid economic development, its unfair distribution mainly lies in the fact that the public goods is controlled by a small number of people and interest groups, and the fact that the capitalized excess income is distributed only within the department. Moreover, as these public goods are often concerned with livelihood and security of the people, a few actual controllers with better bargaining chips are more likely to have monopoly power with the power sector, leading to high public service charges.

Some expressways have become "income generating machines" controlled by interest groups with nominal expressways becoming de facto "private roads", changing the nature of public goods. In 2009, the tolls of The First Group were as high as 3.2 billion yuan while the daily maintenance expenditure was only 66.793 million yuan[1]. The gross profit rate of listed Nanjing Shanghai Expressway in 2010 was as high as 74%. The operating profit margin of Chengdu-Chongqing and Wuzhou Development in Sichuan was 66% and 67% respectively[2]. Expressway profiteering directly makes worker income super-high, seriously deviating from worker's human capital. For example, in 2010, per capita pre-tax annual income of Nanjing-Shanghai Expressway reached 105,000 yuan with only less than 10% of the staff having a bachelor's degree or above; per capita pre-tax annual income of Wuzhou Development reached 145,000 yuan with 80% of its front-line personnel and logistics personnel. The excess capitalized income of public goods is essentially the high cost borne by the public and occupied by a small number of actual controllers. This serious unfair distribution has intensified social conflict.

In addition, factor capitalization has given rise to "power capitalization". Due to the temptation of huge interest and imperfect supervision, there are rent-seeking corruption, power and money trading and opportunism in the market transactions of state-owned resource factors. For example, government departments or officials make use of land, mineral resources, enterprise listing, construction planning and other rights for rent-seeking. Government and business colluded to divide the income of factor capitalization. The destructive power capitalization bred in factor capitalization has become one of the main causes of unfair distribution of capitalized income. Moreover, it is more likely to cause public discontent and intensify social conflict.

---

1 Financial Circles: "The First Group receives 3.2 billion a year with less than 70 million daily maintenance expenses", http://finance.jrj.com.cn/industry/2011/06/17073010227612.shtml, June 17, 2011.

2 Southern News Network: "Gold Road: Turnway Gross Interest Rate of 73.77%", http://news.qq.com/a/201106 "10/000834.htm, June 10, 2011.

(IV) Cause of Unfair Distribution: No Reasonable Distribution Mechanism for Public Assets Income

Lack of reasonable distribution mechanism for income from factor capitalization results in the private possession of public income, the institutional source for unfair distribution. By summarizing unfair income distribution in factor capitalization in China, the essence of unfair distribution is private possession of public income through two ways.

First, unfair distribution of initial capitalized income. When state-owned resource factor is traded through the market for the first time, realizing one-off capitalized income, that is, assets without price becoming valuable capital, resulting in a huge amount of new wealth, the government has not made it clear how to be reasonable and fair in its distribution so that a small number of people take too big a share of the income. Second, unfair distribution of capitalized income flow. In the capitalization of state-owned resource factors, new wealth or income flow can be generated every year, but as the right of distribution is controlled by a few people, the income flows to some groups without being shared by the whole people, which is the biggest cause of unfair initial distribution.

In initial capitalization, unfair income distribution fails to reflect the market value of state-owned resource factor, which reduces the wealth that can be distributed by the state and the whole people. There are two situations in factor capitalization: ownership transfer and right of use (right of management) transfer, the former including collective land collection and occupation, private contracting of state-owned enterprises and the latter including mineral resources transfer and expressway transfer. No matter which property right is transferred, there will always be private excessive possession of this one-time public income of initial capitalization by private individuals. One cause is direct erosion of state-owned assets without compensation. Without owners' authorization to deal with state-owned resources, actual controllers convert state-owned assets into private assets illegally through power abuse, improper relations, etc., causing the loss of state-owned assets. Capitalized income being wholly owned by private individuals who directly obtain huge wealth will harm the interests of state-owned resources' owners, the direct erosion and plunder of national wealth and the most evident unfair income distribution. The other cause is trading state assets at distorted prices. Due to serious information asymmetry, serious lack of supervision, and factor price manipulation in the non-standard market, state-owned resource factor is traded at distorted prices, resulting in under-pricing and cheap buying. The part below market price is rent-seeking space and most of value-added income is divided up by minority interest groups, causing serious damage to national wealth.

Actual controllers have the say in distribution of capitalized income flow income because for a long time, the income distribution of state-owned resource factor lags behind without clear procedures and rules, leading to unfair income distribution. The first cause is absence of distribution system. If mineral resources management right is transferred to private individuals, the state receives very little income from this one-time transfer as capitalized income flow is handed over to the state only as low tax for mineral resources exploitation. For lack of a reasonable income distribution system, huge profits are entirely taken by the operators. The second situation is that the unreasonable and imperfect distribution system. Although, according to the current institutional arrangements, the relevant income distribution system requires state-owned enterprises to hand in a certain proportion of profits, the state receives very low proportion of profits, most of which are still diverted within state-owned enterprises. The distribution mechanism of value-added income of collective land is also unreasonable as the distribution proportion of village collective and villagers is too low. The third situation is the improper and irregular distribution mechanism. For example, the state-owned enterprises or the public sector transfer profits from the main business to other non-main business through improper and irregular operations, resulting in a sharp decline in the income distribution, or even asking for state financial subsidies, with real profits intercepted and divided up by a small number of people of the enterprise.

Therefore, in view of the unfair income distribution in factor capitalization in China, it is necessary to clearly define property rights so as to avoid excessive possession of public income by private individuals and to strengthen the control of state-owned resources so as to avoid being controlled by a small number of people or interest groups, and it's also necessary to establish a reasonable income distribution mechanism so as to ensure that the public income can be equitably shared by all the people.

III. Solution to China's Income Distribution Problem

As Confucius once says, "the problem lies not in the scarcity of resources, but in the uneven distribution". At present, China is faced with not only the widening income gap, but also the fact that widening income gap is, to a large extent, caused by unfair distribution, that is, the crux of income distribution lies in unfair distribution. Therefore, to solve China's income distribution problem, top priority should be given to the elimination of unfair income distribution. We need to speed up economic development on the basis of the elimination of unfair income distribution and improve the redistribution system to gradually resolve widening income gap.

(I) Elimination of Unfair Distribution as the Top Priority

Unfair income distribution is not only an important cause of the widening income gap but a root cause of social conflict and social discontent. Unfair income distribution is neither a problem of development stage nor of market mechanism construction, but a matter of adjustment of interest pattern, construction and enforcement of system and regulations, and it will not be solved on its own with the development of market economy. If income distribution inequality is not eliminated, it is impossible to solve China's income distribution problem.

China's current unfair income distribution is mainly due to the fact that the income of the state-owned economy or the participation of state-owned capital in the market is not reasonably shared by the whole people. Therefore, how to deal with state-owned assets and their income fairly and reasonably becomes crucial to solving the problem of unfair income distribution. In this regard, many people have suggested that in order to eliminate unfair distribution, it is important to continuously weaken state-owned economy with its gradual withdrawal from economy, and some people even have proposed a more extreme method: privatization of state-owned economy. These views are aimed at curing social diseases, but they are wrong prescriptions.

As a socialist country with public ownership playing a dominant role, China should always strengthen its public ownership economy. In fact, it is precisely because of weakening public ownership economy in recent years or continuous loss of state-owned capital that, to some extent, has led to widening income gap and widening gap between rich and poor. After more than three decades reform and development, although public economic sector is still the lifeblood of economic development in terms of function, the proportion of state-owned economic sector continues to decline in terms of composition as state-owned economy has undergone a fundamental change. When the reform and opening up began in 1978, state-owned economy is absolutely dominant in the gross national product, the public sector and non-public sector accounting for 99% and 1% respectively. By the year 2000, the pattern of capital being owned and used mainly by the state and the collective has changed greatly as the capital owned by the residents has exceeded the state-owned capital, even greater than the sum of the state-owned capital and the collective capital. Relevant studies show that, of the total capital of 28.7 trillion in China in 2000, the state, the collective, residents, and Hong Kong, Macao, Taiwan and foreign investment accounted for 34%, 12%, 43%, and 11% respectively (Fan Gang &Yao Zhizhong, 2002). In recent years, there has been the increasing trend of "the withdrawal of state-owned enterprises and the development of private enterprises" in the economic structure with the proportion of public economic sector on a further decline. In 2008, the total capital assets of the country amounted to 14.4078 billion yuan, among which state-owned capital, collective capital, individual capital and foreign capital accounted for 10.50%, 2.76%, 79.92%, and 6.82% respectively (Li Jiguang, 2011). This change in capital structure has inevitably brought about the change in income distribution pattern. As the proportion of private capital in national wealth increases, so will the proportion of private capital income in national income. The extremely uneven possession of private capital inevitably leads to greater income differences among individuals. Therefore, the further weakening state-owned economy will not only bring about a further widening income gap but a further deviation from China's socialism, intensifying social conflict. So, the right way to address income inequality is not necessarily to weaken the status of the state-owned economy. On the contrary, it is quite feasible to achieve the fair distribution of state-owned assets and their income by perfecting distribution mechanism and rules without weakening the status of state-owned economy.

At present, the capitalization of state-owned assets such as land, mineral resources, state-owned enterprises and public goods is the main cause of unfair income distribution. Thus, to eradicate unfair distribution is to stop its loopholes. Therefore, there is an urgent need to perfect the system and rules in the following aspects: First, perfect the land system by clarifying land property rights, reforming collective land collection and occupation system, including land transfer fee in financial budget so as to increase farmers' share of value-added income of the land; Second, establish a more stringent system for the use of mineral resources by levying a resource tax as soon as possible, raising tax standard on the use of mineral resources so as to establish a profit-sharing system for enterprises of mineral resources. Third, improve the management system of state-owned enterprises by strengthening supervision and control, and increasing the proportion of profits state-owned enterprises turn in and including the profits of state-owned enterprises in national budget, and by listing prudently industries of natural monopoly and strategic resources related to livelihood and safety and public goods. Fourth, further standardize the capitalization of public goods by cleaning up such enterprises as highways, municipal transportation and other enterprises having recovered their costs, by supervising strictly the entry of private sector into the field of public goods, and by reducing the cost of public goods and services.

(II) Narrowing Income Gap by Improving Redistribution Mechanism

Generally speaking, the income gap under normal market mechanism is of a phased and controllable nature with clear policy instruments for regulating this income gap. The experience of developed countries has actually provided a good reference and experience for China: the income gap under normal market economy can gradually improve or be bridged by improving redistribution mechanism. Of course, narrowing the income gap should not only take into full consideration the stage characteristics of economic development but the characteristics of China's system and realistic possibility. From the perspective of redistribution, the policy of narrowing the income gap needs to improve in the following aspects.

First, strengthen the role of tax in regulating income distribution by implementing a comprehensive household income tax system to change the current tax system failing to regulate income distribution. On one hand, taxes are to be levied on holding property links as soon as possible, such as property taxes and inheritance taxes; on the other hand, China's personal income tax system is to be reformed by changing from classified collection to household income tax. The personal income tax of China is collected according to its income source. After several adjustments, the exemption amount of salary or income has been raised to 3,500 yuan per month. However, due to the different adaptation tax rates of various income and different expense deduction standards, those taxpayers with many income sources and high combined income can always come up with ways not to pay taxes or to pay less tax while taxpayers with relatively limited income sources will inevitably pay more taxes, resulting in an excessive tax burden on wage earners, the main force of taxpayers. As a result, personal income tax has largely become payroll tax. What's worse, as the income of wage earners in China is growing relatively slow, and the labor share is relatively low, the relatively heavy tax burden makes it difficult for individual income tax to regulate the income gap, and, to some extent, makes it more unfavorable to wage earners in the income distribution pattern. Personal income tax of other countries in the world has adopted comprehensive household income tax system. According to incomplete statistics, among 110 countries or regions collecting personal income tax, 87 of which have adopted comprehensive tax system (Jia Kang & Liang Jiwei, 2012). In 1799, the United Kingdom became the first country in the world to impose personal income tax. In 1909, it changed its tax collection from classified income tax to comprehensive collection. The United States began to collect personal income tax in 1913 with comprehensive tax system. Mexico, Malaysia and other developing countries also implement comprehensive tax system. Therefore, from the role of regulating income distribution, it is urgent to further improve China's personal income tax system. As most countries in the world do, China should implement comprehensive household income tax system as soon as possible.

Second, improve the top design of social security system and enhance the inclusiveness of social security system. The insufficient redistribution of social security system in China adds to the difficulty of narrowing the income gap. Social security system, redistribution means, affects the vitality of economic growth. Internationally, there are two basic social security systems: one is Bismarck system and the other Beveridge system. Bismarck system is characterized by the need for individual contributions and the connection between treatment and payment with little role in regulating income distribution. Countries adopting Bismarck system include Germany, Austria, France, Belgium, Spain and others. Without emphasis on the connection between income and contributions, the Beveridge system aimed to provide a basic social protection emphasizes social equity, having a relatively enormous income distribution effect. Countries adopting Beveridge system include Britain, Denmark, the Netherlands, Switzerland and so on. China's current social security system is a mixture of Bismarck and Beveridge. The social insurance system of urban workers reflects the characteristics of Bismarck system while that of the rural and urban residents mixed the design of Bismarck system and Beveridge system. Because social insurance system of urban and rural residents is of low treatment and insufficient security, generally speaking, China's social security system is more of Bismarck system with its insufficient redistribution function mainly determined by the system itself. Therefore, to improve China's social security system is to start with the top-level design, inclusiveness and fairness of the system, and to give full play its role as redistribution means in the regulation of income distribution. For this reason, implementing the old age allowance system or establishing a unified non-contributory public pension system is to be considered, reforming the current urban workers' pension insurance system, and establishing an occupational annuity system and enterprise annuity system by reducing the proportion of Bismarck system and strengthening the proportion of Beveridge system.

Third, speed up the equal provision of public services and focus on the equal treatment of the migrant population. The biggest injustice in the current provision of public services is that people living in the same area or even in the same city are differentiated and treated differently, especially the rural population, who has long been working in cities and towns. According to the results of the sixth National Census in 2010, China's migrant population has reached 220 million, most of whom are rural migrant workers. Leaving the countryside, they actually are not covered in rural public service and management system since local public service and social welfare take local registration as entry qualification, the floating population excluded from urban public service system in the floating place, the so-called "semi-urbanization" pattern. According to resident population, current urbanization rate has exceeded 54%, but if calculated according to household registration, the population with non-agricultural household registration only accounts for 37% of national population. There is a 17% difference between the two, which means that about 150 million rural residents who leave their homes do not have the same access to public services as urban residents do. The resulting social conflict and problems are increasingly intense, especially the group conflict between floating population and local residents in recent years in some cities. Therefore, to accelerate the equalization of public services, it is imperative to involve as soon as possible the migrant population working and living in the same city or region in the local public service system to narrow the income gap and realize social fairness and justice and to maintain social harmony and stability. For this reason, the state may consider establishing a public service delivery system based on the resident population by speeding up the household registration system reform, and by perfecting the residence permit system. Those who have stable accommodation and jobs in the city and live for more than a certain number of years should enjoy the same education, health care, social security, employment and housing treatment as urban residents do.

Lastly, strengthen the role of taxation in regulating income distribution by enhancing the inclusiveness of social security system and accelerating the equalization of public services so that China's redistribution will be able to play its role in regulating income distribution. If China can also set up the redistribution regulation mechanism as the developed countries, the income gap will be greatly reduced and the widening income gap can be basically narrowed.

Chapter III

Changes and Problems in China's Labor Share

ZHANG Juwei[1]

Labor remuneration share in GDP (hereinafter referred to as labor share), an index to measure laborers' share in initial distribution, is also one of the cores of income distribution whose changes are related to not only national income distribution pattern but economic competitiveness and sustained growth. Statistics show that China's labor share has declined in recent years, but not everyone holds the same view. It will often lead to confusion and misreading of the issue as different statistical calibers are adopted when labor share is compared internationally. When comparable data of employee labor remuneration is adopted to make international comparison of labor share, it is found that China's labor share is quite low due to its low employee employment rate of only 50%. If reaching the average employee employment rate of developed countries of 86%, China's labor share will reach the average level of developed countries and there will be no more low labor share. Of course, when employee labor remuneration is used to measure labor remuneration,

---

1   ZHANG Juwei, Director of the Institute of Population and Labor Economics of the Chinese Academy of Social Sciences, Research Fellow, Doctoral Advisor

labor share changes not only reflect the change in the income distribution pattern but is closely related to the change in the number of employees. Labor share will rise with the increasing number of employees if given wage remains unchanged.

By combining labor share change with employment pattern change, this chapter mainly explores the implications and problems of actual changes in China's labor share with the estimation of the changes in the total wage of Chinese employees (wage earners) and studies of the wage and their differences among different employee groups so as to put forward ideas and opinions for solving the current income distribution problem.

I. Dispute over Labor Share

Labor share has been one of the basic issues in economic research. Mainstream economic theory has long held that labor share is basically stable and is regarded as one of the "characteristic facts" in economic growth (Solow, 1958; Kravis, 1959; Kaldor, 1961). However, judging from the development of the countries across the world, labor share may not be stable with different characteristics in different types of countries: labor share in developed countries tends to remain stable at a high level while labor share in developing countries remains stable at a low level. When on its way to a developed state, labor share in underdeveloped country will keep going up from a low level until it remains stable at a high level (Zhang Juwei, Zhang Shibin 2011).

As historical experience of labor share change is often inconsistent with the prediction of economic theory, labor share change has always been a controversy since Ricardo. The debate over the issue lies not only in the fact that it is difficult to forge a consensus in theory so as to come up with an explanatory theory for income distribution but also in the fact that there are differences in labor share across the world to a large extent. In many cases, labor share change does not really show the actual changes in factor distribution share but shows the measurement difference of labor remuneration in national income accounting.

Labor remuneration may seem to be a simple concept, but it is not simple to do labor remuneration accounting from the perspective of national income. When a person labors for others, his labor remuneration should include any remuneration related to labor. According to the definition of labor remuneration of the United Nations' national income accounting, labor remuneration or employee remuneration includes not only wage, salaries, commissions, bonuses, tips, subsistence allowances, leave and sickness benefits, etc. but social security contributions, family benefits, severance payments, and other benefits paid by employers. However, when a person labors for himself with other production factors such as land, capital, plant and equipment, it will be hard to measure labor remuneration because there is no clear criteria as to how much of the total income should be considered as labor income so that there will be different caliber when calculating the total labor remuneration of a nation.

Generally speaking, there are two statistical calibers for total labor remuneration in the world. One caliber includes not only employee labor remuneration but the mixed income of the non-corporate individual employee from their individual businesses; the other caliber only covers employee labor remuneration. The main difference between the two calibers is whether to include the income of the self-employed. Unless two countries' data are carefully compared with the same caliber, it will be confusing and even misleading.

The UN usually adopts the second caliber in the calculation of employee labor remuneration, the labor income of the self-employed economy included in the operating surplus as mixed income. According to the data released by the UN, labor share varies greatly from country to country. According to *Statistical Yearbook of National Accounts* of the UN, out of 94 countries with data in 1992, Ghana had the lowest labor share of only 0.051 while Ukraine had the highest of 0.77 with 18 countries' labor share being less than 0.30 and 8 countries' being more than 0.60 (Gollin, 2002). Generally speaking, the poorer the country, the lower its labor share; the more developed a country, the higher its labor share.

There is a positive correlation between labor share and GDP per capita.

The reason why there is such a big difference in labor share among countries of different development stages is that their total labor remuneration only covers employee labor remuneration without the labor income of the non-corporate self-employed. There is lower labor share in poor countries with self-employed economy as an important part of their countries; rich countries with self-employed economy as less important part of their countries will have a high labor share. When observed diachronically, labor share tends to rise as the country develops. For example, the share of wage income in national income of the U.K. (labor share) has been on the rise since 1860 from 48.5% between 1860 and 1869 to 72.4% between 1950 and 1959 (See Chart 3-1). At the same time, its rental income fell from 13.7% between 1860 and 1869 to 4.9% between 1950 and 1959; and its profits, interest and mixed income fell from 38.9% between 1860 and 1869 to 22.7% between 1950 and 1959 (Deane & Cole, 1962) .

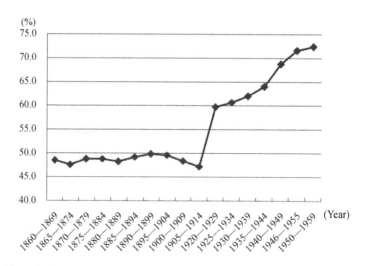

Chart 3-1   Labor Share in National Income of the U.K. (1860-1959)

Source: (Deane, Phyllis & Cole, W. A.,1962)

Labor share of the U.S. has undergone a similar change to that of the U. K. with the employee labor share rising from 55% between 1900 and 1909 to 65.5% between 1947 and 1952 (Johnson, 1954) (See Chart 3-2). Labor share in such countries with rapid economic development as South Korea and Japan has always been on the rise. According to *Statistical Yearbook of National Income Accounts of the UN*, labor share changes in these two countries are found as follows: labor share of South Korea was only about 34% in 1970 and has been on a steady rise with its rapid development of industrialization and urbanization and has been stable after reaching about 50% in 1990. Labor share of Japan was about 42% in 1970, 8% higher than that of South Korea and rose to about 53% in 1975 and has been stable ever since.

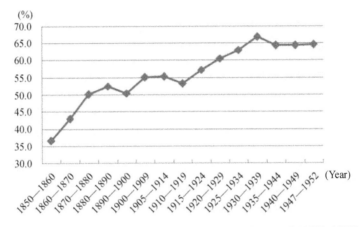

Chart 3-2 Labor Share in National Income of the U.S.(1850-1952)

Source: D. Gale Johnson, 1954.

China has only labor share data with the first caliber, that is, China's labor remuneration includes not only employee labor remuneration but labor income of the self-employed. Is China's labor share too low when compared internationally? How's China's labor share in the world? For lack of the data of the same statistical caliber, it's impossible to answer these questions by comparing China's labor share with that of other countries. Otherwise, it will only lead to incorrect or even ridiculous conclusion.

Compare China's labor share with that of foreign countries with different caliber according to the statistics published by the United Nations. The results of several countries' labor share show that labor share of developed countries is generally stable at between 50% and 60%. For example, labor share of the United

States was 57% in 2007; labor share of the United Kingdom was 60% in 2005; and labor share of Germany was 54% in 2008. Labor share of developing countries is much lower than that of developed countries. For example, India's labor share was 30% in 2008; the Philippines' was 28% in 2008. Labor share of some developing countries was less than 10%. According to the results of GDP accounting with the regional income method of the National Bureau of Statistics, China's labor share was 45% in 2010, close to that of many developed countries and much higher than that of typical developing countries (such as India and the Philippines). In this way, there does not seem to be the so-called China's low labor share. That's why some people still don't think China's labor share is too low or in a downward trend. For example, some people think that China's labor share, lower than that of developed countries, is not low compared with that of other developing countries and isn't in a serious decline (Jia Kang et al. 2010). Others believe that China's labor share is on the rise instead of on the decline (Hua Sheng, 2010).

So, the current debate over China's labor share is not entirely the income distribution problem itself but the misreading of the issue of labor share to a certain extent. In order to understand whether China's labor share is too low and on a decline, it is necessary to make international comparison with comparable data so as to observe the actual labor share changes. In view of this, this chapter attempts to study China's labor share and its changes with the international statistical caliber.

II. China's Actual Labor Share Changes

So far, China has not had an official and widely acknowledged labor share data. Different people or different researches using different data sources to some extent prevents people from understanding the problem. First, look at labor share changes from various data sources published by the National Bureau of Statistics.

(I) Labor Share Changes with the First Caliber based on Data from the National Bureau of Statistics

The total labor remuneration from various data sources published by the National Bureau of Statistics adopts the first statistical caliber including not only employee salaried wage but labor income of the self-employed. Currently, there are three data sources: GDP accounting data of the regional income method, input-output table and funds flow table.

The labor share obtained with GDP accounting of the regional income method has been the most widely used data source with its temporal continuity and long temporal span. However, because of China's graded accounting system, the intervention of local government in the regional GDP accounting tend to cause the local GDP aggregated to be higher than its national accounting data, resulting in the inaccuracy of national labor share. This data source indicates that labor share rose from 49.64% to 53.68% between 1978 and 1984 and remained relatively stable at 50% between 1985 and 1998 and was on the decline after 1999 and declined sharply especially after 2004 till it reached a record low of 39.74% in 2007 and rebounded to 46.62% and 45.01% respectively in 2009 and 2010, roughly the same level as before 2004.

It must be pointed out that the National Bureau of Statistics has made adjustment in statistical caliber in labor share accounting. Total labor remuneration prior to 2004 includes labor income of the self-employed which consists of household operating income of farmers and the operating income of individual businesses in cities and towns. After the 2004 national economic census, the above statistical caliber of labor remuneration has changed in that the operating income of individual businesses in cities and towns as the operating surplus of enterprises is not included in labor remuneration. At the same time, there is no more operating surplus in agriculture. The sudden decline in labor share in 2004 mainly resulted from this change in the statistical calibre. So far, the National Bureau of Statistics hasn't accounted for the sudden rise in labor share starting in 2009. A reasonable guess may be that the statistical calibre has been readjusted to pre-2004 status.

The second data source of labor share is input-output table. This less used data is relatively accurate or comprehensive because the input-output table requires a great deal of research and accounting with detailed breakdown of the industry, making it possible to measure labor share of different sectors. The data are insufficient, discontinuous and lag behind. So far, the National Bureau of Statistics has compiled nine value input-output tables of 1987, 1990, 1992, 1995, 1997, 2000, 2002, 2005 and 2007. The results obtained from the input-output tables show that labor share has declined greatly since 1997 from 54.87% in 1997 to 41.36% in 2007, a decline of more than 13% within a decade. But there has been a slight decline from 47.23% in 1987 to 41.36% in 2007, a decline of less than 6%.

Up till now, the third data source of labor share has been the widely used funds flow table which the National Bureau of Statistics began to compile from 1992 up to 2008. After the 2004 economic census, the National Bureau of Statistics has revised the labor remuneration data in the funds flow table according to the results of the census so that there has been two series of funds flow table data, one being the backtracking adjusted data and the other being non-backtracking adjusted data. The latter series dropped sharply in 2004 while the former became more stable. After backtracking adjustment, China's labor share was 54.59% in 1992, 52.78% in 1995, and decreased to 47.79% in 2008 (See Table 3-1). The problem with the data of the funds flow table lies in the fact that in non-economic census years, labor remuneration data are often estimated based on the assumption that labor remuneration growth and disposable residents' income growth are of the same rate, leading to an overestimation of labor remuneration (Bai Chong'en, Qian Zhenjie, 2009).

Table 3-1 compares labor share changes from three data sources. The input-output table has the highest data before 2000 while the funds flow table has the highest data after 2000. Comparatively speaking, the labor share of regional income method is the lowest among the three, the downward trend being the most stable. Both the regional income method and the input-output table show the sharp decline in labor share while the change in funds flow table is relatively stable. Thus, it can be said that the data of the funds flow table have been adjusted systematically with a relatively consistent statistical caliber and that the regional income method data and the input-output table not having been adjusted in this way is still under the influence of the change of statistical caliber.

Table 3-1   Labor Share with Different Data Sources (%)

Year	Regional Income Method	Input-output Table	Funds Flow Table	
			Adjusted	Unadjusted
1987	52. 02	47. 23	—	—
1988	51. 69	—	—	—
1989	51. 55	—	—	—
1990	53. 31	46. 72	—	—
1991	52. 12	—	—	—
1992	50. 04	45. 23	54. 59	63. 47
1993	49. 49	—	51. 43	61. 49
1994	50. 35	—	52. 30	60. 17
1995	51. 44	57. 89	52. 78	60. 00
1996	51. 21	—	52. 10	57. 86
1997	51. 03	54. 87	53. 00	58. 71
1998	50. 82	—	52. 52	58. 72
1999	49. 97	—	52. 60	59. 65
2000	48. 71	54. 06	50. 46	59. 55
2001	48. 23	—	49. 63	58. 54
2002	47. 75	48. 38	50. 42	59. 45
2003	46. 16	—	49. 20	58. 90
2004	41. 55	—	47. 04	50. 60
2005	41. 40	41. 73	50. 30	50. 30
2006	40. 61	—	49. 10	49. 10
2007	39. 74	41. 36	48. 00	48. 00
2008	—	—	47. 79	47. 79
2009	46. 61	—	—	—
2010	45. 01	—	—	—

Source: The National Bureau of Statistics (1) < Historical Data of China's Funds Flow Table (1992-2004)>; (2) < China Statistical Yearbook (2010) >; (3) Data of Input-Output Table published by The National Bureau of Statistics

From the above three data sources of China's labor share, although there has been significant decline in China's labor share, people still debate over the extent to which the labor share has declined or even over whether it has declined due to the change in statistical caliber. Therefore, it is of vital importance to study labor share changes with a universal statistical caliber.

(II) Labor Share Changes with the Second Caliber based on Author's Estimation

The problem caused by different statistical calibers can be avoided by measuring employee labor remuneration covering only the clearly defined and easily handled remuneration of wage earners. However, the National Bureau of Statistics has never published any data on labor remuneration with this caliber in China.

Analyzing the funds flow table has enabled us to estimate China's total employee labor remuneration as the funds flow table provides an access to labor remuneration of non-financial enterprises, financial enterprises, government departments and residents, according to which employee sector can be distinguished from self-employed sector. Specifically, the total national employee labor remuneration can be obtained by adding the labor remuneration of employee sector including both enterprises (including non-financial enterprises and financial enterprises) and government departments. Residents' labor remuneration is obtained through self operations, that is, labor income of the self-employed. According to this classification, changes in employee labor share between 1992 and 2008 are shown in Table 3-2. As is seen, employee labor share was 33.28% in 1992 and 30.26% in 2008, fell by more than 3%, not much of a decline. In view of the fact that employee labor share, the universal statistical caliber, can be used for international comparison. China's labor share was 30.26% in 2008, only about half the average of developed countries and almost the same as that of some developing countries such as India and the Philippines, a typical characteristic of developing countries. Therefore, it's indisputable that China's labor share is indeed low.

Table 3-2   Employee Labor Share and Self-employed Labor Share Estimated with the Data of Funds Flow Table (%)

Year	Labor Remuneration in Total GDP			Labor Remuneration in Sectoral GDP	
	Total	Employee Sector	Self-employed Sector	Employee Sector	Self-employed Sector
1992	54.59	28	21. 31	47.53	71. 08
1993	51.43	31. 77	19. 66	43. 71	71. 98
1994	52.30	31. 86	20. 44	44. 84	70. 61
1995	52.78	32. 65	20. 13	45. 35	71. 88
1996	52.10	32. 05	20. 06	45. 68	67. 22
1997	53.00	32. 42	20. 58	46. 30	68. 66
1998	52.52	31. 37	21. 15	45. 31	68. 74
1999	52.60	31. 14	21. 46	45. 33	68. 54
2000	50.46	29. 17	21. 29	43. 00	66. 18
2001	49.63	28. 87	20. 76	41. 57	67. 96
2002	50.42	30. 62	19. 80	42. 86	69. 34
2003	49.20	30. 33	18. 86	42. 75	64. 95
2004	47.04	29. 57	17. 46	41. 07	62. 37
2005	50.30	31. 44	18. 86	43. 61	67. 57
2006	49.10	30. 68	18. 42	42. 48	66. 31
2007	48.00	30. 11	17. 89	41. 54	65. 03
2008	47.79	30. 26	17. 53	41. 22	65. 90

Source: the National Bureau of Statistics: (1) *Historical Data of China's Funds Flow Table (1992-2004)*; (2) *China Statistical Yearbook (2010)*

In order to verify the estimation results based on funds flow table, the total annual employee labor remuneration can be estimated based on the survey data of annual urban and rural residents' income in *China Statistical Yearbook* published annually by the National Bureau of Statistics by adding up the urban and rural residents' income excluding the income of the self-employed. Of course, the total labour remuneration obtained through this approach may be underestimated, as respondents tend to understate their income, but such systemic errors do not seem to have much effect on observing labour share changes. The data of urban and rural residents' income provides the most complete total employee labor remuneration with continuity and the longest time span. According to estimation from this data source, China's employee labor remuneration (or salaried labour remuneration, equivalent to employee labor remuneration in this chapter) share was 23.55% in 1985, 26.95% in 2010 with a mere growth of 3.5% in 25 years, the highest of which reached 29.92% in 2003.

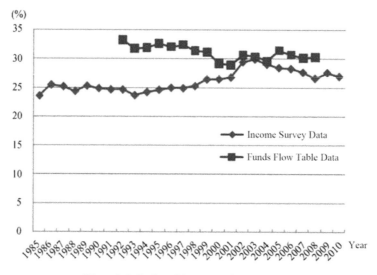

Chart 3-3 Labor Share (1985-2010)

Chart 3-3 shows labor share changes estimated based on funds flow table and survey of urban and rural residents' income respectively. It can be seen from this chart that in either estimation, China's labor share hasn't experienced any serious decline but remains steadily low. The difference between the two series of data is that labor share based on funds flow table is higher than that based on the income survey, especially in earlier period. After 2003, the gap between the two series has greatly narrowed, which proves the assumption that there is an overestimation of labor remuneration in earlier data of funds flow table while there is somewhat an underestimation of labor remuneration in survey data of residents' income. Anyway, data on labor share with the same statistical caliber is obtained, from which a conclusion can be drawn that China's labor share hasn't experienced any serious decline but remains steadily low. So, does this relative stability of labor share mean that there is no serious problem in income distribution pattern? Only with a clear understanding of the real implications of employee labor share changes can a clearer judgment be made on the problem.

III. Definition of Labor Share Changes

With the caliber of employee labor remuneration, labor share will be clearly defined and internationally comparable and reflect labor income changes against capital income, showing the extent to which economic growth translates into labor income growth. In fact, labor share means more than this. The number of employees also affects labor share. Assuming the total output, profits and wage remain unchanged, as the number of employees or employees in total employment grows, so does labor share. Labor share, therefore, can measure the economic development to some extent. The more developed, the higher the employment rate, thus the higher labor share. Labor share of OECD developed economies is mostly high with a high employment rate (wage workers). Conversely, backward developing countries where agriculture is still their main employment sector tend to have a low employment rate and a low employee labor share.

Generally speaking, when a country's employee employment process is over, as in most developed countries, a relatively stable labor share can reflect the extent to which social wealth is transformed into labor income. However, for developing countries whose employee employment is still going on, their low labor share cannot be directly interpreted as the low real wage of workers as changes in employment pattern must be taken into account. Since currently China is developing rapidly, its labor share changes not only implies its change in income distribution pattern but the changes in its employment pattern.

In fact, China's current low labor share is mainly caused by its relatively low employee employment rate. Since China is still a developing country, there has been a major change in its employment pattern from self-employment to employee employment, that is, on its way to employee employment. Employee employment is employees working for their employer who pays for their labor remuneration while self-employment, simply put, means no employer paying for labor remuneration. There are two main types of self-employment in China. One is the business operations in rural areas with households as their own labor force and related capital inputs so as to have output and income through land, whose net income is reflected in the difference between input and output. The other type of self-employment is the individual industrial and commercial businesses in urban and rural areas, commonly referred to as individual businesses. It should be pointed out that the business operations of individual businesses that are carried out entirely by individuals or family members is self-employment. However, according to the existing laws, individual businesses may hire employees. As long as the number of employees does not exceed a certain number, individual businesses will be still regarded as self-employment employing workers whose income is paid by individual businesses.

Employee employment tends to be more stable with higher income and better security than self-employment. It is a symbol of social progress and development for a country's employment pattern to change from self-employment to employee employment. China's employee employment is generally low with a wide urban and rural gap. Urban employee employment rate has experienced a rapid decline and then a slow growth since the reform and opening up. In 1978, urban employee employment rate was close to 100%[1], but with the continuous acceleration of labor market reform, employment continued to differentiate with a declining employment rate, which fell to only 50.91% in 2003. Since then, however, there

---

1 According to the employment statistics in *China Statistical Yearbook* published by the National Bureau of Statistics, urban employment is divided as follows: State-owned units, collective units, joint-stock cooperative units, associated units, limited liability companies, joint stock limited companies, private enterprises, investment units of Hong Kong, Macao and Taiwan businesses, foreign investment units and individual businesses. This chapter regards all employment as employee employment except urban individual businesses.

has been a growth in urban employee employment rate which rose to 54.31% in 2010. There has been a steady upward trend in rural employee employment[1]. In 1978, the majority of rural employment is self-employed with a

high rate of 91% and an employee employment rate of only 9%. In 2010, the self-employed employment rate fell to 54% while the employee employment rate rose to 46%, the two being almost equal. By combining both urban and rural employment, China's employment pattern is characterized by a trend of incessant employee employment with a constantly declining self-employment rate from 69% in 1978 to 35% in 2010 and with a steady growth in employee employment rate from about 30% in 1978 to 50% in 2010.

Up to now, developed countries have completed its economic regularization and employee employment with a high employee employment rate and a relatively high labor share. According to the data of the International Labor Organization, the average employee employment rate in developed countries and EU economies was about 86% in 2008, and even as high as 90% in some countries, such as Australia 88.2%, France 89.5%, Germany 88.4%, Japan 86.5%, the U.K. 86.6%, and the U.S. 93%. Compared with these countries, China's employee employment rate is quite low, a root cause of China's low employee labor share. If its employee employment rate will reach an average of around 86% of OECD countries with wage being unchanged, China's labor share should reach about 55%, relatively high even compared with developed countries so that basically there will be no more small low labor share.

Although China's low employee employment rate can justify its current low labor share, there indeed are serious problems in China's income distribution pattern when combining labor share changes with employment pattern changes. In terms of employment pattern changes, employee employment was stagnant between 1992 and 2003, but after 2003 the employee employment rate has been

---

1 According to the National Bureau of Statistics, this chapter regards employment in rural township enterprises and private enterprises as employee employment.

on a rapid rise from 38.5% in 2003 to 45.6% in 2008. However, labor share fails to reflect employment pattern change. According to the previous data estimated with funds flow table, labor share remained basically stable between 1992 and 2008 and basically unchanged especially between 2003 and 2008 (30.33% in 2003 and 30.26% in 2008). A constant rise in the employee employment rate and a relatively stable labor share implies a decline in real wage. The ratio of labor share to employee employment rate can indicate how real wage declines. By definition, a growth in this ratio means a growth in real wage and a decline in this ratio means a decline in real wage. Chart 3-4 shows the change in the ratio of labor share to employment share between 1992 and 2008, fluctuating between 86% and 81% between 1992 and 2002, but since 2003 there has been a steady decline from 78.78% in 2003 to 66.35% in 2008, a decline by a 12.43% within five years (See Chart 3-4).

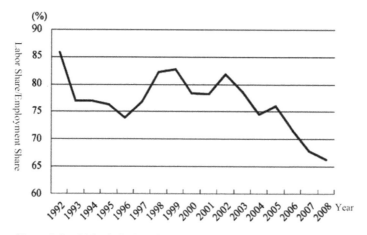

Chart 3-4　China's Labor Share Estimated with Funds Flow Table

IV. China's Income Distribution Problem

What is the overall wage level of wage earners (employees) in China? Is there a downward trend in real wage as is seen above? What are the wage differences and its changing trend among different groups of wage earners? These are quite intriguing open questions. Since the National Bureau of Statistics' wage data cover only urban employees instead of all employees, it would be inappropriate to use only the wage data of urban employees accounting for only a third of all employees (wage earners), as is reported by the National Bureau of Statistics. For example, in 2010 the total number of national urban employees reached 127 million only accounting for 33.35% of the total national employees of 380 million. Therefore, there must be other answers to the above question.

The estimation of both total number of employees and the total employee labor remuneration in this chapter, an indirect estimation of the wage level of wage earners, as well as more detailed urban wage information published by the National Bureau of Statistics will help to answer the questions. Moreover, according to the data available, all employees can be categorized as "urban unit employees" and "other employees", the latter referred to as migrant workers when studying their wage differences. According to the estimation in this chapter, there were 253 million "other employees" in China in 2010. According to the National Bureau of Statistics, there was about 220 million urban migrants, of which there are about 150 million migrant workers while there are about 190 million employees engaged in non-agricultural employment in rural areas, therefore, all together there was about 340 million rural employees and urban migrant workers. There are about 114 million urban flexible employees, most of whom are migrant workers. Deducting 114 million from 340 million will get 226 million which is very close to 253 million, the number of "other employees". Therefore, it is roughly believed that "other employees" are actually migrant workers.

Two sets of data will be adopted to estimate the total national employee labor remuneration, one based on funds flow table and the other based on the survey of urban and rural residents' income. But which set of wage estimation is more reliable or more practical? Judging from the estimated results, the wage level based on funds flow table may be overestimated while the wage level based on the survey of urban and rural residents' income is more reasonable and practical.

According to the estimated results of funds flow table, the average wage of all employees and that of other employees were both much higher than that of urban unit employees for quite a long time after 1992. For example, the average wage of all employees in 1992 was 3,494 yuan, 28% higher than that of urban unit employees, and the average wage of other employees in 1992 was as high as 4,560 yuan, 68% higher than that of urban unit employees, all of which seems unreasonable beyond doubt as urban unit employees, formal group of wage earners, were paid no lower than the average wage of all employees, let alone the average wage of other employees even in the early 1990s. In this sense, the total labor remuneration based on funds flow table is likely to be overestimated. The earlier, the more serious as after 2003, there is no more of such phenomenon. The wage changes based on the survey of urban and rural residents' income is more reasonable. Table 3-3 presents the average annual monetary wage and wage changes of all employees and that of urban unit employees and that of other employees since 1985 based on urban and rural residents' income survey.

Table 3-3   China's Wage Estimated with Urban-Rural Residents' Income Survey

Year	Total Labor Remuneration (100 million yuan)			Average Annual Monetary Wage (yuan)		
	All Employees	Urban Unit Employees	Other Employees	All Employees	Urban Unit Employees	Other Employees
1985	2124	1419	705	1098	1148	1011
1986	2616	1702	913	1261	1329	1150
1987	3036	1928	1108	1379	1459	1259
1988	3664	2377	1287	1583	1747	1348
1989	4296	2658	1637	1859	1935	1748
1990	4639	3008	1631	1975	2140	1729
1991	5365	3394	1971	2208	2340	2013
1992	6630	4009	2621	2585	2711	2414
1993	8363	5000	3364	3036	3371	2645
1994	11664	6920	4744	4179	4538	3746
1995	14965	8410	6555	5141	5500	4744
1996	17772	9447	8325	5946	6210	5672

contd.

Year	Total Labor Remuneration (100 million yuan)			Average Annual Monetary Wage (yuan)		
	All Employees	Urban Unit Employees	Other Employees	All Employees	Urban Unit Employees	Other Employees
1997	19650	9717	9933	6679	6470	6898
1998	21315	9488	11827	7914	7479	8301
1999	23692	10106	13586	8829	8346	9226
2000	26245	10855	15390	9789	9371	10107
2001	29356	12091	17265	10903	10870	10927
2002	35395	13502	21893	12840	12422	13112
2003	40632	15175	25457	14167	14040	14244
2004	46386	17526	28860	15555	16024	15284
2005	52587	20614	31973	16790	18364	15910
2006	61159	24120	37039	18673	21001	17416
2007	73469	29422	44047	21517	24932	19714
2008	83559	34993	48566	23653	29229	20795
2009	94089	40343	53746	25765	32736	22214
2010	108127	47424	60702	28397	37147	23983

Table 3-3 shows that the average annual monetary wage for all employees rose by 24.86 times from 1,098 yuan in 1985 to 28,397 yuan in 2010; during the same period, GDP per capita rose by 33.99 times from 857 yuan to 29,991 yuan so that average monetary employee wage growth is lower than GDP per capita growth. Therefore, it's a further verification of the relatively slow growth in wage earners' labor remuneration compared with GDP growth.

With the relatively slow wage growth of all employees, what is the wage growth difference between urban unit employees and other employees? The change in the ratio of nominal monetary wage to nominal GDP per capita which eliminates the effect of price factors can better reflect wage changes relative to economic growth. Chart 3-5 shows that the ratio of average wage of urban unit employees to GDP per capita and the ratio of other employees to GDP per capita are of the same trend before 2003, both a downward trend and then an upward trend. However, after 2003, there has been a fundamental change in that urban employee wage growth has basically kept pace with GDP growth with a stable ratio of average wage to GDP per capita. However, wage growth of other employees lagged behind GDP growth with a significant declining ratio of average wage to GDP per capita from 1.35 in 2003 to 0.80 in 2010 by a decrease of 0.55.

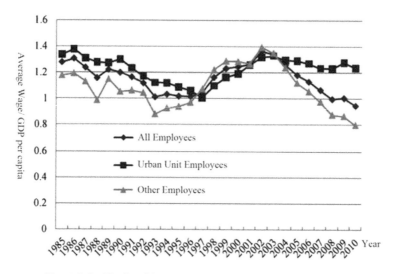

Chart 3-5   Ratio of Average Earners' Wage to GDP per capita

Real wages have experienced a roughly similar change. In 1985, the average wage of all employees, of urban unit employees, and of other employees was 1,098 yuan, 1,148 yuan, and 1,011 yuan respectively with a ratio of 1: 1.05: 0.92, which remained the same until 2003. After 2003, there was a fundamental change, highlighted by the fact that the average wage of urban unit employees grew at a faster rate while the average wage of other employees grew relatively slow with a ratio of the three at 1: 1.31: 0.85 by 2010.

The above estimation indicates that there hasn't been any significant differences between wage of urban unit employees and wage of other employees (or migrant workers) for quite a long time until 2003, which comes as a surprise to many, who are under the impression that the wage of migrant workers (other employees) has risen rapidly in recent years as "labor shortage" and "job recruitment difficulties" have intensified. How is it possible that wage of other employees grows more slowly than in the past? But that may be the case. Other studies with micro-survey data have drawn a similar conclusion to ours in this chapter.

For example, with microscopic sampling survey data (CHNS, China Health and Nutrition Survey), Chang Jinxiong and Wang Danfeng (2010) found that for a long time in the past, the wage of informal urban employees (similar to migrant workers) has been always higher than that of formal employees (similar to urban unit employees). In 1997, the average monthly wage of formal employees, informal employees was 991.21 yuan and 1,007.44 yuan with a ratio of 0.98. Since then, there has been a more rapid wage growth of formal employees and a relatively slow wage growth of informal employees with a ratio of 1.15, 1.29, and 1.30 in 2000, 2004 and 2006. The current wage gap between formal employees and informal employees is ever widening rapidly.

After wage changes and differences between urban unit employees and other employees, wage changes and wage differences among different groups of urban unit employees will be discussed. Chart 3-6 shows the changes in GDP per capita and the changes in the ratio of monetary wage of urban unit employees to GDP per capita since 1978. It can be seen from the chart that the nominal GDP per capita of 29,992 yuan in 2010 is 77.7 times the nominal GDP per capita of 381 yuan in 1978, showing a rapid growth since 1978, meanwhile the average nominal wage of urban unit employees of 37,174 yuan in 2010 is 59.4 times the average nominal wage of urban unit employees of 615 yuan in 1978, a wage growth being 18 times smaller than GDP growth, which means wage growth of urban unit employees is also relatively slower than GDP growth. The average monetary wage of urban unit employees was 1.61 times GDP per capita in 1978, but dropped to 1.24 times in 2010, which means that the average wage of urban unit employees has fallen by nearly 30% compared to GDP per capita. Specifically, there has been a downward trend in the average wage of urban unit employees between 1978 and 1997 with a ratio of average wage to GDP per capita declining from 1.61 in 1978 to 1.01 in 1997, and the wage of urban unit employees has been growing slowly after 1997.

The ratio of average wage to GDP per capita has grown from its lowest in 1997 to 1.33 in 2003, which is relatively stable in recent years (See Chart 3-6).

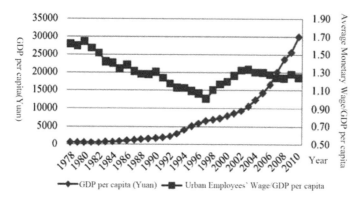

Chart 3-6   Ratio of Average Urban Employees' Wage to GDP per capita

According to the National Bureau of Statistics, urban unit employees can be further divided into state-owned units, collective units and other units, among which, other units mainly include joint-stock cooperative units, limited liability units, foreign-invested units, and so on. Chart 3-7 shows the ratio of average employees' wage of the above three urban units to GDP per capita since 1978.

As can be seen from Chart 3-7, before 1997, there was a downward trend in the ratio of average employees' wage of three urban units to GDP per capita, among which the decline in urban collective units is the largest with its ratio falling from 1.33 in 1978 to 0.7 in 1997, down by 88%, followed by state-owned units with its ratio falling from 1.69 in 1978 to 1.04 in 1997, down by 62%, and then other units with its average wage falling from its highest of 1.83 times GDP per capita in 1991 to 1.42 times GDP per capita in 1997, down by 29.3%. After 1997, employees' wage of these three units changed in different directions.

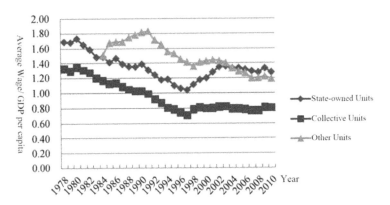

Chart 3-7   Ratio of Average Employees' Wage of Three Urban Units to GDP per capita

Average employees' wage of state-owned units shows a stable upward trend with a ratio of average wage to GDP per capita steadily growing from 1.04 in 1997 to 1.28 in 2010; average employees' wage of collective units has remained at its steady low with a ratio of average wage to GDP per capita fluctuating between 0.7 and 0.8; average employees' wage of other units still showed a significant downward trend with a ratio of average wage to GDP per capita falling further from 1.42 in 1997 to 1.19 in 2010. Among the average employees' wage of these three urban units before 1997, "other unit" employees is the highest, followed by "state-owned unit" employees, the lowest being "collective unit" employees. Current average wage of state-owned units is the highest, followed by other units, collective units still being the lowest.

In all, there was a downward trend in the overall national employees' wage with different wage changes among different employees. Other employees' wage is relatively lower than urban unit employees' wage. Among urban unit employees, state-owned unit employees' wage keeps pace with the growth rate of GDP per capita while there was a serious downward trend in collective unit employees' wage and other unit employees' wage. In labor market, there's almost no wage growth of low income earners while there is a relatively fast wage growth of high income earners, giving rise to wage "polarization".

V. Conclusion and Suggestions

In accordance with the commonly used international statistical caliber, this chapter estimates China's real labor share changes. Combined with employment pattern change, this chapter also calculates the total wage and the changes of China's wage earners, discusses the wage differences of different wage earners, and comes to some understanding and opinions.

First, China's absolute labor share is indeed low when measured by employee labor remuneration mainly caused by the low employee employment rate. If the employee employment rate reaches the level of developed countries, China's labor share will also reach the average level of developed countries and there will be no more low labor share. Moreover, low labor share can not be interpreted as low wage. The total wage changes must be studied with the employment pattern change.

Second, even if there isn't any wage growth, when measured by employee remuneration, labor share should grow as employee employment rate increases. From this perspective, there is indeed serious income distribution issue in China in that China's labor share remains relatively stable despite a continuous growth in the employee employment rate, resulting in a decline in the real wages of wage earners and an income distribution pattern unfavorable to employees.

Third, since the reform and opening up, the overall wage of Chinese wage earners has experienced a down-up-down trend. The current downward trend began in 2003, and for most of the period before 2003, there has been a relatively reasonable wage for wage earners. In fact, in the early stage of reform and opening up, many scholars have been concerned about and discussed the issue of "wage swallowing up profit" (Dai Yuanchen, E. Hon-ming Li, 1988; Tang Zongkun, 1992), believing that wage was too high instead of being too low. The current situation is the opposite with slow wage growth and "profit swallowing up wage".

Fourth, with the overall wage growing slow, wage changes in different groups of wage earners also diverge: the lower wage employees earn, the slower the wage growth; the higher wage employees earn, the faster the wage growth, giving rise to wage "polarization" in labor market.

In general, the slow growth of the overall employee wage, especially of the low income employees, is getting serious. How to achieve a reasonable wage growth is the key to the improvement of the current income distribution.

Fundamentally speaking, the wage of wage earners is mainly determined by the supply-and-demand in the labor market, and the key reason for the slow wage growth is still caused by the fact that labor supply exceeds demand. In this case, to improve employees' wage requires employment expansion. Only when the labor resources is scarce is it possible to achieve wage growth. To this end, the transfer of rural labor force is to be sped up so as to improve non-agricultural employment. Although China's rural labor transfer has made great achievements, the employment rate in the agricultural sector is still very high (29.57% in the primary sector in 2014 with 227 million people), making it the largest source of informal employment. If the number of people employed in the agricultural sector does not continue to decrease, employee employment rate and formal employment will not improve, making it impossible to improve wage. At the same time, economic development and structural transformation is to be sped up by constantly improving employee employment and formal employment. If employees transferred to the non-agricultural sector cannot find suitable jobs, they will have to choose self-employment of an individual nature, which will not contribute to wage growth.

Of course, to achieve reasonable growth in labor remuneration requires systems and the government to play its role in setting up normal wage growth mechanism. In view of this, measures are to be taken as follows: first, dynamically adjust minimum wage in accordance with economic and social development so as to guarantee the rights of low-wage earners to share the economic growth; second, strengthen labor protection by strictly enforcing the labor contract law so as to further improve the labor contract system and labor protection system, labor supervision, and the tripartite coordination mechanism for wage growth; third, promote the wage collective bargaining system so as to enhance the rights of the workers in wage determination. In all, China's current market environment is generally favorable to capital as cities adopt preferential policies to attract domestic and foreign capital. As workers, low middle-income workers in particular, often fail to get better protection after their labor rights are damaged, it is urgent to create a fair market environment favorable to workers by carrying out the wage collective bargaining system so as to enhance workers' rights in wage determination, which is actually the key measure to ensure reasonable wage growth with the mechanism.

Chapter IV

Wage Changes and Wage Growth in China: Should Wage Grow?

ZHANG Juwei, ZHAO Wen[1]

China has become one of the upper middle income countries in the world with its GDP per capita of over US $8,000. But its economic slowdown has caused concern about the middle-income trap (Gill & Kharas, 2007). The key to overcoming the middle-income trap is sustained industrial competitiveness (Cai Fang, 2011). If industrial competitiveness can continuously improve, economy will continue to grow and employment will expand so that the "middle income trap" will be easy to solve (Ma Xiaohe, 2010). To maintain and improve industrial competitiveness, there must be reasonable wage growth. If wage growth deviates from labor productivity and total factor productivity, there soon will be no more industrial competitiveness (Park Bokyeong, Huang Yanghua, 2013).

There have been researches into China's wage. Comparing China's industrial

---

1 ZHANG Juwei, Director of the Institute of Population and Labor Economics of the Chinese Academy of Social Sciences, Research Fellow, Doctoral Advisor; ZHAO Wen, Associate Research Fellow of the Institute of Population and Labor Economics of the Chinese Academy of Social Sciences.

labor productivity and wages with enterprise data, Du Yang and Qu Yue (2009; 2012) found that labor productivity grows faster than wage growth before 2007. Li Wenpu et al. (2011) found that unit labor costs in China's manufacturing sector kept falling between 1999 and 2009 while a study by Cheng Chengping et al (2012) found that despite wage growth, China's manufacturing industry has become more competitive globally. However, Harry X. Wu (2013) found that since 2008 the total factor productivity (TFP), unit labor costs and marginal capital return have deteriorated sharply, contrary to the conclusion of the above studies.

From a macro perspective,with the fundamental changes between labor supply and labor demand, there has been intense recruitment issue in enterprises and a rapid wage

growth of migrant workers so that it has been taken for granted that there is no more labor advantage and no more economic growth in China. China's labor share keeps falling, which seems to contradict the wage growth of migrant workers. Is China's employees' wage high or low? Is the previous wage growth reasonable? Is there room for wage growth? Will wage growth have an impact on industrial competitiveness? This chapter is intended for the above questions.

This chapter estimates and analyzes employees' wage and its changes and discusses the reasonable wage growth with profits, comparative labor productivity and comparative total factor productivity. Part One estimates and analyzes the wage and wage changes of all employees' and employees in different industries and sectors. Part Two discusses the room for wage growth by comparing wage changes, comparative labor productivity, profits and comparative total factor productivity. Part Three is conclusion and suggestions.

I. Wage Changes

Since only wage data of urban unit employees accounting for one-third of all employees are published by the National Bureau of Statistics, China is still in need of wage data of all employees. Our previous study (Zhang Juwei, 2012a) calculated wage and all employees' wage changes by estimating number of all Chinese employees and its total labor remuneration, changes of all employees and found that since the reform and opening up, the average employees' wage has experienced the trend of first falling and then rising and then falling again. The highest average wage appeared around year 2002 with the ratio of nominal monetary wage to nominal GDP per capita at 1.37 which dropped all the way to 0.91 in 2012. If all employees are divided into urban unit employees (urban unit workers) and other employees (mainly those employed in private enterprises and township enterprises), urban unit employees' wage growth basically keeps pace with GDP per capita growth with the ratio of wage to GDP per capita at 1.24 in 2012 while other employees' wage growth has lagged far behind GDP per capita growth with the ratio of nominal per capita wage to GDP per capita declining from a record high of 1.39 in 2002 to 0.72 in 2012 (See Chart 4-1).

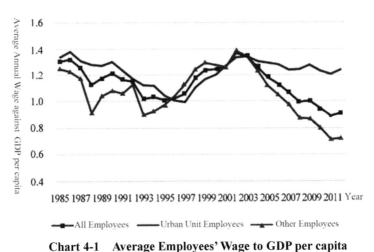

Chart 4-1   Average Employees' Wage to GDP per capita

Source: Website of the National Bureau of Statistics (http://data.stats. gov.cn /).

(I) Wage Changes in Certain Industries

What is the wage trend of urban unit employees in different industries? When discussing income distribution, the wage gap between industries, high wage in certain monopolistic industries in particular, has always been the focus of public opinion. As monopolistic industries with their possession of resources and administrative privileges obtain excess profits by non-marketized means, monopoly is believed to be the major cause for the wage gap between industries and enterprises. Since these monopolistic profits or rents are turned into employee income or welfare in different ways, the income of employees in monopolistic industries often exceeds that of competitive industries, giving rise to a widening residents' income gap.

The employment statistics of *China Statistical Yearbook* are about the wage of urban unit employees of 19 industries. Chart 4-2 is about the top five industries with the highest wage. Between 2003 and 2012, there was an upward wage trend in finance and mining while there was a downward wage trend in such sectors as information transmission, software and information technology services, scientific research and technological services, production and supply of electricity, heat, gas, and water.

In 2012, average wage ratio of finance, information transmission, software and information technology services, scientific research and technological services, production and supply of electricity, heat, gas, and water, mining to that of urban unit employees was 1.92:72:1.48:1.24:1.22:1.

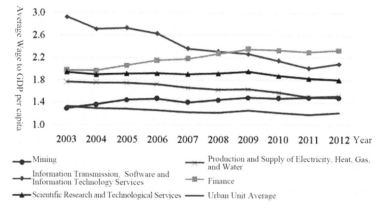

Chart 4-2   Average Urban Unit Employees' Wage: High-waged Industries

Source: Website of the National Bureau of Statistics (http://data.stats. gov.cn /).

In all, wage growth in the top five industries have kept pace with GDP growth. In terms of the ratio of nominal wage to GDP per capita, wage growth in financial industry exceeds GDP growth while the significant wage decline from a high level in information transmission, software and information technology services is similar to the wage in other industries. Several other high-waged industries have basically kept pace with GDP growth.

Chart 4-3 shows that the wage of the five industries with the lowest wage has always been on the decline since 2003. Construction, accommodation and catering, residential services, repair and other services are the five low-end labor-intensive industries, whose wage is very similar to each other with labor mobility. In 2012, the average wage ratio between agriculture, forestry, animal husbandry and fishery, accommodation and catering, water conservancy, environment and utility management, residential services, repair and other services, construction to urban unit employees is 0.49: 0.67: 0.69: 0.75: 0.78: 1. In all, wage growth lags behind GDP growth in industries with the lowest wage, whose real wages are on the decline.

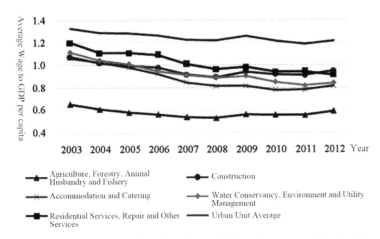

Chart 4-3   Average Urban Unit Employees' Wage: Low-waged Industries

Source: Website of the National Bureau of Statistics (http://data.stats. gov.cn/).

In the longer term, the wage gap between industries has changed considerably (See Chart 4-4). In the early 1990s, there was almost no wage difference between manufacturing, financial and real estate industries, whose absolute wage was almost the same as the average urban unit employees' wage. Since then, the wage of financial sector has grown rapidly with an average wage of 89,743 yuan in 2012 while the wage of manufacturing industry has been on a slow decline with an average wage of 41,650 yuan in 2012. And the average wage of monopoly industries with unique benefits of housing, income outside wages, etc. such as electricity, telecommunications, finance, insurance, tobacco, oil, etc. is two to three times the average wage of other industries, the real income gap between these two groups being far wider.

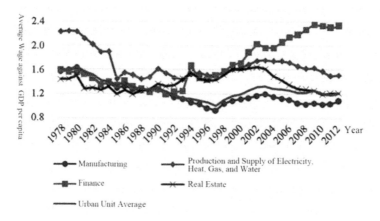

Chart 4-4　Average Employees' Wage of Certain Industries

Source: Website of the National Bureau of Statistics (http://data.stats. gov.cn/).

To some extent, the widening industry income gap is caused by both institutions and policies. There has been no resources tax, regulation tax on monopoly profit and so on in China's fiscal and taxation system. Since there is no reasonable distribution system and transparent budget mechanism for both state-owned enterprise income and land circulation income and when the price of resource commodity rises and the vast majority of income is converted into enterprise income or local government income, enterprises get not only operating income but the resource income which is supposed to be part of the national distribution system. Therefore, it is necessary to establish a more sound fiscal and taxation system to make resource income part of the national finance so as to benefit the whole nation.

The widening industry income gap is also caused by human capital gap between industries as the marketization reform has improved both capital return and human capital return. Human capital has had a growing impact on the income gap. Dynamic analysis shows that human capital accounts for 44.4% of wage Gini coefficient growth (Chen Yuyu, et al., 2004) and that the education-income correlation and education return growth have led to educational accountability growth, resulting in serious wage inequality. After the reform and opening up, human capital has become increasingly important with market regulation as distribution model and with distribution according to the contribution of production factors. Table 4-1 shows the great human capital difference between industries based on the educational level of China's employees. During industrialization, the new technological revolution has brought about the division within the working class, the skill bias in employment, polarization in both occupation and wage where high-skilled workers with high human capital enjoy more job opportunities and rapid wage growth while low-skilled workers with low human capital enjoy fewer job opportunities and slow wage growth, the internal division shown best in service industry. Different human capital intensity has also resulted in the widening industry income gap.

Table 4-1   Education of Chinese Employees by Industry (2012)

Industry	Average Years of Education	Industry	Average Years of Education	Industry	Average Years of Education
Total	9. 69	Information Transmission, Computer Services and Software	10. 45	Water Conservancy, Environment and Utility Management	11. 32
Agriculture, Forestry, Animal Husbandry and Fishery	7. 84	Wholesaling and Retailing	9. 93	Residential Services and Other Services	9. 81
Mining	10. 39	Accommodation and Catering	11. 37	Education	14. 01

contd.

Industry	Average Years of Education	Industry	Average Years of Education	Industry	Average Years of Education
Manufacturing	10. 18	Finance	13. 20	Health, Social Security and Social Welfare	13. 46
Production and Supply of Electricity, Heat, Gas and Water	12. 25	Real Estate	11. 70	Culture, Physical Education and Entertainment	12. 42
Construction	9. 43	Leasing and Business Services	12. 00	Public Administration and Social Organizations	13. 71
Transport, Warehousing and Postal services	10. 55	Scientific Research, Technical Services and Geological Prospecting	13. 72	International Organizations	11. 73

Source: calculated according to *China Labor Statistical Yearbook* (2013).

(III) Wage Changes of Certain Groups

i. Civil Servants' Wage Changes

At present, there has been a great controversy over whether civil servants' wage should be raised or not. On one hand, the ever rising fever of the "national examination" seems to illustrate civil servants' high wage; on the other hand, there is constant mention about the poor livelihood of grass-roots civil servants. The discussion about a large number of gray income in national income and the corrupted civil servants have aroused people's imagination of civil servants' real income. To answer the question whether civil servants' wage should be raised, civil servants' real wage is to be compared with that of other groups with similar human capital, such as those employed by state-owned units or urban units.

Both *China Statistical Yearbook* and *China Labor Statistical Yearbook* published by the National Bureau of Statistics provide the average wage of party and government officials, the so-called civil servants. According to the data published by the National Bureau of Statistics over the years, civil servants' wage is as follows. Before 1998, the average civil servants' wage was basically the same as that of state-owned units and urban units, sometimes slightly lower. At that time, the wages of foreign investment units, Hong Kong, Macao and Taiwan investment units were one and a half times that of civil servants. As a result, the 1990s saw the intellectuals and civil servants going for business. The drain of civil servants directly leads to a shortage of government personnel and low working efficiency, resulting in low wages. In response to this situation, the Government decisively raised civil servants' wage in 1999, reaching a record high in 2002 and declining ever since. The wage decline accelerated after 2010 (See Chart 4-5), the annual average civil servants' wage being 46,207 yuan in 2012.

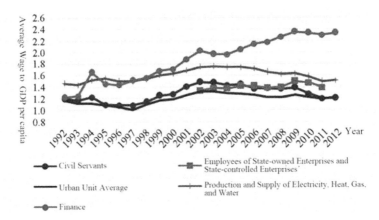

Chart 4-5   Comparison of Civil Servants' Wage with Other Groups' Wage

Source: Website of the National Bureau of Statistics (http: //data. stats. gov. cn/)

The current average civil servants' wage is slightly lower than the average urban unit employees' wage. Chart 4-6 is the comparison of civil servants' wages with those of other urban units. Compared with other industries with a similar human capital such as education, health, culture and social organization, the civil servants' wage is lower, far lower than that of the financial industry, the information industry, and such state-owned enterprises and state-controlled enterprises as the production and supply industry of electricity, gas and water. According to the statistics, in 2012 the average number of years of education of civil servants, of the production and supply of electricity, gas and water, information transmission, computer services and software, finance, scientific research, technological services and geological prospecting, education, health, social security and social welfare, culture, physical education and entertainment was 13.4, 12.25, 10.45, 13.20, 13.72, 14.01, 13.46, and 12.42 respectively. In all, compared with groups with similar human capital, civil servants' wage is relatively lower.

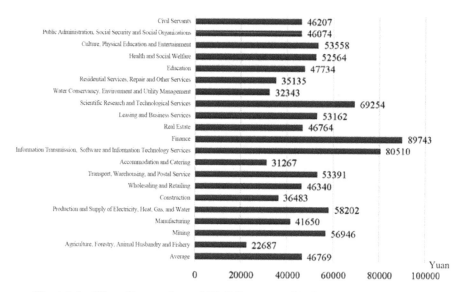

Chart 4-6   Wage Comparison of Civil Servants with Other Industries in 2012

Source: Website of the National Bureau of Statistics (http://data. stats. gov. cn/)

ii. Migrant Workers' Wage Changes

Migrant workers are a rapidly expanding employment group. According to China's first National Agricultural Census, there were 139 million migrant workers across the nation in 1996, including 72 million outbound ones and 67 million local ones. By 2012, there were 263 million migrant workers nationwide, 124 million more than that of 1996 with an annual growth rate of 4.1% including 163 million outbound ones, 91 million more than that of 1996 with an annual growth rate of 5.3% and 99 million local ones, 32 million more than that of 1996 with an annual growth rate of 2.5%.

Among all employees, the great majority of migrant workers work in township enterprises and private enterprises in urban and rural areas as an important part of employee employment. Employment employees are composed of urban unit employees and "other employees", most of whom are migrant workers. There wasn't any wide wage gap between urban unit employees and other employees (migrant workers) in the past. Significant differences occurred after 2003. As is shown in Chart 4-7, according to *National Survey Report on Migrant Workers and Rural Household Survey Yearbook* released by the National Bureau of Statistics, the per capita monthly income of outbound migrant workers grew by an average of 8.7% between 2001 and 2007, whose wage growth rate was significantly slower than that of urban unit employees. Due to the survey method, migrant workers' wage released by the National Bureau of Statistics is on the low side. The adjusted migrant workers' wage by relevant studies (Zhao Wen & Zhang Zhanxin, 2013) is quite close to our calculated wage of "other employees", indicating that our estimation of migrant workers' wage is reliable. Migrant workers' wage growth began in 2008. And between 2007 and 2012, the per capita monthly wage of outbound migrant workers increased by 16.7%, a growth rate nearly doubling that of the previous period. Since 2011, there has been no significant difference between the average wage of migrant workers and that of employees in urban private enterprises. Even so, the ratio of average wage of urban unit employees to that of migrant workers in 2012 was still 1.74: 1.

There is a downward trend in the overall wage of all employees across the nation. In terms of sector, the wage gap between monopolized industries such as finance, telecommunications, etc. and other industries continues to widen while wage in labor-intensive industries such as manufacturing, accommodation and catering is relatively lower. So civil servants' wage was already below urban units' average wage in 2012; migrant workers' wage rose slightly, but was still far from that of other groups. Research suggests that the wage gap among migrant workers is narrow (Feng Yi & Li Shi, 2013). In the labor market, the more disadvantageous the low-income workers, the more difficult it is for their wage to grow while the higher the wage, the more rapid it is for their wage to grow, giving rise to income "polarization" of the workers.

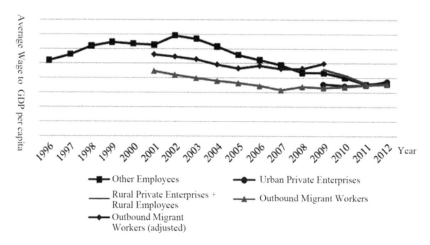

Chart 4-7   Migrant Workers' Wage in Urban Private Enterprises

Sources: NBS website (http://data. stats. gov. cn/).

II. Is There Room for Wage Growth: Comparison with Profits and Productivity

Whether wage should grow or not must be studied by comparing changes in profits and productivity. In theory, if profits growth of an enterprise or industry is brought about by an improvement in operating performance rather than monopoly or administrative intervention, there will be an improvement in labor productivity and total factor productivity, thereby making wage growth possible without weakening competitiveness because of wage growth; Conversely, profits growth does not mean wage growth. Judging from national income distribution pattern, the rapid growth of the ratio of China's corporate surplus to GDP means that there is reasonable room for China's overall wage growth, but it doesn't apply to every industry. If the national corporate surplus is mainly contributed by a few industries and profits in most industries barely increase, there isn't going to be nationwide wage growth.

Since it's relative wage changes rather than absolute wage changes that is mentioned, comparative productivity rather than productivity changes is employed to examine wages and profits in industries and sectors. As comparative labor productivity and comparative total factor productivity refer to the ratio of sector productivity to national productivity, labor productivity and total factor productivity of the nation and every industry needs to be calculated. C-D method is adopted to calculate the total factor productivity (TFP) as follows:

$$TFP_{i,j} = \frac{Y_{i,j}}{K_{i,j}^{\alpha_j} \left(L_{i,j} H_{i,j} \right)^{(1-\alpha_j)}}$$

Among them, Y, K, L and H represents the output of an industry or sector, the capital stock, the number of employees and the number of years of their education respectively, i and j the specific year and the sector respectively, α capital output elasticity. In this chapter, labor productivity refers to average labor productivity rather than marginal labor productivity, the average labor productivity being:

$$APL_{i,j} = \frac{Y_{i,j}}{L_{i,j} H_{i,j}},$$

In many studies, assuming that the production function is a power function, labor productivity and marginal labor productivity are in fact the same thing if capital output elasticity is invariable. Labor productivity and total factor productivity of related industries and sectors is measured based on a brand-new database established after a long period of research which for the first time has completed the data between 1978 and 2011 on capital stock, number of employees, years of education, and output of a total of 6,324 employee sectors and self-employed sectors in three state-owned and non-state-owned industries at provincial level including 2-digit sub-industrial data on capital stock, number of employees, years of education and output data of such industries as 6 mining industries, 30 manufacturing industries and 3 production and and provision industries of electricity, heat, gas and water. According to our previous study of capital output elasticity, capital output elasticity of the national and employee sector capital output elasticity, of industrial and secondary industries and of the tertiary industry is set at 0.597, 0.826 and 0.604 so that the changes in profit and comparative productivity in China's industries and sectors will be studied.

(I) Changes in Total Enterprise Profits and Comparative Total Factor Productivity

Here, changes in total enterprise profits are studied with funds flow table. Chart 4-8 is changes in the ratio of both total enterprise profits and of net production tax to GDP in initial distribution. It can be found that the ratio of total enterprise profits to GDP declined slightly from the early 1990s to its lowest of 16% in 1998, then began to rise rapidly, reaching its highest of 27% in 2008 and then began to drop to 24% in 2011. The ratio of net production tax to GDP rose from 13% in the early 1990s to 16% in 1998 and dropped to 11% in 2000 and 13% in 2011 according to statistical data. In initial distribution, since GDP without total profits and net production tax is total labor remuneration, the decline in Chinese employees' overall wage results from both enterprise profits growth and net government production tax growth. Since net production tax grows slower than enterprise profits, decline in overall employees' wage is mainly caused by enterprise profits growth. In this sense, Chinese employees' overall wage should rise instead of declining.

Take another look at total profits changes of the secondary and tertiary industries. Chart 4-9 is the ratio of total profits of the secondary industry to GDP and comparative total factor productivity changes. Due to TFP mistakes caused by statistical problems of the secondary industry, comparative total factor productivity of industry is calculated by using the statistical data of above-scale industries. Before 2007, the ratio of total profits of the secondary industry to GDP kept pace with comparative total factor productivity. Then, as the ratio of industry to national productivity fell, so did the ratio of total profits of above-scale industrial enterprises to GDP. However, productivity changes cannot account for profit growth in 2010, which requires further study.

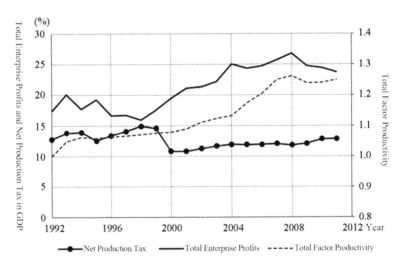

**Chart 4-8   Ratio of both Total Enterprise Profits and of Net Production Tax to GDP
and Total Factor Productivity in Initial Distribution**

Sources: http: //data. website.stats. gov. cn/.

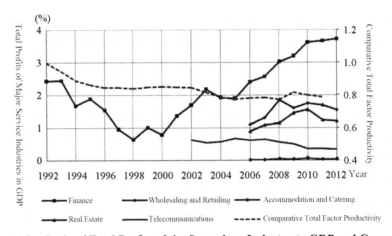

**Chart 4-9   Ratio of Total Profits of the Secondary Industry to GDP and Comparative
Total Factor Productivity**

Sources: http://data. stats. gov. cn/.

Financial industry has got the fastest profits growth among the tertiary industry
which includes banking, securities, and insurance. Chart 4-10 is the changes in
ratio of total profits of financial industry to GDP. In 2000, total profits of financial

industry was 79.4 billion yuan with its ratio to GDP less than 1% by 2011 and was 1.7359 trillion yuan with its ratio to GDP more than 4% in 2011. Between 2000 and 2011, its total profits growth was 1.15 times GDP growth in the same period. However, comparative total factor productivity of the tertiary industry shows a downward trend in the same period. Chart 4-10 is the ratio of total profits of industries' such as wholesale and retail, accommodation and catering, real estate and telecommunications to GDP is 802.32 billion yuan, 16 billion yuan, 630 billion yuan and 179.73 billion yuan respectively in 2012. The ratio of wholesale and retail, accommodation and catering, real estate to GDP goes up and down while the ratio of telecommunications industry to GDP has been on the decline since 2012.

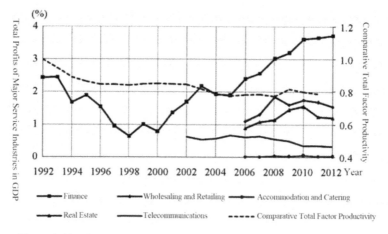

Chart 4-10   Ratio of Total Profits of Major Service Industries to GDP

Source: http://data. stats. gov. cn/.

Deducting total above-scale industries' profits and the total profits of some tertiary industries such as finance, wholesale and retail, accommodation and catering, real estate and telecommunications from total enterprise profits with national income accounting is enterprise profits balance, which is mainly from tertiary industry such as transportation, warehousing and postal service as well as below-scale industries, construction enterprises (small-medium enterprises) and below-scale tertiary industrial enterprise (small-medium enterprises). As operating profits of transportation, warehousing and postal services were modest with 61.578 billion yuan in 2012, only 0.1% of GDP, enterprise profits balance mainly reflects total profits changes of small-medium enterprises. Chart 4-11 is the ratio of total SME profits to GDP, which declined very rapidly between 2008 and 2010, not only reflecting the impact of statistical calibre adjustment, the impact of the international financial crisis but the fact that there doesn't seem to be any reasonable room for wage growth in SMEs.

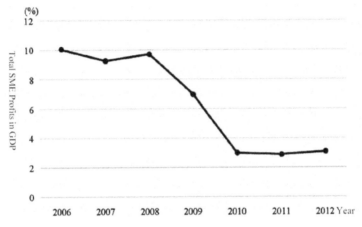

Chart 4-11 Ratio of Total SMEs Profits to GDP

Source: http://data. stats. gov. cn/.

(III) Comparison between Wages, Profits and Productivity

Since total industries' profits changes as are seen above fail to show their actual profit growth, study of actual profit growth needs to eliminate the impact of industry scale changes so that industry profit index is adopted, referring to the ratio of total profits of an industry or an enterprise to the total profits of all industries or enterprises, divided by the ratio of its added value to GDP. Profit index being about 1 indicates that an industry or enterprise has achieved an average profit. Profit index being on the rise means profits have risen compared to that of other industries or enterprises in the previous time and vice versa.

Take a look at wages, profits and productivity in state-owned and non-state-owned industries. In the 1980s, there was "wage swallowing up profit" (Dai Yuanchen & E. Hon-ming Li, 1988; Tang Zongkun, 1992), too high wages which still exists in some state-owned sectors. Chart 4-12 is a comparison of wage and profits between above-scale state-owned and above-scale non-state-owned industries. State-owned industries' wage is higher with the ratio of average wage to GDP per capita now reaching 1.4, where there has been a slow upward trend since 2003 with low profits, basically keeping pace with wage. Therefore, there isn't any profit swallowing up wages in the state-owned sector maintaining a reasonable wage growth. Since wage growth depends on the growth of enterprise profits or labor productivity, currently there is no room for wage growth. There is a great wage difference in different state-owned enterprises and its overall high wage may not apply to any enterprise, some higher while others lower. Take manufacturing industry in 2011 for example, wage of its 143,000 employees of the tobacco industry averaged 99,893 yuan while wage of its 184,000 employees of the nonmetallic mineral industry averaged only 30,485 yuan, very serious wage polarization in different sectors of state-owned industries. It seems that reform is the only way out for state-owned companies with low average wage because of the difficulty of raising wages. It is a completely different picture for the non-state-owned sector: first is low wage with the ratio of average wage to GDP per capita being about 1 and overall decline trend since 2003; next is considerable enterprise profits growth exceeding 2. Both shows that in non-state-owned sector there was serious profit swallowing up wage characterized by unreasonable wage growth and ample room for wage growth. Some studies have suggested that wage differences between state-owned and non-state-owned sectors are mainly determined by employees' human capital (Luo Rundong et al., 2014).

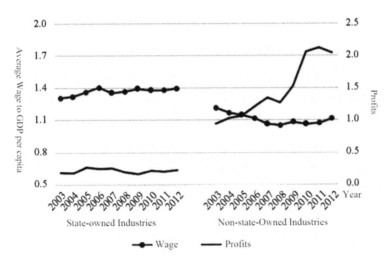

Chart 4-12   Wage and Profit between State-owned and Non-state-Owned Industries
Source: NBS website (http: // data.stats. gov.cn/.

Does productivity growth make room for wage growth? As is shown in Chart 4-13, between 2003 and 2012, comparative labor productivity of state-owned industries grew rapidly and comparative total factor productivity remained unchanged while those of non-state-owned industries were on the decline. Difference in comparative total factor productivity (CTFP) between China's state-owned and non-state-owned industries is caused by inefficiency of capital allocation (Liu Wei, Li Shaorong, 2001; Song, 2011). In contrast, private enterprises are characterized by their efficient productivity and relatively weak financing ability, a major factor deterring China's economic development. As Chinese financial institutions favor state-owned enterprises, private enterprises have to rely on retained profits, personal savings and informal channels to finance their operations and development, one of the reasons why China's total enterprise profits have been on the decline and why non-stated-owned industries can't afford wage growth.

It's worthwhile to study the relationship between middle-upstream industry and downstream industry covering the relationship between state-owned and non-state-owned economy and the relationship between light industry and heavy industry, import sector and export sector, monopoly economy and competitive economy as well. Industries are divided into energy industry, basic material industry and finished and semi-finished product industry based on the concept of upstream and downstream. Higher wage and lower profits of energy industry in the upstream industry reflect the characteristics of monopoly economy, as is shown in Chart 4-14. Lower wage and higher profits of basic material industry in the lower-middle stream industry and the finished and semi-finished product industry reflect the characteristics of competitive economy.

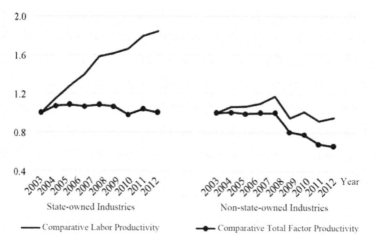

Chart 4-13　Comparative Labor Productivity and Comparative Total Factor Productivity of both State-owned and Non-state-owned industries

Source: NBS website (http: // data.stats. gov.cn/).

As is shown in Chart 4-15, comparative labor productivity of energy industry has grown rapidly with its comparative total factor productivity keeping pace with national economic growth. The rapid decline in comparative labor productivity and comparative total factor productivity of basic material industry after 2007 is possibly due to rising prices of overseas raw materials and overcapacity. Accordingly, comparative productivity of finished and semi-finished industries also declined after 2007. In terms of room for wage growth, despite already high wage, energy industry's rapid growth of labor productivity makes much room for wage growth. After 2008, labor productivity of basic material industry has kept pace with national growth but with limited wage growth. After 2008, comparative labor productivity of finished and semi-finished product industry has improved with certain room for wage growth.

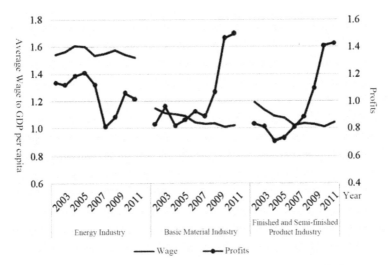

Chart 4-14   Comparison of Wages and Profits in Upstream Industry and Downstream Industry

Source: NBS website (http: // data.stats. gov.cn/).

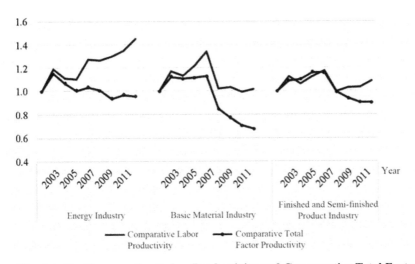

Chart 4-15   Comparative Labor Productivity and Comparative Total Factor Productivity of Upstream and Downstream Industries

Source: NBS website (http: // data.stats. gov.cn/).

Chart 4-16 compares wages and profits in industries of manufacturing, mining, construction, production and supply of electricity, gas and water and that of finance industry. Manufacturing and construction, two lowest-paid industries with highest concentration of migrant workers, are characterized by low wage and a slow downward trend with their ratio of average wage to GDP per capita between 2003 and 2012 declining from 1.2 to 1.08 in manufacturing industry and from 1.07 to 0.95 in construction industry. That wage change here is basically the same as migrant workers' wage change shown before confirms the conclusion that the wage of low wage group is declining. So, is there room for wage growth in these two industries? The rapid upward trend of the profits in manufacturing industry since 2008 has proven that manufacturing industry has entered a golden period of improvement and development despite "shortage of migrant workers" and "recruitment issue" which may weaken its competitiveness and development potential. Despite the low profits of construction industry, there has been a steady upward trend since 2003, proving that both manufacturing and construction have reasonable room for wage growth. Characterized by its relatively high wages and high profits, slow wage growth and fluctuating profits, the mining industry, quite different from manufacturing industry and construction industry, has shown a rapid upward trend with reasonable wage change and little room for wage growth.

The two industries with the highest wages, production and supply of electricity, gas and water and finance, are both monopolies with high wages and high profits. However, there are differences between them. Financial industry shows an upward trend in both wage and profits while production and supply of electricity, gas and water shows a downward trend in wage with rapid profit growth. Through a comprehensive analysis of these two industries, a conclusion is made that both industries are high-waged with profit growth, financial industry in particular, showing that there is still room for further wage growth, but given their monopoly nature, their rapid profit growth is more likely due to its monopoly nature than to its efficiency (Ye Linxiang et al., 2011; Lu Zhengfei et al., 2012). Since bank interest rates, water and electricity prices are subject to government pricing, high wages and high profits in financial industry and the production and supply industry of electricity, gas and water actually reflect the relationship between monopoly economy and competitive economy, between state-owned economy and private economy, between real economy and virtual economy. Therefore, for these two monopoly industries with high average wage, even if there is room for wage growth, it is not reasonable for these enterprises through monopoly to gain high profits, which should be shared by all citizens through a tax or public finance.

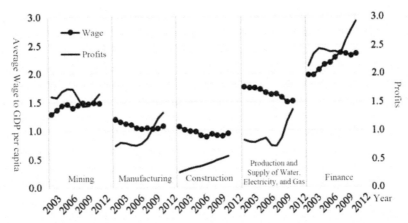

Chart 4-16 Comparison of Wages and Profits in Some Industries (2003-2012)

Note: water, electricity, gas industry refers to production and supply industry of electricity, gas and water.

Source: NBS website (http://data.stats. gov.cn/).

III. Conclusion and Suggestion

In modernization, with employment pattern changing from self-employment to employee employment, China's current trend of employee employment is a true reflection of healthy economic development. The total number of Chinese employees in 2012 was 417 million, 54% of total employment, 82% of total non-agricultural employment. However, in employee employment, labor share has not grown simultaneously, indicating that wage growth lags behind GDP growth and overall employee wage has declined (Zhang Juwei, 2012b). By industry, wage growth of industries with the highest wage has roughly kept pace with GDP growth with wage growth of financial industry even exceeding GDP growth while wage growth of industries with the lowest wage lags behind GDP growth with wage decline in real wages of civil servants and migrant workers. Civil servants, seemingly better-paid, better-welfare, stable and secure, has always been the dream job of many university graduates. However, civil servants' wages have been on the decline after reaching relatively high in 2002, keep declining since 2010 at a faster pace until below the average wages of urban unit employees in 2012. Although migrant workers' nominal wage has grown rapidly in recent years, their real wages are still far lower than that of urban unit employees and its wage growth has not only lagged behind that of urban unit employees, let alone GDP growth.

Should wage grow? Will wage growth lead to a decline in industrial competitiveness? In initial distribution of national income, total wage of salaried workers corresponds to the rapid enterprise profit growth, indicating that total wage decline results from enterprise profit growth, which shows the reasonable and feasible wage growth of salaried workers. However, the problem is not that simple. Profit share growth in national income distribution does not necessarily mean that profits of every sector and industry grow simultaneously. If profit growth is limited to some industries, it is not likely to raise the overall wage. At present, the relationship between state-owned sector and non-state sector, upstream industry and downstream industry, monopoly industry and competitive industry, real economy and virtual economy is worrying. After the analysis in this chapter, the strong position of state-owned sector, upstream industry, monopoly industry and financial sector in wages and profits is further strengthened. Therefore, as far as wage growth is concerned, importance should be attached to wage structure contradictions rather than national wage growth.

State-owned sector is characterized by higher wages and lower profits with wage changes keeping pace with profit changes since 2003, thus no room and condition for further wage growth. Above-scale non-state-owned sector is a completely different picture in that it is characterized by lower wage, a declining overall trend since 2003 but considerable profit growth, indicating much room for wage growth. By industry, although monopolies with high wages, such as the production and supply industry of electricity, gas and water and financial industry have shown a trend of rapid profit growth with conditions for wage growth, high wages are not a sufficient reason for further wage growth when wages are already very high because profit growth of these monopolies mainly results from monopoly rather than improvement in enterprise efficiency. China should benefit all its citizens with rapidly grown enterprise profits by means of public finances. Competitive industries, such as manufacturing and construction with vast majority of migrant workers, low wages but relatively slow wage growth, have enough reason for wage growth. Moreover, because of steady profit growth of these industries, there is also room for wage growth. Therefore, wage growth in these industries is both reasonable and feasible.

In all, China's overall wage do need to grow, the lower wage group in particular. Slow wage growth mainly exists in the non-state-owned sector and competitive industry, which means that China's market-oriented wage determination mechanism is not yet perfect. The solution to this problem is to set up a reasonable wage growth mechanism under market conditions.

Historically, relatively slow Chinese employees' wage growth is somewhat related to supply and demand change in labor market. For a long time in the past, labor market has been faced with an almost unlimited labor supply so that labor factor price is below its marginal output, the basic conclusion of Lewis model, which is hard for wage to grow. However, with supply-demand labor force change, there is no more infinite labor supply and workers' wage changes with supply-demand labor change. In fact, difficulties in hiring and recruitment do not seem to be reflected in reasonable wage growth, indicating that reasonable wage growth mechanism is not yet in place.

In order to establish normal wage growth mechanism, the following measures are to be considered: first, strengthen labor protection by strictly enforcing labor contract law, further perfecting labor contract system and labor protection system, strengthening labor supervision and improving the tripartite coordination mechanism to ensure wage growth; Second, enhance workers' right to speak in wage determination by promoting wage collective bargaining system; Third, in wage determination make workers and enterprises the main body of the market rather than the minimum wage system which can protect the workers to a certain extent under the condition that labor supply seriously exceeds labor demand and which will become a hindrance to reasonable wage growth when labor demand exceeds labor supply. Nowadays, as many enterprises pay their workers minimum wage, workers have to work overtime for wage growth. As a result, "employment difficulties" caused by the supply-demand labor changes have not brought about reasonable wage growth.

Chapter V

Tax System Reform and National Income Distribution

CHEN Wendong, LIU Zuo[1]

Income gap issue must be solved properly in building an all-round well-off society in China. Reasonable regulation of income distribution has caused great concern from the CPC Central Committee, the National people's Congress, the State Council and people from all walks of life.

Approved by the Fourth Session of the Eleventh National People's Congress on March 14, 2011, *The Outline of the Twelfth Five-year Plan for National Economic and Social Development of the People's Republic of China* proposes in national income distribution to adhere to and improve distribution system with distribution according to work as its main body as well as multiple distribution modes by being efficient and fair in both initial distribution and redistribution especially being fair in redistribution so as to promote reasonable and orderly

---

1   CHEN Wendong: Research Fellow, Institute of Taxation Science, State Administration of Taxation; LIU Zuo, editor-in-chief, China Tax News Office; expert member, Tax Administration Review Commission of State Administration of Taxation; Vice President, China Fiscal and Tax Law Research Association.

income distribution pattern and narrow the widening income by raising both the proportion of residents' income in national income distribution and the proportion of labor remuneration in initial distribution so as to promote regulatory redistribution mechanism with taxation, social security, transfer payment as its main means by adjusting tax base and tax rate structure of personal income tax, raising expense deduction of earned income, lightening tax burden of middle-low income earners, enhancing tax regulation of high income earners, and by establishing and improving property tax system.

At the 18th National Congress of the Chinese Communist Party on November 8, 2012, Hu Jintao, General Secretary of the CPC Central Committee, delivered a report entitled *Unswervingly Advance along the Road of Socialism with Chinese Characteristics to Build an All-round Well-off Society.* The report proposes that in order for the development results to be shared by the people, income distribution system reform must be deepened by making residents' income growth keep up with economic development and making labor remuneration growth keep up with labor productivity growth and by raising both the proportion of residents' income in national income distribution and the proportion of labor remuneration in initial distribution, trying to be efficient and fair in both initial distribution and redistribution especially being fair in redistribution and improving initial distribution mechanism according to their participation and contribution of such factors as labor, capital, technology, management and regulatory redistribution mechanism with taxation, social security, transfer payment as its main means.

On February 3, 2013, the State Council approved and transferred *Opinions on Deepening Income Distribution System Reform* including some measures on taxation submitted by the National Development and Reform Commission, the Ministry of Finance and the Ministry of Human Resources and Social Security. On November 12, 2013, *Decisions of the CPC Central Committee on Issues of Comprehensively Deepening Reform* adopted by the Third Plenary Session of the 18th Central Committee of the Communist Party of China (CPC) proposes reasonable and orderly income distribution pattern by protecting labor income, making labor remuneration growth keep up with labor productivity growth, and raising the proportion of labor remuneration in initial distribution, and by improving regulatory redistribution mechanism with taxation, social security and transfer payment as its main means, and enhancing tax regulation.

As one of the main means of the government to regulate income distribution, tax system is to play its important role in national income distribution. Since the implementation of tax sharing fiscal management system (hereinafter referred to as tax sharing system) in 1994, the average annual growth rate of China's tax revenue has gradually exceeded the average annual growth rate of gross domestic product (GDP), and the proportion of tax revenue in national income has grown so that the role tax revenue has played in the regulation of national income distribution has been gradually acknowledged and hoped for but should never be exaggerated. Only through scientific and rational analysis can tax system and policies play a better role. This chapter attempts to theoretically explain the regulatory function of tax system from the perspective of national income distribution and puts forward relevant reform suggestions.

I. National Income Distribution Pattern

Theoretically, national income is a country's economic aggregate in a certain period. Under SNA statistical system, different calibers have been adopted for different research purposes, such as gross domestic product (GDP), gross national income (GNI), national disposable income and so on. The main distribution pattern of national income refers to the distribution of national income among government departments, enterprises and residents (hereinafter referred to as government, enterprises and residents).

National income distribution consists of initial distribution and redistribution[1] and in a broader sense "The Third Distribution".

---

1 Initial distribution consists of income formation and initial income distribution.

Initial distribution of national income refers to the distribution of part of gross national income (GNI) directly related to production factors since all production is inseparable from such production factors as labor, capital, land and technology. In market economy, a certain amount of remuneration will be paid to obtain these factors, thus giving rise to initial income distribution for factor providers. With production factor price determined by supply and demand, initial distribution in market economy is regulated and standardized by the government through taxation, laws and regulation without immediate intervention. Redistribution is the second income distribution in which factor income is transferred and re-regulated between main income earners by the government through various channels based on initial distribution results. Through redistribution, main income earners get the income for final consumption, savings and investment, that is, disposable income.

In the current statistical system, funds flow table reflects fund flow in national economy and reports the disposable income obtained by enterprises, government and residents after initial distribution and redistribution. Accounting of Chinese funds flow consists of physical transaction and financial transaction. Physical transaction accounting is mainly about income distribution, funds flow direction and funds flow volume of institutions and whole economy as well as the inflow and outflow of funds between these institutions. Funds flow table shows how the income created by production is distributed and transferred among institutions involved in production and how institutions' disposable income is consumed and saved, and funds gap and financing of non-financial investment in various institutions.

According to their economic nature, all units and individuals of economic activities can be divided into five sectors: household sector (residential sector), non-financial enterprises, financial institutions, government departments and departments that have economic dealings with non-resident units (foreign departments), among which, non-financial enterprises and financial enterprises can also be merged into enterprise sector.

Physical transactions in funds flow table consist of initial distribution and redistribution of income, reflecting national income distribution pattern, that is, initial distribution pattern (factor income pattern) and redistribution pattern (final distribution pattern). The first stage of initial distribution, income formation, is direct distribution of results of production and operations, i.e., the added value, from which the government gets net production tax[1]. enterprises get fixed assets depreciation and operating surplus and residents get their labor remuneration, reflecting that contribution of each main income earner to the national income plays a fundamental and decisive role in the formation of main distribution pattern and scale distribution pattern[2]. The second stage of initial distribution is the distribution of property income on the basis of income formation. Property income is the interest, dividend, bonus, rent, royalty and other income from financial investment, land lease, patent assignment and other business activities, which is the expenditure of departments that use the property. After the above two stages of distribution, initial distribution pattern comes into being with the government, enterprises and residents getting their own original income respectively.

Based on initial distribution, recipients of each original income obtain some transferred income from other income earners through various forms and procedures while transferring part of the income obtained from initial distribution including income tax paid by various institutions. Such regular transfers between various departments as social insurance payments, social insurance benefits, social benefits, etc. completes national income redistribution, thus the final distribution

---

1   Net production tax is the balance of production tax minus production subsidy. Production tax is all kinds of taxes, surcharges and fees levied by the government on production, sales and business activities of production units and on the use of certain production factors (such as fixed assets, land and labor) as a result of audit activities. Production subsidy, contrary to production tax, is the government's unilateral expenditure transfer to production units, regarded as negative production tax, including policy loss subsidy, price subsidy and so on. Please refer to the explanation of the main statistical indicators in *China Statistical Yearbook*.

2   Scale distribution pattern is the quantity difference and change law of the internal income of each income earner in income distribution and redistribution. Please refer to *Empirical Analysis of China's National Income Distribution Pattern of the Present Stage, Finance and Trade Economy* by Liu Yang (No. 11, 2002).

pattern, the real and available income share of each income earner representing fullest and most accurately distribution of a country's national income over a certain period of time.

Based on funds flow table over the years is the scale and proportion of initial distribution of national income and final disposable income in different departments (See Table 5-1 and Table 5-2). The data show it is an indisputable fact that residents' income share (proportion) keeps declining in both income pattern of initial distribution and redistribution.

Table 5-1 Sectoral Income and Proportion in Initial Distribution

Year	Enterprise		Government		Resident		Total
	Income (100 million yuan)	Proportion (%)	Income (100 million yuan)	Proportion (%)	Income (100 million yuan)	Proportion (%)	National Income (100 million yuan)
1994	7588.4	16.3	9168.5	19.7	29913.2	64.1	46670.1
1995	8705.4	15.1	11565.1	20.1	37224.4	64.7	57494.9
1996	10381.5	15.5	11522.5	17.2	44946.6	67.2	66850.6
1997	11829.7	16.2	13237.1	18.1	48061.4	65.7	73128.2
1998	12982.8	16.9	13498.2	17.5	50495.2	65.6	76976.2
1999	13654.7	17.0	14563.8	18.1	52360.7	65.0	80579.2
2000	19324.3	19.7	12865.2	13.1	65811.0	67.2	98000.5
2001	23122.2	21.4	13697.3	12.7	71248.7	65.9	108068.2
2002	25694.2	21.6	16600.0	13.9	76801.6	64.5	119095.7
2003	30077.0	22.3	18387.5	13.6	86512.5	64.1	134977.0
2004	40051.2	25.1	21912.7	13.7	97489.7	61.1	159453.6
2005	45026.4	24.5	26073.9	14.2	112517.1	61.3	183617.4
2006	53416.4	24.7	31373.0	14.5	131114.9	60.7	215904.4
2007	68349.9	25.7	39266.9	14.7	158805.3	59.6	266422.0
2008	84085.8	26.6	46549.1	14.7	185395.4	58.7	316030.3
2009	84169.6	24.7	49606.3	14.6	206544.0	60.7	340320.0
2010	97968.3	24.5	59926.7	15.0	241864.5	60.5	399759.5
2011	112212.5	23.9	72066.9	15.4	284282.9	60.7	468562.4

According to Table 5-1, the arithmetic average ratio of the proportion of government, enterprises and residents in initial distribution pattern of national income between 1994 and 2008 is 14.7: 23.6: 61.7. In 1994, the year of tax reform, the ratio of the above three was 19.7: 16.3: 64.1; in 2008, it was 14.7: 26.6: 58.7. In comparison, the government revenue proportion fell by 5%, enterprise income proportion rose by 10.3%, and residents' income proportion fell by 5.4%. Comparing data of 2008 with the average, the government's proportion remains unchanged with enterprises' proportion rising by 3% while residents proportion falling by 3%. Since 2001, government income, mainly from production taxes, have accounted for roughly 14.3% of national income and enterprise income has been on the rise by more than 20% while residents' income has kept falling to around 60% since 2004, and fell below 60% in 2007 and 2008 with the lowest in 2008 down by 8.4% from its highest in 1996. After adjustments in recent years, the ratio between the three was fine-tuned to 15.4: 23.9: 60.7 in 2011. Compared with 1994, government revenue proportion fell by 4.3% while enterprise income proportion rose by 7.6% and residents' income proportion fell by 3.4%. Things are changing for the better.

Table 5-2   Sectoral Disposable Income and Proportion

Year	Enterprise		Government		Resident		Total
	Income (100 million yuan)	Proportion (%)	Income (100 million yuan)	Proportion (%)	Income (100 million yuan)	Proportion (%)	National Income (100 million yuan)
1994	7495. 5	16. 0	8427. 9	18. 0	30862. 0	66. 0	46785. 4
1995	9618. 8	16. 7	9504. 6	16. 5	38491. 2	66. 8	57614. 6
1996	9092. 6	13. 6	11492. 8	17. 1	46442. 9	69. 3	67028. 3
1997	10568. 6	14. 4	12878. 1	17. 5	50121. 3	68. 1	73568. 0
1998	11086. 2	14. 3	13555. 9	17. 5	52688. 6	68. 1	77330. 7
1999	11587. 7	14. 3	15046. 4	18. 6	54354. 3	67. 1	80988. 4
2000	17670. 3	17. 9	14314. 1	14. 5	66538. 7	67. 5	98523. 0
2001	20581. 6	18. 9	16324. 2	15. 0	71865. 3	66. 1	108771. 1
2002	23241. 2	19. 3	19505. 9	16. 2	77423. 3	64. 4	120170. 4
2003	27206. 0	19. 9	21946. 8	16. 1	87268. 5	64. 0	136421. 2
2004	36322. 3	22. 5	26517. 6	16. 4	98508. 9	61. 1	161348. 8
2005	40088. 5	21. 6	32573. 7	17. 6	112910. 2	60. 8	185572. 4
2006	46990. 5	21. 5	39724. 9	18. 2	131426. 4	60. 2	218141. 8
2007	59492. 5	22. 1	51192. 1	19. 0	158558. 6	58. 9	269243. 2
2008	72557. 1	22. 7	60544. 1	19. 0	185926. 3	58. 3	319027. 5

contd.

Year	Enterprise		Government		Resident		Total
	Income (100 million yuan)	Proportion (%)	Income (100 million yuan)	Proportion (%)	Income (100 million yuan)	Proportion (%)	National Income (100 million yuan)
2009	72576. 8	21. 2	62603. 3	18. 3	207302. 4	60. 5	342482. 5
2010	85275. 7	21. 2	74116. 3	18. 4	243121. 7	60. 4	402513. 7
2011	94169. 6	20. 0	90203. 2	19. 2	285772. 6	60. 8	470145. 4

From the final disposable income, the arithmetic average ratio of the proportion of government, enterprises and residents in disposable income distribution of national income between 1994 and 2011 is 18.0: 20.2: 61.8. In 1994, the ratio was 18.0: 16.0: 66.0. In 2011, that ratio rose to 19.2: 20.0: 60.8. In comparison, government's proportion rose by 1.2% and enterprises rose by 4.0% while residents fell by 5.2%. Comparing data of 2011 with the average, government's proportion rose by 1.2% while enterprises fell by 0.2% and residents fell by 1%.

With the average value as its standard, compare the proportion of disposable income with that of initial distribution, enterprises' proportion fell by 3.4% while government's proportion rose by 3.3% and residents' proportion rose slightly by 0.1%. After redistribution, there has been government disposable income growth and a slight change in residents' disposable income proportion while enterprise disposable income proportion decreases, indicating that enterprise income tax plays its regulative role. However, as the bulk of the net enterprise income tax is converted into government revenue, the government's transfer payments to residents are clearly inadequate. Through the description above, it is indisputable that residents' income has declined in both initial distribution and redistribution of national income. Therefore, the 17th CPC National Congress report, the 18th National Congress report and the outline of the 12th Five-Year Plan approved by the National People's Congress (NPC) proposes the increase in the proportion of residents' income in national income. Many people believe that the decline of residents' income in national income distribution lies in initial distribution, but there are different views on whether it is the government or enterprises that have swallowed up residents' income in initial distribution. Through Table 5-1 and Table 5-2, it is believed that although there is much more detailed analyses, the decline in residents' income is mainly due to the ever rising proportion of enterprises in initial distribution instead of production tax growth. At the same time, the government has greatly increased its income by imposing income tax (especially the income tax collected from enterprises) in redistribution and there has been insufficient transfer payment to residents, another major cause.

Therefore, taxation in national income distribution should be studied separately from income pattern formed by the two distributions by classifying the current tax system based on the statistical indicators of national income and by analyzing the role taxation plays in initial distribution and redistribution and the ways for taxation reform.

II. Tax System Factors in National Income Distribution

National income distribution pattern results from a series of distribution processes. In order to investigate the influence of taxation on national income distribution pattern, it is quite necessary to examine taxation in each stage of national income distribution and analyze the function of tax system and tax finance in national income distribution.

(I) Taxation Classification

At present, there are two kinds of taxation classification in both theory and practice: one is to divide tax into direct tax and indirect tax based on tax burden transfer: tax burden that can not be transferred is direct tax; tax burden that can be transferred is indirect tax. However, in real economy and tax collection, tax burden transfer is complicated as it is difficult to define whether tax burden can be transferred and how much tax can be transferred so that it's difficult to distinguish direct tax from indirect tax. So these traditional, more academic concepts of tax theory doesn't work in practice. The other is to classify taxes into goods and service tax, income tax, property tax, etc., according to taxation object. In production, circulation and services, the tax on goods and services is the goods and services tax, including value-added tax, customs duty; the tax on income is the income tax including enterprise income tax and personal income tax; the tax on property is property tax including real estate tax, car and boat tax. This kind of intuitive, simple tax classification is adopted by countries across the world.

China's current 18 kinds of taxation is classified into four categories according to taxation object: (1) goods and services tax including value added tax, consumption tax, vehicle purchase tax, business tax and customs duties which are levied in production, circulation and services according to the taxpayer's sales income (quantity), operating income and the price (quantity) of imported and exported goods. (2) income tax including enterprise income tax, personal income tax and land value-added tax of income tax nature which are levied in income distribution according to profits made by enterprises or income earned by individuals. (3) Property tax including property tax, urban land use tax, cultivated land occupation tax, deed tax, resource tax, car and boat tax which are levied according to property owned and used by taxpayers. (4) other taxes including stamp duty, urban maintenance and construction tax and tobacco tax.

There is no property tax and deed tax in the Tibet Autonomous region for the time being. In addition to taxation, the state stipulates that there are two non-tax revenue items collected by tax authorities: additional education fees and construction expenses for cultural undertakings. The provincial government may also stipulate that social insurance premiums shall be levied by tax authorities (at present, there are mainly four items, namely, basic old-age insurance premiums, basic medical insurance premiums, unemployment insurance premiums and industrial injury insurance premiums) with handling fund of waste electrical appliances and electronics levied by tax authorities and the customs respectively.

Goods and services tax, levied in production and sales can regulate production, circulation and consumption, such as value-added tax, consumption tax and tariffs; income tax can regulate taxpayers' income, such as enterprise income tax and personal income tax; property tax collected on property acquisition, holding and transfer can regulate taxpayers' wealth, such as deed tax, real estate tax, inheritance tax and gift tax.

(II) Production Tax and Income Tax and Their Structure

According to the interpretation of China Statistical Yearbook (2013), production tax in current statistical index system refers to all taxes, surcharges and fees the government imposes on production units engaging in production, sales and business activities for their use of certain production factors (such as fixed assets, land, labor) as a result of their production activities. Production subsidy, contrary to production tax, refers to the government's unilateral expenditure transfer to production units as negative production tax including policy loss subsidies, price subsidies, and so on. Net production tax is the balance after production subsidies is deducted from production tax.

In accordance with China's current tax system, production tax should include all kinds of taxes except income tax, first, production (sales) tax, that is, price tax included in the price of goods and services, mainly sales tax, consumption tax, city maintenance and construction tax and resource tax. In enterprise accounting, the above-mentioned taxes are recorded into current production (operation) expenses through "operating tax and additional" account which belongs to the added value of production and is part of initial distribution of national income. Second, VAT, from microscopic perspective, is not included in the price of goods and services sold by taxpayers, not constituting the added value of accounting under enterprise accrual basis. However, from the perspective of macroeconomic operation, part of the total value added tax payable by all enterprises in the current period obtained by the government in initial distribution is first paid by enterprises, becoming the final burden of disposable income by various sectors through redistribution. Therefore, VAT also belongs to production tax in initial distribution of national income. Third, management expense tax mainly include deed tax, real estate tax, urban land use tax, cultivated land occupation tax, car and boat tax, stamp duty and so on. Lastly, all kinds of fees that constitute costs and expenses of the enterprise such as mineral resources compensation fee and cultural construction fee.

Income tax mentioned in statistical index of national income corresponds to the enterprise income tax and personal income tax in China's current tax system. Reflected in redistribution, social security contributions are also classified as income tax. Since China's social security contributions have not yet been incorporated into tax system, social security contributions will not be addressed in this chapter when it comes to the impact of taxation and tax policies on national income distribution.

Table 5-3   Tax Structure since China's Reform and Opening up (%)

Year	Proportion of Goods and Services Tax	Proportion of Income Tax	Proportion of Property Tax
1978	83. 6	10. 4	0. 2
1985	58. 8	34. 3	0. 9
1994	72. 0	14. 8	3. 8
2000	67. 5	18. 5	4. 2
2005	64. 5	26. 3	5. 5
2010	60. 8	27. 4	7. 0
2012	57. 8	29. 6	8. 4

In recent years, due to economic structure change, enterprise profits, property income and personal income, property growth, tax system improvement and tax collection and management, the proportion of China's income tax and property tax revenue in total tax revenue has gradually increased although the proportion of goods and services tax revenue in total tax revenue has declined gradually (See Table 5-3).

It can be clearly seen from Table 5-3: first, in 2012, production tax revenue was still the main source of Chinese tax revenue, accounting for about 60% of total tax revenue while income tax accounted for less than 30% of total tax revenue, which is consistent with the high proportion of goods and services tax and low proportion of income tax in China. But starting from 1994, the proportion of goods and services tax in tax revenue fell by 14.2% in 2012, far exceeding the rising proportion of property tax in total tax revenue over the same period

(4.6%). The proportion of production tax in total tax revenue declined while the proportion of income tax in total tax revenue rose by 14.8% over the same period. In recent years, the proportion of income tax in total tax revenue has gradually increased, indicating that China's tax structure is in gradual optimization. Due to characteristics of tax system above, the irreplaceable role of production tax in initial distribution of national income must be taken into account in discussing tax regulation of China's national income, which is significantly different from the traditional understanding that tax policies mainly play its role in redistribution of national income. Traditional viewpoint is made from the perspective of value composition and circulation of economic aggregate. Therefore, great importance should be attached to the role of taxation in initial distribution of national income from the practice of national economy with the expectation that taxation will regulate initial distribution of national income.

III.Impact of Tax System on National Income Distribution and its Reform

(I) Impact of Production Tax on Initial Distribution of National Income and its Reform

Main reason for the decrease in the proportion of residents' income in initial distribution of national income is that enterprise income swallows up residents' income so that the idea of reducing the proportion of production tax to raise the proportion of residents' income does not seem appropriate. First, in the current initial distribution pattern of national income, the proportion of production tax is small and relatively stable so that government tax revenue is not the main reason for the widening income gap in initial distribution. Second, instead of ensuring that the proportion of residents' income increases significantly, the reduction in the proportion of production tax is likely to translate into enterprise income. For example, when the state exempted some meat, poultry and egg products from VAT, the retail prices of these products did not fall, but there has been enterprise income growth.

However, production tax does play its role in initial distribution of national income because most production tax is part of national income distribution, prior to distribution of wage, enterprise profits, and income tax collection which is beneficial to the state in raising financial revenue. Production tax has been an important part of national income distribution and there is a counter-balance between production tax, enterprise income and residents' income, which has an immediate effect on economic resources allocation and economic development efficiency.

In short, from a macro perspective, taxation, an effective tool for regulating resources allocation and income distribution, plays a vital role in initial distribution of national income. Any change in the proportion of production tax income is the inevitable result of tax participation and guidance in resource allocation, which can promote transformation of economic development mode, reasonable distribution of national income and motivation and efficiency of stimulating workers to create wealth. Moreover, from a micro perspective, the internal structure adjustment of production tax and tax element reform of each taxation can be of significance.

i. VAT and Business Tax

In current tax system, value-added tax (VAT), a major goods and services tax, is levied on all kinds of good s and services. Theoretically speaking, as VAT is somewhat regressive in social economic regulation and control, it's impossible to curb tax burden transfer which is realized by changing price and output and is directly related to supply elasticity and demand elasticity of commodities. Generally, demand elasticity for life necessities is less than demand elasticity for luxury goods so that low-income people spend a larger part of their income on life necessities and high-income people spend a smaller part of their income on life necessities. Levying VAT results in higher burden rate of VAT of the low income group and low burden rate of the high income group so that it is difficult for VAT to regulate personal income distribution. However, as is mentioned earlier, VAT, the largest tax in China, takes the lead in initial distribution of national income and is paid by enterprises first until in retail VAT is borne by consumers with their disposable income. In terms of total quantity, VAT can regulate the income of three sectors at the macro level. In this sense, the regulation of VAT in income distribution is strategic rather than tactical.

Although VAT generally does not directly regulate personal income distribution, it can weaken its regressive effect by adjusting tax system elements. For example, there is a lot of room for operation in tax rate adjustment. In China's current VAT system, agricultural products, grain replicas, edible vegetable oils, edible salt, tap water, heating, gas, books, newspapers and other goods are subject to a low tax rate of 13%, most of which belong to primary product because of its small demand elasticity, low price, short production chain. One of the main functions of VAT is to promote specialized cooperative development and production as well as business structure rationalization. Because of its low price and short production chain, to reduce VAT rate of goods mentioned above or even to exempt them won't affect collaboration, production and business structure between production departments of these primary products. In addition, according to Engel's law, as income increases, the proportion of residents' expenditure on these goods in their total income will continue to fall. Therefore, a proper reduction or even exemption of VAT for essential primary products will not only directly reduce indirect tax burden on low-income groups so as to increase their real income but help to narrow the income gap between different resident groups.

Reform of expanding VAT levy scope—conversion of business tax to VAT (for short "Business Conversion to VAT") has made steady progress and will be fully implemented from May 1, 2016, thereby eliminating double tax in current business tax system. This reform also helps to reduce total tax burden on goods and services and its proportion in total tax revenue so as to make room for increasing the proportion of income tax in total tax revenue, to strengthen direct tax regulation of income distribution, and to promote the reasonable disposable income for all departments.

Specifically, main measures of perfecting VAT include adjusting its levy scope, tax rate and collection rate, and cleaning up tax preference and so on. (1) Expand levy scope and speed up "business conversion to VAT". At the same time, impact of "business conversion to VAT" on local fiscal revenue and levy scope of tax authorities must be dealt with and appropriate revenue compensation measures must be taken, such as increasing the proportion of local share of value-added tax revenue or transfer payment of central fiscal in local finance. In the long run, it is necessary to perfect local tax system as soon as possible, create a stable and sustainable major tax for local tax, and reasonably determine relevant tax authority's collection and administration. (2) Adjust tax rate and collection rate. At present, base rate of China's VAT (17%) is too high and should be gradually reduced to that of the average developing countries (under 15%). Tax rate on necessities such as food, clothing and medicine can be reduced first, or even exempted their VAT. When "business conversion to VAT" is over, it's time to reduce tax rate. In order to balance tax burden, collection rate of small scale VAT payer should be adjusted accordingly when adjusting levy scope and tax rate of VAT. (3) Continue to clean up the preference. Clean up obsolete and other inappropriate preferences in a timely manner, for they are not only inconsistent with the theory and basic principles of VAT but also not conducive to strengthening the collection and management. (4) Set an exemption volume. In order to take proper care of small and micro enterprises and individuals with low income, promote employment and balance tax burden, starting point of VAT should be changed into exemption as soon as possible, and raise starting point of VAT appropriately according to economic development, wage, price and other factors. Current starting point of monthly sales of 5,000–20,000 yuan was set at the end of 2008. After several years, it has become significantly lower because now small and micro enterprises and individuals with a monthly sales of no more than 20, 000 yuan are gradually declining. At the same time, real income of some small and micro enterprises and individuals has not increased much or even reduced because of rising prices.

ii. Consumption Tax

With economic and social development, consumption and its structure of Chinese people have changed fundamentally. Some problems in current consumption tax system have seriously affected its regulation and control. To sum up, such problems as limited levy scope and unreasonable tax rate can be solved by doing as follows. First, expand its levy scope by collecting tax on some special consumer goods. Generally speaking, when income reaches a certain level, the proportion of consumer spending on high-end consumer goods in their total expenditure will be increasingly raised for high income group. Once corresponding expenditure is set, it will not easily change, that is, the high-income group shows a relatively low demand elasticity. Therefore, if supply remains unchanged, the part of the tax paid by operators in initial distribution of national income tends to be transferred to high-income group. Second, adjust consumption tax rate structure according to China's current social and economic situation so as to make it more in line with the government's goal of regulation and control. Take into account characteristics of some restricted consumer goods to further increase its applicable tax rate; reduce tax rate of some goods that were originally luxury ones which, with economic development, turn out to be average consumer goods now. For example, consumption tax levied on high-quality cosmetics and jewelry is no different from that on average cosmetics, gold and silver jewelry, which is not conducive to reasonable consumption habits and to realization of the government's goal of regulation and control. High quality consumer goods should be treated differently from average consumer goods with a higher consumption tax rate. With the increase in people's income and consumption level, it's proposed to reduce consumption tax rate until exempt from consumption tax for average cosmetics, gold and silver jewelry which has become daily consumer goods.

Specifically, main measures for consumption tax improvement can be adjusting tax levy scope, tax rate and tax standard, taxation procedures, etc. (1) Adjust levy scope. There should be tax on luxury goods and high consumer goods (such as private jets and high-end furniture, electrical appliances, clothing, food, beverages, etc.) and no more tax on non-consumer goods (such as alcohol, car tyres, etc.). There should be tax on resources items and environmental protection items (such as batteries, disposable plastic products, vehicle purchase, etc.) (2) Adjust tax rate (tax standard). In order to regulate taxation, there should be proper tax increase on some luxury goods, high-end consumer goods and dutiable consumer goods (such as cigarettes, wine, cosmetics, jewelry, firecrackers, fireworks, refined oil, motorcycles, automobiles, golf products, high-end wrist watches, yachts, solid wood floor) that are unfavorable to resources and environment. In recent years, there has been a general increase in consumption tax rate (tax standard) for tobacco, alcohol and certain luxury goods. Such consumer goods as gasoline, and diesel with ever rising prices shall be taxed on ad valorem basis instead of volume quotas. (3) Adjust taxation procedures. As long as conditions for tax collection and administration permits, production taxation should be changed into sales taxation, intra-valorem into extra-valorem by levying trial retail taxation on precious jewelry, jade, refined oil, motorcycles, cars, high-end watches, yachts and other consumer goods. (4) Levy local consumption tax or local added consumption tax. Due to great differences in income and consumption levels among different regions, local consumption tax or local added consumption tax may be allowed to be levied at retail level of some dutiable consumer goods.

iii. Resource Tax

For a long time in China, pricing of resource products has not taken into full account sustainable exploitation of resources as it fails to consider both acquisition costs caused by the use or exploitation of resources and its impact on future generations due to its improper use of resources. In this way, resource rent, not reflected in price, naturally becomes excess profit of resource exploiters, operators who exploit all national resources getting a large amount of rent income that should be collected by the state through excess profits. This unreasonable pricing model is not only unfavorable to rational exploitation of resources but gives rise to the widening income gap and unfair initial distribution of national income. Since March 26, 2006, the state has levied a special income on excess income obtained by oil extraction enterprises from sale of domestic crude oil because price exceeds a certain level, a crucial measure in rational regulation of income of oil mining enterprises but with limited regulation of oil extraction enterprises.

In addition, since most resource tax items are still taxed on quota, their resource tax revenue has not gradually grown with the rising price of resource products, causing resource mining enterprises to obtain a large amount of excess profits, which is not conducive to initial distribution of national income distribution. Therefore, reform the collection method of resource tax as soon as possible by implementing both ad valorem tax and quota tax. At the same time, raise both tax rate and tax standard of resources. In view of high profits of some state-owned resource mining enterprises, increase state-owned enterprises' capital return and restrict their wage growth and welfare growth.

Specifically, measures to improve resource tax can be adjustment of taxpayers, levy scope, tax base and tax burden. (1) expand levy scope by taxing on such natural resources as land, forest, grassland and water, further reflecting the principle of compensated use of state-owned natural resources; (2) adjust resource product price and reform charging system by abolishing improper tax reduction and tax exemption, by raising tax rate and tax standard in order to save resources and protect the environment, and by regulating resources differential income of resource mining enterprises to increase fiscal revenue; (3) turn quota tax of dutiable resources with frequent and large price changes into ad valorem tax so as to maintain tax burden balance and fiscal revenue stability.

In addition, in order to simplify taxation system and avoid the adverse impact of resource tax on the price of resource products and double taxation on resource products and their processed products, a special income tax rate shall be imposed on resource mining enterprises with reference to the practice of certain countries.

iv. Real Estate Tax

Real estate tax system is also an important measure to regulate income distribution. In order for real estate tax to play its effective role in regulating income distribution, it is necessary to improve real estate property right registration system and the real estate appraisal system. Measures to improve real estate tax are to simplify tax system, expand tax base, design reasonable tax rate and delegate proper tax power. (1) simplify tax system with unified real estate tax consistent with that in other countries by merging collection tax items with certain reasonable and taxable government fees and charges in real estate, the former including current property tax, urban land use tax, cultivated land occupation tax, deed tax and stamp duty; (2) expand tax base by covering individual housing and rural areas and by levying tax according to assessed value of real estate. At the same time, provide appropriate tax-exemption items and exemptions (value or area, or both value and area standards) for low-middle-income group; (3) implement differential real estate tax rate according to regions and types of real estate. For example, applicable tax rate for real estate in small and medium-sized cities and for average residential building can be reasonably low while applicable tax rate for real estate in large cities and for high-end homes, golf courses, productive and operative real estate can be reasonably high; (4) decentralize tax power to make real estate tax the main local tax and main tax revenue source for city (county) government with its economic development so that under unified national tax system, local governments will be given greater administrative authority (including appropriate adjustment of tax objects, taxpayers, tax base, tax rate, tax reduction and exemption and other basic elements of tax) by adapting to country size, actual situation of different economic development to increase its fiscal revenue and regulate its economy with real estate tax according to local conditions.

It takes time to implement real estate tax reform which involves economic interests of a large number of enterprises, other units and individuals and the government real estate tax and fee system reform, real estate registration, real estate value assessment and new real estate tax collection system. Therefore, this reform requires full, careful decision-making, and gradual implementation by starting from big cities and then medium-sized cities, small cities and rural areas after gaining successful experience in pilot cities. At the same time, this reform should be closely combined with construction of China's local tax system, overall tax system reform, fiscal and taxation system reform, and other related reforms in order to achieve better social benefits and reduce resistance to reform and reform costs.

(II) Impact of Income Tax on Redistribution of National Income and its Reform

i. Enterprise Income Tax Measures to improve enterprise income tax are to establish legal corporate income tax, standardize tax base, adjust tax rate and tax preference.

(i) Establish legal corporate income tax. With gradual establishment and improvement of legal corporate system, enterprise income tax should be turned into legal corporate income tax, which, together with personal income tax, constitutes a complete income tax system.

(ii) Standardize Tax Base New enterprise income tax law, its implementation regulations and supporting documents have been published and carried out one after another, but specific tax base provisions still need to be formulated and current laws and regulations need to be perfected in practice. Great importance should be attached to the following issues: first, link enterprise income tax system with current enterprise financial and accounting system, and at the same time, in order to ensure the state's financial revenue and reflect specific state policies (such as encouraging scientific and technological progress, environment and resource protection, energy conservation and emission reduction, development of specific regions and industries, employment placement, etc.). Second, deal with the close connection within enterprise income tax system including the connection between tax law and its implementing regulations and supporting documents, and the connection between regulation provisions, etc. Third, deal with the connection between enterprise income tax law and other tax laws and regulations, such as personal income tax law, provisional regulation of value-added tax, company law and accounting law, etc. Fourth, learn from beneficial experience in building income tax system of foreign enterprises and better adapt to the needs of foreign economic exchanges in the light of China's national situation.

(iii) Reduce Tax Rate In early 2014, enterprise income tax rate of 76 countries and regions is less than 25%, accounting for 35.3% of 215 countries and regions levying enterprise income tax. Enterprise income tax rate of 13 countries and regions is less than 25%, accounting for 48.1% of 27 countries and regions around China levying enterprise income tax. To improve enterprise competitiveness and attract foreign capital, an increasing number of countries and regions will reduce or continue to reduce their enterprise income tax rate so that China's enterprise income tax rate should be appropriately reduced, too.

(iv) Handle Tax Preferences Although new enterprise income tax system has regulated tax preferences, with economic and social development, new situations and problems will continue to arise, appropriate countermeasures will be taken (In recent years, the state has stipulated a large number of preferential measures for enterprise income tax in disaster relief and reconstruction in areas affected by natural disasters). After implementation expiration of original tax preferences, many of them may continue to be implemented for a long term (such as agriculture, urban employment, the disabled, culture, western region development).

(v) Create Exemption Provisions for Small-profit Enterprises to Safeguard Employment and People's Livelihood.

ii. Personal Income Tax

Personal income tax is generally believed to be the most effective income regulation tax. However, due to relatively small number of personal income taxpayers in China, the proportion of personal income tax income in total tax revenue is too low (only about 6% in recent years), which limits the due function of income regulation. Starting from September 2011 when standard for deducting salaries and expenses is raised to 3,500 yuan per month, tax level is limited to seven levels, and minimum applicable tax rate is reduced to 3% so that personal income tax payers drop sharply. Moreover, the largest income source of personal income tax is wages, and salaries while main income source of high-income earners, besides wages, and salaries, is operating income, labor remuneration, investment income, property income, etc., thus making it impossible for progressive tax rate system to give full play of regulating income distribution. The fundamental way out lies in the transformation of tax mode based on comprehensive collection supplemented by classified collection.

Specifically, measures to improve personal income tax is to expand levy scope, change levy mode, adjust tax base and tax rate, strengthen coordination between personal income tax and enterprise income tax, and clear up tax preference.

(i) Expand Tax Levy Scope. First of all, according to the current practice in most countries, the time limit of determining that resident taxpayers "have no domicile in China but have resided in China for one year" should be changed into 183 days in order to better safeguard China's tax rights and interests. Second, levy on all kinds of taxable personal income according to economic development and ability of tax collection and administration.

(ii) Change Levy Mode. According to the current practice in most countries, turn levy mode with different income sub-items into a combination of comprehensive collection and classified collection with comprehensive collection as main levy mode in order to balance tax burden, protect low-income group and strengthen income regulation of high income earners. However, under current system of personal income tax collected and administrated by local tax bureau and financial management system shared by both central government and local government, it is difficult to implement comprehensive collection system.

Before adjusting both management system of tax authorities and financial management system, some transitional measures may be taken, such as levying personal income tax on an annual basis rather than a monthly basis, pre-levying personal income tax on a monthly basis and collecting and paying at the end of the year; some taxation items should be collected annually; deduction before tax and tax rate should be adjusted rationally; system and management of personal income tax should be further improved by those people earning 120,000 yuan or more per year; and so on. These measures can not only reasonably adjust personal income tax burden of most personal income tax taxpayers but improve personal income tax management system to pave the way for combined levy mode of both comprehensive collection and classified collection with the former as its major mode.

(iii) Set Reasonable Tax Base. Basic costs of life of taxpayers and their dependents, specialized expenses such as insurance, housing, medical care and education (training), and special expenses of children, the elderly, the disabled and persons in difficult areas or with hazardous occupations (jobs) should be reasonably determined and adjusted according to wage, price and exchange rate. In order to improve work efficiency, the National People's Congress may be requested to authorize the State Council to adjust deductible standards above regularly in accordance with principles stipulated in tax law. However, under current personal income tax system of classified collection, it is impossible to provide a detailed expense deduction mode so that the only option is to moderately raise deduction standard of basic living expenses.

(iv) Adjust Tax Rate. In early 2014, the highest tax rate of personal income tax of central or local governments of 146 countries and regions is less than 40%, accounting for 81.6% of 179 countries or regions levying personal income tax. The highest tax rate of personal income tax of central or local governments of the 26 countries or regions around China is no more than 40%. By contrast, China's 45% of maximum marginal rate in terms of personal income tax is significantly higher. At the same time, it should be noted that an increasing number of countries or regions are preparing to reduce or continue to reduce maximum marginal rate of personal income tax. Under current classified levy mode of personal income tax in China, it is difficult to balance applicable tax rate and income tax burden from different classification and overall tax burden of taxpayers with many income items.

In addition, personal income tax levied on wages and salaries in China is subject to seven levels of progressive tax rates, more than those of other countries or regions. Therefore, after personal income tax reform in China, a reasonably-designed 5-level progressive tax rates for comprehensive increase of 5%, 10%, 20%, 30% and 40% can be adopted so as to design level distance of every tax rate. Before mode changes, release tax rate table of wages, salaried income and individual business income and reduce tax rate level and maximum tax rate.

(v) Strengthen Coordination between Personal Income Tax and Enterprise Income Tax. Income tax treatment of individual industrial and commercial households, sole proprietorship enterprises and partnership enterprises shall be basically the same as that of legal corporate enterprises. Tax exemption, tax reduction or integrated tax credit can be adopted to solve double collection of both enterprise income tax and personal income tax so as to reduce or even eliminate tax on dividends and bonuses. In fact, it may be relatively simple and easy for enterprises to exempt from personal income tax on dividends and bonuses after paying enterprise income tax.

(vi) Clean up tax preference. Outdated and other inappropriate tax preference should be cleaned up in a timely manner. Tax exemption and tax reduction should be provided for talented people who make outstanding contributions to society and low-income people in difficult circumstances.

IV. Factors Affecting Tax System in "The Third Distribution"

The so-called "The Third Distribution" is another round of regulation of disposable income based on redistribution of national income through various charitable activities or undertakings organized by non-profit organizations, non-governmental organizations and civil society organizations (in general terms, social organizations and groups other than government organizations, market organizations, etc., the so-called "The Third Sector") as a supplement to the government redistribution on the part of society in form of mutual assistance. "The third distribution" mechanism, different from market mechanism and government administrative mechanism, can be a complement to market and the government, a bridge between private sector and public sector.

However, many scholars disagree with the concept of "The Third Distribution" put forward by Professor Li Yining of Peking University, arguing that "The Third Distribution" is neither in line with international practice nor with China's national conditions. Theoretically, social donations and charity is still considered as "the second distribution" and is of the same nature as tax and public welfare expenditure. Moreover, from international experience, the development of philanthropy must be based on appropriate institutional arrangements and social values.

(I) Distribution and Tax System of "The Third Sector"

Up till now, "the third sector" development has just started in China. Compared with other countries and regions, "the third sector" in China still plays a quite limited role mainly because there are only a small number of social organizations and private non-enterprise units with limited fund for distribution, charity donation of 50.9 billion yuan in 2009, accounting for 0.17% of GDP that year, less than 5% of China's fiscal revenue. The United States contributed $300 billion in 2008, about 2% of its $14 trillion GDP that year, 10% of its $3 trillion revenue. In 2009, there were 1,843 foundations in China[1] while there are over one million, over 160,000 and over 80,000 charitable organizations in the U. S., the U.K. and Canada respectively. In 2009, there were fewer than 20, 000 people, over 9 million and 600,000 charity employees in China, the U. S. and the UK respectively[2].

---

1   "The Guiding Program for the Development of Chinese Charity (2011-2015)" issued by the Ministry of Civil Affairs on July 15, 2011 shows that by the end of 2010 there has been 2,200 foundations registered in the civil affairs department.

2   Wang Zhenyao, "Charities in Contemporary China: Status Quo, Path, Prospect", July 20, 2010, China Social Sciences Journal. According to Beijing Charitable Development Report (2013), at the end of 2012, there were 536 charitable social organizations in Beijing with 7,951 employees, and a total worth of 7.622 billion yuan of charitable donation from 2008 to 2012. As is reported on November 29, 2013 in Shenzhen Special Zone Paper, there are 20,000 philanthropic practitioners with more than 800,000 registered volunteers in Shenzhen's 1,407 charitable social organizations and 65 registered foundations. The city's annual charitable donations has reached more than 1.08 billion yuan. Its 30,000 public welfare and charitable projects has benefited people across the country.

Reasons for these differences cannot be explained only by "custom and moral influence" of different nationalities and societies. In developed countries, donation system related to tax collection are two-fold. On one hand, enterprises and individuals involved in donation and public charity can get certain tax exemption and tax reduction; on the other hand, high inheritance tax and gift tax is adopted to restrict asset transfer, enabling citizens and enterprises with huge wealth to put their own income, part of their property either as government tax for public purpose through the "tax-finance-public expenditure" channels or as social contribution for public purpose through "social donations-charitable foundations-philanthropy" channels.

In China's tax practice of "the third distribution", on the one hand, tax laws stipulate that enterprises and individuals and recipients of donations will enjoy preferential treatment of income tax deduction proportionately; on the other hand, tax collection and management of non-profit organizations is not strict enough as some non-profit organizations are engaged in profit-making, neither paying taxes nor under tax administration. Obviously lack of administration of donation organizations and their activities as well as limited tax preference obviously will not be able to promote charity and collect funds for "the third distribution".

(II) Tax Policy of "The Third Distribution" Development

First, improve tax collection and administration of the third sector. According to *Detailed Rules for Implementation of the Law of the People's Republic of China on Tax Collection and Administration*, non-profit organizations shall, within 30 days after the occurrence of their tax obligations, go through tax registration and declaration with tax authorities, which is not conducive to the third sector administration by tax authorities and easily leads to tax evasion in the third sector. Therefore, it is suggested that upon establishing the third sector, tax registration and strict tax declaration system will be adopted with the latter as an independent legal obligation whether out of tax obligation or not. Moreover, registration authorities, business authorities, and tax authorities should establish information exchange system with all "the third sector" so that tax authorities will know establishment, alteration, and cancellation of "the third sector".

Second, distinguish commercial activities from non-commercial activities of "the third sector" followed by different tax treatment. According to research of the Department of Laws and Regulations of the State Administration of Taxation as well as the practice of the United States, treat differently commercial activities and non-commercial activities of non-profit organizations according to tax policy, which can be divided into four categories: first, tax exemption for non-profit organizations which provide services or welfare to the whole society or for a specific group for free; Second, tax exemption when benefits of the beneficiary is not equal to benefits obtained although there is money or other benefits between the non-profit organization and beneficial person. Third, tax imposition when service sales between non-profit organization and beneficiaries is regarded as production of an enterprise and as business activity. Fourth, tax exemption for income for charity purpose during circulation of asset value-keeping, value-added activity (asset operations) of non-profit organizations[1].

Third, improve donation tax system. According to current tax system in China, improvement of donation tax system should include the following: first, according to agreements between China and other countries on avoiding double taxation on income, establish donation tax system for the third sector making donation in other countries; Second, there shall be more non-profit organizations enjoying preferential treatment of donation tax with annual inspection system for "the third sector" donations so as to cancel in time "the third sector" organizations which fail to meet requirements; Third, according to policy guidance of the country, deduction rate before tax should be imposed on donation from different "third sector" organizations.

---

1   Research Group of Policy and Law Department of State Administration of Taxation: *Study on Tax System of Non-profit Organizations*, Taxation Research Journal, No. 12, 2004.

Chapter VI

State-owned Enterprises and National Income Distribution

GUO Dongjie[1]

There does exist widening income gap in China. As is pointed out in *The 2012 Report on Household Income Inequality in China*, the Gini coefficient of household income in China in 2010 was 0.61; the Gini coefficient within urban households and within rural households is 0.56, and 0.60 respectively, well above the global Gini average of 0.44. In January 2013, the National Bureau of Statistics published the Gini coefficient of national residents' income between 2003 and 2012, 0.479, 0.473, 0.485, 0.487, 0.484, 0.491, 0.490, 0.481, 0.477, 0.474 respectively. Horizontally compared, official figures are small and have even been falling back since 2009, contrary to true feelings of the general public. The incalculable illegal income (i.e., labor remuneration income or property income that does not pay personal income tax) makes people feel indignant. Furthermore, after years of irregular development, there's been widening gap in household wealth. At the same time, in China's industrialization, labor share does

---

1   GUO Dongjie Associate Professor of School of Economics and Trade Management, Zhejiang University of Technology, Master's Tutor

not grow as other industrialized countries do. On the contrary, there has been an "atypical" situation of maintaining stability or even falling at low level ("Social Security Green Book", 2012). The public put blame on state-owned enterprises for a powerful country with poor people. As an important practitioner of China's economic system reform, the reform mode and operation mechanism of state-owned enterprises has been frequently challenged by the public--What role have state-owned enterprises played in national income distribution? In addition, the public is more concerned about how to promote income distribution system reform and how to narrow the gap between rich and poor to build a powerful country with rich people.

I. Nature and Responsibility of State-owned Enterprises

According to neoclassical economics, an enterprise is regarded as the "black box" of making products whose behavior is abstracted as production planning of profit maximization or cost minimization to achieve optimal production level under the constraints of technology, market and economic conditions. Coase (1937)'s analysis of enterprise nature goes beyond neoclassical economics: "transaction costs leads to the emergence of the enterprise whose marked sign is the substitution of price mechanism." In other words, an enterprise is an organization that has the same function as market coordination mechanism to save transaction costs. Sometimes, in order to achieve its production function, enterprises need to obtain production factors from production factor owner, which leads to the separation of ownership and management rights. Accordingly, Jensen and Meckling (1976) believe that an enterprise is an organization that, like most other organizations, is a legal fiction whose function is to act as a "connecting point" for a set of contracts between such individuals as labor owners, material and capital providers, and product consumers.

New institutional economics regards the enterprise as a contract hanging on to the "interest" goal of the enterprise established by neoclassical economics, ignoring the subject nature of the enterprise as an independent subject with rights, obligations and responsibilities. Obviously, this view is consistent with the traditional civil law believing that the enterprise is a certain property complex containing both material and immaterial factors, as the object of rights, and belonging to enterprise owners, which, to a certain extent, was absorbed by the personality of business owners (Wang Yanmei, 2012). In legal practice, business ownership has been included in civil property right, the enterprise being the object of civil property right and enterprise owners bearing full responsibility for enterprise debt. However, with social progress, this organizational form which depends on enterprise owner can not meet the needs of capitalist economic development anymore. Modern commercial law endows the enterprise with some legal personality such as a unity of rights, legal relations and factual relations, organized by contract by re-regulating ownership power and contractual freedom, thus breaking through the concept of enterprise in civil law and possessing the following three legal attributes: first, independent; second, engaging in a kind of legal behavior of obtaining remuneration in the market; and third, well-planned and well-targeted in its continuing operation.

In terms of enterprise nature, there has never been any distinction between private enterprises and state-owned enterprises in either economics or law. Judging from the history of world economy, state-owned enterprises, no unique product of socialist countries, also exist in capitalist countries. SOEs have been part of social and economic life for profound historical reasons: first, the state-owned enterprise is product of political function as well as product of economic development. As private economy is not conducive for the rulers to control economy, nor for them to carry out their political intentions, the government will naturally invest in enterprises. Second, SOEs meet the need of reasonable distribution of social wealth. "Distribution, by its decisive characteristics, is always the inevitable result of a society's relations of production and exchange as well as the historical premise of that society", however, "distribution, not merely the negativity of production and exchange, in turn affects production and exchange[1]".Therefore, both Marx and Engels, the founders of communism, attach great importance to the core position of state-owned enterprises in public-owned economy.

After the founding of the People's Republic of China, due to restriction of the situation home and abroad and limited ideology, ownership of means of production by the whole people took the form of state ownership, unified management and unified profits and losses for a long period of time. Enterprises have become appendages of state organs without business autonomy at all as their production is stipulated by the state's unified plan; enterprises have no independent economic interest as their profits are turned over to the state which subsidizes their losses. In view of state-owned enterprises' nature under planned economy, the representative theories are: Korner's "shortage" theory (1986), Ogagi Lontaro's theory (1993) of "No enterprises in China", Liu Shijin's theory (1995) on "Community Units", He Fan & Zhang Yuyan's theory (1996) on "boundary rigidity". These theories explain the existence and behaviors of state-owned enterprises from different angles, but they have not really made any breakthrough in both theory and practice. Deng Xiaoping has made great contributions to socialist political economy by clearly pointing out that both planned economy and market economy are means of developing production and regulating economy as a matter of operating mechanism both socialism and capitalism can adopt instead of a matter of basic economic system to distinguish socialism from capitalism. *Decision of the CPC Central Committee on Comprehensively Deepening Economic System Reform* made at the Third Plenary Session of the 12th CPC Central Committee pointed out that "in accordance with Marxist theory and socialist practice, ownership can be properly separated from the right to operate". According to *The Decision*, state-owned enterprise reform is based on the concept of state ownership, enterprise's independent management and self-responsibility for profits and losses, which requires enterprises to become

---

1   Engels: *Anti-Durin Theory*, People's Press, 1999.

independent economic entities, independent producers and managers, and legal persons with certain rights and obligations.

So far, the establishment of modern enterprise system has become the guide for state-owned enterprise reform, state-owned enterprises that have bid farewell to planned economy have begun to restore their original market features and regain their subjective status. Therefore, state-owned enterprise nature and practice should include both production decision and property right and law regulation as state-owned enterprises, main body of market and required registration as legal persons, must abide by corresponding laws. Among them, it's of vital importance that both state-owned enterprises and private enterprises should engage in fair market competition, otherwise, market economy order will inevitably be destroyed. Report of the 18th National Congress of the CPC pointed out that "We will unswervingly encourage, support and guide non-public economic sector development so as to ensure that all forms of ownership use production factors equally in accordance with law, participate in fair market competition and are equally protected by law". In economics, the establishment of state-owned enterprises is to solve the externality caused by the inconsistency between enterprise objectives and social goals to provide public goods and quasi-public goods not fully developed by market mechanism. Goods with the government as its only buyer or whose production process needs strict control should be provided by state-owned enterprises while other products by private economy. Many scholars believe that under market economy, in addition to profit targets, SOEs, as institutional arrangement and government policy tool, should take on more social goals, such as economic growth, price stability, full employment and common prosperity, rather than "social responsibility" of average private enterprises. Based on this expectation, the government allows state-owned enterprises to enjoy priority over other market subjects, which violates fair value standard of law. In addition to defects in property right system, "the absence of owner" inevitably magnifies the moral hazard in principal-agent of state-owned assets. Frankly speaking, if there are many state-owned assets and enterprises in entire economic system, the government will inevitably favor and protect state-owned enterprises in rule making and macro-control. Focusing on private enterprises with supervision, regulation and control will divide the whole economy. First, survival space of private enterprises is suppressed because they can not enter relevant industries, fail to hire outstanding talent (welfare gap) and give rise to financing difficulties; Second, state-owned enterprises are becoming more and more concentrated in certain industries, and various monopolies have greatly hindered the development of market mechanisms, causing a series of serious problems, such as production inefficiency, internal control, extravagance and so on.

II. SOE Reform

SOE reform, the first of its kind, can be roughly divided into four stages. In the first stage, between 1979 to 1986, state-owned enterprises became economic entities responsible for their own profits and losses and managed on its own through decentralization with part of residual control right and claim right and without changing their ownership and support of commercial law. In the second stage, between 1987 and 1992, there has been a breakthrough in ownership of state-owned enterprises. At that time, there were two reform courses: one is contract system, transfer of operation right rather than ownership. The other is stock system characterized by multiple property rights and optimization of internal governance structure. In the third stage, between 1993 and 2002, the Third Plenary Session of the 14th CPC Central Committee proposed to establish modern enterprise system with the goal of "clear property right, clear power and responsibility, separation of government administration and enterprise management, scientific management". *Decision on Implementation of Financial Management Mechanism of Tax Sharing System* stipulates that state-owned enterprises need not turn in profits to the state within a certain period of time except a certain proportion of revenue with the rest left to enterprises for their laid-off workers, pensions, etc. *Decision on Several Important Issues Concerning State-owned Enterprise Reform and Development* clearly defines reform strategy of "developing major enterprises and letting go of minor ones" and "great majority of state-owned enterprises' withdrawal from competitive industries and developing into national security industries, natural monopolies, public welfare industries providing public goods, few key high-tech industries, and backbone enterprises of pillar industries." The fourth stage, from 2003 up to now, under the policy of "further promotion of state-owned capital going to vital industries and key areas of national security and national economic lifelines, and further control of state-owned economy by playing a leading role in reform", newly established SASAC (The State-owned Assets Supervision and Administration Commission of the State Council) regards "merger and reorganization" and "integration and expansion" as target of its new round of SOE reform. Central enterprises accelerated asset restructuring and structure adjustment with 196 in 2003 declining to 117 in 2012 with its absolute domination in oil, electricity, tobacco, post and telecommunications industries. Between 2002 and 2011, total assets of state-owned enterprises rose from 7.13 trillion yuan to 28 trillion yuan and tax payment rose from 292.6 billion yuan to 1.7 trillion yuan. At the same time, management system reform of state-owned assets has been deepened in an all-round way with laws such as *Law of State-owned Assets* promulgated one after another, further protecting state-owned assets. In 2007, the state tried out "state-owned capital operating budget" system stipulating that central enterprises should turn in 5% to 10% of its net profit to the Ministry of Finance. An overall tax collection adjustment was made in 2011 with an upward adjustment of 5%, involving four types of enterprises: first category is tobacco, petroleum and petrochemical, electricity, telecommunications, coal and other resources monopolies with 15% collection rate; second category is iron and steel, transportation, electronics, trade, construction and other general competitive industries with 10% collection rate; third category includes military industry, transformed scientific research institutes and so on with 5% collection rate; and fourth category is policy companies such as China General Grain Reserve Corporation with exemption from state-owned capital income. In addition, another result of this reform stage has been continued withdrawal of private capital from so-called "important industries and key areas", such as refining and marketing of petroleum and petrochemical industries and coal industry in Shanxi Province. "Advancement of SOEs and withdrawal of private enterprises" is about to appear. It is no doubt that state-owned enterprise reform liberates productive forces, cultivates numerous market competitors, strengthens non-public economy, giving momentum to rapid economic growth. As is shown in charts 6-1 and 6-2, proportion of state-controlled and collective economies in gross industrial output fell from 54.6% and 35.62% in 1991 to 26.18% and 1.31% in 2011 while proportion of other economies in gross industrial output rose from 6.01% to 90.79%. Accordingly, number of state-controlled and collective economies fell from 20.7% and 77.5% to 5.3% and 1.6% while number of other economies rose from 1.7% to 93.1%. However, SOE reform strategies and methods have always been heatedly discussed by society with controversy over its fairness and feasibility. Specific problems are as follows: first, state-owned assets loss; second, placement and compensation of laid-off workers; and third, preservation of state-owned enterprise monopoly, and fourth, preservation of entrustment agent of state-owned enterprises.

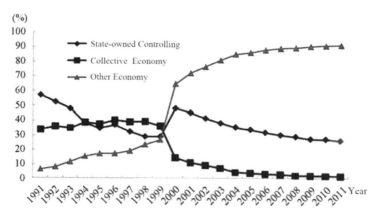

Chart 6-1   Proportion of Different Economic Types in Gross Industrial Output Value

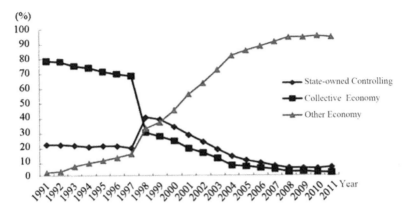

Chart 6-2   Proportion of Different Economic Types in Industrial Enterprises

Some scholars believe that China's state-owned enterprise reform doesn't involve their owners, let alone owners' rights. Reform started from operation right, then possession right, and lastly ownership so that state-owned enterprise workers and workers across the nation has become object of reform and bystanders (Liu Yongji, 2002). On the one hand, in state-owned enterprise reform, as staff and workers do not have labor ownership, thus no possession institutions to exercise their ownership, and unable to protect their labor ownership, including right to work, right to protect. Some state-owned enterprises "become privatized" by "reducing employees to achieve efficiency", by speculating with bureaucratic capital and putting workers' ownership under their own names so as to transfer state-owned property right to private property right, exacerbating contradiction between capital and labor and worsening income inequality of whole society. On the other hand, the government continues to control state-owned enterprises through centralization system, essence of which is "capitalization" of state-owned assets, that is, operating state-owned assets for profits: "bureaucratic" operations (both ranks and management appointed by leaders), lack of democratic and legal supervision, and identity exchanges between management and officials, i.e. corporate senior executives gaining access to policies and resources by entering the government while government officials cash in power by entering an enterprise, giving rise to powerful capitalism characterized by vested interest groups controlling social and public resources, thus ruining the goal of common prosperity of socialism with Chinese characteristics.

III. Corporate Governance and Income Distribution of Privatized ESOs (Employee Stock Ownership)

In the mid-1980s, in order to solve capital investment problem, some operators and employees of collective enterprises spontaneously choose ESOs. After that, with flourishing stock-sharing system, small and medium-sized state-owned enterprises and more collective enterprises gave ESO a try. Promulgation of company law in 1993 recognized modern enterprise system as its reform core. As basic mode of property right reform, employee stock ownership was widely adopted by stated-owned enterprise reform. The author, an employee of an accounting firm back then, witnessed state-owned enterprises reform and carried out relevant research on some restructured enterprises in Hangzhou (Yao Xianguo, Guo Dongjie, 2004). Then, what have become of them a decade later? Is there any improvement in employees' income distribution? The author revisited them. My findings are as follows.

(I) Is there perfect corporate governance mechanism in restructured enterprises?

Among the 15 restructured enterprises revisited, there is absolutely no modern corporate governance mechanism. In the 11 enterprises that retain state-owned shares (proportion of which ranges from 10% to 40%), natural person stockholders (generally, operators) and employee shareholding associations have the right to participate in shareholders' meetings by law, enjoy voting rights, and elect corporate directors and supervisors. In actual operation, chairman of the board of directors is often nominated and recommended by an asset management company representing state-owned shares. Moreover, in making major corporate decisions, there goes again state-owned enterprise style. Such administrative tendency has seriously prevented restructured enterprises from development, board of supervisors being virtually powerless in most enterprises. Except operators, the proportion of employee stock shares is low, which can only be managed through chairman of ESOP, further weakening trade unions. Among enterprises without state-owned shares, Enterprise A's governance mechanism has gone to the other extreme: chairman alone has the say even if ESOs have dominant stocks. Chairman does behave at his own will: setting up a small treasury, embezzling enterprise property and employees' equity, giving rise to poor operating performance, "book loss" every year, and intensity between manager and staff. Two sides brought the issue to Hangzhou municipal party committee and municipal government. The then Hangzhou city leaders gave order as follows: "Trade unions can play their role in fighting for workers' rights by investigating and improving employees' income." As a result, chairman was investigated and sentenced to six years' imprisonment. Enterprise B is small with stocks owned by natural persons and with neither state-owned shares nor employee shareholding associations. According to *Provisions of Company Law*, Enterprise B can develop modern corporate governance mechanism. However, general manager of Enterprise B mentioned that although operation autonomy has been expanded, the enterprise has rented the house of asset management company, both party construction and trade union are all set up in operating company, and are often given assignment, such as donations, attending to its retirees, participating in "Project Spring Wind". Since the enterprise does not make sound economic sense with unenthusiastic natural person shareholders and incomplete enterprise reform, it's all for the best if the enterprise is auctioned or merged by major companies. Enterprise C with average profits pointed out that its internal affairs are often interfered by asset management company. As the interviewee summed up, defects of governance mechanism of restructured enterprise are those with power assumes no responsibility while those with responsibility has no power.

(II) Does ESOP Improve Employees' Income Distribution?

ESOP fails to narrow the income gap between managers and shareholding employees, only to widen the income gap between shareholding employees and non-shareholding employees. Most respondents believe that "with the loss of state-owned assets, restructuring has made some people rich first" and that operators "rely on policy and luck to make a fortune" rather than create wealth to become rich. As chairman of Enterprise D quipped: "if our enterprise land had not been part of Hangzhou's urban planning and construction land in restructuring, I would have become a billionaire. Yes, though it's a dream that can never come true, I do have a lot of shares."

In fact, most operators of former state-owned enterprises have realized their dreams of making a fortune. When reconstructing, operators often get tens or even hundreds of times as many shares as average employee and become the biggest beneficiaries of SOE reform. In addition, operators' income have been marketized after restructuring. How is it possible to the narrow gap between the two? As employees of Enterprise E say, "they work for life quality; we work to live a hand-to-mouth existence." Among 15 enterprises, annual income of chairman of companies with average profits is usually 4 to 6 times average income of their shareholding employees; annual income of chairman of companies with high profits is usually 8 to 12 times average income of their shareholding employees, excluding job expenses that interviewees mention from time to time. The 15 cars costs Enterprise E with only 100 employees nearly a million a year, eroding its profits. After restructuring, operators of four listed companies tend to increase job consumption, "soft constraint". At the same time, a difficult task for restructured enterprises retaining state-owned shares is to maintain and increase state-owned share value. In addition, during state-owned enterprise reform, most employees except "laid-offs" as a result of "reducing staff to improve efficiency" were given a certain number of shares. With passage of time, new employees who can't get their shares from the company get no capital income, causing their income to be significantly lower than shareholding employees. Some restructured enterprises often implement a variety of labor contract system with equal work and different pay, further widening employees' income gap.

(III) Ownership Structural Changes of Restructured Enterprises

As most interviewees pointed out, although state-owned enterprise reform is a measure the government had to take, hasty introduction of ESOP system, a temporary form, will inevitably give rise to all sorts of problems. Ownership structural changes of 15 restructured enterprises seem to suggest that ESOP system is doomed.

Restructured enterprise F retained no state-owned shares. Later, its demolished factory was given land compensation of as much as 2 billion yuan, thus triggering complaints from retirees, employees whose shares were repurchased at a low price (according to articles of association during restructuring, most enterprises repurchase shares at book value of their net assets or multiplied by a coefficient) and non-shareholding employees, all of whom ask for compensation. After futile negotiations, those employees filed a petition. In order to maintain social stability, asset management company was forced to buy back employees' shares at 1: 11, and meanwhile, non-shareholding employees were given one-off compensation, so once again Enterprise F became a state-owned holding enterprise.

Two restructured enterprises have listed successfully in recent years. According to China Securities Law and relevant regulations of China Securities Regulatory Commission, sponsors of to-be-listed companies should not exceed 200 and companies must thoroughly clean up such phenomena as trade union shareholding, shareholding associations and shares nomination before listing. Relevant regulations do not allow listed companies option issuing, stock appreciation rights and other equity incentives. Enterprise G and H had to repurchase their employees' shares at 1: 4.8 and 1: 5.5 respectively for listing to their employees' satisfaction.

Three restructured enterprises have been acquired by other companies more or less with the "administrative push". State-owned shares of Enterprise I were not sold while shares of both natural persons and employees were acquired at 1: 10. Its chairman of board of directors owned 1 million shares and became a multimillionaire overnight. After the accident of Chairman of Board of Directors of Enterprise A, new investors were introduced under the guidance of municipal government. After voting at shareholders' meeting and shareholding meeting, shares of natural persons and employees were acquired at 1: 5.5. Restructured Enterprise J without retaining state-owned shares has been constantly fighting between two major factions due to different management concepts, affecting its normal operations. Driven by asset management company, the enterprise's entire stake was acquired by a large Shanghai company at 1: 4.6, purchase price of full equity being 0.46 billion yuan. It is reported that Enterprise J's current annual sales revenue has reached more than 13 billion yuan with a net profit of about 600 million yuan.

Restructured Enterprise K left its parent company to become an employee-owned company with 10% state-owned shares. After a year of running alone, all shares were repurchased at 1: 3.5 because of operational needs of former state-owned enterprises, thus a wholly-owned subsidiary of state-owned enterprises.

Enterprise B consists of only 21 natural person shareholders at restructuring. Originally, chairman of Board of Directors held 17.5% of shares and owned 75% of shares after buying shares from natural person shareholders who quit or retire, the enterprise being gradually "privatized." According to chairman, as a competitive industry with average corporate performance and with old employees who have poor management concepts, outdated knowledge and almost no enthusiasm for work, he had to pay a great price to acquire shares that employees find it hard to part with. Even with absolute control over shares, chairman still has a lot to complain.

While their ownership structure has not changed significantly, the remaining seven enterprises have experienced fine-tuning. Some enterprise managers quit or retire with their shares transferred to other managers. Some shareholding employees quit, their shares repurchased by employees' shareholding associations or transferred to other employees. Some well-performed enterprises have transferred repurchased shares or extra shares added to them to non-shareholding technical and professional backbone. In any case, a common issue here is share repurchase price. Although most restructured enterprises have made regulations for share transfer often linked to enterprise net assets. But after a few years, the regulations do not seem reasonable because asset prices have soared in recent years so that book prices do not reflect real assets, triggering conflicts between shareholding employees and the enterprise. When Enterprise E was being restructured, its regulations failed to mention employees' share transfer, causing those employees who quit or retire to hold more than 50% of shares. Is this still an employee-owned enterprise?

Interviewees commented that restructured enterprises often face two serious problems: one is that "old employees priding themselves on being old do not comply with company law and overprotect their own rights." This may seem too much but it is with enough reason to say so because many restructured enterprise employees have been engaged in group petition. As is in restructuring of Enterprise F, executives and enterprise leaders met many times to ask employees to buy shares, but some of them refused to do so. Later, when getting relocated, the enterprise received a huge amount of land compensation so that these employees could not wait but to spontaneously gather themselves together to file a petition, so-called "protecting their rights." Local government was on all guard and had to spend money to buy peace.

The other problem is that there is no written law on ESOP, ESOP operation lacking legal norms. From the practice in the past decade, there has been three forms of ESOP: one is to register and set up corporation legal person. Since corporation legal person must be non-profit organizations, this form was suspended in 1999 by the Ministry of Civil Affairs. Another form is to set up employee shareholding meeting by relying on legal status and capacity of trade union. In this case, shareholding meeting not fulfilling legal registration procedures does not have independent rights and action capacity under the guise of the position, rights, and obligations of trade unions, violating existing laws on trade union regulations. Still another form is that through principal agent, a certain number of shareholding employee representatives selected by all shareholding employees register and set up shareholding companies. For lack of credibility in entrustment process, rights and interest of most non-registered shareholding employees depend entirely on credibility of registered shareholding employees, posing greater potential risks.

IV. Income Distribution of Capitalized State-owned Monopolies

(I) Monopoly Formation and Industrial Distribution of Retained State-owned Enterprises

By the end of 20th century, more than 70% of China's state-owned enterprises had suffered losses and were in difficult financial situation, forcing the government to restructure state-owned enterprises and its financial system. Small and medium-sized state-owned enterprises got privatized so as to stay out of competition first by "focusing on large enterprises and letting go of small ones". Then, in the name of making bigger and stronger, retained state-owned industries cultivate monopoly power with low labor cost and monopoly position of such upstream industries as energy, transportation, telecommunications, etc. by "maintaining and increasing value", causing product market to become highly competitive while factor market becomes highly monopolized. Li Rongrong (2008), former director of SASAC, noted in *Qiushi* that 82.8% of assets of state-owned enterprises of central government are in such industries as petroleum and petrochemical, electricity, national defense, communications, transportation, mining, metallurgy, machinery, providing China with almost all the crude oil, natural gas and ethylene, basic telecommunications services and most value-added services; about 55% of national electricity generation, 82% of total turnover of civil aviation transportation, 89% of total turnover of goods transported by water, 48% of national automobile output, 60% of national added-value steel, 70% of national hydro-power equipment, and 75% of thermal power equipment. As is shown in Chart 6-3, the proportion of total assets of central enterprises in China's state-owned enterprises rose from 46% in 2001 to 51.6% in 2010 (the highest being 55.2% in 2008) and the proportion of total profits dropped from 79.7% to 63.4%. Thus, central enterprises have been playing a vital role in China's economy.

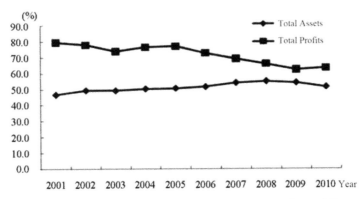

Chart 6-3   Proportion of Total Assets and Total Profits of Central Enterprises in National SOEs

In the wake of global financial crisis, the government adopted more drastic economic policies to tighten economic control by expanding state-owned enterprises, resulting in a reduction in the market capacity of private enterprises. In many key industries, a "tangible hand" firmly grasps core resources such as finance, energy, land resources, transportation, and education industry, all of which is under the control of monopoly state-owned enterprises. In 2012, China's state-owned and state-owned holding enterprises (excluding state-owned financial enterprises) had total operating income of 42.37696 trillion yuan and total profits of 2.19596 trillion yuan (net profit of 1.6068 trillion yuan). Total operating income and total profits of central enterprises (including enterprises under central management and enterprises affiliated to departments) was 26.05585 trillion yuan and 1.50454 trillion yuan, with 85.7% of total operating income and 81.3% of total profits made by 117 central enterprises. Yuan Zhigang et al. (2010) took as an example a total of 1,604 enterprises (562 private enterprises and 1,042 state-owned enterprises) listed in Shenzhen and Shanghai stock exchanges in 2008 to estimate monopoly power of state-owned enterprises in certain industries with market concentration. It is found that the proportion of state-owned enterprises is positively related to market concentration. Aggregate proportion of private enterprises in all industries with market concentration of less than 50% is more than 82%, significantly higher than that of state-owned enterprises, becoming major force of intense market competition in China. The proportion of private enterprises in all industries with market concentration of over 50% is less than 18%, much lower than that of state-owned enterprises, 55%. It can be seen that strengthening monopoly power and retrogressive marketization are accompanied by increasing concentration of assets and profits of state-owned enterprises. According to Economic Freedom Index of the Heritage Foundation/Wall Street Journal, mainland China's economic freedom was 51% in 2010, ranking 140th among 183 economies in the world, almost the same as Russia (50.3%), Viet Nam (49.8%), the Laos (51.1%), Bangladesh (51.1%), Argentina (51.2%), significantly lower than Taiwan, China (70.4%), South Korea (69.9 %), Japan (72.2%), Hong Kong, China (89.7%). But under the halo of world's second in terms of GDP, "China model" is about to emerge, underlying crisis ignored or overlooked.

(II) Paradox between Profit and Efficiency of State-owned Enterprises

Between 2001 and 2009, China's average return on equity of state-owned and state-owned holding industrial enterprises and that of non-state-owned industrial enterprises is 8.16% and 12.9% respectively. Affected by financial crisis, net interest rate on sales, return on equity and profit to cost ratio of central enterprises in 2012 was 4.2%, 7.2% and 6.1% respectively. This shows that nominal performance of state-owned and state-owned holding enterprises is not good enough. Even so, this may not be real performance because they have been enjoying a great variety of preferential policy, such as financial subsidies, financing costs, land and resource rents, etc. "If 6 trillion yuan of unpaid costs and subsidies due to preferential policy were deducted from nominal profit and real enterprise costs were restored to book financial data, average real return on equity of state-owned and state-owned holding industrial enterprises between 2001 and 2009 would be -1.47%". Moreover, in sharp contrast to huge nominal profits, total factor productivity (TFP) of state-owned enterprises has declined in recent years, indicating that profits of state-owned enterprises do not result from technological progress and improved management. So where does huge profit come from? The answer is monopoly and preferential policy. Yuan Tangjun (2009) found that non-manufacturing agriculture, mining, coal, oil and natural gas mining, as well as total factor productivity (TFP) have all declined to varying degrees, with oil and gas mining being the most serious. Average productivity of most industries, except manufacturing industries such as furniture and printing, shows an upward trend. Between 1999 and 2004, productivity of most listed companies in automobile, electronic, electrical and general machinery industries has greatly improved, most of which are competitive private enterprises.

In addition, between 1999 and 2004, efficiency of new listed companies in oil and natural gas mining, coal, construction, petroleum products, metals and electric power industries was not high, which had an obviously negative impact on TFP of their industries. Resource allocation efficiency in most enterprises has greatly reduced, especially in metal, rubber and plastics manufacturing industries and oil and gas mining industries, most of whose listed companies/SOEs are protected by the state. Luo Deming et al. (2012) constructed a stochastic dynamic general equilibrium model by introducing monopolistic competitive intermediate product manufacturers and endogenous entry-exit selection to portray state-owned and private enterprises faced with policy distortions in factor market with different stochastic processes of total factor productivity growth. Through calibration, quantitative models show that resource misalignment resulting from policy distortions results in very serious efficiency losses.

(III) Income Distribution of State-owned Enterprises' Internal Staff

Time can change everything. Now state-owned enterprise profits are getting better day by day. As is shown in Table 6-1, though the number of SOEs fell by nearly half between 1999 and 2010, their total assets and total profit grew to 4.4 times and 18.7 times the original figure, profits growing from 46.5% to 60.0%. With increased book profits of state-owned enterprises, state-owned employees' income also increases. As Chart 6-4 shows, before 2003, average state-owned unit employees' wage was lower than that of other units, and then surpassed the latter. Average central enterprises' wage in particular is much higher than that of other units. In 2010, average central enterprises' wage, state-owned units' wage, other units' wage, and collective units' wage was 56,960 yuan, 39,471 yuan, 35,843 yuan, and 22,430 yuan respectively.

Table 6-1   Profits and Losses of National State-owned Enterprises

Year	Number of Enterprises (10,000)	Total Assets	Total Profits (100 million yuan)	Profits of Profitable Enterprises (100 million yuan)	Losses of Loss-making Enterprises (100 million yuan)	Profits (%)
1999	21. 7	145288. 1	1145. 8	3290. 7	- 2144. 9	46. 5
2000	19. 1	160068. 4	2833. 8	4679. 8	- 1846	49. 3
2001	17. 4	166709. 6	2811. 2	4804. 7	- 1993. 6	48. 8
2002	15. 9	180218. 9	3786. 3	5588. 8	- 1802. 5	50. 1
2003	14. 6	199709. 8	4769. 4	7589. 1	- 2819. 8	47. 4
2004	13. 6	215602. 3	7368. 8	10429. 4	- 3060. 6	48. 0
2005	12. 6	242560. 1	9579. 9	12005. 9	- 2426	50. 1
2006	11. 6	277308. 1	12193. 5	15701. 1	- 3507. 5	53. 4
2007	11. 2	347068. 1	17441. 8	21220. 4	- 3778. 6	56. 5
2008	11. 0	416219. 2	13335. 2	19863. 7	- 6528. 4	56. 8
2009	11. 1	514137. 2	15606. 8	20983. 8	- 5377	58. 6
2010	11. 4	640214. 3	21428. 2	27715. 5	- 6287. 3	60. 0

Source: *China Financial Statistical Yearbook* over the years

In addition, the income gap between industries is also surprising. In 2010, national average employees' wage was 36,539 yuan while industries whose average wage above 50,000 yuan were as follows: securities (168,116 yuan); air transport (91,913 yuan), software (86,137 yuan); banking (81,533 yuan); tobacco products (78,675 yuan); computer services (76,839 yuan); research and testing (60,493 yuan); professional and technical services (58,677 yuan); water transport (56,482 yuan); press and publication (56,267 yuan); oil and gas mining (55,099 yuan); telecommunications and other information transmission services (54,785 yuan); pipeline transport (52,167 yuan); production and supply of electricity, heat, gas and water (51,273 yuan). It is not difficult to find that most high-income industries are state-owned monopolies.

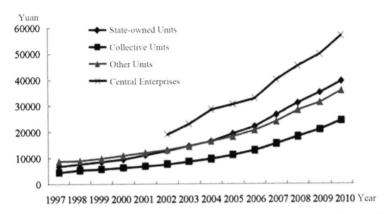

Chart 6-4   Average Wage of On-the-Job Staff and Workers of Different Economic Units

But average wage tends to conceal the fact that there were income gap between different jobs within SOEs. In 2004, *The Implementation Rules of Interim Measures for Compensation Management of Central Enterprise Senior Executives* advocated a performance-oriented annual salary system for senior executives of state-owned enterprises, thus widening the income gap between senior executives of state-owned enterprises and average employee. According to annual report of state-owned listed companies, a great number of state-owned executives earn more than 1 million annual salary. According to SASAC's pay appraisal system, senior executives' income is generally divided into basic wage, performance pay, bonuses and benefits, only basic wage and benefits known to the public while performance pay and bonuses mostly not announced. Other categories of award income, annual fee, housing provident fund, enterprise annuity and so on have not been included in calculation, let alone "bottomless" duty consumption. In 2009, the joint multi-ministerial *Guidance on Further Standardizing Compensation Management of Senior Executives of Central Enterprises* issued a "salary restriction order" for senior executives in all sectors of central enterprises, but its effectiveness is doubtful, as there is evidence that revenue from most state-owned senior executives keeps growing, according to annual report of recent years. In addition, dual identity of China's state-owned enterprise senior executives as both "associate officials" and "quasi-entrepreneurs" may result in them being neither subject to administrative supervision law nor bound by market rules, thus leading to corruption and bribery, prevalence of extravagance and embezzlement of state capital which has caused public discontent. In economics, enterprises have always been striving to maximize their profits. When total income exceed total costs, enterprise will make excess profits; when totals costs exceed total income, enterprises will suffer losses. Clearly, high income for state-owned internal staff come from high monopoly profits or high government subsidies when enterprises suffer losses. For now, the core goal of most monopolies is to pursue as much profits as possible, ignoring their social responsibility. In addition, "absence of owners" has led to uncertainty as to who is in charge of state-owned assets with no one responsible for its bankruptcy and with rampant "insider control". Although quite a number of state-owned enterprises have undergone corporate reform, most act as a government agency that operates bureaucratically instead of an independent economic entity. In monopoly profits distribution, insiders conspire with staff and workers to turn in profits as little as possible and increase income share of operators and average employee.

(IV) Influence of State-owned Monopolies on National Income Distribution

In constituent item of income of gross domestic product in national economic accounting, labor remuneration represents residents' income share, employees' income (or labor remuneration). Enterprise surplus is equal to undistributed profit in enterprise financial statement, and depreciation of fixed assets comes from profit of enterprise deferred tax payment, both of which can be regarded as income share acquired through production factor distribution of capital, land and resources in their narrow sense, that is, enterprise income, net production tax being government tax revenue. As is shown in Table 6-2, since 1978, China's labor share has been on the rise and reached its peak of 56.5% in 1983, but it has been on the decline since then and fell to 39.74% in 2007, a decline of 16.76%. Over the same period of time, in sharp contrast to continuous decline of labor share, enterprise income share in GDP rose by about 12% and government tax revenues in GDP rose slightly by about 2%. In 2008, affected by financial crisis, numerous small and medium-sized enterprises went bankrupt and enterprise income share in GDP fell from 45.45% in 2007 to 38.18% in 2009. Labor share increased from 39.74% in 2007 to 46.62% in 2009. Then, as economy slowly recovers, labor share begins to decline slowly again while government tax revenues unaffected by the financial crisis have been on a slight rise. On the whole, regardless of financial crisis, it is believed that China's labor remuneration grows though labor share falls and that both enterprise income share and government income share in GDP show a relative upward trend. This shows that over the past few decades of industrialization, return rate of capital, land and other resources is rising fast, which has constantly been eroding labor share, causing a serious decline in residents' income share.

Compared with that of the world in industrialization, China's current labor share is steadily small. Zhang Juwei and Zhang Shibin (2012) found that between 1850 and 1920, average labor share in the United States was 76%. Labor share of South Korea in the 1950s when it began to industrialize was even smaller than China's and was 41.4% in 1970, the same as China in the 1980s, then it rose dramatically, and in 1990 it was bigger than that of China by 15%. In 1910, Japan's labor share was 55% and reached 67% in 1960. It can be seen that the proportion of constituent items of China's income in GDP is extremely imbalanced, reflecting the imbalance between investment and consumption structure in economic structure changes as well as continuous decline in marginal output effect--the marginal value change of labor factor in laborers' industrial transfer.

Table 6-2   Initial Distribution of National Income since Reform and Opening up

Year	GDP (100 million yuan)	Employees' Income (Labor Remuneration)		Enterprise Income (Depreciation of Fixed Assets and Operating Surplus)		Government Income (Net Production Tax)	
		Amount (100 million yuan)	Proportion (%)	Amount (100 million yuan)	Proportion (%)	Amount (100 million yuan)	Proportion (%)
1978	3381.37	1684.41	49.81	318.93	37.43	431.25	12.75
1985	8365.76	4446.53	53.15	825.86	34.38	1043.18	12.47
1990	18021.21	9601.47	53.28	2129.83	33.67	3996.20	11.68
1995	57535.19	29596.8	51.44	7457.09	36.29	7056.76	12.27
1996	67764.16	34703.64	51.21	8634.17	35.89	8736.67	12.89
1997	76339.65	38954.4	51.03	9958.12	35.32	10420.29	13.65
1998	82558.51	41960.46	50.83	10932.51	34.92	11768.96	14.26
1999	88215.62	44082.16	49.97	11847.27	35.14	13136.3	14.89
2000	98504.13	47977.69	48.71	13854.88	35.99	15078.57	15.31
2001	108545.745	52351.29	48.23	15113.93	36.14	16967.57	15.63
2002	120571.03	57576.79	47.75	16643.55	36.66	18794.46	15.59
2003	139250.04	64271.53	46.16	19376.47	38.07	21962.09	15.77
2004	1675887.12	69639.64	41.55	23624.01	44.38	27919.21	14.12
2005	197789.03	81888.02	41.40	29521.99	44.48	27919.21	14.12
2006	231053.35	93822.83	40.61	32726.66	44.83	33641.84	14.56
2007	275624.62	109532.27	39.74	39018.85	45.45	40827.52	14.81
2009	365303.69	170299.71	46.62	49369.64	38.18	55531.11	15.20
2010	437041.99	196714.07	45.01	56227.58	39.74	66608.73	15.24
2011	521441.11	234310.26	44.94	67344.51	39.45	81399.26	15.61

Source: Historical Data on China's GDP Accounting (1952-2004), China Statistical Yearbook, 1996-2012.

Theoretically, there are reasons for a country's declining labor share: first, in globalization, capital is more mobile, more profit-driven and has more bargaining power than labor. Dividing factor income into "competitive income" and "rent under incomplete competition", Harrison (2002) argued that globalization has strengthened bargaining power of capital and that labor does not or rarely shares "rent under incomplete competition" in this "bargain" with capital. Second, as long as labor and capital are inter-replaceable, capital-enhanced technological progress will lead to labor share decline. Therefore, along the path of balanced economic growth, when labor-enhanced technological progress appears, labor share remains stable; On the path to a steady state, if there is capital-enhanced technological progress, labor share tends to decrease (Acemoglu, 2003). Third, supply and demand in labor market, protection (trade union power), the way to make payment contract will be directly related to labor share (Bentolina, 2003). In addition, there are other factors affecting labor share, such as human capital, policy tendency, development stage and so on.

Why does China's labor share remain steadily low or even decline? Comparing labor remuneration of various countries in the world, Li Daokui et al. (2009) studied changing law of labor remuneration in some developed countries and put forward the hypothesis that labor share and economic development are "U" related to each other and that China is still in its "U" downward range. Zhang Juwei and Zhang Shibin (2012) held that although China's low labor share is related to its agricultural labor share being much higher than that of the second, tertiary industry and its economic structure change from agriculture to non-agricultural industry, the key reasons still lie in long-term low labor share of the second and tertiary industry and in the fact that employees' wage growth rate is lower than economic growth rate and labor productivity growth rate and that both capital-expanded technological progress and economic growth depends on international trade and FDI and that there is no labor protection in labor market as well as that there has been monopolistic use of resources and financial factor.

Distorted by systems and policies, reform of factor markets (including labor market, capital market, land market, energy market, etc.) is in a slow process and has not made any substantial progress. In labor market, as household registration system is difficult to take its initial step to change and social security system is still under construction, there is dual division between urban and rural areas so that high-quality labor force unwilling to go to private enterprises tend to go to institutions and state-owned enterprises with material benefits. In capital market, it is very difficult for private enterprises to obtain financial support, be it direct or indirect financing. As is shown in Chart 6-5, loan balance of large, medium-sized and small state-owned shareholding enterprises in 2010 is 9.414672 trillion yuan, 4.29663 trillion yuan and 2.112199 trillion yuan respectively, that of large, medium-sized and small private holding enterprises is 1.497176 trillion yuan, 3.49285 trillion yuan, and 4.125564 trillion yuan respectively. However, there are far more private enterprises than state-controlling enterprises. Combined with Charts 6-1 and 6-2, financing efficiency of enterprises of different ownership can be measured, that is, gross industrial output value divided by loan balance of the year. Results showed that financing efficiency of state-owned economy, collective economy and other economies was 117.5%, 36.5% and 543.0% respectively. Clearly, other economies have far more loan output than the first two, in other words, other economies should have received more financial support.

Private enterprises are still not given the same opportunity of fair competition as state-owned enterprises in terms of access to factor market and policy support. Since it is difficult to enter monopoly industries as state-owned enterprises do, such as post and telecommunications, finance and insurance, culture and education, health care and other high-end services, private enterprises can only over-invest in competitive fields such as manufacturing industries where investment is allowed, causing serious overcapacity of manufacturing industry and making it impossible to increase the proportion of tertiary industry. In 2011, fixed assets investment of state holding, collective and private holding enterprises in manufacturing sector was 1.33294 trillion yuan, 374.55 billion yuan and 7.36494 trillion yuan respectively while fixed assets investment of state holding, collective and private holding enterprises in service sector was 8.66457 trillion yuan, 1.30291 trillion yuan, and 6.22950 trillion yuan respectively. As a result, China's service sector has long been unable to achieve effective improvement, accounting for less than 40% of GDP. In contrast, the proportion of service industry in GDP is about 70% in western developed countries, and more than 50% in emerging countries such as India and Russia. In addition, as the most important assets, land belongs to private sector in most countries while China's urban land is owned by the state with rural land owned by collectives, farmers having no substantial assets that can be mortgaged. Since state-owned enterprises can obtain land, energy, mineral resources and other scarce factor assets at low prices, in rapid industrialization and urbanization, these assets value increased significantly faster than the growth of GDP. This kind of institutional arrangement determines substantial income growth of various scarce factors, which causes the ever widening income gap between state-owned enterprises, government departments, and residents.

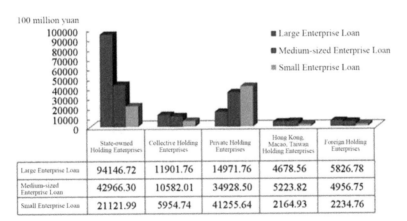

	State-owned Holding Enterprises	Collective Holding Enterprises	Private Holding Enterprises	Hong Kong, Macao, Taiwan Holding Enterprises	Foreign Holding Enterprises
Large Enterprise Loan	94146.72	11901.76	14971.76	4678.56	5826.78
Medium-sized Enterprise Loan	42966.30	10582.01	34928.50	5223.82	4956.75
Small Enterprise Loan	21121.99	5954.74	41255.64	2164.93	2234.76

Chart 6-5   Loan Balance of Large, Medium-sized and Small Enterprises of China's Financial Institutions in 2010

V. Innovating ESOP System to Narrow the Income Gap in Privatized Enterprises

The development of ESOP in the United States and Europe who have achieved their aim of narrowing the gap between rich and poor, alleviating labor-management relations and sharing social development shows that establishment and perfection of this system is of a gradual process. ESOP in China is only a kind of reconstruction of enterprise ownership whose implementation purpose, implementation process and implementation result are completely different from western ESOP system. Moreover, for lack of enough legislative support and fiscal and tax incentives in China, it is inevitable that its ESOP system will be "alienated", resulting in an endless series of problems and inconsistency between practice and theory. In all, previous state-owned enterprise property rights reform was unsuccessful and unfair, leaving behind a lot of historical problems. Therefore, the government established property rights trading centers to make state-owned shares withdraw through listed trading instead of deepening state-owned enterprise reform in the form of ESOP. Obviously, reformers have yet to understand the true meaning of ESOP, let alone reasons for development of ESOP in the U.S. and Europe since ESOP is used as a means to reform property rights of state-owned enterprises. Now that problems arise, they simply "abandon ESOP system to act as if it were damaged goods." In fact, problem doesn't lie in ESOP itself but in lacking careful design, legal support and necessary external environment. Moreover, ESOP system applies not only to state-owned enterprises but also to non-state-owned enterprises; it can apply not only to large public enterprises but also to small private enterprises. How can China draw lessons from development experience of ESOP in the U.S. and Europe and innovate China's ESOP system so as to narrow social income gap? The suggestions are as follows.

First, introduce or perfect laws to establish legal status of ESOP and to clarify nature, rights and obligations of ESOP. Second, amend company law and related provisions in securities law not conducive to ESOP development. For example, a listed company will be allowed to buy back its shares to encourage its employees to hold stocks or equity incentive and ESOs will be adding exception conditions of listing restrictions on the number of shareholders. Third, by combining employee shareholding system with social insurance system, supplementary old-age security system for enterprises will be established and improved. For China, introduction of such employee shareholdings will help make up for serious shortfall in current social pension insurance account, making it the second pillar of China's social security system. Fourth, relevant policies will allow and encourage banks and other financial institutions to provide low-interest loans for ESOP or mortgage (pledge) loans, and amortization. For example, employees are allowed to pledge shares to obtain required loans; Enterprises implementing ESOP will enjoy a discount at bank loans. Fifth, tax law and tax policy will be revised to solve problems of overlapping tax payment faced by ESOs which are composed of multiple entities such as ESOP employee, natural person shareholder of stockholding companies, stockholding company, entity operating company, etc. At the same time, financial institutions such as banks that provide credit support to ESOs may be given a percentage reduction in loan interest income. Part of personal income tax may be exempted concerning dividends of employee reinvesting or increasing their shares in their company. Tax exemption shall be granted as employees' shares contributed directly from enterprise wage funds and welfare funds. Sixth, improve stock markets by providing possible trading platforms for development of ESOP to realize incentive distribution mechanism of ESOP.

If China's ESOP system can innovate according to suggestions above, it will surely be able to play its role and achieve the goal of narrowing income gap and sharing value-added dividends between owners of "two factors". This new system of employee shareholding system will become an effective economic form of socialist basic system to achieve the ultimate prosperity in future.

VI. Deepening State-owned Enterprise Reform to Improve National Income

Monopoly enterprises constantly squeeze competitive profits of downstream private enterprises, causing labor share to decrease year by year and social income gap to widen rapidly. In this process, social vested interest group gradually came into being, hindering the deepening of China's market economy reform so that behavior of monopoly state-owned enterprises is too far from its nature. It is urgent for us to re-examine historical status and role of state-owned enterprises and to promote a new round of state-owned enterprise reform and factor market reform. Can the government hold on to ownership of enterprises and guarantee public ownership of socialism? Not necessarily. Some state-owned enterprises have become private property of "outstanding entrepreneurs", and some state-owned enterprises have become personal gold mines for government officials, this part of state-owned capital having been transformed into private capital or "power capital". In market economy, the key is to set up constitutional governance framework of state-owned enterprises to restrain participants' behavior with system strength and to realize the goal of justice and efficiency of socialist market economy with Chinese characteristics. The suggestions are as follows.

First, rid labor market segmentation and improve investment in human capital. The key to break monopoly profit and improve labor remuneration lies in giving full play to the leading role of market mechanism in allocating labor resources and realizing free migration of labor force. Prerequisites for formation of supply and demand mechanism and competition mechanism in labor market is market fairness, competition and unification. The final formation of competition mechanism in labor market should be carried out step by step on the premise of perfecting labor contract system, straightening out labor relations and establishing and perfecting social security system. In addition, it's necessary to increase investment in human capital, continuously improve labor productivity, and gradually realize mechanism of proportionate growth of wages and national economy. And it's necessary to improve internal wage distribution system, market regulation, independent enterprise distribution, government supervision and guidance of wage distribution mechanism.

Second, open up some monopoly industries and introduce market competition mechanism. Irrationality of excessive industrial income gap is often intertwined with rationality of widening income gap caused by differences in knowledge and skills. To this end, there is a need to study equal pay for equal work rather than universal convergence. It is necessary to control industrial income gap, break monopoly and control high income of monopoly industries. The government should eliminate discriminatory policies in factor market and stop giving state-owned enterprises and private enterprises different user cost of factors. State-owned enterprises who make use of all kinds of rare resources at low prices and obtain resources rent at premium must pay resource tax. At the same time, proceeds rate of state-owned enterprises needs to be further raised, whose use should be different from that of average fiscal revenue so as to better serve people's livelihood. In view of different monopoly types of state-owned enterprises, the government should distinguish between competitive business and natural monopoly and regulate them more effectively. Natural monopoly needs strict regulation so as to promote public welfare while competitive business does not need regulation, open to private capital directly. It is necessary to break monopoly and to introduce market competition mechanism in administratively monopolistic industry. To improve efficiency, state-owned enterprises should withdraw completely from competitive industries and eliminate barriers to market for private economy.

Third, explore new management mechanism for state-owned enterprises, implement status of independent legal persons of state-owned enterprises, take the market as basis and company law as the yardstick so as to give equal status and fair opportunities to compete to all kinds of market subjects. In this way, particularity of state-owned ownership cannot be emphasized, nor can state-owned enterprises be given more social responsibility. Otherwise, it will result in disruption of market competition order. Even if state-owned enterprises appear to be prosperous, social welfare will be a net loss. In current society, ownership and management is to be separated. All that state-owned assets supervisor should do is to innovate management system of state-owned enterprises and thoroughly implement independent legal person of state-owned enterprises. To innovate manager system, state-owned enterprises must carefully handle relationship between manager appointment system and principle of Party cadre's management, draw a clear line between government and enterprises, and turn long-term administrative appointment and removal system into open appointment system through talent market. It's quite a matter of course for "entrepreneurs" with their talent who become managers selected by the market to get high income. In order to find a feasible and effective way to coordinate relationship between the two, the British golden stock system is to be drawn lesson from. Theoretically, once a state-owned enterprise is transformed into a joint-stock company, the government selling all its state-owned stocks will no longer be enterprise shareholder and will not have the right to interfere in the enterprise and the manager in any form; meanwhile the enterprise will no longer rely on state funding. However, if the government loses control of enterprises that have a significant bearing on national economy, people's livelihood and national security, it may be detrimental to survival and development of its country.

Fourth, to redefine role of trade unions and strengthen participation of state-owned workers in its governance. With democracy and legal restriction, reforming administrative centralization system and putting administration and management of state-owned enterprises under laborers' democratic supervision can make its reform a success. Most Western European countries have implemented participation of company representatives through legislation, that is, workers' representatives get involved in decision-making instead of workers in order to redistribute power within the company so that laborers' interests, management interests and shareholder interests can be equal. Representative participation often takes two forms: an employees' committee and representatives in the board of directors, the former connecting employees and management while the latter being employee representatives who enter the board of directors on behalf of employees' interests. From the perspective of course and mode of Chinese state-owned enterprise reform, employees' interests are always ignored and functions and power of trade unions are increasingly restricted so that trade unions have become puppets in today's state-owned enterprises as managers have taken control, resulting in more inequality in income distribution within state-owned enterprises. Now, it's time to re-examine significance of state-owned trade unions, redefine role of trade unions, and strengthen their democratic management and establish an effective internal supervision and check-and-balance mechanism.

VII. Conclusion

Efficiency originates from market competition and rule of law is the basis of fair competition. The essence of state-owned enterprise reform is to cultivate countless independent legal persons for market economy, thus creating a lasting development power and support system. In this process, both privatization and capitalization have widened social income gap without exception. Theoretically speaking, widening income gap in transitional countries is not against law of economic development. The key lies in the fact that China's income gap and gap between rich and poor have far exceeded international warning line, becoming a potential threat to social harmony and stability. Privatization reform mode through ESOP is mainly questioned by "fairness". Although there are still many problems in restructured enterprises, after all, it has achieved the improvement of Pareto efficiency. At present, what needs to be done is innovation of employee stock ownership system to achieve common prosperity. Capitalization reform mode through shareholding system transformation is mainly questioned by "feasibility". Monopoly power of state-owned enterprises protected by policy in "important industries and key fields" is getting increasingly stronger only to end up with low productivity, serious internal control, widening industrial income gap, increasingly compressed non-public economy living space, which has aroused the whole society's vigilance. In the long run, economy as a whole will lack momentum. Therefore, it's time to deepen factor market reform, break down industrial monopoly, treat market subjects equally; carry out independent legal person status of state-owned enterprises, explore new management mechanism for state-owned enterprises; redefine role of trade unions, and strengthen employees' participation in governance of state-owned enterprises.

Chapter VII

Economic Growth and Residents' Income Distribution--How to Achieve China's Residents' Income Growth

ZHANG Juwei, ZHAO Wen[1]

Both the Third Plenary Session and the Fourth Plenary Session of the 18th CPC Central Committee put forward by 2020 the grand goal of doubling gross domestic product (GDP) and per capita urban and rural residents' income of 2010 and building a well-off society in an all-round way. For now, it is no easy task. Current economic downtown is intensifying. If residents' income growth is still slower than GDP growth as it used to be, it will be very difficult to achieve the goal of doubling residents' income. How to maintain rapid residents' income growth under sustained economic downturn has become a major issue that must be taken seriously.

---

1   ZHANG Juwei, Director of the Institute of Population and Labor Economics of the Chinese Academy of Social Sciences, Research Fellow, Doctoral Advisor; ZHAO Wen, Associate Research Fellow of the Institute of Population and Labor Economics of the Chinese Academy of Social Sciences.

While per capita urban and rural residents' income generally has grown rapidly between 2011 and 2014, growth rate of both urban and rural residents' income have declined since 2012, and growth rate of per capita disposable urban residents' income in 2014 was only 6.8%, the lowest in 15 years. According to this calculation, in order to achieve the goal of building a well-off society in an all-round way, growth rate of average annual per capita disposable urban residents' income between 2015 and 2020 should not be less than 6.67%; growth rate of average annual per capita net rural residents' income should not be less than 5.24%; growth rate of average annual per capita disposable national residents' income should not be less than 5.81%; and average annual GDP growth rate should not be below 6.63%. This chapter mainly analyzes the relationship between economic growth and residents' income growth, characteristics of China's residents' income growth and factors affecting residents' income growth, and puts forward some countermeasures and suggestions for residents' income growth.

I. Residents' Income Growth

(I) Current Residents' Income Growth

Data released by the National Bureau of Statistics include both urban residents' income and rural residents' income, the former being disposable income, the income after wage income, net operating income, property income and transfer income minus personal income tax and personal social security expenditure and the latter being net income, the income after wage income, household operating income, property income and transfer income minus household operating expenditure, expenses of taxes and fees, depreciation of productive fixed assets, and gift expenditure of relatives and friends in rural areas. Although there are some statistical differences between urban and rural residents' income, two income sources include all the following four parts: wage income, operating income, property income and transfer income.

Since the last quarter of 2012, the National Bureau of Statistics has implemented urban and rural integration household survey reform, unified name, classification and statistical standard of urban and rural residents' income. After selecting 160,000 urban and rural resident households across the country, it has carried out a direct investigation and calculated per capita disposable national residents' income. In order to maintain annual comparability, the National Bureau of Statistics continued to publish data of per capita net rural residents' income and per capita disposable urban residents' income.

Since the National Bureau of Statistics publishes per capita disposable urban and rural residents' income only after 2012 and since a longer period of time of this data is needed when studying residents' income, it is necessary to weigh per capita disposable urban residents' income and per capita net rural residents' income according to urban and rural population so as to obtain approximate data to replace per capita disposable national residents' income. As far as situations between 2012 and 2014 are concerned, there is little difference between weighted national residents' income data and urban-rural statistics published by the National Bureau of Statistics, indicating that weighting method to calculate residents' income can basically reflect real urban and rural residents' income.

In 2013, per capita urban residents' household income was 29,547 yuan, among which wage income (the most important component), transfer income (the second important component), net operating income and property income is 18,929.8 yuan, 7,010 yuan, 2,797 yuan 810 yuan, accounting for 64%, 24%, 9% and 3% of per capita annual urban residents' household income respectively. Classified income statistics between 1990 and 2013 including nominal income with price factor, urban residents' wage income, net operating income, property income and transfer income has increased by 16 times, 149 times, 52 times, and 22 times respectively. Therefore, net operating income and property income are relatively fast growing part of urban residents' income.

Per capita net rural residents' household income in 2013 was 8,895.9 yuan, among which wage income (the most important component), household operating income (self-employed operating income and farming household income), rural residents' property income and transfer income, relatively less than that of urban residents with low proportion in net income, is 4,025 yuan, 3,793.2 yuan, 293 yuan and 784 yuan, accounting for 45%, 42%, 3% and 9% of per capita net rural residents' household income. Classified income statistics between 1990 and 2013 including nominal income with price factor, rural residents' wage income, household operating income, property income and transfer income has increased by 29 times, 7 times, 24 times and 46 times respectively on average. As the government has subsidized agricultural production and started new countryside construction since 2004, rural residents' transfer income began to grow rapidly, transfer income in 2013 being eight times higher than that in 2003.

Table 7-1   National Per Capita Disposable Income of Resident (yuan)

Year	Data Released by NBS	Weighted Data	Year	Data Released by NBS	Weighted Data
1991	—	976	2003	—	4993
1992	—	1125	2004	—	5645
1993	—	1385	2005	—	6367
1994	—	1870	2006	—	7211
1995	—	2363	2007	—	8567
1996	—	2814	2008	—	9939
1997	—	3070	2009	—	10965
1998	—	3250	2010	—	12508
1999	—	3478	2011	—	14582
2000	—	3712	2012	16511	16669
2001	—	4059	2013	18311	18599
2002	—	4519	2014	20167	20542

Note: The data released by the National Bureau of Statistics is per capita disposable national residents' income published by the National Bureau of Statistics. The weighted data is per capita disposable national residents' income calculated according to urban and rural resident population in this chapter.

Take a look at urban and rural residents' income from 1978 to 2013, per capita disposable national residents' income reached 18,310.8 yuan. Among them, wage income, operating income, property income and transfer income accounted for 57%, 19%, 8%, and 16% respectively.

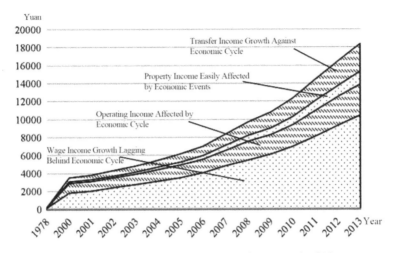

Chart 7-1 Residents' Income Growth Structure in China

Source: *China Statistical Yearbook* over the years

(II) Main Characteristics of Residents' Income Growth

Gross domestic product (GDP) of 2014 was 63.6463 trillion yuan, an increase of 7.4% over the previous year. Annual residents' consumer price rose by 2.0% over the previous year, annual urban residents' consumer price rising by 2.1% and annual rural residents' consumer price rising by 1.8% respectively. Annual per capita disposable national residents' income is 20,167 yuan, an increase of 10.1% over the previous year, a real growth of 8.0% after price factor, annual per capita disposable urban residents' income being 28,844 yuan, an increase of 9.0% over the previous year, a real growth of 6.8% after price factor, and annual per capita net rural residents' income being 10,489 yuan, an increase of 11.2% over the previous year, a real growth of 9.2% after price factor.

i. Residents' Income Growth Lagging Behind Economic Growth

In most of the past 30 years, residents' income growth has been lagging behind economic growth. From 1978 to 2014, average annual growth rate of urban and rural residents' real income is 8.5%. However, average annual growth rate of GDP is 9.7%, 1% more than that of urban and rural residents' income. In all, urban and rural residents' income growth did not outperform GDP growth. The same is true over periods of time. As Table 7-2 shows, during The Eighth Five-year Plan, The

Ninth Five-year Plan, The Tenth Five-year Plan, and The Eleventh Five-year Plan, residents' income growth rate was lower than economic growth rate by 2.2%, 5.3%, 0.8%, 1.9% and 2.4% respectively. In terms of urban and rural areas, from 1978 to 2014, both per capita disposable urban residents' income growth rate and per capita net rural residents' income growth rate were higher than GDP growth rate for 10 years, and lower than GDP growth rate for 27 years. Since 1991, per capita net rural residents' income growth rate has been lower than economic growth rate for 19 consecutive years, resulting in slow improvement of rural residents' living conditions and rapidly widening urban-rural income gap which reached its highest ratio of 3.33:1 in 2007. It is worth noting, however, that since 2010, urban-rural income ratio has narrowed to 2.75:1 in 2014, the same as that of 2000, because of rapid growth in rural residents' income thanks to rapid national residents' income growth, exceeding economic growth for the first time for three consecutive years.

Table 7-2   Annual Growth Rate of per capita Income of Urban & Rural Residents (%)

Year	GDP Growth Rate	Growth Rate of per capita Disposable Income of Urban Residents	Growth Rate of per capita Net Income of Rural Residents	Growth Rate of per capita Disposable Income of Urban and Rural Residents	GDP Growth Rate-- Growth Rate of per capita Disposable Income of Urban Residents	GDP Growth Rate-- Growth Rate of per capita Net Income of Rural Residents	GDP Growth Rate-- Growth Rate of per capita Disposable Income of Urban and Rural Residents	
1991	9.2	7.2	2.0	0.5	2.0	7.2	8.7	
1992	14.2	9.7	5.9	5.9	4.6	8.3	8.3	
1993	14.0	9.5	3.2	5.8	4.4	10.8	8.1	5.3
1994	13.1	8.5	5.0	11.7	4.6	8.1	1.4	
1995	10.9	4.9	5.3	11.2	6.0	5.6	-0.3	
1996	10.0	3.9	9.0	12.0	6.1	1.0	-2.0	
1997	9.3	3.4	4.6	7.4	5.9	4.7	1.9	
1998	7.8	5.8	4.3	6.8	2.1	3.5	1.0	0.8
1999	7.6	9.3	3.8	8.4	-1.7	3.8	-0.7	
2000	8.4	6.4	2.1	4.5	2.0	6.3	3.9	
2001	8.3	8.5	4.2	7.1	-0.2	4.1	1.2	
2002	9.1	13.4	4.8	10.7	-4.3	4.3	-1.6	
2003	10.0	9.0	4.3	7.6	1.0	5.7	2.4	1.9
2004	10.1	7.7	6.8	5.4	2.4	3.3	4.7	
2005	11.3	9.6	6.2	8.4	1.7	5.1	2.9	

contd.

Year	GDP Growth Rate	Growth Rate of per capita Disposable Income of Urban Residents	Growth Rate of per capita Net Income of Rural Residents	Growth Rate of per capita Disposable Income of Urban and Rural Residents	GDP Growth Rate-- Growth Rate of per capita Disposable Income of Urban Residents	GDP Growth Rate-- Growth Rate of per capita Net Income of Rural Residents	GDP Growth Rate-- Growth Rate of per capita Disposable Income of Urban and Rural Residents
2006	12. 7	10. 4	7.4	9. 0	2. 3	5. 3	3. 7
2007	14. 2	12. 2	9.5	10. 1	2. 0	4. 7	4. 1
2008	9. 6	8. 4	8.0	7. 5	1. 2	1. 6	2. 1
2009	9. 2	9. 8	8.5	11. 0	- 0. 6	0. 7	-1. 8
2010	10. 4	7. 8	10.9	6. 7	2. 7	- 0. 5	3. 7
2011	9. 3	8. 4	11.4	8. 1	0. 9	- 2. 1	1. 2
2012	7. 7	9. 6	10.7	12. 2	- 1. 9	- 3. 0	-4. 5
2013	7. 7	7. 0	9.3	8. 1	0. 7	- 1. 6	-0. 4
2014	7. 4	6. 8	9.2	8. 0	0. 6	- 1. 8	-0. 6
							2.4
							-1.1

Source: calculated on the basis of *China Statistical Yearbook* over the years

Although many factors may lead to residents' income growth being slower than economic growth, one reason worth mentioning is that residents' income growth target lags behind economic growth target in economic development planning. According to The Eighth Five-Year Plan (1991-1995), economy will grow at average annual rate of 6%, employees' wage will grow at 2% annually and per capita net rural residents' income will grow by 3.5% annually. According to The Tenth Five-Year Plan (2001-2005), average annual economic growth rate will be about 7%, both annual growth rate of per capita disposable urban residents' income and growth rate of per capita net rural residents' income will be 5%. The Eleventh Five-Year Plan (2006-2010) states that GDP will grow at average annual rate of 7.5% and annual per capita disposable urban residents' income and annual per capita net rural residents' income will grow by 5%. According to The Twelfth Five-Year Plan (2011-2015), gross domestic product (GDP) will grow at annual average of 7% and annual per capita disposable urban residents' income and annual per capita net rural residents' income will grow by more than 7% respectively. In terms of planning targets, except for The 12th Five-Year Plan, residents' income growth target is lower than economic growth target.

In terms of achievements, real economic growth rate tends to be significantly faster than planning targets while residents' income growth though above planning targets still lags considerably behind economic growth rate (See Table 7-3), slow growth of rural residents' income in particular. During The 11th Five-Year Plan, real GDP growth rate hit 11.2% but growth rate of urban residents' income was only 9.7% and growth rate of rural residents' income is only 8.9%. During The 10th Five-Year Plan, average annual economic growth rate was 9.5%, exceeding its target growth rate by 2.5% but real growth rate of rural residents' income was 5.3%, only exceeding the target rate by 0.3%.

Table 7-3   Economic Growth and Residents' Income Growth: Planning Targets and Achievements (%)

	"Tenth Five-Year Plan": 2001-2005		"Eleventh Five-Year Plan": 2006-2010		"Twelfth Five-Year Plan": 2011-2014	
	Planning Targets	Achievements	Planning Targets	Achievements	Planning Targets	Achievements
Average Annual GDP Growth Rate	7	9.5	7. 5	11. 2	7	8
Average Annual Growth Rate of Per Capita Disposable Income of Urban Residents	5	9.6	5	9.7	7	7.9
Average Annual Growth Rate of per capita Net Income of Rural residents	5	5.3	5	8.9	7	10. 1

ii. "Counter-cyclical" Residents' Income Growth

China's residents' income growth is also characterized by its "counter-cyclical economic growth". According to the division of China's economic cycle by Liu Shucheng (2011), China's economic growth since 1990 can be divided into four stages. As is shown in Chart 7-2, period between 1990 and 1992, and between 1999 and 2007 witnessed economic upturn and period between 1992 and 1998, and between 2007 and 2014 witnessed economic downturn. "Counter-cyclical" phenomenon refers to the fact that residents' income growth tends to be slower in economic upturn with rapid growth while residents' income growth tends to be faster in economic downturn with slow growth.

During economic upturn, GDP growth rate was 9.2% in 1991, 5.3% higher than previous year while growth rate of per capita disposable urban residents' income was 7.2%, 1.2% lower than previous year. Between 2003 and 2004, GDP growth rate was 10%, 0.9% higher than previous year while growth rate of per capita disposable urban residents' income was 9%, 4.4% lower than previous year. During economic downturn, GDP growth rate was 7.8% in 1998, 1.5% lower than previous year while growth rate of per capita disposable urban residents' income was 5.8%, 2.4% higher than previous year. GDP growth rate was 7.7% in 2012, 1.6% lower than previous year while growth rate of per capita disposable urban residents' income was 9.6%, 1.2% higher than previous year.

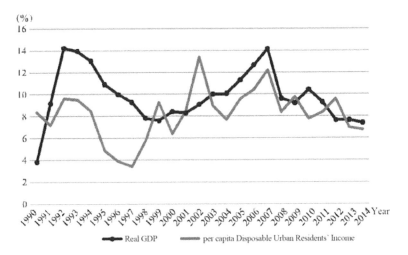

Chart 7-2   Urban Residents' Income Growth and Economic Cycle

In terms of quarterly data, "counter-cyclical" phenomenon in residents' income growth was ever more evident. Between the first quarter of 2008 and the first quarter of 2009, per capita disposable urban residents' income grew significantly from 5.5% to 11.2% while economic growth fell sharply from 11.2% to 6.6%. Between the first quarter of 2009 to the first quarter of 2010, per capita disposable urban residents' income fell sharply from 11.2% to 6.4% while economy grew significantly from 6.6% to 12.4%. There has been a new counter-cycle between the first quarter of 2010 to the first quarter of 2012 and has continued to this day. Viewed from years between 1992 and 1994 and between 2006 and 2007 with highest economic growth rate, economy grew more than 12% while residents' income did not grow more than 12%. Viewed from years in 1990, 1999 and 2012 with lowest economic growth rate, economy grew less than 8% while residents' income grew more than 8%. A closer look at Chart 7-3 shows that faster residents' income growth often occurs during economic transitional period and economic downturn. The last time when such a phenomenon occurred was during Asian financial crisis between 1998 and 2004, and between 1986 and 1991.

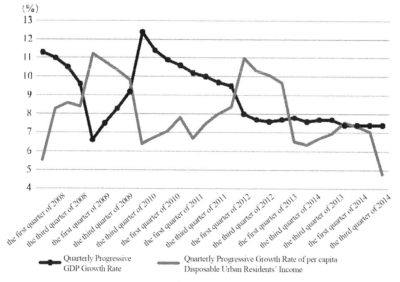

Chart 7-3　GDP Growth and Urban Residents' Income Growth: Quarterly Progressive Growth

Counter-cyclical phenomenon in residents' income growth reflects different mechanism of production factor sharing benefits of economic growth. In labor market, if wage is rigid, it's difficult to adjust wage with fluctuations in economic growth. As a result, when economy grows faster than expected because wage cannot achieve the same growth rate as economy, accelerated benefits of economic growth tend to become capital income; on the contrary, when economy grows slower than expected, costs of slow economic growth will be more borne by capital because wages cannot fall quickly. Because labor share in residents' income is much higher than capital (property) income, residents' income growth appears to be slower when economic growth accelerates while residents' income growth appears to be faster when economic growth decelerates.

However, on flexible labor market, wage growth can synchronize with economic growth, thus there will be less "counter-cyclical" residents' income growth. In sharp contrast to China, wage income growth synchronizes with economic growth in the United States (See Chart 7-4). Generally speaking, the more flexible labor market, the more labor factor can get market returns according to marginal productivity, the less wage stickiness, the more efficient market will be. In this sense, China's "counter-cyclical" residents' income growth, to a certain extent, reflects that China's labor market needs improvement, reasonable wage growth mechanism in particular.

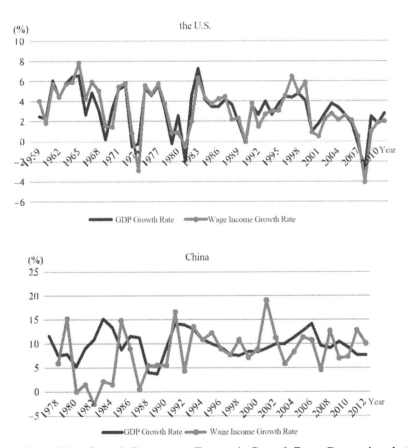

Chart 7-4   Wage Growth Rate versus Economic Growth Rate: Comparison between China and the U.S.

"Counter-cyclical" residents' income growth is also related to investment-driven economic growth mode. China's economy used to be mainly driven by investment. In the years with rapid economic growth, investment growth was faster but consumption growth was insufficient. As a result, the proportion of residents' income in national income would decline accordingly. In a critical period of economic crisis, this feature is even more obvious. During the Asian financial crisis in the late 1990s and global economic crisis in 2008, there was counter-cycle between economic growth rate and growth rate of urban residents' income. As China faces external shocks and national economy has experienced great ups and downs. In response to spread of global economic crisis in 2009, China launched a big investment plan, leading to a rebound in its economic growth rate in 2010 which declined in 2009. Growth rate of urban residents' income was higher than growth rate of GDP per capita in 2009 and went down accordingly in 2010. In the long run, decline in urban residents' income relative to economic growth rate is caused by investment-driven economic growth mode.

Ratio of per capita residents' income to GDP per capita is adopted to observe "counter-cyclical' residents' income growth. Per capita Residents' income accounted for 0.45 of GDP per capita in 1978, rose to 0.63 in 1983, returned to 0.45 of 1978 in 2005 after a series of downturn, and fell further to 0.41 in 2011. In the early years of reform and opening up, years with rapid decline in the proportion of residents' income in GDP was often years with rapid economic growth. Years with increasing proportion of residents' income in GDP was often years with declining economic growth rate, residents' income growth and economic growth being "counter-cyclical".

(III) De-synchronization in Residents' Income Growth and GDP Growth

i. Differences between GDP Composition and Residents' Income Composition

Fundamentally speaking, residents' income growth and economic growth are out of step because of difference between GDP composition and residents' income composition. In income method of GDP accounting, GDP includes such components as labor remuneration, operating surplus, depreciation of fixed assets and indirect tax, in which operating surplus and depreciation of fixed assets can be classified as capital income while indirect tax belongs to government revenues. Residents' income is divided into such components as labor remuneration, property income, operating income and transfer income. There is a correspondence between GDP and residents' income: labor remuneration in GDP corresponds to labor remuneration of residents' income, capital income in GDP corresponds to property income in residents' income, and indirect tax in GDP corresponds to transfer income of residents' income. "Operating income" of residents' income needs to be accounted for. In national income accounting, added value in individual economic sectors or self-employed economic sectors is generally called "mixed income" since it is very difficult to distinguish between labor remuneration and capital income. Many countries, developed countries in particular, tend to list this income component as "mixed income" in GDP accounting while China's income method of GDP accounting divides this income component into labor remuneration and capital income with a certain proportion. Therefore, residents' operating income corresponds to "mixed income" in GDP accounting. According to our calculations, GDP created by China's self-employed sectors, or individual economic sectors accounted for 20% of total GDP in 2013. Chart 7-5 shows correspondence between GDP accounting and residents' income.

Because of difference between GDP composition and residents' income composition, it is very difficult for residents' income growth to keep pace with economic growth. In current China's national income distribution pattern, labor remuneration, capital return, indirect tax, and mixed economic components accounts for about 31%, 36%, 13%, and 20% respectively. But in residents' income, labor remuneration accounts for 70% to 80% of urban residents' income and 50% of net rural residents' income which tends to be on the rise. Capital income accounting for high proportion in national income accounts for low proportion in residents' income, be it urban residents' income or rural residents' income. And the proportion of property income is very low in both national income and residents' income as it is difficult for residents to obtain property income through capital market, which makes it difficult for capital return in GDP to convert into residents' income. As can be seen from Chart 7-5, capital return accounts for 36% of GDP but residents' property income only accounts for about 8% of residents' income. Because of this, the direct result of long-term declining labor share in China's national income distribution is that residents' income growth can not keep up with economic growth.

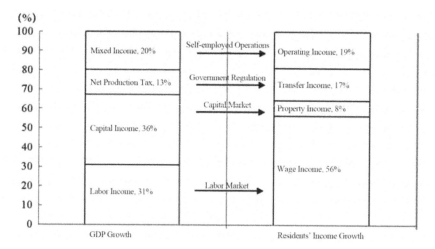

Chart 7-5 Correspondence between GDP Accounting and Residents' Income

With their own characteristics, it is difficult for both operating income growth and transfer income growth in residents' income to keep pace with economic growth. The source of residents' operating income is urban and rural individual household income and farmers' household operating income with low growth rate, which is closely related to economic cycle. In 1997, operating income declined for four consecutive years as a result of the Asian financial crisis. With improved economy, operating income has grown for eight consecutive years. In recent years, affected by international and domestic economic downturn, operating income growth has been on continuous decline. Transfer income is all the transfer payment to residents' households made by the state, units, social organizations as well as income transfer between residents' households, including individual withdrawal benefits and retirement benefits from the government, unemployment benefits; dismissal compensation from the unit to the individual, insurance claims, housing provident funds, gifts and maintenance between households, and so on. Transfer income is national regulation of gap between rich and poor with inclination towards the disadvantaged groups to prevent effects of economic fluctuations on residents' income. In terms of actual effects, Chinese residents' transfer income can counteract economic fluctuations but fails to keep pace with economic growth. During 2008 economic crisis, growth rate of residents' property income declined significantly from 30% in 2007 to 5% in 2008 while growth rate of transfer income rose from 12% in 2008 to 19% in 2009.

ii. Change in National Income Distribution Pattern not Conducive to Residents' Income Growth

National income distribution between sectors affects residents' income growth (Liu Shangxi, 2012). Change in China's income distribution pattern since 1992 can be calculated based on funds flow table published by the National Bureau of Statistics. In terms of initial distribution, between 1992 and 2008, both government income and enterprise income were on the rise with enterprise income rising from 17.37% to 25.26%, up by 7.81% and with government income rising from 16.57% to 17.52%, up by 1%. But residents' income is on the sharp decline from 66.06% to 57.23%, down by 8.83%, which mainly attributed to the rise in enterprise income.

After redistribution, national income distribution pattern still shows that the proportion of enterprise income and government income increases while residents' income decreases. Between 1992 and 2008, enterprise income rose from 11.70% to 21.60%, up by 9.9%, government income rose from 19.96% to 21.28%, up by1.32%, residents' income decreases from 68.34% to 57.11%, down by 11.32%. Compared with initial distribution pattern, redistribution makes enterprise income decrease, government income rise, and residents' income fluctuate slightly. In 2012, enterprise income fell by 4.24%, residents' income rose by 0.37% and government income rose by 3.91%. Government income grows through redistribution.

Table 7-4   Change in National Income Distribution Pattern: Initial Distribution and Redistribution (%)

Year	Initial Distribution			Redistribution			Redistribution-Initial Distribution		
	enterprise	gover-nment	resident	enterprise	gover-nment	resident	enterprise	gover-nment	resident
1992	17. 37	16. 57	66. 06	11. 70	19. 96	68. 34	- 5. 67	3. 39	2. 28
1993	20. 10	17. 29	62. 61	15. 73	19. 65	64. 62	- 4. 37	2. 36	2. 01
1994	17. 77	17. 08	65. 15	14. 53	18. 51	66. 96	- 3. 25	1. 43	1. 82
1995	19. 53	15. 22	65. 25	16. 22	16. 55	67. 23	- 3. 31	1. 33	1. 98
1996	16. 90	16. 62	66. 48	13. 69	17. 88	68. 44	- 3. 21	1. 25	1. 96
1997	16. 90	17. 08	66. 02	13. 10	18. 30	68. 60	- 3. 80	1. 22	2. 58
1998	16. 19	17. 74	66. 06	13. 45	18. 13	68. 41	- 2. 74	0. 39	2. 35
1999	17. 81	17. 15	65. 05	14. 70	18. 10	67. 20	- 3. 11	0. 95	2. 15
2000	18. 96	17. 65	63. 39	16. 60	19. 20	64. 20	- 2. 36	1. 55	0. 81
2001	20. 19	18. 50	61. 31	17. 50	20. 50	62. 00	- 2. 69	2. 00	0. 69
2002	20. 32	19. 14	60. 54	18. 00	21. 00	61. 00	- 2. 32	1. 86	0. 46
2003	20. 93	19. 37	59. 70	18. 20	22. 00	59. 80	- 2. 73	2. 63	0. 10
2004	25. 99	16. 34	57. 68	23. 27	18. 90	57. 83	- 2. 72	2. 56	0. 15
2005	23. 19	17. 45	59. 37	20. 76	20. 04	59. 20	- 2. 43	2. 59	- 0. 16
2006	23. 15	17. 90	58. 95	19. 86	21. 44	58. 70	- 3. 29	3. 55	- 0. 26
2007	23. 57	18. 30	58. 13	20. 22	21. 94	57. 84	- 3. 35	3. 64	- 0. 29
2008	25. 26	17. 52	57. 23	21. 60	21. 28	57. 11	- 3. 65	3. 77	- 0. 11
2009	24. 69	14. 55	60. 59	21. 29	18. 36	60. 81	- 3. 40	3. 81	0. 22
2010	24. 40	14. 93	60. 24	21. 24	18. 46	60. 55	- 3. 16	3. 53	0. 31
2011	23. 72	15. 23	60. 09	19. 90	19. 07	60. 40	- 3. 82	3. 84	0. 31
2012	22. 67	15. 59	61. 50	18. 43	19. 50	61. 87	- 4. 24	3. 91	0. 37

Source: *1992-2004 Historical Data of China's Funds Flow Table by the National Bureau of Statistics; China Statistical Yearbook*

Be it initial distribution or redistribution, national income distribution is characterized by the decline in residents' income. In initial distribution, national income distribution is oriented to enterprise income whose growth caused nearly 90% of the decline in residents' income while the remaining 10% of the decline in residents' income is caused by government income growth. In redistribution, government income rose further while enterprise income fell, causing a slight residents' income growth. Among them, before 2004, residents' income share increased in redistribution compared with initial distribution, decreased after 2004, but the decline was not significant, and then increased slightly after 2009. In 2012, government income growth in redistribution was largely caused by the decline in enterprise income. Therefore, in redistribution, national income distribution pattern is mainly government-oriented.

To sum up, main factors affecting residents' income growth are enterprise income growth in initial distribution and orientation towards government in redistribution. Because GDP composition is different from residents' income composition, achievements of economic growth can not be transformed into residents' income in time and effectively, resulting in residents' income decline in the national economy.

II. Major Problems Hindering Residents' Income Growth

Residents' income growth is slow. On the one hand, labor remuneration share in national income is ever declining; on the other hand, the fast growing capital income, relatively large proportion of national income, is difficult to transform into residents' property income. At the same time, because of its low position in labor market and its much dependence on wage income, low-income groups' income grows slow, an important reason hindering residents' income growth.

(I) Slow Growth of Labor Remuneration, Major Residents' Income Components

Labor share decline has become one of the major issues in China's income distribution. According to regional income method GDP accounting data, China's labor share rose from 49.64% to 53.68% between 1978 and 1984 and remained relatively stable at above 50% between 1985 and 1998. After 1999, it declined and fell to 46% in 2011. In addition, data in both Input-output Table and Funds Flow Table show a similar downward trend in labor share. When labor share declines, residents' wage income growth rate will be lower than economic growth rate. As wage income is the most important residents' income component, labor share declines, especially in economic downturn, is main cause for slow growth of residents' income.

Labor share decline causes the proportion of residents' income in GDP to decrease. Funds Flow Table 7-5 is composition of residents' income sources in initial distribution. As is seen, the proportion of residents' income in GDP fell from 66.1% in 1992 to 61.5% in 2012 as a result of residents' income growth lagging behind economic growth. Among this, labor share fell from 54.6% to 49.4%, down by 5.2%. In initial distribution, the proportion of labor remuneration in residents' income also fell from 82.6% to 80.3%. As labor remuneration is major residents' income component, residents' income decline mainly results from labor share decline.

Table 7-5　Composition of Residents' Income Sources in Initial Distribution (%)

Year	Labor Remuneration in GDP	Property Income in GDP	Operating Retention in GDP	Residents' Income in GDP
1992	54. 6	4. 4	7. 1	66. 1
1993	51. 4	5. 1	6. 0	62. 5
1994	52. 3	5. 8	6. 9	65. 0
1995	52. 8	4. 9	6. 5	64. 2
1996	52. 1	5. 2	8. 2	65. 5
1997	53. 0	4. 3	8. 0	65. 3
1998	52. 5	4. 3	8. 2	65. 0
1999	52. 6	3. 4	8. 2	64. 2
2000	52. 7	3. 1	10. 5	66. 3
2001	52. 5	2. 7	9. 8	65. 0
2002	53. 6	2. 5	7. 7	63. 8
2003	52. 8	2. 4	8. 5	63. 7
2004	50. 6	2. 4	8. 0	61. 0
2005	50. 4	2. 4	8. 0	60. 8
2006	49. 2	3. 3	8. 1	60. 6
2007	48. 1	3. 7	7. 9	59. 7
2008	47. 9	3. 8	7. 3	59. 0

contd.

Year	Labor Remuneration in GDP	Property Income in GDP	Operating Retention in GDP	Residents' Income in GDP
2009	49. 0	3. 3	8. 3	60. 6
2010	47. 5	3. 2	9. 5	60. 2
2011	47. 0	4. 0	9. 1	60. 1
2012	49. 4	4. 7	7. 4	61. 5

Source: *1992-2004 Historical Data of China's Funds Flow Table by the National Bureau of Statistics; China Statistical Yearbook*

With working force ever growing, labor share decline means not only slow growth of wage income but downward trend of real wage, as can be seen clearly from ratio of wage to GDP per capita. By estimating total number of Chinese employees and aggregate remuneration of Chinese employees, all employees' wage and its changes can be measured. Results suggest that since reform and opening up, average employees' wage has been experiencing a trend of decline first and then rise and then decline (Zhang Juwei, 2012). The highest average wage was around 2002, ratio of nominal monetary wage to nominal GDP per capita being 1.37, falling all the way to 0.86 in 2013. If all employees are divided into urban unit employees (urban unit workers) and other employees (mainly those employed by private enterprises and township enterprises), urban unit employees' wage growth basically keeps pace with GDP growth with wage growth rate to GDP per capita being 1.25 in 2013. Other employees' wage growth has lagged far behind GDP per capita growth with nominal per capita wage to GDP per capita from its highest in 2002 of 1.39 down to 0.61 in 2013. Low-income employees' wage (represented by migrant workers) relative to economic growth has fallen to a record low. This not only widens income gap within workers' groups but makes life more difficult for lower-income groups.

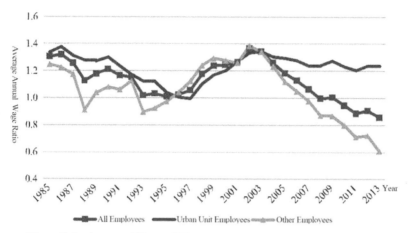

Chart 7-6   Average Wage of Wage Earners Relative to GDP per capita

Source: Zhang Juwei, Zhao Wen, "*Should Wage be Increased?--Observation on Changes of Employees'*
Compensation in China", in Analysis on the Prospect of China's Economy (2014), Social Sciences
Academic Press(China), 2014.

As can be seen from this, the major change in current national income
distribution pattern is that the declining proportion of residents' income in national
income is mainly caused by the decline of labor share.

(II) Low Proportion and Slow Growth of Residents' Property Income

Residents' property income mainly comes from free movable property income
and immovable property income. Compared with other market economies, the
proportion of China's residents' property income is relatively low. The proportion
of residents' property income in residents' income has remained at about 15%,
nearly 20% in the 1980s in the United States while only 8% in China. High
proportion of property income indicates a well-performed capital market and that
residents can get capital income through capital market investment.

In China's national income distribution pattern, income is more oriented to
capital factor. In initial distribution, the proportion of property income in residents'
income is relatively low, about 7.6% so that residents can hardly share capital
return. Distortion of capital market further exacerbated slow growth of residents'
property income. China's residents' property income comes mainly from securities
market transactions and interest income. However, because of capital market

control in China, interest rate of user cost of capital is low, which fundamentally distorts price information of capital market. Residents can only obtain a small amount of property income from limited channels. In GDP growth, major capital factor income component is converted into enterprise income. Imperfection of capital market makes capital return rate of initial distribution shrink greatly when transformed into residents' income, which slows down residents' income growth. Thus, despite rapid economic growth, the proportion of residents' property income in GDP in initial distribution has remained below 6% since 1992 with a record low of 2.4%.

Instability of China's residents' property income makes it rather risky for residents to invest, suppressing residents' demand for property income and further lowering the proportion of property income, leading to its slow growth. After China's entry into WTO and with acceleration of China's integration into global economy, impact of major economic events on China's residents' property income extended. As is often the case, during inflation (austerity), economic crisis, or financial market reform, property income will inevitably go through significant changes. As is shown in Chart 7-7, 1997 Asian financial crisis, 2008 sub-prime mortgage crisis in the U.S. and 2008 European debt crisis all caused China's residents' property income to fluctuate greatly. This makes vast majority of residents more willing to deposit their savings in banks rather than engage themselves in higher-yielding investment. Maintaining stability of financial markets and controlling investment risks will help increase China's residents' property income.

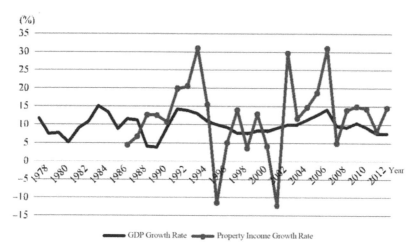

Chart 7-7   GDP Growth Rate and Growth Rate of both Property Income and Transfer Income in China

Source: calculated according to *China Statistical Yearbook* over the years

(III) Slow Income Growth of Low-income Groups

According to the National Bureau of Statistics, China's Gini coefficient reached 0.481 in 2010 and 0.474 in 2012 with serious polarization. Some studies even suggest that China's Gini coefficient reached 0.61 in 2010 with urban Gini coefficient being 0.56 and rural Gini coefficient being 0.60 (Gan Li, 2013). Growing income inequality means that when total residents' income growth is relatively slow, income growth of low-income groups is even slower, posing as the major issue in China's income distribution (Su Hainan, 2012).

Based on statistics of 2009, 10 income groups are divided. Residents' income of the lowest group accounted for only 1.4% of all residents' income and 4.7% of residents' income of the highest income group while residents' income of the highest group accounted for 28.9% of all residents' income (See Table 7-6). Residents with higher income save more with higher consumption expenditure than residents with lower income.[1] Among urban residents, the 5% residents with the lowest income tend to spend more on their daily consumption than their

---

1   Savings in its broad sense includes savings, housing purchases, property purchases and gifts.

income with negative savings growth for many years; about 8% of the income of the 10% of residents with the lowest income can save or buy property while 38% of the income of the 10% of residents with the highest income save and buy property. Among rural residents, on average, 20% of residents with the lowest income consume more than average income with negative savings growth. In 2010, average savings rate of rural residents was 14%, in which savings rate of the lowest 20% of rural residents was -23% while savings rate of the top 20% of rural residents was 26%. In urban and rural areas, income growth rate of the 20% urban residents with the lowest income has increased after 2009 while income growth rate of the 20% rural residents with the lowest income showed a continuous downward trend.

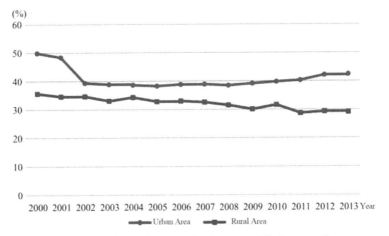

Chart 7-8 Comparison of per capita Income with Average Income of 20% Residents with the Lowest Income

Table 7-6 Proportion of 10 Different Income Groups in Total Residents' Income (%)

Year	1980	1985	1990	1995	2000	2001	2002	2003	2004	2005	2006	2007	2008	2009
Group 1	2.0	3.2	2.8	2.1	1.9	1.7	1.6	1.5	1.6	1.5	1.5	1.5	1.5	1.4
Group 2	3.1	4.6	4.2	3.5	3.2	3.1	2.9	2.8	2.9	2.9	2.9	2.9	2.9	2.8
Group 3	5.4	5.6	5.2	4.4	4.2	4.2	3.9	3.8	3.8	4.0	3.9	3.9	3.9	3.9

contd.

Year	1980	1985	1990	1995	2000	2001	2002	2003	2004	2005	2006	2007	2008	2009
Group 4	7.2	6. 2	6. 3	5. 5	5. 5	5. 3	5. 0	4. 8	4. 8	5. 0	5. 2	5. 1	5. 9	6. 6
Group 5	8. 5	8. 1	7. 5	6. 8	6. 6	6. 6	6. 3	6. 1	6. 1	6. 6	6. 7	8. 1	8. 3	7. 9
Group 6	9. 8	8. 7	9. 0	8. 5	8. 5	8. 4	8. 0	7. 9	7. 9	8. 9	10.0	9. 4	8. 8	8. 7
Group 7	11.5	10.8	11. 3	10.8	10.7	10. 8	10.3	10.7	11. 4	11.7	11.0	10.3	9. 7	9. 7
Group 8	13.2	13.3	13. 1	13.9	14. 1	14. 6	14.4	14.0	13.0	13.1	12.7	12.8	12.7	12.9
Group 9	15.6	16.1	16.7	17.5	18. 1	17. 7	17.3	17.0	16.9	16.8	16.9	17.0	17.1	17.2
Group 10	23.8	23.3	23. 8	27.0	27. 1	27. 7	30.3	31.5	31.8	29.4	29.2	29.0	29.2	28.9

Source: *China Statistical Yearbook.* All residents are divided into 10 equal groups.

From figures above, the income gap among residents is widening in both urban and rural areas with slow income growth of low-income groups although there has been a slight improvement in urban low-income residents since 2011. In 1980, average income was in Group 6, and by 2009, it had reached Group 8, indicating that more residents' income was below average. According to the National Bureau of Statistics, median per capita disposable urban residents' income in 2011 was 19,118 yuan, 2,692 yuan lower than per capita disposable income. In 2011, median per capita net rural residents' income was 6,194 yuan, which was 783 yuan lower than per capita net rural residents' income.

Since residents in higher income group have more savings and capital return has been increasing compared with labor return in recent years, there has been widening income gap between residents in high income group relying on operating income and property income and average resident relying on wage income. Either property income or operating income is return of residents' wealth accumulation resulting from early income growth. That is to say, without widening wage income gap in the previous years, there will be no widening gap between operating income and property income in recent years. It is generally believed that China's rapidly widening income gap stems from widening income gap between urban and rural areas and income gap between urban residents and between rural residents since the mid-1990s. Specifically, these income gaps are between industries, sectors and people at different levels. After entering the 21st century, income of low-income group is getting worse and worse, which is inseparable from China's widening income gap.

Viewed from changing trend, deterioration of residents' income distribution, which mainly began in the mid-1990s, coincides with deepening of state-owned enterprise reform and reform of urban employment and social security system. This time consistency, not a coincidence, results from marketization reform in which old equalitarianism wage distribution is gradually replaced by distribution according to factor contribution so that income gap between individuals and households is widening.[1] In deepening state-owned enterprise reform, the impact of large number of laid-off employees on labor market has also contributed to urban residents' income distribution gap. Regional income gap, major form of urban residents' income gap, was shown in the first stage of state-owned enterprise reform (1988-1995). Economic reform caused urban residents' income gap to widen, shown in the second stage of state-owned enterprise reform (1995-1999).[2] Increased unemployed households and decreased household income contributed more than 78% to Gini coefficient growth between 1995 and 1999. In addition, employees' income decline from loss-making enterprises also caused the widening income gap in this period. Widening gap in urban residents' income distribution will not only have an impact on consumption, investment and social stability but give rise to problems such as urban poverty.

---

1   With reference to Li Shi (2004), *"A Review of Income Inequality in China"*, The Research Institute of Economics of CASS Working Paper.

2   With reference to Meng Xin (2004), *"China's Economic Reform and Urban Income Gap"*, in *The Price of Economic Transformation* (ed.) Li Shi, Sato Hiroshi, China Financial and Economic Press.

III. Countermeasures and Suggestions for Residents' Income Improvement

In the long run, it is necessary to improve residents' income by accelerating reform, improving labor market, capital market and initial distribution and redistribution as well as establishing long-term mechanism of reasonable residents' income growth and distribution. To be specific, in initial distribution, wage income will improve through labor market by creating more employment opportunities through industrialization and urbanization and by accelerating rural labor transfer; property income will improve through capital market; operating income will improve by developing efficiency agriculture and encouraging individual economy. In redistribution, great importance should be attached to the role transfer payment plays in counter-cyclical regulation and narrowing income gap so as to improve income of low-income groups. In order to achieve 2020 goal of doubling the 2010 GDP and per capita urban and rural residents' income, it is of vital importance to ensure the implementation of following policies.

First, it's necessary to maintain bottom line of economic growth. Judging from experience, there is a correlation between growth rate of residents' income and economic growth rate in that the decline in economic growth rate will eventually lead to the decline in residents' income growth rate. As a result, bottom line of economic growth must be maintained. According to current situation, in order to achieve the year 2020 goal of doubling the 2010 GDP and per capita urban and rural residents' income, per capita disposable urban residents' income is to grow at average annual rate of no lower than 6.67%, and per capita net rural residents' income is to grow at average annual rate of no lower than 5.24%, and per capita national residents' income is to grow at average annual rate of no lower than 5.81%, and gross domestic product (GDP) is to grow at average annual rate of no lower than 6.63%.

Second, it is necessary to improve labor share. After Lewis' Turning Point, labor market developed in favor of employees. Employees and enterprises, main body of labor market, should be allowed to determine their wage growth. It is necessary to change economic growth mode of by breaking down capital market monopolization, correcting factor price distortion, and perfecting market formation mechanism of factor price, interest rate in particular. With continuous improvement in labor market, capital market reform has become the key to formation of fair and reasonable national income distribution pattern and labor share improvement.

Third, it is necessary to ensure a reasonable wage growth. Interest relationship between industries and sectors needs adjustment for all industries, employment-intensive industries in particular, to achieve reasonable profits, thus creating external conditions for wage growth with strengthened labor protection, wage collective bargaining system, enhanced workers' right to speak in wage determination, improved labor contract law and labor contract system and labor protection system, labor supervision, and improved tripartite coordination mechanism to ensure wage growth and minimum wage based on hourly wage so as to protect workers' right and interests and ensure work flexibility.

Fourth, it is necessary to expand the proportion of property income and enable residents to share capital income. Improve factor market and speed up capital market reform. Here are how it will be done: first, speed up marketization of interest rates by eliminating capital market monopolization and administrative interference, breaking down discrimination against and barriers to private capital so as to form a unified, open financial system with orderly competition, and to establish a fair and competitive market environment and to give full play to the decisive role of market in resource allocation and eliminate the influence of non-market mechanism on income distribution. Second, improve urban and rural land factor market, rationalize the mechanism of state-owned land market transaction and income distribution, promote rural land ownership, and clear and orderly rural land market so as to establish a fair and reasonable income distribution mechanism for rural land factor.

Fifth, it is necessary to give play to the role of social security so as to improve the income of low-income groups. Here's how it will be done: first, speed up the promotion of social security system covering urban and rural residents by focusing on subsistence of low-income groups and provide subsistence for poor people against the background of declining financial income growth. Second, comprehensively promote the establishment of national basic public service system with innovative ways of providing public services, encourage private capital to be part of social program development, and develop and perfect social insurance system. Third, importance should be attached to making social security standard consistent with China's current economic development with implementation of social security based on subsistence.

Sixth, it is necessary to encourage entrepreneurship, improve capital, knowledge, technology, management and other factors to be part of distribution mechanism. Current China's income distribution problems arise because factors hasn't been able to play their roles in income distribution, knowledge and technology in particular, hindering market vitality and social creativity. In the environment of mass entrepreneurship and innovation, it is necessary to perfect distribution policy conducive to transfer and transformation of scientific and technological achievements which will be priced into shares and share out dividends with high-end talents and new entrepreneurs they deserve.

Chapter VIII

Impact of Labor Market Changes on Income Distribution

Recently, the National Bureau of Statistics published an important indicator reflecting urban and rural residents' income distribution--Gini coefficient. Results show that urban and rural residents' income gap has gradually narrowed since 2009. Despite mixed public reaction to the results, the apparent changes in labor market in recent years have indeed contributed to narrowing income distribution gap. From the perspective of public policy, in order to further narrow income gap in the future, what causes unfair income distribution will be eliminated and positive means to narrow income gap will continue playing their role through reform deepening and labor market development.

I. Positive Changes in Labor Market

Viewed from labor market, employment expansion and wage convergence among

---

1   DU Yang, Research Fellow of Institute of population and Labor Economics, Chinese
     Academy of Social Sciences, doctoral supervisor.

different groups are positive means to narrow income distribution gap among different groups. When labor market reform makes labor flow possible, rural labor force must react to urban and rural labor price difference, which caused, according to our observations, the ever growing labor flow, especially rural-to-urban migration. China's labor flow and migration motivated by higher income has direct impact on income distribution--employment expansion effect and wage convergence effect.

First, there's been growing rural labor flow from low-productivity sectors to high-productivity sectors. Because of low productivity in the agricultural sector, employment in non-agricultural sectors has brought about employment expansion and income growth, main impetus for positive transformation of income distribution. Rapid non-agricultural wage growth will raise the opportunity costs of agricultural labor accordingly. If agricultural labor price is to reflect cost of agricultural labor input, it is not difficult to find that migrant workers' wage of non-agricultural labor is similar to agricultural employees' wage. As Chart 8-1 shows, since 2003 the proportion of migrant workers' wage to agricultural employees' wage has been on the decline at about 1.16 in 2011, the two being very close.

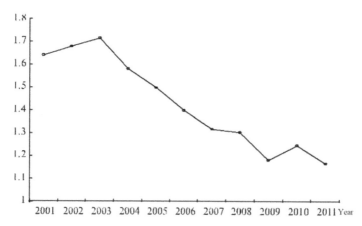

Chart 8-1   Ratio of Migrant Workers' Wage to Agricultural Employees' Wage

Source:The author calculated according to *The Cost of Agricultural Products Data* and rural household survey data.

Second, with large-scale labor flow, economic development and population age structure change, supply and demand in labor market tend to change significantly with new characteristics different from those of dual economy. One prominent aspect is that average worker wage is starting to grow at a faster rate. Therefore, wage effect and employment expansion effect together have become an important driving force to improve income distribution. According to rural household survey data of the National Bureau of Statistics, annual compound growth rate of migrant workers' average wage grew from 6.7% at constant prices between 2001 and 2006 to 12.4% between 2006 and 2011. In the latter period, migrant workers' wage have grown faster than urban workers' wage.

Although this change in labor market does have an effect on income distribution, theoretical expectations have been lacking empirical evidence mainly because it is still difficult to obtain comprehensive statistics to keep track of rapid changes in China's labor market. Although there has long been a discussion on lacking statistical data for urban and rural structural changes (Ravallion & Chen, 1999), new changes in labor market will have a far-reaching influence. On the one hand, with large-scale labor flow, it is difficult for statistical system based on dual economy of urban-rural division to cover labor flow. The departments concerned are implementing the sampling system of urban-rural integration in an intensive manner. But with current statistical system, it is difficult to observe positive and important effects of employment expansion on income distribution improvement. On the other hand, it is difficult to obtain enough micro-information on urban-rural divided statistical samples. For these reasons, it is impossible to have convincing research that can fully reflect the impact of labor market changes on income distribution.

A correct understanding of the relationship between labor flow and income distribution will also help us to further improve labor market policy and income distribution policy. What should be seen is that both employment expansion effect and low income groups' wage growth effect have become the driving force of positive transformation of income distribution. However, in terms of the effect of labor market policies, the two are not always consistent with each other, especially when labor market has experienced a turning point. Establishment of labor market system also attach more importance to employment protection and improvement of employment quality due to the changing situation. To be sure, tougher labor market regulations will not have an obvious negative impact on employment growth at a time of rapid economic growth and big labor demand. However, once economic growth suffers a serious negative blow (such as international financial crisis) or long-term potential growth rate is in downward trend, then it may be more difficult for employment expansion to keep pace with wage growth. In this case, it is time for decision-makers to make labor market policies consistent with the goal of income distribution improvement.

II. Employment Expansion Conducive to Initial Distribution Improvement

It is generally believed that income gap in developing countries is mainly caused by the relative undercapitalization and abundant labor force. In this case, capital return can be high due to capital scarcity. On the one hand, it is difficult for workers to be part of initial distribution for lack of employment opportunities; on the other hand, oversupply in labor market caused low labor return. Top priority for entities with dual economy to narrow income gap is creating as many employment opportunities as possible for workers to be part of initial distribution. Income gap is likely to narrow only when the poor can take full advantage of their most important endowment--their labor force. Transition of developing countries from dual economic structure can be realized through continuous transfer of labor force from the agricultural sector to the non-agricultural sector. If marginal productivity of surplus labor in agricultural sector is zero, employment in the non-agricultural sector not only improves productivity of labor factor but narrows (originally) income gap between surplus labor and non-agricultural sector worker.

There is no denying that there's been employment expansion in China's non-agricultural sector over the past three decades. According to data of the National Bureau of Statistics, total employment in the non-agricultural sector in 2010 was 0.483 billion, 0.127 billion more than 0.356 billion in 2000. Although accuracy of total employment statistics remains controversial (Du & Wang, 2011), it can be observed that rapid employment expansion in the non-agricultural sector based on two years of economic census data: average annual growth rate of non-agricultural employment between 2004 and 2008 was 7.2%, which means that abundant rural labor flow from the agricultural sector to the non-agricultural sector and that an increasing number of workers get to be part of initial distribution.

Unfortunately, it is difficult to fully reflect the effect of large-scale labor flow on current urban-rural statistical system, especially the effect of rural labor flow to urban areas on income distribution. For lack of urban-rural integrated household survey sampling scheme, it is difficult to accurately reflect the income changes brought about by labor flow. On the other hand, from statistical analysis, calculation of income inequality index usually is only about persons with income (greater than zero), ignoring observation value of negative income or zero income. As employment expands, workers with zero income getting low income are accordingly included in inequality index. Therefore, widening income gap came into existence. Although there is no actual data for this phenomenon, the following simulation is to show how income distribution improvement caused by employment expansion is ignored.

10,000 observation values are randomly chosen with normal distribution in income. But in initial state, some people do not get employment opportunities, whose income is zero. Example in Table 8-1 contains 807 observation values of zero income. Therefore, income inequality index of observed income workers can be obtained. With employment expansion, the otherwise unemployed labor force received lower non-agricultural income. Initial state is interpreted as situation before employment expansion and the second observation as the situation after employment expansion.

As is shown in Table 8-1 (1), when income inequality is measured before employment expansion, Gini coefficient is 0.31 and Theil index is 0.16 if observation value (the income) less than zero is not included in inequality index. Including observed value (the income) less than zero, Gini coefficient will be 0.40. After increase in employment opportunities, if newly increased employees are mostly in relatively low-income sectors, Gini coefficient after employment expansion is 0.34 and Theil index is 0.19. It can be seen that inclusion of income less than zero in the calculation of income distribution index has become the key to analysis of income distribution. If all the samples are to be considered, employment expansion is bound to narrow income gap; if a selective sample is considered, the effect of employment expansion on income distribution improvement may be overlooked.

Table 8-1   Simulation of Employment Expansion Effect on Income Distribution

	Before Employment Expansion (1)	Including Zero Income (2)	After Employment Expansion (3)
Observation Value	10000	10000	10000
Observation Value Including Zero Income	807	807	0
Observation Value Including Inequality Index	99193	10000	10000
GE(-1)	1. 01	—	0. 95
GE(0)	0. 22	—	0. 25
GE(1)	0. 16	—	0. 19
GE(2)	0. 15	0. 25	0. 18
Gini	0. 31	0. 40	0. 34

Source: The author calculates according to the data of Urban Labor Market Survey.

Of course if the effect above is all about calculation, researchers can obtain more real measurement of income distribution by adjusting calculation method. However, under current statistical system, sampling schemes of many surveys cannot effectively reflect both labor flow effect and employment expansion effect, inevitably making our income distribution analysis go like Table 8-1 (1) .

Employment expansion effect on income distribution can be studied with microcosmic data collected by China Urban Labor Market Survey. In the following empirical model, determinants of per capita household income are regressed first in order to observe influence of employment variables on per capita household income based on controlling other income determinants. Specific regression equations is as follows:

$$y_i = \alpha_0 + \alpha_1 EMP_i + \alpha_3 HE_i + \alpha_4 SE_I + \alpha_5 AGE_i + \alpha_6 AGE_i^2 +$$
$$\alpha_7 H_i + \alpha_8 ML_i + \alpha_9 FL_i + \alpha_{10} SIZE_i + \sum_{j=2}^{5} CT_j = \varepsilon_i$$

The left part of the equation is per capita household income. Regression variables are the proportion of employed household members, years of education of head of household and the spouse, average family age and its square, and average family health condition, the proportion of male and female labor force in the household, family size and urban virtual variables. Regression results of income determination equation are shown in Table 8-2. Employment, a major determinant of per capita household income, is significantly positive in three rounds of regression. But the real concern is the extent to which employment affects income distribution. In order to achieve this goal, inequality index of per capita income household is decomposed based on income determination model so as to study the effect of different factors on income distribution.

Table 8 - 2   Determinants of Urban Household Income

Year	2001		2005		2010	
Proportion of Employed Household Members	693.49	11.70	10505.76	13.75	1255.5	11.36
Years of Education of Heads of Household	24.20	6.66	530.53	8.5	91.6	10.10
Years of Education of the Spouse	4.48	1.44	15.03	0.34	1.8	0.20
Average Family Age	2.84	0.29	-281.58	-2.4	-28.4	-2.42

contd.

Year	2001		2005		2010	
Square of Average Family Age	0.14	1.36	4.37	3.74	0.5	3.93
Average Family Health Condition	52.29	3.41	560.68	3.06	140.7	6.41
Proportion of Male Labor In Household	195.81	3.17	6753.28	4.4	-198.3	-0.70
Proportion of Female Labor In Household	52. 03	0.60	7500. 04	4. 59	-216.9	-0.69
Family Size	-55. 31	-3.85	- 38. 64	-0. 19	-25.3	-0.98
Wuhan	-412.09	-13.00	-6413.11	-13.38	-551.4	-7.59
Shenyang	-480. 2	-14.83	- 6712. 6	-14.49	-876.9	-13.51
Fuzhou	-243.62	-6.13	-3643.29	- 7.02	-576.4	- 8. 00
Xi'an	-488.17	-14.85	-6442.76	-14.04	-789.2	-11.16
Constant Term	-317.25	-1.34	-1713.28	- 0.6	217.1	0. 83
R^2	0.24		0.40		0.25	
N	3490		2499		3526	

Source: The author calculated according to the data of *Urban Labor Market Survey*

Regression-based decomposition of income gap index is a recently-developed research method with advantages over traditional method of grouping decomposition of inequality index (Fields, 1998; Bourgignonet et. al. 1998, Morduch & Sicular, 2002). For example, the former takes into account contribution of continuous variables to inequality index and controls endogenetic problem of grouping decomposition. Here the regression results of Table 8-2 will be adopted to decompose Theil index of urban household income. The basic method is as follows.

Following the basic concept proposed by Shorrocks (1982), inequality index can be expressed as the weighted sum of household income:

$$I(y) = \sum \alpha_i(y) y_i \qquad (1)$$

Where *I(y)* is aggregate inequality index, such as Theil index, Gini coefficient, variation coefficient, etc., *yi* is per capita household income *i, ai (y)* is the weight applied to each household which varies with different income gap measurement indicators. Each regression factor in the regression equation contributes to inequality index. Contribution of factor *k* (explanatory variables and residuals in regression models) to aggregate inequality index sk can be expressed as follows:

$$s^k = \frac{\sum_{i=1}^{n} a_i(y) y_i^k}{I(y)} \qquad (2)$$

Since each income source in equation/formula (2) depends on regression coefficient *βk* in the table and absolute level of *xki* of each factor of household *i*, regression-based income gap decomposition can be expressed as:

$$s^k = \hat{\beta}_k \left(\frac{\sum_{i=1}^{n} a_i(y) x_i^k}{I(y)} \right) \qquad (3)$$

Sources of Theil index, aggregate income gap index and regression-based decomposition in this chapter are:

$$I_{TT}(y) = \frac{1}{n} \sum_{i=1}^{n} \frac{y_i}{\mu} \ln\left(\frac{y_i}{\mu}\right) \qquad (4)$$

and

$$s_{TT}^k = \frac{\frac{1}{n} \sum_{i=1}^{n} y_i^k \ln\left(\frac{y_i}{\mu}\right)}{\frac{1}{n} \sum_{i=1}^{n} y_i \ln\left(\frac{y_i}{\mu}\right)} \qquad (5)$$

Therefore, Theil index of per capita household income can be factor-decomposed according to regression results in Table 8-2. Our estimates suggest that household income inequality is on a downward trend in several rounds of regression from 0.285 in 2001 to 0.231 in 2010, as is measured by Theil Index. Because factor-decomposed income inequality index is divisible and additive, factors in Table 8-2 are combined according to category whose result is shown in Table 8-3. Results of Table 8-3 show that employment expansion is conducive to narrowing income gap. From data analysis of three rounds of surveys, other factors (such as labor quality, family structure and family size, etc.) being stable, income inequality between urban households measured in terms of Theil index has shrunk by 14% to 23% only through employment expansion. Similarly, it can be inferred that overall employment expansion over the past 30 years which has made the best of the large number of rural labor force has the same effect. Viewed from other factors, both human capital growth and change in demographic characteristics play a positive role in narrowing income gap, but inter-regional gap is still a major source of income gap.

Table 8-3   Sources of Income Gap: Decomposition Based on Regression Results

	2001	2005	2010
Theil Index of per capita Household Income	0.285	0.261	0.231
Proportion of Employment Household Members	-14.1	-22.5	-13.5
Human Capital	-25. 0	-45. 5	-41.9
Demographic Characteristics	-117. 6	-4. 7	-14.5
Regional Factors	111. 0	29. 0	35.9
Regression Residual Term	120. 9	136. 0	128.8

Source: The author calculated according to data of *Urban Labor Market Survey.*

III. Effect of Labor Flow on Income Distribution

As is mentioned earlier, due to limited data, it is still difficult to study changes in aggregate income gap caused by both large-scale rural to urban labor flow and Lewis Turning Point. But basic trends in China's labor market and economic development have shown that the effect of labor market is conducive to income distribution improvement. Regardless of other factors that cause income gap, labor market development itself will gradually narrow wage income gap. The following is labor flow and its effect on income distribution from three aspects.

(I) Income Convergence among Migrant Workers

First, as a response to income gap, labor flow itself is supposed to promote the integration of labor market and narrow workers' income gap, especially income convergence among migrant workers. Previous empirical analysis (Cai, Du & Zhao, 2007) indicates a trend of migrant workers' wage convergence and labor market integration. With labor market changes, income growth rate of low-income groups began to accelerate, which will inevitably drive migrant workers' income gap to gradually narrow. Similarly, according to data of three rounds of urban labor market survey, income gap changes among migrant worker groups and calculated results of income gap with different measured indicators are shown in Table 8-4.

Table 8-4   Income Gap among Migrant Workers

	CULS2001 (a)	CULS2005(b)	CULS2010 (c)	(c/a - 1)× 100%
p90/p10	5. 854	5. 000	3. 750	- 35. 9
p90/p50	2. 614	2. 500	2. 000	- 23. 5
p10/p50	0. 447	0. 500	0. 533	19. 2
p75/p25	2. 003	2. 000	2. 400	19. 8
GE (-1)	0. 321	0. 210	0. 202	- 37. 1
GE(0)	0. 262	0. 183	0. 168	- 35. 9
GE(1)	0. 291	0. 195	0. 175	- 39. 9
GE(2)	0. 443	0. 253	0. 220	- 50. 3
Gini	0. 396	0. 334	0. 319	- 19. 4
A (0.5)	0. 129	0. 090	0. 082	- 36. 4
A (1)	0. 231	0. 167	0. 155	- 32. 9
A (2)	0. 391	0. 296	0. 288	- 26. 3

Source: The author calculates according to data of *Urban Labor Market Survey.* ①

There are four types of indicators in Table 8-4: percentile ratios, generalized entropy, Gini coefficient and Atkinson index. Although all the indicators can show different aspects of changes in migrant workers' income gap, the overall downward trend of income gap index is consistent. Compared with 2001, Gini coefficient and Theil index fell by 19.4% and 40% respectively in 2010. Thanks to a general average worker's wage growth, average income ratio of top 10% of migrant workers with the highest income to lowest 10% of migrant workers with the lowest income in 2001 was 5.85 and dropped to 3.75 in 2010 with a decline rate of 35.9%. It can be inferred that with Lewis Turning Point, supply and demand change of average worker in labor market is the major cause of migrant workers' income convergence.

(II) Income Convergence in Urban Labor Market

Despite migrant workers' income convergence and narrowing migrant workers' income gap, it has become a great concern whether migrant workers entering urban labor market will give rise to low-income groups in urban areas and lead to widening income gap in urban labor market. To answer this question, first of all, it needs to be understood whether migrant workers in urban labor market is still income gap determinant. Review of labor flow policy and household registration system reform has shown that, from the perspective of employment and wage determination, adequate labor market system reform has further weakened the role of household registration in wage determination with increased liberalization of labor market. In order to empirically verify the impact of resident status on wage determination, samples of migrant workers are mixed with samples of local urban workers and added a virtual variable of "whether or not a migrant identity" to control personal characteristics and regional characteristics of labor market (urban variable) so that changes in coefficient of migrant identity variable was studied. Regression results are shown in Table 8-5.

Table 8-5   Role of Migrant Identity in Wage Determination

	CULS2001	CULS2005	CULS2010
Migrant Identity (migrant workers = 1)	-0.107 (3. 85) ***	-0.087 (2.95) ***	- 0.048 (2.38)**
Years of Education	0. 102 (25. 21)	0. 098 (20. 60)	0. 11 (30. 98)
Experience	0. 005 (1. 89)	- 0. 001 (1. 09)	0. 018 (6. 48)
Square of Experience	- 0. 0 (-1. 20)	- 0. 0 (1. 12)	- 0. 0 (-5. 13)
Gender (Male=1)	0. 21 (10. 50)	0. 24 (11. 07)	0. 18 (11. 05)
Urban Virtual Variable	Yes	Yes	Yes
Observation Value	6260	6535	7940
R^2 Adjusted	0. 31	0. 42	0. 37

Note: The value in parentheses is t statistical value. *** is significant at 1% level and ** is significant at 5% level.

It is found that regardless of other variables, the role of household registration system in wage determination is gradually weakening. As is shown in Table 8-5, regardless of other variables, average wage of migrant workers in 2001, lower than that of local workers by 11% , by 9% in 2005 and 5% in 2010. Considering the ever expanding migrant workers flowing into cities, total migrant workers in 2009 was 1.73 times that of 2001 and income convergence between migrant workers and local urban workers is bound to be an important force in narrowing the overall wage gap in labor market.

Of course, increased competitiveness on labor market and weakening role of household registration in wage determination are only one of requirements for narrowing wage income gap between migrant population and local urban population. If there are significant differences in endowment between the two, normal operations of labor market will further widen income gap between these two groups. Due to education expansion, education measured by number of years of schooling in urban labor market tends to shrink between these two groups. Average number of years of education of local urban workers in 2001 was 11.65 years, 1.41 times that of migrant workers, and was 12.55 years in 2010, 1.31 times that of migrant workers. Meanwhile, extended urban work experience has enabled migrant workers to get higher income. In order to observe directly changes in wage income gap in urban labor market between these two groups, three rounds of Chinese urban labor market data are adopted to get income inequality index of urban labor market between local urban labor force and migrant workers. Calculation results of various income inequality indicators are shown in Table 8-6.

Table 8-6 Changes in Income Gap in Urban Labor Market

	CULS2001(a)	CULS2005 (b)	CULS2010 (c)	(c/a-1)×100%
p90/p10	5. 619	5. 000	4. 625	-17. 7
p90/p50	2. 458	2. 500	2. 220	- 9. 7
p10/p50	0. 438	0. 500	0. 480	9. 6
p75/p25	2. 400	2. 400	2. 557	6. 5
GE (-1)	0. 333	0. 266	0. 228	-31. 5

contd.

	CULS2001(a)	CULS2005 (b)	CULS2010 (c)	(c/a-1)×100%
GE(0)	0. 232	0. 214	0. 184	-20. 7
GE(1)	0. 247	0. 223	0. 185	-25. 1
GE(2)	0. 352	0. 291	0. 224	-36. 4
Gini	0. 371	0. 359	0. 332	-10. 5
A (0.5)	0. 112	0. 103	0. 088	- 21. 4
A (1)	0.207	0. 192	0.168	- 18. 8
A (2)	0.400	0. 347	0.313	- 21. 8

It is observed that total wage gap in urban labor market, including migrant workers, is gradually narrowing. Gini coefficient decreased from 0.37 in 2001 to 0.33 in 2010. Theil index decreased from 0.25 to 0.19. And other measured inequality indicator have also declined to varying degrees.

It is worth noting that although change in Gini coefficient has received the most attention from different fields, different income gap measurements have different implications for understanding income distribution changes. The larger the parameter value of generalized entropy is, the more sensitive the index value of measuring inequality is to income gap at distribution top of income (high-income earners). The larger the parameter of Atkinson index is, the more sensitive the index value of measuring inequality is to the income gap at distribution bottom of income (low-income earners) while Gini coefficient is sensitive to median income earners (mode).

Measured indicators of inequality in Table 8-6 do show varying degrees of changes. Taking generalized entropy for example, GE (-1) and GE (2) sensitive to income bottom differences and income top differences declined by 31.5% and 36.4% respectively between 2001 and 2010. Income inequality indicator sensitive to income middle of distribution hasn't changed much: Gini coefficient has decreased by only about 11%. Change in Atkinson index sensitive to income top and income bottom of distribution also reflected this characteristic, falling by 21.4% and 21.8% respectively while Atkinson index sensitive to income middle of distribution decreased by 18.8%.

Thus, both rural labor force in urban labor market and change in supply and demand in labor market may bring about changes in total urban income gap: because of rapid growth in average worker's wage, income difference of the group at income bottom of distribution in urban labor market will undergo significant change, such as GE (-1) and A (2) indicate if successful migrant workers perform so well that income gap between groups at income top of distribution in urban labor market will change significantly as GE (2) and A (0. 5) indicate.

The impact of labor flow on income gap is reflected in income changes between different groups, which calls for more indicators for more comprehensive observation and measurement of this change. Insensitivity of measured indicator of income difference, such as Gini coefficient, does not mean that income distribution has not improved.

(III) Changes in Overall Income Differences

Although microcosmic data on urban labor market show that there is income convergence among migrant workers and that wage differences between migrant workers and local urban workers are gradually narrowing, it does not necessarily mean that labor flow and Lewis Turning Point has a significant impact on overall income gap because urban-rural income gap has always been regarded as the most important component of overall income gap. However, current statistical system fails to effectively include migrant workers in urban and rural income surveys, so there may be a serious sampling deviation in the survey (Park, 2007), resulting in the overestimation of income gap (Cai & Wang, 2009).

Unfortunately, there is no representative and chronological overall data to analyze changes in total income difference, including migrant workers. However, sampling data of 1% of national population in 2005 is available to study what impact the inclusion of migrant workers in statistical system of current urban-rural income will have on estimation of income distribution. The first column in Table 8-7 is usually estimation of urban and rural income gap including rural labor force and urban local population while the second column covers migrant workers.

Results show that if migrant workers are included, income difference index will fall.

It can be predicted that the larger the labor flow, the higher the migrant workers' wage income, and the greater the deviation caused by neglecting migrant workers in estimation of income gap. Table 8-7 is based on sampling data of 1% of national population in 2005. According to a survey by the Rural Department of the National Bureau of Statistics, 0.126 billion migrant workers in 2005 had average monthly wage of 821 yuan (2001 prices); migrant workers has increased by 15.6% in 2009 with a real wage growth of 48.7%. Therefore, it can be imagined that overestimation of overall income gap caused by neglecting migrant workers will be more serious.

Table 8-7   Urban and Rural Income Differences: Deviated and Undeviated Estimation

	Rural Employees + Urban Employees	Rural Employees + Urban Employees + Migrant Workers	Changes (%)
p90/p10	10. 642	10. 145	-4.67
p75/p25	3. 604	3. 694	2.50
GE(-1)	0. 668	0. 657	-1.65
GE(0)	0. 422	0. 408	- 3. 32
GE(1)	0. 425	0. 407	- 4. 24
GE(2)	0. 740	0. 705	- 4. 73
Gini	0. 484	0. 474	- 2. 07
A(0. 5)	0. 190	0. 183	- 3. 68
A(1)	0. 344	0. 335	- 2. 62
A(2)	0. 572	0. 568	- 0. 70

Source: The author calculated based on sampling survey of 1% of national population in 2005.

IV. Conclusion

Although in general China's labor market has not been able to achieve a fully free labor flow, labor market reform has been fully effective in the past 30 years in that policies and systems restricting labor flow have been effectively cleaned up so that there has been larger scale of labor flow, especially transfer of rural labor force from agriculture to non-agriculture. Empirical studies also show that market mechanism plays an increasingly important role in employment decision and wage formation, which makes rural and urban wage income gap gradually narrow.

Our research shows that both labor market reform and larger-scale labor flow are undoubtedly positive means to narrow income gap. According to the analysis of this chapter, labor flow improves income distribution through two effects. First, employment expansion effect has enabled more people to be part of initial distribution, improving income distribution. Unfortunately, limited statistics have made it difficult for us to have a comprehensive assessment of this effect. Second, income convergence effect has narrowed income gap. When economy faces Lewis Turning Point, full labor flow will lead to income convergence of different groups, the driving force to narrow income gap. Our observations show that income gap among migrant workers, between urban workers and migrant workers, and between urban and rural areas is likely to be narrowed by labor flow. Microcosmic data analysis based on urban labor market shows that increasing employment expansion (mainly migrant workers) in recent years is the driving factor in narrowing income gap.

Therefore, currently, it can be said that employment expansion effect brought about by labor market development and income convergence brought about by labor flow are playing a positive role in narrowing income gap. There is reason to believe that after Lewis Turning Point, major labor market results will shift towards a more favorable income distribution improvement and convergence with Kuznets Turning Point is well on the way.

Considering that there are many other factors (welfare, asset income, etc.) that affect income distribution, more empirical evidence is needed to judge overall income gap so as to observe the relative influence of labor income on income distribution pattern and change in overall income distribution trend.

Of course, labor market reform is far from over. The most important and arduous task is social protection system reform with permanent household registration system as its core. Although there is the goal of equalization and integration of social protection and public service among different groups, systematic reform of permanent household registration system still has a long way to go. When labor market has undergone changes, household registration system reform can further stimulate the possible stagnation of labor flow, enabling employment expansion and labour flow to play their role in further narrowing income gap.

Chapter IX

Informal Employment and Income Gap between Urban Employees

GAO Wenshu, XUE Jinjun[1]

I. Informal Employment

Informal employment initially refers to working in the informal sector. The term of informal sector was first put forward in the 1972 Kenya report by the International Labor Organization (ILO). The report points out that most of the people working in cities do not work in the modern formal sectors, but the "working poor" employed in the informal sector, including small-scale enterprises ungoverned by the state or national law, peddlers, carpenters, mechanics, cooks, etc., as are distinguished from large enterprises governed and supported by the state (ILO, 1972). Subsequently, informal employment included employment in informal sector of enterprises and households and informal employment in the

---

1 GAO Wenshu, Research fellow, Institute of Population and Labor Economy, Chinese Academy of Social Sciences, Doctoral Supervisor; XUE Jinjun, Professor & Doctoral Supervisor, School of Economics, Nagoya University, Japan

formal sector. Difference between the informal sector and informal employment is that the former emphasizes registered status of the workplace and the latter emphasizes undeclared work for legal, social insurance and tax purposes. It's an international consensus that informal employment does not comply with Labor Law (OECD, 2004).

In order to provide guidelines for informal employment statistics in different countries, the International Labor Organization (ILO) issued *Guideline Concerning Statistical Definition of Informal Employment* in 2003, the most authoritative guideline for defining informal employment up till now. *Guideline* combines types of units in which employees work and employment status of individuals to specifically define whether workers are engaged in formal or informal employment. Workplaces are divided into the formal sector, the informal sector and the household sector. Employees are divided into self-employed workers, employers, domestic workers, employees and members of production cooperatives with employment status (except domestic workers) further divided into "formal" and "informal". Three unit types are set as "line" and employment status as "column" to form a matrix. Each grid in the matrix corresponds to a specific characteristic of a worker, which can be divided into formal and informal workers (ILO, 2003).

The ILO statistical definition framework for informal employment is shown in Chart 9-1. All white grids marked with numbers in the Chart constitute all informal employment. Among them, Grids 1 and 2 is informal employment in the formal sector; Grids 3, 4, 5, 6, 8 is informal employment in the informal sector; Grids 9 and 10 is informal employment in the household sector and Grid 7 is formal employment in the informal sector.

According to definition of ILO (2003), informal employment consists of the following five categories of workers: domestic workers, self-employed workers in informal sectors and household sectors, employers in informal sectors, members of production cooperatives in informal sectors and employees engaged in informal work. However, the International Labur Organization also points out that, as informal employment varies from country to country, countries should have statistical definitions of informal employment in accordance with their specific circumstances and priorities. That is to say, the International Labor Organization can only give basic standards to define informal employment, and countries need to come up with specific standards based on their national conditions and basic standards of the International Labor Organization.

Unit Type	Employment Status								
	Self-employed Workers		Employers		Domestic Workers	Employees		Members of Production Cooperatives	
	Informal	Formal	Informal	Formal	Informal	Informal	Formal	Informal	Formal
Formal Sector					1	2			
Informal Sector	3		4		5	6	7	8	
Household Sector	9					10			

Chart 9-1 Definition Framework of Informal Employment by ILO

Source: ILO(2003). *Guideline Concerning Statistical Definition of Informal Employment*, http://www. ilo.org/global/statistics-and-databases/standards-and-guidelines/guidelines-adopted-by-international- conferences-of-labour-statisticians/WCMS_087622/lang-en/index.htm.

Following basic framework of ILO (2003), here is China's definition of informal employment. Types of production units are still divided into formal sectors, informal sectors and household sectors. Among them, formal sectors are organizations and institutions, state-owned and state-owned holding enterprises, collective enterprises, private enterprises and other types of units; informal sectors are individual industrial and commercial households; household sectors are households that produce or employ domestic workers for their own purposes. The reason why individual industrial and commercial households are regarded as informal sectors is that its small scale with no more than seven employees, consistent with standards defined by the International Labor Organization for informal sectors, that is, small number of unregistered employees (ILO, 1993). Employment status of workers is divided into four categories: employees, employers, self-employed workers and domestic workers. Since there are no production cooperatives in China's urban areas, category of members of production cooperatives in the ILO classification of employment status is omitted. "Employees engaged in informal work", according to OECD (2004) standards, are employees who do not have formal labor relations without protection of labor laws, that is, those who have not signed formal labor contracts or those who have signed labor contracts without social insurance such as pension and medical care. At the same time, following international practice, the agricultural sector is excluded from informal employment.

Thus, China's informal employees are actually composed of the following four parts of non-agricultural workers: domestic workers; self-employed workers in the informal sector and the household sector; employers in informal sectors; and employees engaged in informal employment. This way, relevant survey data are adopted to measure the proportion, size and characteristics of China's informal employment.

II. Informal Employment in Chinese Cities

(I) Proportion and Scale of Informal Employment in Chinese Cities

Measurement of the proportion and scale of informal employment requires high quality microcosmic survey data because to find out whether a laborer is engaged in formal or informal employment means collecting information on employment status of the laborer and type of production unit he works for. To obtain overall information on the proportion and scale of informal employment in the whole country or region as China requires large-scale sampling survey data, preferably census data. In more than a decade, China has conducted four census surveys, namely, the Fifth Census in 2000, sampling survey of 1% of national population in 2005, the Sixth Census in 2010 and sampling survey of 1% of national population in 2015. Among them, sampling survey data in 2005 is the most authoritative on the proportion and scale of informal employment in China since it provides information on types of work units and employment status of employees.

In sampling survey of 1% of national population in 2005, employment status of workers was divided into four categories: employees, employers, self-employed workers and domestic workers; types of work units include organs, organizations, institutions, state-owned and state-owned holding enterprises, collective enterprises, individual industrial and commercial households, private enterprises, other types of units, land contractors and other eight categories. The survey also provides important information about workers' labor contracts, social security and monthly income. With this survey data, there're four categories of informal workers: domestic workers, self-employed workers in informal and household sectors, employers the in informal sector, and employees in the informal sector with statistical definition of China's informal employment proposed in accordance with basic framework of ILO (2003) excluding agricultural workers. Among them, employees engaged in informal employment are workers employed who fail to sign labor contracts or who sign labor contracts without basic pension or basic medical care.

Analysis sample of nearly 500,000 people can be obtained by retaining only sample of urban workers aged 16 and above excluding agricultural workers from 1/5 sample of 1% of national population in 2005. Weighted by sampling weights, the proportion of non-agricultural workers in urban China engaged in informal employment is 58.85%, or nearly 60% of urban employees are engaged in informal employment. In 2005, China's urban employees reached 0.277 billion, 0.163 billion of which were engaged in informal employment. As is seen, the number of informal workers is very large. Moreover, the proportion of migrant workers engaged in informal employment (70.90%) is far higher than that of urban local workforce (52.78%); the proportion of urban workers engaged in informal employment in eastern region of China, 60.93%, is much larger than that in central region of China; the proportion of urban workers engaged in informal employment in central China is 56.73%, slightly higher than that of the western region (See Table 9-1). Since sampling survey data of 1% of national population in 2005 is the only census data in China that can define and measure informal employment in accordance with the ILO (2003) standard, results above should be the most important reference data on the proportion and scale of informal employment in Chinese cities.

Table 9-1   China's Urban Informal Employment (%)

	Local Labor	Migrant Labor	Total Employees
Eastern Region	54. 24	70. 63	60. 93
Central Region	52. 66	71. 16	56. 73
Western Region	48. 26	72. 16	54. 66
National Average	52. 78	70. 90	58. 85

Source: calculated according to sampling survey data of 1% of national population in 2005.

(II) Sector Distribution and Employment Status of Informal Employees

Further analysis shows that 46.93%, 42.06%, and 11.01% of China's informal employment is in formal sectors, informal sectors and household sectors. In terms of employment status, 63.49%, 30.68%, 4.10%, and 1.73% of all informal workers are employees in enterprises and individual industrial and commercial households, self-employed workers, domestic workers, and employers (See Table 9-2).

Table 9-2   Sector Distribution and Employment Status of Formal and Informal Employees (%)

		Informal Employees	Formal Employees	All Employees
Sector	Formal Sector	46. 93	90. 19	64. 73
	Informal Sector	42. 06	8. 45	28. 23
	Household Sector	11. 01	1. 36	7. 04
Employment Status	Self-employed Workers	30. 68	0. 00	18. 06
	Employers	1. 73	8. 27	4. 42
	Domestic Workers	4. 10	0. 00	2. 41
	Employees in Enterprises or Self-employed Sectors	63. 49	60. 87	62. 41
	Formal Staff and Employees in Organs and Institutions	0. 00	30. 85	12. 70

Source: calculated based on sampling survey data of 1% of national population in 2005.

(III) Basic Characteristics of Informal Employees

In terms of personal characteristics, typical informal employees are unmarried, not well-educated young female migrants from agriculture households. 42.39% of informal employees is female, 2% higher than that of formal employees. Unmarried informal employees accounted for 21.40%, 8% higher than that of formal employees. More than 80% of informal employees are under 45 years old with an average age of 35.52, about 2 years younger than formal employees. Average number of years of education for informal employees is 9.42 years, far below that of formal employees (12.41 years) as more than 70% of them are junior high school graduates and below. Migrant workers account for 40.37% of informal employees, compared with 23.69% of formal employees. 59.26% of informal workers are from agriculture households while only 13.97% of formal employees are from agriculture households (See Table 9-3). It can be seen that there are significant differences in gender, age, marital status, education, resident status and household registration between informal and formal employees.

Table 9-3   Personal Characteristics of Informal Employees (%)

		Informal Employees	Formal Employees	Total Employees
Gender Composition	Male	57. 61	59. 09	58. 22
	Female	42. 39	40. 91	41. 78
Marital Status	Unmarried	21. 40	13. 88	18. 30
	Married	78. 60	86. 12	81. 70
Average Age (years of age)		35. 52	37. 62	36. 38
Age Distribution	16—24	20. 58	10. 55	16. 45
	25—34	31. 53	33. 10	32. 17
	35—44	29. 76	34. 60	31. 75
	45—54	14. 04	18. 65	15. 94
	55—64	3. 27	2. 86	3. 10
	65and above	0. 82	0. 23	0. 58
Average Years of Education (years)		9. 42	12. 41	10. 65

contd.

		Informal Employees	Formal Employees	Total Employees
Educational Background	Primary School or Lower	17. 75	3. 37	11. 82
	Secondary Schools	54. 32	24. 67	42. 10
	High School	21. 13	32. 63	25. 87
Educational Background	College	4. 91	24. 43	12. 96
	University and Above	1. 89	14. 90	7. 25
Resident Status	Migrant Population	40. 37	23. 69	33. 50
	Local Residents	59. 63	76. 31	66. 50
Household Registration	Agricultural	59. 26	13. 97	40. 59
	Non-agricultural	40. 74	86. 03	59. 41

Source: calculated according to sampling survey data of 1% of national population in 2005

In terms of job characteristics, informal work is characterized by long working hours, low income without labor contracts and social security. On average, informal employees have to work 52.62 hours per week, 8 hours more than formal employees. Average monthly income of informal employees is only 888.57 yuan, 70% less than that of formal employees (1290.74 yuan). The average hourly income of informal employees is only 4.29 yuan, about 40% lower than that of formal employees (7.09 yuan). Formal employees have all signed labor contracts, most of which enjoy such social security as pension, medical care and unemployment insurance while less than 20% of informal employees have signed labor contracts and enjoyed social insurance (See Table 9-4).

Table 9-4　Job Characteristics of Informal Employees (%)

	Informal Employees	Formal Employees	All Employees
Average Working Hours per Week	52. 62	44. 82	49. 41
Average Monthly Income (yuan)	888. 57	1290. 74	1055. 99
Average Hourly Income (yuan)	4. 29	7. 09	5. 47

contd.

	Informal Employees	Formal Employees	All Employees
Signing Labor Contracts (%)	14. 15	100. 00	57. 29
Social Insurance (%)			
Pension	15. 94	79. 32	42. 02
Basic Medical Care Insurance	23. 06	83. 85	48. 07
Unemployment Insurance	5. 92	58. 14	27. 41

Source: sampling survey data of 1% of national population in 2005

In terms of industrial distribution, about 90% of informal employment is in five industries: manufacturing, wholesale and retail and catering, social services, construction, transportation and storage and postal services, accounting for 31.9%, 30.6%, 9.7%, 9.2% and 8.7% of informal employment respectively, other industries being basically less than 2%. Moreover, the proportion of formal employees in five major industries above is significantly lower than that in the informal sector while in the rest of industries, the proportion of formal employees is higher than that of informal employees, the latter being mostly in monopoly industries (See Chart 9-2).

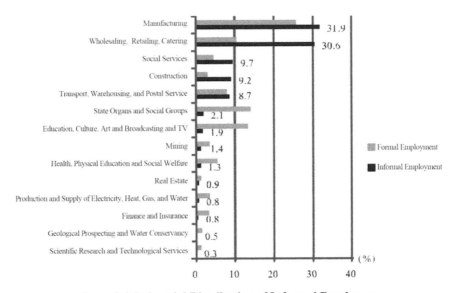

Chart 9-2 Industrial Distribution of Informal Employees

Source: Based on sampling survey of 1% of national population of 2005

In terms of unit type, 70% of informal employees are in individual industrial and commercial households (with 42.1% of informal employees) and private enterprises (with 28.1% of informal employees) while other units have few informal employees. Reversely, 70% of formal employees are in government institutions and organizations and state-owned enterprises with formal employees in individual industrial and commercial units and private enterprises being only about 8% and 10% respectively (See Chart 9-3).

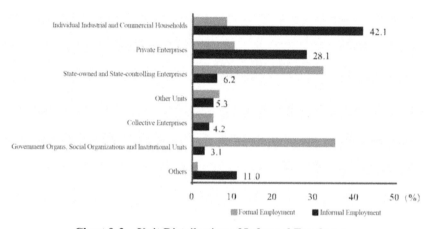

Chart 9-3   Unit Distribution of Informal Employees

Source: Based on the sampling survey of 1% of national population of 2005

III. Informal Employment and Employees' Income Gap

(I) Average Income Gap between Informal Employees and Formal Employees

As has been pointed out, there is widening income gap between formal and informal employees. The average monthly income of formal employees is 1290.74 yuan, 1.45 times that of informal employees, which was 888.57 yuan (See Table 9-4). Since informal employees work longer hours, hourly income gap between the two is wider than monthly income gap. Calculations show that average hourly income of formal employees is 7.09 yuan, about 1.65 times that of informal employees, which is only 4.29 yuan. Moreover, informal employees' income is significantly lower than that of formal employees, either for migrant or for local urban employees. Among migrant labor force, average hourly income of formal employees is 5.70 yuan, 1.41 times that of informal employees which is 4.05 yuan. Among urban local labor force, average hourly income of formal employees is 6.81 yuan, 1.68 times that of informal employees, which is only 4.05 yuan (See Table 9-5).

Table 9-5 Work and Income of China's Urban Employees

	Migrant Labor			Local Labor		
	Informal Employment	Formal Employment	Total	Informal Employment	Formal Employment	Total
Average Monthly Income (yuan)	910.89	1217.99	962.05	818. 69	1223.35	1011.72
Average Weekly Working Hour	56.46	52.57	55.83	51. 16	44.08	47.82
Average Hourly Income (yuan)	4.05	5.70	4.33	4.05	6.81	5.38

Source: Based on the sampling survey of 1% of national population of 2005.

(II) Estimation of Employees' Income Inequality Index

Judging from comparison of average income of different employees above, income gap between migrant and local labor force and income gap between informal and formal employees reflects income inequality in China's urban labor market. However, with the average value masking distribution of employees' income, actual income inequality can't be seen. In order to know about actual income inequality, relevant income inequality index is to be adopted. There are many indices to measure income inequality, such as Gini coefficient and generalized entropy.

Calculation of Gini coefficient points to China's widening income gap of urban employees with Gini coefficient of hourly income reaching 0.39. Moreover, income inequality of informal employees whose Gini coefficient is only 0.37, higher than that of formal employees whose Gini coefficient is 0.35. Further comparison shows that income inequality of migrant labor force measured by

Gini coefficient is greater than that of local urban labor force in either informal or formal employment (See Table 9-6).

Calculation of generalized entropy index reveal the same trend as that of Gini coefficient, that is, income inequality of informal employees is greater than that of formal employees. In both formal and informal employment, income inequality of migrant labour force is bigger than that of local urban employees. For example, first Theil index of hourly income of informal employees and formal employees is 0.28 and 0.24 respectively. Within both formal and informal employment, first Theil index of migrant labour force is also significantly higher than that of local urban labor force (See Table 9-6).

Table 9-6   Gini Coefficient and Theil Index of China's Urban Employees'
Income

	Informal Employees			Formal Employees			All Employees
	Migrant Labor	Local Labor	Total	Migrant Labor	Local Labor	Total	
Gini Coefficient	0.37	0.36	0.37	0.39	0.34	0.35	0.39
Theil Index One (T_1)	0.29	0.27	0.28	0.28	0.21	0.24	0.29
Theil Index Two (T_0)	0.23	0.22	0.22	0.25	0.19	0.21	0.25

Source: Based on sampling survey of 1% of national population of 2005

(III) Theil Index Decomposition of Income Inequality

Increasing income inequality among China's urban workers, income gap between migrant workers and local workers, income gap between formal employees and informal employees has given rise to a question: How does this income gap between different groups of workers affect overall income inequality? In other words, how much does income gap between different groups of employees contribute to overall income inequality?

Theil index decomposition method is adopted to calculate gap between informal and formal employees, inter-group gap, whose contribution to overall income inequality of China's urban workers is 13.68%. Gap within informal employees group and gap within formal employees group, intra-group gap, whose contributions to overall income inequality is 51.09% and 35.23% respectively. Further analysis shows that, for both informal and formal employees, inter-group gap between migrant and local urban labor force doesn't contribute much to income inequality, both less than 4% (See Table 9-7). This shows that income gap within informal workers is the most important source of income gap of China's urban employees and that income gap between informal employees and formal employees also contributes a lot to overall income inequality and that income gap between migrant and local labor also has an impact on income inequality, but to a lesser extent.

Table 9-7 Theil Index Decomposition of Income Gap between China's Urban Employees

	All Employees			Informal Employees			Formal Employees		
	Informal Employees	Formal Employees	Total	Migrant Labor	Local Labor	Total	Migrant Labor	Local Labor	Total
Theil Index 2	0.22	0.21	0.25	0.23	0.22	0.22	0.24	0.19	0.21
Population Proportion (%)	58.06	41.94	100.00	40.66	59.34	100.00	2376	76.24	100.00
Intra-group Contribution (%)	51.09	35.23	86.32	42.51	56.46	98.97	27.15	68.98	96.13
Inter-group Contribution (%)	—	—	13.68	—	—	1.03	—	—	3.87

Source: Based on the sampling survey of 1% of national population of 2005

(IV) Regression Equation-based Decomposition of Income Gap

Theil index decomposition of income gap based on different sub-samples or labor groups can be adopted to analyze the extent to which overall inequality originates from inter-group differences and intra-group differences. It is of great significance to analysis of overall inequality composition and causes of the increase or decrease of inequality. However, there are two defects in this sub-sample decomposition method. First, decomposition results depend on group number. In general, inter-group contribution tend to grow as group number increases. Second, differences between subsamples are often determined by grouping category variables. For example, income gap between informal and formal employees does not necessarily reflect or reflects more than market discrimination against informal employees, as there may also be differences in education, experience, etc. between the two groups. It is debatable to simply attribute inter-group contribution to grouping category variables without controlling other variables (Wan Guanghua, 2008). Therefore, regression equation-based decomposition of income gap is adopted here to control influence of other variables so as to explain main influencing factors and their contribution to income gap between China's urban workers.

According to Mincer equation (Mincer, 1974), employees' income is a function of his own education, experience and other related variables, i.e., In $y=\sum\beta jxj$, with y denoting employees' income, x related explanatory variable of income, j the number of explanatory variables, and β coefficients of related explanatory variables. Thus, income gap between informal employees and formal employees can be expressed as Formula (4), with i denoting informal employees and f formal employees. Of course, in analyzing income gap between migrant and local labor, i denotes migrant labor and f local labor.

$$ln y_f - ln y_i = \sum \beta_{fj} x_{fj} - \sum \beta_{ij} x_{ij} = \sum \beta_{fj} (x_{fj} - x_{ij}) + \sum (\beta_{fj} - \beta_{ij}) x_{ij}$$

(1)

The first item in Formula (1) $\sum\beta fj(xfj-xij)$ is called income gap caused by differences in endowment or stock (xj) of explanatory variables between formal employees and informal employees, such as income gap caused by higher average education of formal employees. The second item in $\sum(\beta fj-\beta ij)$ xij is called income gap caused by difference in regression coefficient of explanatory variables between two types of employees, such as income gap caused by different education return rate. The second item, referred to as unexplanatory part, indicates that two types of employees with the same personal characteristics receive different incomes, often interpreted as market discrimination against low-income groups such as informal employees. This income decomposition method and idea is the famous Blinder-Oaxaca decomposition method (Oaxaca, 1973).

Based on sampling survey data of 1% national population in 2005, first regression analysis of determinants of employees' income is made based on Mincer Equation, and then Blinder-Oaxaca decomposition method is analyzed with factors affecting income gap among different groups of employees. In the regression model, employees' income is expressed as logarithm of hourly income, and explanatory income variables includes not only classic variables such as number of years of schooling, work experience (by age minus years of education minus school age or 6 years of age), square of work experience, but also variables with personal characteristics such as gender, marriage, household registration, etc. and employees' profession, occupation, unit type and region and so on. Regression results of determinants of employees' income are shown in Table 9-8.

Regression results show that education has a significant positive impact on employees' income both for all employed workers and for formal or informal employees. Work experience also has a significant positive impact on employees' income, but the sign of square regression coefficient of work experience is negative, indicating that income return rate of work experience is characterized by its marginal decline. Meanwhile, gender (being male) and marital status (being married) also have a significant impact on income. All these results reflect consistency of China's reality and human capital theory with practices of other nations.

However, regression results show that either formal or informal employment has a significant impact on employees' income. After controlling human capital variables such as education and experience, as well as related variables such as gender, marital status, industry and region, workers engaged in informal employment earned 25.64% less than those in formal employment. This conclusion further confirms previous statistical description that there is a significant income gap between informal and formal employees. In addition, nature of household registration is also an important determinant of employees' income. Other conditions being unchanged, non-agricultural household employees' income is significantly higher than that of agricultural households, but impact of household registration on income is not significant within formal employees.

Regression results also show that human capital return rate is quite different between formal and informal employees. Return rate of education and experience of formal employees is way higher than that of informal employees, education regression coefficient of formal employees and of informal employees being 9.19% and 4.95% respectively and work experience regression coefficient of formal employees and of informal employees being 1.31% and 0.63% respectively.

Table 9-8   Regression Results of Workers' Income Determinants

	All Employees	Informal Employees	Formal Employees
Formal/Informal Employment (Formal=1)	-0.2564 *** (0. 0022)	---	---
Years of Education	0.0679 *** (0.0004)	0.0495 *** (0. 0005)	0.0919*** (0.0006)
Work Experience (Year)	0.0099 *** (0. 0003)	0.0063 *** (0. 0004)	0.0131 *** (0.0005)
Square of Work Experience	-0. 0002*** (0. 0000)	- 0. 0001 *** (0. 0000)	- 0. 0001*** (0.0000)
Gender (Male=1)	0. 1802 *** (0. 0017)	0. 2200 *** (0. 0023)	0.1267 *** (0.0025)
Marital Status (Married=1)	0. 0293 *** (0. 0029)	0. 0435 *** (0. 0139)	0.0129** (0.0065)
Household Registration (Agricultural=1)	- 0. 0273 *** (0. 0021)	-0.0214 *** (0. 0025)	0.0040 (0.0042)
Industries	controlled	controlled	controlled
Occupation	controlled	controlled	controlled
Unit Type	controlled	controlled	controlled
Region	controlled	controlled	controlled
Intercept Term	1. 0561 *** (0. 0082)	1. 3037 *** (0. 0129)	0. 5613 *** (0. 0116)
Sample Size	455239	256953	198286

contd.

	All Employees	Informal Employees	Formal Employees
Value F	8555. 30 ***	2469. 72 ***	2906. 35 ***
R^2 Adjusted	0. 3366	0. 1999	0. 2759

Note: ***,**,* represents significance at levels of 1%, 5% and 10% respectively; standard deviation is in brackets.

Blinder-Oaxaca decomposition of income equations of formal and informal employees shows that 73.51% of income gap between informal and formal employees can be explained by such stock factors as low education of informal employees and 26.49% is determined by coefficient differences in income factors, or market discrimination against informal employees. Further analysis shows that education is the most important factor affecting income gap between formal and informal employees. As average number of years of schooling for informal employees (9.42 years) was significantly lower than that of formal employees (12.41 years), difference in this educational stock accounted for 42.85% of income gap between the two. Education return rate of informal employment being significantly lower than that of formal employment accounted for 47.48% of income gap between the two (See Table 9-9). Therefore, the most important way to narrow income gap between formal and informal employees is to improve education of informal employees and reverse market discrimination against informal employment.

Table 9-9   Blinder-Oaxaca Decomposition Results of Income Gap between Formal and Informal Employees

	Explanatory Part (Stock Difference)		Unexplanatory Part (Coefficient Difference)	
	Value	Percentage (%)	Value	Percentage (%)
Logarithmic Income Difference (0. 5160)	0.3793	73.51	0.1367	26.49
Contribution Factors: Years of Education	0.2211	42.85	0.2450	47.48
Work Experience	-0.0022	-0.43	0.0870	16.86

contd.

	Explanatory Part (Stock Difference)		Unexplanatory Part (Coefficient Difference)	
	Value	Percentage (%)	Value	Percentage (%)
Gender	0.0010	0.19	- 0.0295	-5.72
Marital Status	0.0059	1.14	- 0.0535	-10.37
Household Registration	0.0067	1.30	0.0086	1.67
Other	0.1468	28.45	-0.1209	-23.43

IV. From Informal Employment to Formal Employment

(I) Significance of Regularization of Informal Employment

Undoubtedly, informal employment has been playing a positive role in relieving employment pressure, creating opportunities for income growth, expanding domestic consumption demand, and accelerating industrialization and urbanization, etc. Since informal employment is completely under the influence of market law, with more applicable technology and with market playing a key role in allocation of capital, labor force and other resources, informal employment has also significantly improved allocation efficiency of labor resources.

However, negative impact of informal employment is also very obvious. First, workers' rights and interests are vulnerable to infringement. Much informal employment in the formal sector, to a large extent, results from enterprises evading minimum wage legislation, social security benefits and welfare expenditures, directly damaging legal rights and interests of employees. Second, informal employment lacks technological innovation. Because of unstable labor relations of informal employment, organizations often lack the motivation of systematic technical training for employees in informal employment, which hinders scientific and technological innovation and its application in production. Last, informal employment can cause national economy to hover at low level. For lack of a sense of stability in the informal sector and lack of long-term development goals and corresponding development strategies in many business units, many employees only work for a short period, making it is difficult for informal sectors to develop towards specialization in a highly competitive environment. In addition, an excessively low professional structure is not conducive to further urban modernization.

Moreover, under the influence of their working environment, economic and social status and mode of thinking, informal workers will gradually develop deviant behaviors, lifestyles and values different from those of formal employees. This difference reflects not only their individuality but in the entire group of informal employees, leading to spatial segmentation of informal employment and formal employment which will result in exclusion of informal employees from formal employees--employment discrimination, and further reduce the possibility of informal employees entering the formal sector and cause permanent demotion of employees' employment status (Yang Fei, Liu Pengfei, 2008).

(II) Determinants of Formal Employment

Probability of workers engaged in informal employment is regarded as the function of their personal characteristics, human capital characteristics and their occupation, trade and region, etc., and Probit Model is adopted to make a regression analysis of workers' employment choices so as to find out factors that make it easier for workers to become formal employees. In regression analysis, variable is whether the worker will be engaged in formal employment, value "yes" being 1, and value "no" being 0. Independent variables include migrant labor force, years of schooling, work experience, gender, marital status, household registration, unit type, occupation and region.

Regression results of Probit Model (See Table 9-10) show that employment status of workers and human capital status have a significant impact on their formal employment. Other things being equal, probability of migrant labor force engaged in formal employment is 6.09% lower than that of local labor. Probability of agriculture household workers engaged in formal employment is 19.59% lower than that of non-agriculture household workers. This suggests that China's urban labor market discriminates against migrant and agriculture household workers. Higher human capital will significantly increase probability of formal employment. Keeping other conditions unchanged, probability of workers engaged in formal employment will increase by 3.39% as number of years of education increases by 1 year. Probability of formal employment will increase by 0.9% as number of work experience increases by 1 year. These findings mean that to promote formal employment, it is necessary to improve human capital, such as years of education of workers, and to eliminate discrimination in labor market against migrant and agriculture household workers.

In addition, gender, marital status, occupation, industry, unit type and region of workers also have a significant impact on their formal employment. Other conditions being equal, probability of formal employment is higher for male than for female and higher for the married than for the unmarried. In terms of unit type, probability of formal employment is the highest in government organs and institutional units, followed by state-owned and state-owned holding enterprises, followed by other types of enterprises, collective enterprises, private enterprises and individual industrial and commercial households. In terms of occupation, probability of formal employment is the highest for unit leaders, followed by clerical personnel, professional and technical personnel, production, transportation and equipment operators and commercial service personnel. In terms of industry, probability of formal employment is the highest for manufacturing workers, followed by transportation, wholesale and retail, and catering, social services, and construction workers being the lowest. In terms of regions, other conditions being equal, probability of formal employment is the highest in the eastern region, followed by the western region, and the central region being the lowest. All this means that in employment regularization, great importance should be attached to females and the unmarried, to workers in private enterprises and individual industrial and commercial households, to key industries such as construction and social services, and to the central and western regions.

Table 9-10　Regression Results of Probit Model of Formal Employment

	Marginal Effect	Standard Error	Average
Migrant Labor Force (Yes=1)	- 0.0609 ***	0.0006	0.34
Years of Education	0.0339 ***	0.0001	10.65
Work Experience (Years)	0.0009 ***	0.0000	18.74
Gender (Male=1)	0.0261 ***	0.0006	0.58
Marital Status (Married=1)	0.0572 ***	0.0009	0.82
Household Registration (Agricultural=1)	- 0.1959 ***	0.0007	0.59
Unit Type (Organs and Institutions=1)			
State-owned and State-owned Holding Enterprises	- 0.1572 ***	0.0012	0.17
Collective Enterprises	- 0.3146 ***	0.0008	0.05
Individual Industrial and Commercial Households	- 0.5428 ***	0.0008	0.28
Private Enterprises	- 0.4835 ***	0.0007	0.21
Other Unit Types	- 0.2949 ***	0.0009	0.06
Other Units	- 0.4295 ***	0.0004	0.07
Occupations (Unit Leaders=1)			
Professional and Technical Personnel	- 0.0400 ***	0.0016	0.16
Clerks and Related Personnel	- 0.0289 ***	0.0017	0.10
Commercial Service Personnel	- 0.1116 ***	0.0015	0.32
Production, Transport, Equipment Operators	- 0.0893 ***	0.0015	0.38
Other Occupations	- 0.1552 ***	0.0035	0.01
Industries (manufacturing=1)			
Construction	- 0.1776 ***	0.0011	0.07
Transport, Warehousing, Postal Services, Communications	- 0.0880 ***	0.0011	0.09
Wholesaling, Retailing, Catering	- 0.0888 ***	0.0011	0.22
Social Services	- 0.0920 ***	0.0012	0.08
Education, Culture, Radio and Television	- 0.1306 ***	0.0016	0.07
Government Organizations and Social Organizations	- 0.1607 ***	0.0014	0.07

contd.

	Marginal Effect	Standard Error	Average
Other Industries	- 0.0588 ***	0.0011	0.12
Region (Eastern Region=1)			
Central Region	-0.0902 ***	0.0007	0.28
Western Region	-0.0585 ***	0.0009	0.14
Sample Size	468797		
LR chi2 (26)	250000 ***		
Pseudo. R^2	0.3997		

Note: *** , **, * represents significance at levels of 1%, 5% and 10% respectively; standard deviation is in brackets.

V. Conclusion

According to the ILO (2003) statistical definition guide on informal employment, China's informal employment is specifically defined as domestic workers, self-employed workers in informal sectors and household sectors and employers and employees in informal sectors. With sampling survey data of 1% of national population in 2005, the proportion of informal employment in China's urban areas was 58.85%, among which the proportion of migrant workers in informal employment was 70.90%, much higher than that of local urban labor force of 52.78%. Informal employment is characterized by longer working hours, lower income, rarely being able to sign labor contracts, and generally lacking social security. Most informal employees are females and unmarried young migrant labor force and agriculture households with less education. Informal employment is mainly in manufacturing, wholesale and retail and catering, social services and construction, nearly 70% of informal employment being in individual industrial and commercial households and private enterprises.

There is widening income gap between migrant and local workers and between formal and informal employees in Chinese cities. Average monthly income of formal employees is 1.45 times that of informal employees. Hourly income of formal employees is 1.65 times that of informal employees. In terms of income inequality index, Gini coefficient of hourly income for China's urban employees is 0.39, widening income gap. With Theil index decomposition, gap between informal and formal employees, inter-group gap, makes its contribution to overall income inequality of urban employees in China is 13.68%; gap within informal and formal employees, intra-group difference, make their own contribution to overall income inequality: 51.09% and 35.23% respectively. All this indicates that income gap within informal employees is the most important source of income gap among urban employees in China, and income gap between informal employees and formal employees also contributes a lot to overall income inequality.

Regression analysis of Mincer Equation shows that related variables such as education and experience being unchanged, informal employees' income is 25.64% lower than formal employees' income. Blinder-Oaxaca decomposition shows that 73.51% of income gap between informal and formal employees ascribes to such stock factors as low education of informal employees and that 26.49% ascribes to market discrimination against informal employees. Further analysis shows that education is the most important factor affecting income gap between formal and informal employees. Therefore, the most important way to narrow income gap between formal and informal employment is to improve education of informal employees and to diminish market discrimination of informal employment.

Informal employment plays a positive role in employment opportunities, but it has its negative effect. Rights and interests of workers are vulnerable to infringe on and informal employment lacks technological innovation. Both wide income gap between informal and formal employment and discrimination against informal employment goes against social justice and economic development. Therefore, it is necessary to promote employment regularization. Regression analysis of this chapter shows that employment status and human capital of employees have a significant impact on their formal employment. In order to promote employment regularization, it is necessary to raise human capital, such as education, and to eliminate discrimination of labor market against migrant labor and agriculture household workers. In addition, gender, marital status, occupation, industry, unit type and region of employees also have a significant impact on their formal employment. This means that in employment regularization, greater importance should be attached to females and the unmarried, to employees in private enterprises and individual industrial and commercial households, and to key industries such as construction and social services, and central and western regions.

Chapter X

Social Security and Income Distribution

GAO Wenshu[1]

Social security and income distribution concerning national economy and people's livelihood has an enormous impact on social stability and economic development. After years of development, great progress has been made in China's social security system in that a new social security system compatible with market economy has basically been set up including social insurance, social assistance and social welfare. But widening income distribution gap of Chinese residents has raised concern of the whole society. International experience shows that social security system can play an important role in income redistribution as "regulator" of income distribution as well as "safety net" and "stabilizer" of society. Experience of major developed countries shows that social security, the most important means to regulate residents' income distribution, is able to play a much larger role than taxation. Therefore, what role will China's social security play in regulating income distribution and what are the problems with China's society security system?

---

1   GAO Wenshu, Research fellow, Institute of Population and Labor Economy, Chinese Academy of Social Sciences, Doctoral Supervisor.

In order to curb the further widening income gap, great importance should be attached to income redistribution effect of social security. It's time to adopt social security to regulate income distribution gap by further increasing financial input in social security and raising the proportion of social security expenditure in financial expenditure and to improve social security of rural residents by changing city-oriented social security expenditure and increasing national financial input in rural social security.

This chapter includes the following parts: regulation effect of social security on income distribution, impact of social security on residents' income distribution with survey data, empirical study of "inverse regulation" effect of social security on urban-rural income gap, and a summary and policy recommendations.

I. Regulation Effect of Social Security on Income Distribution

(I) Basic Function of Social Security: Income Redistribution

Social security is a system with which a country provides safety and security to basic life of its social members through distribution and redistribution of national income according to law. Its essence is to maintain social equity and promote stability. Generally speaking, social security system includes three components: social assistance, social insurance and social welfare. Social assistance is to help poor people and their families by providing them with the lowest living security. Social insurance, main component of whole social security system, is aimed at the laborer group and provides basic living security for the insured. Social welfare is social care and service for all citizens, aimed at improving their quality of life. China has also included social preferential treatment system, protection of its servicemen and their families, in its social security system. Social security, one of the most important institutional arrangements in social economy, has become social "safety net" and "stabilizer".

Importance has always been attached to the relationship between social security expenditure and income distribution by economic theorists. It is generally believed that social security can greatly improve uneven income distribution. Traditional Keynesianism believes that social security expenditure, an important component of transfer payment, can act on national income through transfer payment multipliers so as to change income pattern and prevent income gap from widening with income transfer and redistribution between different members of society on the part of government. Old school of welfare economy represented by Pigou holds that based on law of diminishing marginal utility, income can be transferred from the rich to the poor with social security system to achieve equalization of income distribution and improve social welfare. New welfare economy represented by Hicks and Samuelson argues that income redistribution through social security can achieve Pareto improvement and improve total social utility (Li Zhi, 2011).

Social security's regulation of residents' income distribution is mainly reflected in raising and issuing social security funds from members of society with income whose expenditure object or beneficiary group is mainly low-income group or disadvantaged group. With higher income and lower risk of poverty or disease, high income group usually needs to make more contribution to raising social security funds though less likely to receive social security funds. On the other hand, low income group tends to contribute less to social security funds but is more likely to be funded by social security system. Therefore, such kind of universal levying and focused payment of social security has made possible residents' income redistribution and narrowing income gap. Since recipients do not have to contribute to social security and as long as they fall victim to poverty, they can get assistance from social security, reflecting income redistribution effect of social security. Income redistribution effect of social security embodies the principle of social equity and forms mechanism of social security system to narrow the gap between rich and poor and to promote equal income distribution, thus social security system being the "regulator" of social income distribution.

Of course, different models of social security system result in different income redistribution mechanism, path, scope and intensity. If the government adopts pay-as-you-go system, social security funds will mainly come from the working population and will go to retired groups, reflecting inter-generational income redistribution. If the government adopts full fund system (that is, according to future needs of social insurance, set up a fund with collected premiums to ensure future payment needs), this horizontal income redistribution is mainly reflected in social security fund transfer from rich households to poor households (Zhao Guizhi & Wang Yanping, 2010).

From specific social security programs, redistribution effect of social assistance is the most direct and obvious. Social assistance is to help the poor in society on the part of the state through financial expenditure, which does not require recipients to bear any obligation to pay. As long as his life is in trouble or his income is below a certain standard, the state has the obligation to provide financial support enabling him to live at subsistence level. Residents' subsistence living security system is typical and vital component of social assistance. Social assistance is, in essence, financial transfer payment funded by tax revenue from both central and local governments through financial allocation, not only directly affecting residents' income distribution but effectively alleviating poverty.

Social welfare does play its role in narrowing income distribution gap. Social welfare is economic subsidy, material assistance and service facilities provided by the state and local governments for specific groups such as the elderly, the disabled, orphans and so on, such as old-age allowance, free compulsory education, welfare home for the elderly and children, and so on. In developed countries, social welfare has become "inclusive" welfare treatment covering all their citizens and welfare projects include education program, medical care program, old-age care program and other developmental security programs. Social welfare funding generally comes mainly from central and local finance and partly from social groups and private donations. Social welfare are distributed solely based on conditions of incapacity to work, loss of dependants, etc., as well as needs of life and development. Main beneficiaries are groups such as the elderly, children and the disabled, catering for weak group and low-income group in resident's income distribution. It is one of the important channels for social security to regulate resident's income distribution.

Social insurance affects income distribution in an indirect and complicated way. Since social insurance is an employment-related insurance, raising and issuing its funds is generally related to payment of wages and years of payment and follows the principle of paying more, getting more and paying less, getting less. Social insurance is individual self-help by nature. When collecting social insurance premiums (or taxes), countries generally emphasize the principle of a combination of both proportional collection of income of the same wage and reasonable burden by prescribing the upper and lower limits of legal collection base so as to protect different interests of high and low income group without affecting enthusiasm of high income people to pay taxes and fees while lightening burden of low-income people. Some countries, such as Sweden, set starting point for members of society to pay social security taxes (or fees), that is, members of society below a certain income level can be exempted from social security taxes (or fees) (Tao Jikun, 2010). Judging from real situations in different countries, low-income workers are often main beneficiaries of social insurance (Zhao Haoran, 2010).

(II) International Experience of the Regulation Effect of Social Security on Income Distribution

After market distribution, initial income distribution, production factor owners get their own income, market income, mainly including wage income and capital income. With sound market mechanism, market distribution is mainly determined by efficiency. In general condition, market distribution is quite unequal. To make sure that residents' income gap does not get too wide, governments will regulate market distribution first through social security income transfer, mainly including social security retirement benefits, medical insurance subsidy, unemployment assistance, work-related injury insurance payment and poverty relief, etc, thus remarkably reducing inequality in market distribution. Total residents' income includes market income and all kinds of transfer income. Another important means for the government to regulate income distribution is taxation, which can narrow income distribution gap through personal income tax and social security tax. Income after social security transfer payment and tax regulation forms disposable or net residents' income. Usually, inequality of disposable or net residents' income is much lower than inequality of market distribution, reflecting regulation effect of social security and taxation on income distribution.

Data show that almost all economies are not equal in market income distribution, 13 in 42 economies in Chart 10-1 having Gini coefficient of market income of over 0.5. Gini coefficient of market income in the rest 29 economies is basically over 0.4 except Switzerland and the Netherlands, whose Gini coefficient is less than but quite close to 0.4. Gini coefficient of market income of Sweden, known for its income equality, is 0.468. This shows that market income inequality is inevitable under market economy. However, after the regulation of social security and taxation, income distribution inequality has greatly improved.

Effective redistribution of 17 economies, mainly Western European and Nordic countries, in Chart 10-1 reduces Gini coefficient of market income by over 35%. After redistribution, Gini coefficient of their disposable income is generally below 0.3. Effective redistribution of 10 economies, mainly southern Europe and Anglo-Saxon countries, have reduced Gini coefficient of market income by 15% to 35% so that Gini coefficient of final income was basically below 0.4 after redistribution. Ineffective redistribution of 15 economies, mainly in Latin America including Hong Kong, China, Singapore and Russia, have reduced Gini coefficient of market income by up to 15%. In Brazil and Chile, taxation and benefits have not brought about any improvement in income inequality (Wang Shaoguang, 2012).

Regulation effect of social security on income distribution is quite effective in developed countries. Studies show that around the 1990s, social security reduced Gini coefficient of Sweden, Germany, and the U. S. by about 40%, 30%, and 10% respectively (Erivk, 1998). Between 1980 and 2000, social security reduced Gini coefficient of Sweden, Germany and the U.S. by 41.14%, 28.33% and 12.44%

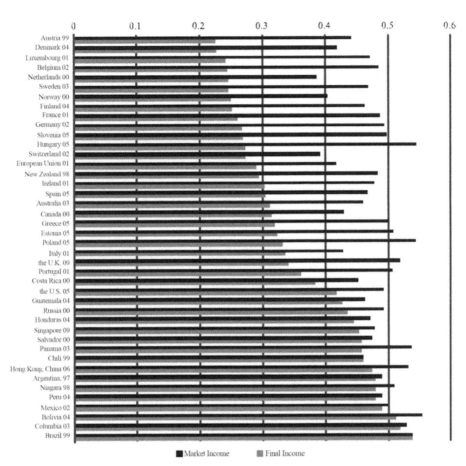

Chart 10-1   Gini Coefficient of Market Income and Final Income of Countries and Regions

Source: Wang Shaoguang, *The Income Inequality in Hongkong*, in Jinjun Xue (ed.) Economic Growth and Income Distribution, Social Sciences Academic Press(China), 2012.

Note: The number after the name of the country in the chart is the year, for instance, "Brazil 99", "Canada 00", and "UK 09" refers to Brazil's data for 1999, Canada's data for 2000, and the United Kingdom's data for 2009 respectively.

respectively (Jesuit & Mahler, 2004). Social security plays a similarly important role in income redistribution in other developed countries (See Table 10-1).

Table 10-1   Regulation Effect of Social Security on Income Distribution in Developed Countries

Nation and Year	Gini coefficient of Market Income	Gini coefficient of Disposable Income	Gini coefficient Reduction due to Social Security	Gini coefficient Reduction due to Social Security (%)
Sweden 1987	0. 47	0. 24	0. 19	39. 49
Sweden 1992	0. 5	0. 25	0. 22	43. 55
Sweden 1980-2000	0. 44	0. 22	0. 18	41. 14
Germany 1984	0. 46	0. 26	0. 14	31. 30
Germany 1989	0. 47	0. 26	0. 14	29. 98
Germany 1980-2000	0. 42	0. 25	0. 12	28. 33
the U.S. 1991	0. 44	0. 35	0. 04	9. 84
the U.S. 1994	0. 46	0. 38	0. 04	7. 98
the U.S. 1980-2000	0. 45	0. 35	0. 06	12. 44
Finland 1987	0. 37	0. 25	0. 07	19. 52
Finland 1991	0. 37	0. 25	0. 08	21. 08
Finland 1980—2000	0. 42	0. 22	0. 15	35. 00
Denmark 1987	0. 45	0. 28	0. 14	30. 34
Denmark 1992	0. 48	0. 26	0. 16	34. 33
Denmark 1980-2000	0. 41	0. 25	0. 13	31. 95
Norway 1986	0. 38	0. 26	0. 08	21. 44
Norway 1991	0. 42	0. 25	0. 13	29. 79
Norway 1980—2000	0. 38	0. 24	0. 11	27. 63
the U.K. 1986	0. 46	0. 3	0. 11	23. 51
the U.K. 1991	0. 47	0. 35	0. 08	17. 95
the U.K. 1980-2000	0. 48	0. 32	0. 12	25. 42

Source: The author collated and calculated the data of Erivk (1998) and Jesuit & Mahler (2004).

International experience shows that social security and taxation are two most important means for governments to regulate income distribution. However, which one has played a bigger role in income distribution regulation, social security or taxation? Many scholars believe that income gap regulation mainly depends on personal income tax, but international experience shows that social security has been playing a far larger role in regulating income distribution gap than taxation (Tao Jikun, 2010). An empirical study by Jesuit & Mahler (2004) of 13 developed countries, including Norway, Sweden, Germany, the U.S. and the U.K., shows that both social security and taxation reduced Gini coefficient by about 40% in these countries between 1980 and 2000, among which contribution of social security to the reduction of Gini coefficient is 74.6% while taxation contributes only 25.4%. Moreover, in all countries, social security contributes more than taxation to narrowing income gap (See Table 10-2), and social security of such countries as France, Sweden and Switzerland contribute more than 80% to narrowing income gap (See Table 10-2). Therefore, it is believed that social security regulation of income distribution is much more effective than taxation, becoming the most effective measure to regulate income distribution gap in developed countries.

Table10-2   Contribution of Social Security and Taxation to Narrowing Income Gap in Developed Countries (1980-2000)

Nation	Gini coefficient of Market Income	Gini coefficient of Disposable Income	Gini coefficient Reduction due to Social Security and Taxation	Contribution of Taxation to Gini coefficient Reduction	Contribution of Social Security to Gini coefficient Reduction (%)
Belgium	0. 47	0. 24	0. 23	28. 0	72. 0
Sweden	0. 44	0. 22	0. 22	17. 5	82. 5
Netherlands	0. 46	0. 26	0. 2	20. 4	79. 6
Finland	0. 42	0. 22	0. 2	24. 9	75. 1
France	0. 47	0. 29	0. 18	12. 0	88. 0
Denmark	0. 41	0. 25	0. 16	21. 2	78. 8
Germany	0. 42	0. 25	0. 17	27. 9	72. 1
the U.K.	0. 48	0. 32	0. 16	20. 7	79. 3
Norway	0. 38	0. 24	0. 14	27. 9	72. 1
Australia	0. 42	0. 30	0. 12	39. 2	60. 8
Canada	0. 41	0. 29	0. 12	33. 0	67. 0
the U.S.	0. 45	0. 35	0. 1	44. 7	55. 3

contd.

Nation	Gini coefficient of Market Income	Gini coefficient of Disposable Income	Gini coefficient Reduction due to Social Security and Taxation	Contribution of Taxation to Gini coefficient Reduction	Contribution of Social Security to Gini coefficient Reduction (%)
Switzerland	0. 40	0. 30	0. 1	12. 4	87. 6
Average	0.43	0.27	0.16	25.4	74.6

Source: Jesuit, D. and V. Mahler (2004), "*State Redistribution in Comparative Perspective: A Cross-National Analysis of the Developed Countries*", Luxembourg Income Study Working Paper, No. 392.

(III) Regulation Effect of China's Social Security on Income Distribution

China's social security system consists of four components: social insurance, social assistance, social welfare and social special treatment. Social assistance mainly provides basic living standards for the poor. Social welfare provides life assistance mainly for the elderly, children and the disabled and other disadvantaged groups. Social special treatment provides material support mainly for servicemen, martyrs and their families. These three kinds of social security schemes are direct financial income transfer so that recipients do not need to bear payment or other obligations as long as they are in poverty or in line with certain conditions. Since recipients are disadvantaged groups, such as the poor and the old and the disabled, effect of these social security schemes on alleviating poverty and narrowing residents' income gap are self-evident.

Regulation effect of social insurance on income distribution is relatively complex. In China's social insurance scheme, work-related injury insurance and child-birth insurance are paid by their units instead of workers themselves. When encountering work-related injury or child-birth condition, workers can enjoy corresponding treatment, reflecting regulation effect of social insurance on income distribution. Workers and their units jointly pay for their medical insurance according to wage. Since medical insurance is paid according to workers' actual medical demand without requiring fixed number of years and contributory amount, its regulation on income redistribution is more effective. Unemployment insurance is paid jointly by both individuals and units mainly according to basic life needs of the unemployed for treatment standard without direct relation to contributory amount. Entitlement duration is related to number of years of contribution. Since higher income and longer employment means less likelihood of unemployment, unemployment insurance benefits tend to be oriented towards low-income, unstable employees. Old-age insurance is based on both individual account and social planning. Fund financing comes from joint payment of individuals and their units. The insured who contribute after a certain number of years and reach retirement age can receive monthly social pension. As pension is mainly determined by contribution of the insured, its regulation effect on income distribution is not effective and further empirical research is needed.

It should be pointed out that old-age insurance and medical insurance in China's social insurance system may give rise to "inverse regulation" in terms of contribution, that is, contribution burden of high-income group is way lighter than that of low-income group because contribution of these social insurance schemes are based on average monthly wage of a worker in the previous year as contribution base for social insurance rather than real wage according to stipulations. However, average monthly wage of a worker in the previous year is three times higher than average wage of local society, which will be contribution base for social insurance. Average monthly wage of a worker is less than 60% of average wage of local society, which will be contribution base for social insurance. This means that those who earn more than three times local average will not have to pay extra social insurance while those who earn less than 60% of local average will have to bear heavier social security burden. In other words, China's current social insurance contribution rate is not progressive but regressive nor of the same proportion.

Take old-age insurance system for example, individual and unit contribute 8% and 20% of approved contribution base respectively. Take for example, a worker in Beijing urban basic old-age insurance, whose average monthly wage in the previous year is 5,000 yuan which is between 60% and 300% of average monthly wage (4,672 yuan) of Beijing's employees in 2012. With his monthly wage as his individual contribution base, contribution rate of the worker and his unit is 8% and 20% respectively. Take for example, a worker whose monthly average wage in the previous year is 20,000 yuan, over 3 times local social average wage, with 3 times 4,672 yuan, 14,106 yuan, as his contribution base, the worker pays 1121.28 yuan, 8% of contribution base, and his unit contributes 2803.20 yuan, 20% of contribution base. Since the worker's real wage is 20,000 yuan, actual contribution rate of this worker in this case is only 5.6% and contribution rate of his unit is only 14.02%. Conversely, if a worker whose average monthly wage in the previous year is only 2,000 yuan, lower than 60% of social average wage (4,672 yuan) in the previous year, his contribution base is not his real wage but 60% of social average wage in the previous year, 2803.20 yuan. Calculation shows that the worker's contribution rate will reach 11.21% and contribution rate of his unit will reach 28.03%. So current old-age insurance is very disadvantageous to low-income people in its design, inverse regulation. The state needs to curb this inverse regulation through social insurance contribution subsidies, reduction and exemption for low-income people.

In addition, significant differences between China's urban and rural social security system will also have an impact on urban-rural income gap. Keeping pace with industrialization, China's urban social security is characterized by its complete security schemes and relatively high level while rural social security lags behind with low level and few security schemes. Current rural social old-age insurance system is advancing with not high coverage rate. New rural cooperative medical insurance and scheme of guaranteeing minimum living standards for rural residents have been established, but security level still needs improvement. Since a considerable amount of social security fund is government's financial fund and if the government invests more funds in urban social security than in rural areas when urban-rural population ratio is basically the same, urban-rural income gap will widen further. Research shows that in rural residents' income source between 1998 and 2007, the proportion of unstable security income from finance in their total income is 3%-5% while the proportion of urban residents' security income from finance is 19%-25%, showing a rising trend (Zhao Guizhi, Wang Yanping, 2010). Studies have compared social security transfer income of urban and rural residents and found that in 2000, 2003, 2005, per capita social security transfer income of urban residents was 10.04 times, 15.45 times and 13.37 times that of rural residents (Tao Jikun 2008). It can be seen that China's current social security payment system is still city-oriented, having a certain "inverse regulation" effect on urban-rural income gap.

Empirical results further confirm that wide urban-rural social security system gap widens China's urban-rural income gap. Yang Cuiying (2004) thinks that there is wide urban-rural social security system gap in China and that instead of redistributing income, current social security system further widens China's urban-rural income gap. Wang Xiaolu and Fan Gang (2005) pointed out that China's social security system and expenditure on education has brought more benefits to upper-middle income group than to low-income group, widening China's urban-rural residents' income gap. In order to narrow the wide urban-rural income gap, Cai Fang (2010) put forward the influence of public policy on income difference and the importance of equal social security policy in narrowing urban-rural income gap in view of Lewis Turning Point.

II. Effect of Social Security on Residents' Income Distribution with Survey Data

(I) Survey Data

The survey conducted in Baoji City, Shaanxi Province in May 2012 with questionnaires was jointly completed by the Institute of Population and Labor Economy of Chinese Academy of Social Sciences and Baoji survey team of the National Bureau of Statistics. In accordance with China's statistical system and random sampling principle, the National Bureau of Statistics selected 100 "accounts" in urban and rural Baoji respectively and carried out annual bookkeeping surveys. In order to ensure that the survey is well-represented, research group first listed designated accounts as survey objects. In order to expand survey sample, research group carries out random sampling of urban and rural communities and then selects households at random in previously selected communities to carry on the survey. In order to fully understand living conditions and policy demands of suffering groups, in addition to random sampling, the research group also included all low-insured community households in the survey with its emphasis on effect of social security on income distribution. Thus the survey covers living information, income and expenditure of a total of 500 Baoji households (300 urban and 200 rural ones), including state accounts.

Final effective questionnaires of this survey cover 842 people in 291 urban households including including 345 low-insured people and 815 people in 198 rural households including 154 low-insured people. Due to over-sampling of urban households and low-insured households: the proportion of urban population (50.81%) of survey sampling is much higher than actual one in Baoji city (26%) and the proportion of urban low-insured population (40.97%) and the proportion of rural low-insured population (18.90%) is also much higher than actual ones (9% and 7%), actual proportion of urban-rural population and actual proportion of low-insured urban-rural households has been weighted respectively so that calculations can better reflect situation of Baoji City.

Weighted calculations of survey data showed that average age of respondents was 40.37 years old, of which 50.68% are males and 49.32% are females. The unmarried and the married accounted for 30.76% and 69.24%; agriculture-registered permanent residents and non-agricultural registered permanent residents account for 69.87% and 30.13%. There are urban-rural differences in demographic features of respondents. Average age of rural respondents was 39.68 years old, lower than that of urban respondents (42.07 years old) and the proportion of the rural unmarried is higher than that of the urban unmarried (See Table 10-3).

Table 10-3   Descriptive Statistical Table of Survey Sample

	Rural Residents	Urban Residents	Total
Gender (%)			
Male	50. 73	50. 54	50.68
Female	49. 27	49. 46	49.32
Average Age (Years Old)	39. 68	42. 07	40.37
Marital Status (%)			
Unmarried	32. 62	26. 16	30.76
Married	67. 38	73. 84	69.24
Household Registration Status (%)			
Agricultural Household Registration	2. 44	98. 13	69.87
Non-agricultural Household Registration	97. 56	1. 87	30.13

Source: The Institute of Population and Labor Economy, Chinese Academy of Social Sciences: *Survey of Social Security and Income Distribution*, May 2012.

In the survey, social security in its broad sense includes four components: social insurance, social assistance, social special treatment and social welfare. Social insurance consists of social old-age insurance, social medical insurance, unemployment insurance, child-birth insurance and work-related injury insurance. Social assistance includes minimum living standards, medical assistance, education assistance, natural disaster relief, housing assistance, temporary hardship assistance. Social special treatment is preferential treatment for special people such as military martyrs and their families. Social welfare consists of old age welfare, child welfare and disabled welfare. It should be pointed out that although employees in public institutions do not participate in social old-age insurance, they enjoy the de facto old-age insurance, that is, retirement pension system and participate in social old-age insurance. Because Baoji city has implemented urban and rural residents' social old-age insurance system, residents' old-age insurance is also regarded as social old-age insurance.

Here, urban and rural residents' income is defined by the National Bureau of Statistics. Total rural household income refers to total income received by rural households and its members from various sources during survey period, which is divided into wage income, household operating income, property income and transfer income according to income nature. Wage income is the income obtained by selling labor to a unit or an individual. Household operating income is the income obtained from production planning and operations by household as production and operation units. Property income is the income that financial assets owners or tangible unproductive assets owners provide funds or tangible unproductive assets to other institutions over which they gain control as a return. Transfer income is ownership of goods, services, funds, assets, etc., obtained by households and their members without paying any counterpart. Net rural household income is equal to total rural household income minus household operating expenses, tax and fee expenses, depreciation of productive fixed assets and gift expenses on rural relatives and friends. Per capita net rural residents' income is average net income of household population. Total urban household income refers to total sum of wage income, operating income, property income and transfer income of household members, not including financial income from sale and loan income. Disposable urban household income is equal to total urban household income minus personal income tax paid by individuals and social security expenditure paid by individuals. Survey shows that per capita disposable urban residents' household income in Baoji City is 19,669.28 yuan and per capita net rural residents' household income was 8,619.56 yuan.

(II) Regulation Effect of Social Security on Residents' Income Distribution

Further analysis is made of the effect of social security on income distribution. As three components of social security except social insurance, social assistance, social special treatment and social welfare don't require payment, income from these social security schemes is entirely transfer income while income from social insurance cannot all be counted as transfer income since social insurance requires recipients to fulfil contribution obligation. Specifically, there are four forms of social old-age insurance, namely, the basic old-age insurance for urban employees, old-age insurance for employees in organs and public institutions, old-age insurance for urban residents, and old-age insurance for rural residents (new rural insurance). Basic old-age insurance reform for urban employees began in 1997, and then began to implement income and expenditure system combining individual accounts with social pooling. Retirees with pension before 1997 haven't made accumulative contribution to pension so that his pension income can be considered entirely as transfer income. Retirees with pension after 1997 contribute to pension as part of their pension income comes from their own past accumulation. Individual contribution proportion of old-age insurance for urban employees and contribution proportion of social pooling is 8% and 20% of his contribution wage respectively so that 28.57% pension income [8%/(8%+20%)] is actually savings from employees' wage in the past and the remaining 71.43% pension income from enterprise contribution and is pooled by the state should be regarded as transfer income as the individual does not pay any of them. Since retirees of government organs and public institutions do not contribute to pension accumulation, the pension they receive can be regarded as transfer income. Only government subsidies of old-age insurance for urban and rural residents implementing full accumulation is regarded as transfer income.

Social medical insurance also adopts methods similar to social old-age insurance. That is, reimbursement income of basic old-age insurance for urban employees' and medical insurance for urban and rural residents after taking away individual contribution will be regarded as transfer income. Income from unemployment insurance is also divided into individual accumulation and transfer income according to the proportion of individual contribution. Child-birth insurance and work-related injury insurance paid by units and pooled by the state instead of employees can be regarded as transfer income.

Calculation shows that social security transfer income is an important source of urban-rural residents' income. The survey shows that per capita social security transfer income for urban-rural residents in Baoji city is 2191.30 yuan, accounting for 17.61% of per capita urban-rural residents' income. Among them, per capita social security transfer income for urban residents is 5001.30 yuan, accounting for 25.43% of per capita disposable urban residents' income. Per capita social security transfer income for rural residents is 702.47 yuan, accounting for 8.15% of per capita net rural residents' income. According to the proportion of social security transfer income for urban-rural residents' income, transfer income of old-age insurance was the highest at 14.50%, followed by medical insurance at 1.83%, then social assistance at 1.05% while the proportion of social welfare and social preferential benefits was quite low at 0.01% and 0.22% respectively.

Social security transfer income not only improves urban and rural residents' income but narrows residents' income gap because of its poverty alleviation and helping the weak. In order to measure regulation of social security transfer income on income distribution, income distribution gap before and after social security income transfer is compared with indexes, including income ratio, Gini coefficient, Theil index and so on, among which Gini coefficient is the most widely used. In this chapter, Gini coefficient is mainly used as index to measure income distribution gap. Both Gini coefficient without social security transfer income and with social security transfer income is calculated. Change in Gini coefficient without and with social security transfer income, actual regulation of social security transfer income on income distribution is calculated, that is, decline amount of Gini coefficient by social security transfer income=Gini coefficient without social security transfer income - Gini coefficient with social security transfer income.

Calculation of survey data indicates that Gini coefficient of per capita urban-rural residents' income without social security transfer income in Baoji City will be 0.44, among which that of urban residents and that of rural residents was 0.43 and 0.40. Gini coefficient of per capita urban-rural residents' income with social security transfer income in Baoji City fell to 0.42, among which that of urban residents fell sharply to 0.34 and that of rural residents fell slightly to 0.39. That is to say, urban-rural residents' income gap has been reduced by 2 Gini points with regulation of social security transfer income, among which urban residents' income gap fell by 9 Gini points and rural residents' income gap fell by 1 Gini (See

Table 10-7). It can be seen that social security transfer income plays an important role in narrowing income distribution gap, especially urban residents' income gap.

Table 10-7 Effect of Social Security Transfer Income (SSTI) on Residents' Income Distribution (Gini coefficient)

	Gini coefficient without SSTI	Gini coefficient with SSTI	Gini coefficient Reduction due to SSTI	Gini coefficient Reduction due to SSTI (%)
Urban Area	0. 43	0. 34	0. 09	22. 76
Rural Area	0. 40	0. 39	0. 01	1. 82
Total	0. 44	0. 42	0. 02	4. 53

Source: The Institute of Population and Labor economy, Chinese Academy of Social Sciences, *Survey of Social Security and Income Distribution*, May, 2012.

Results of measuring income gap with Theil index are similar to those with Gini coefficient. Theil index of per capita urban and rural residents' income without social security transfer income and with social security transfer income in Baoji City will be 0.36 and 0.32 respectively, which shows that social security transfer income has caused Theil index of urban residents to fall by 10.95%. Further calculations show that social security transfer has caused Theil index of urban residents to decline by 39.21% and that of rural residents to decline by 2.78% (See Table 10-8). This further confirms the effect of social security transfer income on narrowing urban-rural income distribution gap, especially on narrowing that of urban residents'.

Table 10-8 Effect of Social Security Transfer Income (SSTI) on Residents' Income (Theil Index)

	Theil Index without SSTI	Theil Index with SSTI	Theil Index Reduction due to SSTI	Theil Index Reduction due to SSTI (%)
Urban Area	0. 36	0. 22	0. 14	39. 21
Rural Area	0. 27	0. 26	0. 01	2. 78
Total	0. 36	0. 32	0. 04	10. 95

Source: The Institute of Population and Labor economy, Chinese Academy of Social Sciences, *Survey of Social Security and Income Distribution*, May, 2012.

III. "Inverse Regulation" Effect of Social Security on Urban-rural Income Gap

Although social security has played a role in narrowing income gap of all residents, it should not be ignored that China's current social security system is still urban-oriented under the influence of long-term planned economy. Urban social security system with wide coverage and good social security has long been established while rural social security system has only been established with low social security. According to data, per capita annual urban residents' social security transfer income in Baoji City has reached 5001.30 yuan, more than 7 times that of rural residents with only 702.47 yuan. Moreover, there is a wide urban-rural gap in all components of social security transfer income (See Chart 10-3).

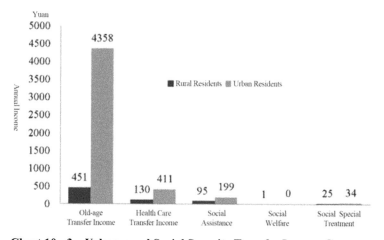

Chart 10 - 3   Urban-rural Social Security Transfer Income Gap

Source: The Institute of Population and Labor Economy, Chinese Academy of Social Sciences, *Survey of Social Security and Income Distribution*, May, 2012.

Wide urban-rural social security gap will inevitably have a negative impact on the already wide urban-rural income gap. Calculation shows that without social security transfer income, per capita urban residents' income is 14,668 yuan and per capita rural residents' income is 7,917 yuan; with social security transfer income, per capita urban residents' income increased to 19,669 yuan and per capita rural residents' income increased to 8,620 yuan. In other words, social security transfer income has caused urban and rural income ratio to increase from 1.85 to 2.28, up by 23.17% (See Chart 10-4). Obviously, current social security has an "inverse regulation" effect on urban-rural income gap.

As Theil index can be decomposed into intra-group and inter-group income gap, changes in contribution of urban-rural income gap to the whole income gap with and without social security transfer income enables us to further understand impact of social security transfer income on urban-rural income gap. Decomposition results of Theil index show that without social security income transfer, inter-group contribution, that is, urban-rural income gap, to the whole income gap is 18.75%. With social security transfer income, inter-group contribution to the whole income gap reached 21.88% (See Table 10-9). It can be seen that social security transfer income has enabled urban-rural income gap to have a greater effect on the whole income gap.

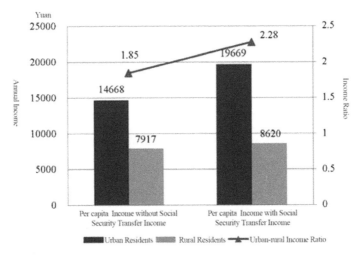

Chart 10 - 4   Effect of Social Security Transfer Income on Urban-rural Gap

Source: The Institute of Population and Labor Economy, Chinese Academy of Social Sciences, *Survey of Social Security and Income Distribution*, May, 2012.

Table 10 - 9   Decomposition of Theil Index of Residents' Income with and without Social Security Transfer Income(%)

	Without SSTI		With SSTI	
	Intra-group Contribution	Inter-group Contribution	Intra-group Contribution	Inter-group Contribution
Urban Area	25.00	18.75	17.19	21.88
Rural Area	56.25		60.94	

Source: The Institute of Population and Labor Economy, Chinese Academy of Social Sciences, *Survey of Social Security and Income Distribution*, May, 2012.

IV. Conclusion and Suggestions

Social security system plays an important role in income redistribution as "safety net", "stabilizer" of society and "regulator" of income distribution. A survey of Baoji City shows that social security system especially old-age insurance and medical insurance can cover both urban and rural residents very well with a participation rate of over 90% and that minimum living security system has helped about 8% of its population. Social security transfer income has accounted for 17.61% of urban-rural residents' income. Social security plays a very important role in residents' income growth and residents' life protection, especially basic life of poor groups.

Social security transfer income not only improves residents' income but narrows income distribution gap. Our survey data show that social security transfer income has caused Gini coefficient of urban-rural residents' income to reduce by 2 Gini points, of which income gap of urban residents is reduced by 9 Gini points and income gap of rural residents is reduced by 1 Gini point. Social security transfer income has caused Theil index of urban-rural residents' income to reduce by 10.95%, of which income gap of urban residents is reduced by 39.21% and income gap of rural residents is reduced by 2.78%.

But it can not be ignored that there is a wide social security transfer income gap between urban residents and rural residents. The survey shows that per capita social security transfer income for urban residents is more than 7 times that of rural residents, and there is a big gap between rural residents and urban residents in all schemes of social security transfer income, further widening the already huge urban-rural income gap. Calculation shows that social security transfer income has caused income ratio of urban and rural areas to grow from 1.85 to 2.28, up 23.17%. Decomposition of Theil index shows that with social security transfer income, contribution of urban-rural income gap to overall residents' income gap has increased from 18.75% to 21.88% with a greater effect of urban-rural income gap on overall residents' income.

Current income gap in China is already wide. In order to curb further widening income gap, first of all, social security should be regarded as the most important means to regulate the income distribution gap. International experience shows that social security has the greatest regulation on income distribution, greater than that of taxation. For a long time, China's regulation of income distribution gap mainly depends on personal income tax and other taxes. Practice has proved that taxation does play an important role in regulating income distribution gap, but drawing lessons from international experience, great importance should be attached to effect of social security on income redistribution by gradually adopting social security to regulate income distribution. Second, social security should be offered more financial input and the proportion of social security expenditure in financial expenditure should be raised because as responsibility of the government, social security, especially social assistance, social preferential treatment and social welfare, must be supported by national finance through financial budget to meet the needs of people in need, and social insurance also needs government financial support and input. Just over 12% of China's public finance are spent on social security, as are data from some well-developed provinces, indicating that there is inadequate public finance and inadequate responsibility of the government to protect people's livelihood (Zheng Gongcheng, 2010). China should increase its financial input in social security, perfect social security system, expand the coverage of social security as soon as possible, improve treatment and focus on the disadvantaged groups such as the elderly, the disabled, widows and widowers, and other low-income groups. From the experience of Sweden, Germany and the U. S. and other countries, the higher proportion of social security expenditure in financial expenditure, the more effective it is to narrow income distribution gap (Tao Jikun, 2010). Due to unreasonable structure of financial expenditure with low proportion of expenditure in social security such as inadequate subsidies and assistance to low-income groups in China, social security can not play an effective role in regulating income distribution gap.

Third, urban-oriented social security expenditure should be reversed so as to curb "inverse regulation" effect of social security expenditure on urban-rural income gap. Inverse regulation of China's social security on urban-rural income gap is mainly due to urban-oriented social security expenditure. It's time to consider defects of current social security system, attach more importance to construction of rural social security system so as to set up a perfect rural social security system as soon as possible by increasing the state's financial input in rural social security and upgrading rural residents' social security. At present, the following aspects should be attached great importance to: first, try our best to improve guarantee of subsistence allowances for rural residents; second, with new rural cooperative medical insurance system having basically achieved full coverage, further increase financial subsidy and improve insurance treatment; Third, increase subsidies of new rural insurance and raise basic pension subsidies.

Chapter XI

Harmonious Labor Relations and Reasonable Wage Growth

QU Xiaobo, WANG Meiyan[1]

I. Wage Formation and Determination Mechanism: International Experience

(I) Wage Formation and Determination Mechanism

i. Main Determinants of Wage Formation Mechanism

Wage formation and determination mechanism in most developed European countries is a relatively complex process that takes into consideration a series of macro factors: labor productivity, enterprise budgets, inflation rates, economic growth, unemployment and employment rate, labor market supply and demand

1 QU Xiaobo, Associate Research Fellow of the Institute of Population and Labor Economics of the Chinese Academy of Social Sciences, Researcher, Doctoral Advisor; CHENG Jie, Research Fellow of the Institute of Population and Labor Economics of the Chinese Academy of Social Sciences; WANG Meiyan, Research Fellow of the Institute of Population and Labor Economics of the Chinese Academy of Social Sciences, Doctoral Advisor.

and healthy economic operations. A small number of countries maintain "index-linked" wage determination mechanism to ensure that they are protected from excessive inflation. Belgium, for example, as a minority in Western Europe, maintains broad automatic "index-linked" wage determination mechanism where wage determination and social insurance profits is linked to consumer price index. In Malta, workers' wage must include a living cost allowance based on inflation rate over the previous year.

Wage formation mechanism in various countries is characterized by universal trend of wage determination decentralization and wage determination system reform through government legislation and administrative regulations. For example, Australia has changed from a centralized determination mechanism with *The National Wage Regulations* to an enterprise bargaining framework with *The Industrial Relations Reform Act* implemented in 1993, the first major symbol of the shift from wage determination to decentralization. *Workplace Relations Act* in 1996 decentralized trade unions, making it easier for workers to form enterprise trade unions. *Australian Workplace Agreements*, an employment contract between the employer and employees, was introduced to create greater flexibility in regulating work and remuneration payment. *Certified Agreements*, a collective agreement on wage and employment, involves employment agreements between employers and bargaining enterprises with trade unions so as to ensure real wage growth and better working conditions with productivity growth. Wage determination framework in the U.S. is also marked by its government labor acts (Zenglein, 2007).

The vast majority of European countries have a wage formation mechanism of collective bargaining between the employer and employee representatives. Despite differences in levels and level of collective bargaining, collective bargaining mechanism coverage in most European countries has reached 80% to 90%, Germany and the U.K. having lower coverage rates of 61% to 70% and 31% to 40% respectively. Collective bargaining wage formation mechanism occurs at different levels. Sector collective bargaining wage determination mechanism plays a major role in Australia, Denmark, Germany, Italy, the Netherlands, Norway, Portugal, Slovenia, Serbia. In Sweden, most corporate wage bargaining determination mechanism takes place under sectoral framework agreements. Collective bargaining mechanism is based on legislation in Ireland where voluntary collective bargaining mixes with industrial relations legislation. Wage determination is structural and wage determination at different levels is interlinked. In Belgium, national collective bargaining is aimed at setting a framework for collective bargaining at sub-level: sectoral level and corporate level. In Ireland, *National Income Policy Agreement* requires corporate collective bargaining to be within its framework. In Spain, sectoral collective bargaining and corporate one within framework of annual national remuneration growth standard has been implemented since 2002, attaching importance to wage moderation in line with real wage criteria.

Unlike European countries, wage determination mechanism in the U.S is shown in Chart 11-1 (Gernigo net et al., 2000). Wage determination system of unionized and non-unionized systems of the U.S. is a combination of legislative, economic and cultural factors, non-unionized wage determination being the major part determining wage of more than 90% of the private sector and 60% of the public sector. The government makes labor market work through legislation with most significant influence on labor market system. Direct government legislation has had an important impact on working conditions in labor market in wage determination framework with federal laws and state laws affecting collective bargaining and wage determination. Considering economic, cultural and political influence, the U.S. has created non-unionized wage determination mechanism with its three core components: wage information, economic information and human resource information.

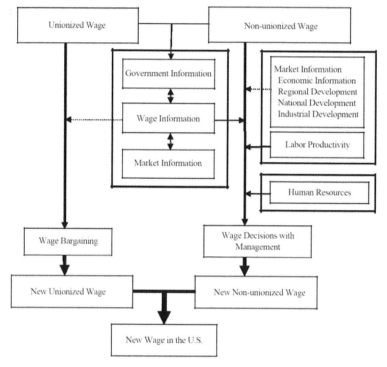

Chart 11-1   Wage Determination Mechanism in the U.S.

ii. Role of Government in Wage Formation and Determination Mechanism

There are significant differences in wage formation between public and private sectors in many countries. Among them, wage formation of private sectors is dominated by collective bargaining, government playing no general role while wage remuneration of the public sector is bargained by many parties with their government making the final decision. In Australia, social groups are also involved in public sector remuneration bargaining but are excluded from formal bargaining. The same is true of the U.K. where public sector remuneration growth is left to the government to decide independently whether or not to adopt or implement. Although more flexible mechanism has been introduced into its public sector wage determination over the past decade, traditional highly-centralized mechanism still dominates in Denmark. In non-union wage determination mechanism of the U.S., the government plays its role in determining low wage and indirect regional wage with contract and subcontract in a certain way, its influence being limited to the nation. Governments in some countries interferes in wage growth if average aggregate wage growth results in a sharp rise in unit labor costs or a decline in enterprise external competitiveness. Governments in other countries such as France, Germany and Portugal sometimes play a role in expanding collective agreements between employers and employees in sectors/industries where wage agreements are not agreed.

Macroeconomic outcomes of collective bargaining wage determination mechanism are difficult to separate from other economic performance determinants. Research literature shows that wage collective bargaining wage determination system, an endogenous variable in the economic, legal and political environment of a country, whose different effect on macroeconomic performance is determined by economic, legal and political environment in period of occurrence and implementation of collective bargaining system (Aidt & Tzannatos, 2002).

(II) Wage Determination and Labor Productivity

In developed European countries and the U.S., labor productivity is not only an important determinant of wage formation mechanism but an important economic indicator which should be taken into account and referred to in most countries' wage determination mechanism, that is, wage determination and growth trend won't have a negative impact on labor productivity. The new wage formation mechanism driven by market forces in the U.S. is highly dependent on wage information provided by the government and workers' labor productivity. Employers take advantage of labor productivity and inflation information to adjust wages to reach agreement with their employees.

Wage development trend of pay moderation in EU countries can be understood as keeping real wage growth below labor productivity growth. In the 27 EU countries, labor productivity grew by 20.3% between 1995 and 2007 and real wages grew by only 13.9%. In countries that have joined the euro zone in particular, there has been more wage moderation with labor productivity rising by 16.9% and real wages rising by only 6.8% over the same period (Keune, 2008). Typical countries of macro wage moderation such as Ireland and Slovenia improve their competitiveness through more modest wage growth compatible with labor productivity. Wage growth in Cyprus is estimated to have been significantly lower than productivity growth over the past decade. In Luxembourg, Tripartite Consultative Council agreed in April 2006 that wage policies must reflect labor productivity of national economy and that Confederation of Luxembourg Enterprise, Luxembourg's main employers' organization, was convinced of the need to modernize automatic wage growth mechanism to ensure that labor productivity is not adversely affected. Australian trade unions and industries have been committed to the principle that current wage standard is calculated based on labor productivity and inflation rate.

Wage of dynamic, innovative and fast-growing sectors driven by modern science and technology, such as IT sector represented by information technology, characterized by high wage and high labor productivity, is not determined by sectoral collective bargaining nor the government. Labor productivity has become the main basis and determinant of wage bargaining at corporate level or between individuals and employer.

A transnational study conducted by the World Bank (The World Bank, 2011) with enterprise and household data shows that productivity linked wage system can potentially increase labor productivity, enables wage growth to keep pace with labor productivity and have positive macroeconomic effect while helping workers to earn money. As a result, firms facing tougher trade environment and skilled workers shortage are more likely to adopt productivity linked wage system.

(III) Role of Trade Unions in Wage Determination

Among the five core labor standards defined by the International Labor Organization (ILO), both freedom of assembly, workers' right to form trade unions out of their own choice, and right of representatives of trade unions and employers' organizations for both wage and working conditions bargaining are two core standards.　Trade unions and trade union organizations undoubtedly play a key role in wage formation and determination mechanism in most European countries where collective bargaining is practised. However, as "collective bargaining" mechanism plays a different role in wage formation and determination in different countries, national, sectoral and corporate trade unions play their different roles. If collective bargaining system works at national level, trade union representatives at national level are important participants, such as Finland and Ireland, where wage determination system is widely attended by tripartite representatives at the national level. In Australia, Germany and the U.K., national trade union representatives are not involved in wage bargaining. If collective bargaining mechanism is mainly based on sectors, sectoral trade unions are important participants in collective bargaining. If "collective bargaining" mechanism mainly occurs at corporate level, employee representatives or trade unions at corporate level are important participants, such as in the U. K., Cyprus, Malta and other countries.

Decline of Trade unions is an important factor for EU to develop wage moderation. In many countries, trade union membership has continued to decline from one-third of European workers to one-fourth between 1994 and 2004. Membership in Australia, Germany, Portugal, Finland and Greece fell by 20% to 30%, with new EU member states falling even more by 50% and with increasingly dramatic membership in the public sector. General decline in trade union membership has led to decline in trade union influence on wage system development, especially in Baltic countries such as Germany, Hungary and the U.K. with low collective bargaining coverage.

Trade unions in most countries do not play a significant role in IT sector wage determination and in setting its wage either at sectoral level or corporate level, but there are exceptions, IT sector wage determination in Sweden is collectively bargained by employers and trade union representatives from IT sector. Collective bargaining of Denmark covers about 60% of workers' wage determination in hardware production sector while collective bargaining coverage is low in software and IT service sectors with weaker trade unions. In addition, unions in

Latvia have an influence on wage determination of state-owned IT sector where unionized social dialogue often takes place in wage bargaining of state-owned telecommunications enterprises.

Although there are major differences in levels and level of collective bargaining wage determination, there is a common feature that trade unions play their role in wage collective bargaining only in the private sector instead of the public sector.

II. Labor Market System Related to Wage Growth: Wage Guidance Price System

With China's labor market development, labor wage and labor supply and demand is increasingly closely related. In 1999, the Ministry of Labor and Social Security issued *The Notice on Establishment of Wage Guidance Price System in Labor Market*, marking preliminary establishment of wage guidance price system in China's Labor Market .

Establishment of labor market wage guidance price system makes it possible for the government labor wage administrative department to make the best of labor market price signal to guide enterprises in carrying out reasonable wage distribution. By introducing market mechanism into their internal distribution, enterprises can reasonably determine wages and wage relations of all personnel, providing important basis for wage collective bargaining; making it possible to promote reasonable price formation in labor market; making it possible to improve workers seeking successful employment and efficiency of labor market operation by providing objective market reference for both labor supply and demand to bargain and determine wage and reducing blindness of labor supply and demand; making it possible to construct a complete labor market system by guiding rational and orderly labor flow, adjusting employment structure between regions and industries and by combining labor price mechanism with labor supply and demand mechanism.

The Notice on Establishment of Wage Guidance Price system in Labor Market stipulates that in accordance with national unified norms and system requirements, administrative departments of labor security shall regularly investigate, analyze, aggregate, process, form and release to public wage prices for different occupations (jobs) in all enterprises so as to guide enterprises for reasonable wage determination and wage relationship and labor market price adjustment.

According to *The Notice on Establishment of Wage Guidance Price System In Labor Market*, wage guidance price in labor market should be determined based on scientific collection and analysis of relevant data with high, median and low digits determined according to *wage price survey method* so as to ensure that wage guidance prices are comparable among different regions. Wage guidance prices should be issued in public employment agencies annually before end of June and be put into computer for enterprises, workers and other people in need for inquiries through labor market information network if possible.

With years of development, wage guidance price system in labor market has made great progress as it covers Beijing, Shanghai and other large and medium-sized cities and gradually goes to small and medium-sized cities. There has been an increasing number of cities and positions for wage guidance price system year by year.

III. Labor Market System Related to Wage Growth: Minimum Wage System

Minimum wage is minimum labor remuneration employers shall pay by law to their employees who provide normal labor within statutory working hours or working hours stipulated in labor contracts signed by law. Some early industrialized countries have already introduced minimum wage system, such as the United States which introduced federal minimum wage in *Fair Labor Standards Act* in 1938. At present, most countries in the world have currently implemented minimum wage system. In 1993, China's Ministry of Labor issued *Minimum Wage Regulations for Enterprises* and began to establish minimum wage system. *Labor Law* of 1994 clearly shows that China implements minimum wage system legally. In 2004, the Ministry of Labor and Social Security promulgated *Minimum Wage Regulations* which promoted full implementation of minimum wage system in China.

Chapter V of *Labor Law of 1994* dealing with wage provisions contains minimum wage, which states "the State implements minimum wage system. Specific minimum wage shall be prescribed by the people's governments of provinces, autonomous regions and municipalities directly under Central Government and reported to the State Council for the record. Wages that unit employers pay their workers must not be lower than local minimum wage. The following factors shall be taken into account in determining and adjusting minimum wage standards: (1) minimum living expenses of the worker himself and his average supporting population; (2) average social wage; (3) labor productivity; and (4) employment; (5) regional economic development differences". It can be seen that *Labor Law* of 1994 containing minimum wage is relatively simple and not very specific.

The introduction of *The Minimum Wage Regulations* in January 2004 marks the implementation of minimum wage system across China. Definition, classification and application scope, and determination and adjustment of minimum wage are detailed, specific and operable in *The Minimum Wage Regulations*. *The Minimum Wage Regulations* points out that minimum wage "means that when the laborer provides normal labor within statutory working hours or working hours stipulated in labor contracts signed in accordance with the law, employers shall pay in accordance with law minimum labor remuneration". Minimum wage generally takes the form of monthly minimum wage and hourly minimum wage, the former applying to full-time employees and the latter applying to non-full-time employees.

Many developed countries adopt national minimum wage, each region making adjustment according to its own social and economic development. *The Minimum Wage Regulations* do not clearly set national standard, but in Article 6 it states: "different administrative regions within provinces, autonomous regions, and municipalities directly under the Central Government may have different minimum wage". *The Regulations* also provides minimum wage adjustment according to local social and economic changes and "minimum wage should be adjusted at least once every two years".

In international experience, minimum wage system mainly involves three aspects: first, labor force covered by minimum wage system; second, setting and adjusting minimum wage; third, monitor and supervision of implementation of minimum wage system.

(I) Labor Force Covered by Minimum Wage System

As *The Minimum Wage Regulations* point out, "these regulations apply to employees who have labor relations with enterprises and private non-enterprise units, and individual industrial and commercial households as well as laborers who have labor contracts with government departments and institutions, social organizations in the People's Republic of China". In other words, minimum wage regulations apply to all employers and workers, that is, all employers and workers must abide by minimum wage system.

Minimum wage system of many countries do not cover the disabled on the grounds that some enterprises actually employ the disabled for humanitarian reasons. Assuming that average productivity of the disabled is generally lower than that of persons with normal working capacity, including the disabled in minimum wage system is unfair to enterprises employing the disabled. Some countries choose to include the disabled in their minimum wage system, but the government will subsidize wage of the disabled to reduce enterprise costs.

As *The Law for Protection of Persons with Disabilities of the People's Republic of China* stipulates, "the state shall, in accordance with law, grant tax preferences and support in production, operation, technology, funds, materials, venues, etc to employer units who have reached, exceeded the proportion of employing persons with disabilities or who have systematically employed persons with disabilities and to persons with disabilities engaged in self-employment". Tax preferences mainly includes preferential policies of VAT, business tax, enterprise income tax and personal income tax. However, employers who enjoy these tax preferences must meet a number of requirements, one of which is that they must pay persons with disabilities no less than local minimum wage.

(II) Setting and Adjusting Minimum Wage

i. Components of Minimum Wage

Minimum wage components are usually very detailed in developed countries. *The National Minimum Wage Regulations 1999* of the U.K. provides strict and detailed rules on wage range for minimum wage (Xie Zengyi, 2008). According to China's *Minimum Wage Regulations*, "As long as laborers provide normal work, wage paid by the employer to laborers shall not be lower than local minimum wage after excluding the following items: First, wage for extended working hours; second, subsidies for such hard working conditions as middle shifts, night shifts, high-temperature, low-temperature, underground, poisonous and harmful environment; third, welfare and preferential treatment for workers stipulated by law, regulations and the state". Clearly, there is lack of clarification and specification as to which components should be included in minimum wage.

For example, individual laborers' social insurance premiums and housing provident funds are usually withheld from workers' wage. There is no provision in *Minimum Wage Regulations* as to whether this component should be included in wage. Regulations vary from city to city. In Beijing and Shanghai, social insurance premiums and housing provident fund paid by individual workers is not minimum wage component as employer units should pay on their own according to regulations. In contrast, Tianjin City stipulates that various social insurance premiums and housing provident funds paid by individual workers is minimum wage component. Nanjing City stipulates that housing provident funds is not minimum wage component while social insurance premiums that individual workers pay is minimum wage component. Urumqi City announces minimum wage both with and without social insurance premiums and housing provident funds paid by individual workers. Whether social insurance premiums and housing provident funds paid by individual workers is minimum wage component or not is not clearly defined in many cities, adding much difficulty to implementation and supervision of minimum wage system and making it impossible to compare minimum wages across cities.

ii. Monthly Wage or Hourly Wage

In many developed countries, such as the U.K., the U.S. and Canada, minimum wage comes in hourly minimum wage. In the U.K., minimum wage is calculated by the hour and there are strict rules on the calculation of working hours in its minimum wage regulations (Xie Zengyi, 2008).

According to China's *Minimum Wage Regulations*, "minimum wage generally comes in both monthly minimum wage and hourly minimum wage, the former applying to full-time employees while the latter applying to part-time employees". Although *Minimum Wage Regulations* clearly defines hourly minimum wage and conversion between monthly minimum wage and hourly minimum wage, there are still difficulty in its implementation. For example, adoption of monthly minimum wage makes it possible for employers' to "abuse regulations" because employers may extend working hours of their employees to meet minimum wage requirement. This way, employers seem to pay workers higher wage but employees work for extended hours. In recent years, some cities set both monthly minimum wage and hourly minimum wage for full-time workers, but most cities only set monthly minimum wage.

Minimum wage coverage of migrant and local urban workers is analyzed based on data from three rounds of China Urban Labor Survey(CULS). Sampling cities, Shanghai, Wuhan, Shenyang, Fuzhou and Xi'an, have so far published only monthly minimum wages for full-time workers. Table 11-1 shows average monthly wage and minimum wage coverage of migrant and urban local workers. Minimum wage coverage of both migrant and local urban workers decreased in 2005 compared with 2001 but increased significantly, reaching nearly 97% by 2010.

Table 11-1 Minimum Wage Coverage in Five Cities: Migrant Workers;

Local Urban Workers

	Migrant Labor		Local Urban Labor	
	Monthly Wage (yuan)	Monthly Minimum Wage Coverage (%)	Monthly Wage (yuan)	Monthly Minimum Wage Coverage (%)
CULS2001				
Male	1007	89. 9	1072	93. 9
Female	775	86. 8	815	88. 1
Total	921	88. 8	963	91. 5
CULS2005				
Male	1140	88.6	1282	88. 9
Female	879	79.1	963	80. 0
Total	1022	84.4	1144	85. 0
CULS2010				
Male	2483	97.7	2564	97. 2
Female	1860	96.7	1953	97. 0
Total	2195	97.2	2303	97. 1

Note: (1) Monthly minimum wage coverage is the proportion of workers whose monthly wage is higher than monthly minimum wage to all workers. (2) Five cities of Shanghai, Wuhan, Shenyang, Fuzhou and Xi'an are calculated in the table.

Source: The author calculated according to CULS2001, CULS2005 and CULS2010.

In 2001, minimum wage coverage of migrant workers was lower than that of local urban workers for both male and female. In 2005 and 2010, minimum wage coverage of migrant and local urban workers became roughly the same. By 2010, minimum wage system has covered vast majority of migrant and local urban workers. In CULS2010, Guangzhou has been added to our sampling city. Guangzhou happens to be a city where both monthly minimum wage and hourly minimum wage are announced for full-time workers. In Guangzhou, vast majority of labor wage is generally higher than monthly minimum wage and hourly minimum wage. In other words, Guangzhou's employers implement minimum wage system. Hourly minimum wage coverage is lower than monthly minimum wage coverage for both migrant and local urban workers. For female migrant workers in particular, hourly minimum wage coverage is lower than monthly minimum wage coverage by nearly 10% (See Table 11-2). This suggests that some workers receiving monthly minimum wage may be paid less than hourly minimum wage because they work longer hours. Therefore, it's quite necessary to implement hourly minimum wage. Changing monthly minimum wage to hourly one would help eliminate discrimination against female workers. Implementation of hourly minimum wage does not mean that all remuneration is calculated based on number of working hours but that when measuring whether wage exceeds minimum wage, working hours should be taken into account in hourly wage calculation.

Table 11-2   Minimum Wage Coverage in Guangzhou: Migrant Labor and Local Urban Labor

	Migrant Labor				Local Urban Labor			
	Monthly Wage (yuan)	Monthly Minimum Wage Coverage (%)	Hourly Wage (yuan)	Hourly Minimum Wage Coverage (%)	Monthly Wage (yuan)	Monthly Minimum Wage Coverage (%)	Hourly Wage (yuan)	Hourly Minimum Wage Coverage (%)
CULS2010								
Male	4801	99.0	22. 2	97. 0	4487	98. 0	23. 4	94. 5
Female	3185	98.9	14. 7	89. 5	3051	97. 1	16. 4	94. 7
Total	4063	98.9	18. 8	93. 5	3819	97. 6	20. 2	94. 6

Source: The author calculated according to CULS2010.

iii. Determining and Adjusting Factors of Minimum Wage

According to *The Minimum Wage Regulations*, China does not have national minimum wage as administrations in provinces, autonomous regions and municipalities directly under the Central Government may have their own minimum wages. In determining minimum wage, the following factors are to be taken into account: minimum living cost of local employees and their dependent population, urban residents' consumer price index, both social insurance premiums and housing provident funds paid by individual workers, average employees' wage, economic development and employment conditions, etc. Widely-used minimum wage determination method is gravity method or Engel coefficient method by first calculating monthly minimum wage and then revising it by considering social insurance premiums and housing provident funds that workers pay, average employees' wage, social assistance and unemployment insurance premiums, employment condition and economic development, etc.

Du Yang, Wang Meiyan (2008) adopted regression model to study minimum wage and its determinants. Studies found that the highest elasticity of minimum wage to average wage is 0.43, and that elasticity of minimum wage to per capita consumption is 0.19, the second most important factor in minimum wage determination, and that elasticity of minimum wage to GDP per capita is relatively low at 0.06 because impact of economic development on minimum wage determination is largely reflected by two variables: average wage and per capita consumption. Urban consumer price index is also a factor in minimum wage determination with little elasticity.

According to estimates from research model, relatively low minimum wage is in those regions with relatively low wage, consumption, economic development and price levels. Some international organizations (such as the World Bank) suggest that productivity, producer price, competitiveness, informal economy scale, GDP growth and unemployment should be taken into account in minimum wage determination instead of income inequality and living cost (consumer prices). As most economists acknowledge, minimum wage is not a tool for poverty alleviation and purchasing power enhancement. Main purpose of minimum wage is to solve the problem of giving employers excessive bargaining chips in wage determination in labor market.

Determining higher minimum wage based on living cost could lead to job losses and more poverty in a region with low productivity, high living cost and extreme poverty.

In addition to identifying the necessary indicators, availability and reliability of these data is also crucial for minimum wage determination in china. If data are unavailable or unreliable, there will be inappropriate minimum wage determination. Productivity is an important factor in minimum wage determination, as is suggested by international organizations, but it may not be easy for local governments to have their local productivity calculated accurately. These problems need to be continuously explored and solved in practice.

According to the World Bank's proposal, ideal model is that minimum wage adjustment is made on its own at a predetermined level and then systematically based on a reliable model. But such models can sometimes be too rigid. When faced with economic crisis, minimum wage adjustment based on the original model may result in massive employment loss since data usually lag behind. It is necessary for policymakers to know whether minimum wage is adjusted on time based on real economic situation.

According to *The Minimum Wage Regulations*, China's minimum wage has been adjusted at least once every two years. Since 1995, the proportion of prefectural cities adjusting minimum wage has shown a relatively stable upward trend (See Chart 11-2). In 2006, 88% of cities raised their minimum wage. In 2008, 70% of cities raised their minimum wage. Financial crisis in 2008 hit China's economy to a certain extent, and in 2009 all 287 prefectural cities did not adjust minimum wage. In 2010, almost all cities (except Chongqing) raised their minimum wage. In 2011 and 2012, more than three in four prefectures adjusted minimum wage.

Both nominal and real minimum wage have shown a remarkable improvement (See Chart 11-3): average nominal minimum wage rose from 195 yuan per month in 1995 to 1,018 yuan in 2012, and average real minimum wage rose from 195 yuan per month in 1995 to 630 yuan in 2011. Growth rate of minimum wage is divided into two stages. Before 2004, growth rate of minimum wage and minimum wage growth is relatively slow; after 2004, it accelerates remarkably.

In region, average minimum wage in eastern, central and western prefectures is on the rise (See Chart 11-4). Average minimum wage in eastern region, central region and western region grew from 225 yuan per month in 1995 to 1,104 yuan in 2012; from 177 yuan per month to 978 yuan; and from 173 yuan per month to 963 yuan. Average minimum wage in central and western regions has always been close, and average minimum wage in eastern region is obviously higher than that in central and western regions.

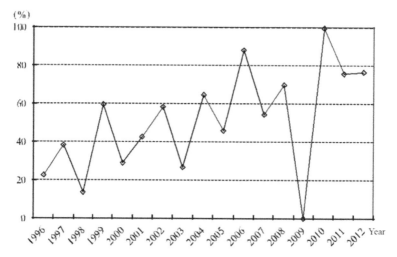

Chart 11-2   Proportion of Cities Adjusting Minimum Wage

Source: The author collates and calculates data about minimum wage from official websites of human resources and social security departments of prefectural cities.

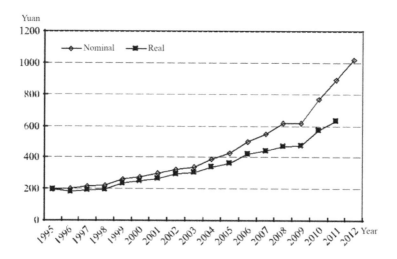

Chart 11-3   Average Nominal and Real Minimum Wage

Note: Real minimum wage is obtained by subtracting nominal minimum wage from aggregate urban consumer price index (constant price in 1995). Source: The author collates and calculates data about minimum wage from official websites of human resources and social security departments of prefectural cities,

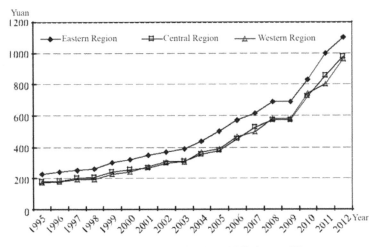

Chart 11-4   Average Regional Minimum Wage

Source: The author collates and calculates data about minimum wage from official websites of human resources and social security departments of prefectural cities.

As is known to all, since 2004, Pearl River Delta Region has suffered from migrant worker shortage which spread to other parts of the country. Even in labor-exporting central and western provinces began to suffer from widespread labor shortage. China's labor supply has undergone fundamental change, unlimited labor supply turning into limited surplus. With the arrival of Lewis Turning Point, wage, other treatment, employment conditions and labor relations were determined by labor market system instead of spontaneous labor supply and demand (Cai Fang, 2008). In 2004, the Ministry of Labor and Social Security promulgated *The Minimum Wage Regulations*, which promoted implementation of minimum wage system across China. The rapid growth of minimum wage since 2004 is a positive response on the part of Chinese government to the ever-changing labor market and is conducive to better protection of workers' interests and rights.

iv. Different Minimum Wages for Different Types of Workers

In many countries, there is different minimum wages for workers of different ages. In the U.K., workers are divided into three age groups: 16-17, 18-22 and over 22 years old. The older the age, the higher minimum wage (Xie Zengyi, 2008). The World Bank also strongly recommends lower minimum wage for younger workers with relatively little experience and low productivity as the same minimum wage for workers of all ages may make employers reluctant to hire young workers. In the medium-to-long term, this may affect economic growth and social productivity improvement.

Minimum wage gap between younger and older workers can be narrowed with age, avoiding a big leap in minimum wage when workers reach a certain age. Studies have shown that a leap in minimum wage is unfavourable to workers of that age who are right before minimum wage growth (Abowd et al., 2000).

The same minimum wage applies to workers of all ages in China. In future, China needs to consider setting different minimum wages for workers of different ages. However, it should be noted that the Cultural Revolution had a great impact on some people's education, in turn, on their human capital acquisition (Cai Fang, Du Yang, 2003). By contrast, these people are less productive and may lose their jobs if higher minimum wage is set for them.

Many countries set lower minimum wage for apprentices and interns who improves their human capital and productivity through apprenticeship or internship. Although paid less during apprenticeship or internship, in future they will be able to take advantage of their improved productivity to earn higher wage. Conversely, if apprentices and interns receive the same minimum wage as formal workers, employers may be reluctant to offer them apprenticeship or internship. China does not have lower minimum wage for apprentices and interns, which should have if necessary.

(III) Monitor and Supervision of Implementation of Minimum Wage System

Even in developed countries, it is generally difficult to implement minimum wage system. All over the world, labor and human resources departments are generally responsible for implementation of minimum wage system. China is no exception. It is human resources and social security department that is responsible for implementation of minimum wage system. But for years, due to limited manpower, few people work in the line of minimum wage. In order to enhance implementation of minimum wage system, first of all, increase manpower and secondly improve working efficiency. Establishment of a network platform with employers will make it possible for employer supervision.

For more effective implementation of minimum wage system, laws and regulations on minimum wage should make detailed provisions on the rights of staff engaged in minimum wage supervision so that they will have the right to obtain from employers timely information about implementation of minimum wage system, and to punish employers for circumventing or violating laws and regulations. When employers violate regulations, there should be detailed punishment regulations. At the same time, employers will be able to appeal.

The Minimum Wage Regulations stipulate that employers shall publicize minimum wage to all its workers within 10 days after its release. If violating this regulation, employers will be ordered by labor security administrative department to rectify its behavior within deadline. If the wage that employers provide is lower than minimum wage, employers will be ordered by labor security administrative department to make up to worker's salary before deadline and be ordered to pay a compensation of 1-5 times the wage that he owes to the worker. On the whole, there is no specific and detailed stipulation in *The Minimum Wage Regulations* concerning supervision power of administrative department of Labor Security Bureau and punishment of employers violating the regulations.

It is government's responsibility to provide access for both employers and employees to have a better understanding of minimum wage system and their rights and obligations with postings in public places, lectures and publicity campaigns, requiring employers to post minimum wage which is of vital importance when minimum wage system is merely established and implemented. China promulgated *The Minimum Wage Regulations* in 2004, marking full implementation of minimum wage system. Governments at all levels should vigorously publicize minimum wage system and achieve its effective implementation.

IV. Wage Collective Bargaining System, Collective Contract System and Trade Unions

Wage collective bargaining system and collective contract system, important systems for labor relations adjustment, have been attached great importance to by departments concerned. A series of laws, regulations and documents providing policy basis have been promulgated and implemented one after another for implementation of collective wage bargaining system and collective contract system. In the past few years, tripartite mechanism of coordinating labor relations has played an important role in promoting wage collective bargaining by giving play to their own functions, complementary to and coordinated with each other. After more than a decade's efforts, wage collective bargaining system and collective contract system has developed with expanding wage collective bargaining system coverage and improved collective contract signing rate.

There are provisions on collective contracts in *The Labor Law 1994* that "enterprise employees may sign collective contracts with their enterprise on labor remuneration, working hours, rest and leave, safety and health at work, insurance and welfare". Labor departments at all levels have actively carried out pilot collective contracts in selected 57 enterprises in Beijing, Guangdong, Fujian and other places. In 1995, pilot work of collective bargaining and collective contract system was carried out in more than 800 enterprises in eight provinces and cities, including Beijing, Guangdong and Fujian, .

In 1997, General Office of the Ministry of Labor issued *Opinions on Wage Collective Bargaining System for Foreign-funded Enterprises* guiding foreign-funded enterprises in the implementation of collective wage bargaining. Both collective bargaining system and collective contract system have gradually been established across China in 1997. In April 1998, the All-China Federation of Trade Unions formulated and issued *Guidelines for Trade Unions to be Part of Wage Collective Bargaining System* which clarified basic requirements for trade unions to implement wage collective bargaining system and implementation of wage collective bargaining system and collective contract system throughout the country.

The Trial Scheme for Wage Collective Bargaining System issued and implemented in 2000 made a comprehensive stipulation about wage collective bargaining system and wage collective contract by clarifying basic rules of wage collective bargaining system between enterprises and employees. *The Trade Union Law*, revised in 2001, stipulates that "Trade unions coordinate labor relations and safeguard labor rights and interests of enterprise employees through equal consultation and collective contract system" and that "Trade unions shall, on behalf of staff and workers, consult on an equal footing and enter into collective contracts with enterprises and public institutions implementing enterprise management".

In 2001, five ministries and associations, including the Ministry of Labor and Social Security, issued *On Full Implementation of Equal Consultation and Collective Contract System* in order to promote equal consultation and collective contract system and speed up cultivation of coordination mechanism between two main bodies of labor relations. Since then, enterprise collective bargaining system has steadily advanced. By 2002, 30 provinces, autonomous regions and municipalities under the direct administration of central government had established a tripartite coordination mechanism for provincial labor relations. By 2003, more than 290,000 enterprises have established wage collective bargaining system.

Collective Contracts Regulations implemented in 2004 further stipulates collective bargaining and collective contracts signing. In 2005, the Ministry of Labor and Social Security, All-China Federation of Trade Unions, China Enterprise Federation and China Entrepreneurs' Association jointly issued *On Full Implementation of Wage Collective Contract System* which stipulates that trade unions on behalf of staff and workers bargain on equal footing, sign collective contract with enterprise representatives or enterprises such as foreign-funded enterprises, private enterprises, township enterprises, especially small enterprises in relatively concentrated areas to achieve full implementation of collective contract system. By the end of 2005, more than 6,600 tripartite coordination organizations had been set up in prefectural cities across the nation, and 340,000 enterprises had established wage collective bargaining system. There are 8,030 and 10,702 national tripartite coordination organizations in 2006 and 2007.

The Labor Contract Law implemented in 2008 is a detailed stipulation about collective contracts. Premier Wen Jiabao proposed in *The Government Work Report* of the First Session of the Eleventh National People's Congress to "promote in enterprises the establishment of wage collective bargaining system, improve wage guidance system, and improve and implement minimum wage system". This is the first time that wage collective bargaining system has been written into government work report, highlighting the importance of wage collective bargaining system in new labor market. In June 2008, National Federation of Trade Unions issued *Opinions of All-china Federation of Trade Unions on Collective Bargaining Instructor Team* and *Opinions of All-china Federation of Trade Unions' Proposal for Collective Bargaining* and again issued *"Guidance of All-China Federation of Trade Onions on Active Industrial Implementation of Wage Collective Bargaining"* in July, 2009.

In April 2008, the Ministry of Human Resources and Social Security held a national symposium on labor relations, proposing The Rainbow Plan for full implementation of wage collective bargaining system and collective contract system. The symposium set development goals for the next five years: establish collective bargaining system and collective contract system in above-scale enterprises in eastern region in 2008 and 2009, then in central region by the end of 2010, and across the nation by the end of 2012. At the same time, regional and industrial collective bargaining system and collective contract system in all types of small and medium-sized enterprises will be promoted by striving to basically establish collective bargaining system and collective contract system in all types of enterprises within five years.

In May 2010, the Ministry of Human Resources and Social Security, All-China

Federation of Trade Unions, and China Enterprise Federation and Entrepreneurs' Association jointly issued "*Full Implementation of The Rainbow Plan to Strengthen Collective Contract System*", aiming to implement collective contract system in all types of unionized enterprises between 2010 and 2012. In 2010 and 2011, coverage of collective contract system will be over 60% and over 80% respectively. For non-unionized small enterprises, regional, industrial collective contracts will be signed to increase coverage. Thus collective bargaining mechanism has gradually improved and effectiveness of collective contracts has been significantly enhanced.

In 2010, National conference on grassroots trade unions construction was held, proposing that enterprises should vigorously promote establishment of trade unions by law so as to implement wage collective bargaining system by law. Conference goal was that in 2010, 2011 and 2012, establishment rate of trade unions in national corporate units should reach over 60%, 75% and 90% respectively and union membership rate of staff and workers should reach over 82%, 87% and 92% respectively so as to fulfill the goal of establishing enterprise trade unions by law.

Judging from establishment and development of trade unions, national grass-roots trade unions remained stable in the 1990s but declined in the late 1990s. Between 2000 and 2002, grassroots trade unions increased by a large margin. Since 2003, there has been a steady increase in grass-roots trade unions, reaching 2.78 million in 2014. Trade union membership remained stable throughout the 90s at about 1,000 million. Since the beginning of the 21st century, trade union membership has begun to grow rapidly, reaching 2,880 million in 2014 (See Chart 11-5).

In early 2011, All China Federation of Trade Unions issued *The Plan of All-China Federation of Trade Unions to Promote Wage Collective Bargaining System between 2011 and 2013.* The plan states that between 2011 and 2013, over 80% of unionized enterprises will have established wage collective bargaining system so that unionized enterprises generally implement wage collective bargaining and all the world top 500 enterprises in China will set up wage collective bargaining system. Annual planning targets between 2011 and 2013 are elaborated and priorities and main measures are proposed in the plan.

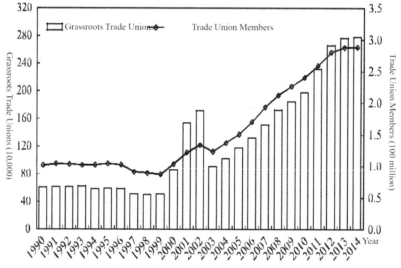

Chart 11-5   Grassroots Trade Unions and their Membership in China

Note: Since 2003, there has been statistical caliber adjustment of number of grassroots trade unions.

Source: The National Bureau of Statistics, *China Statistical Yearbook* (calendar year), China Statistical Press.

With implementation of collective bargaining system and collective contract system, collective contracts have been submitted for examination and approval by labor security departments all over the country and collective contract employees keep growing (See Chart 11-6). In 1998, collective contracts reached 150,000, covering 50 million employees. In 2001, collective contracts increased to 270,000, covering over 70 million employees. In 2002, collective contracts increased by a large margin to 635,000, covering over 80 million employees. In 2009, after implementation of *Labor Contract Law* in 2008, collective contract rose to 703,000, covering over 94 million employees. In 2014, collective contracts reached 1.7 million, covering 1,600 million employees.

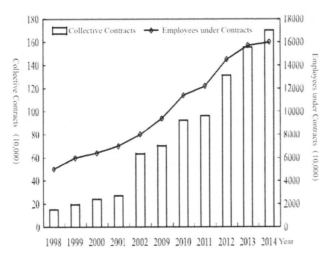

Chart 11-6   Collective Contracts Submitted for Approval by Labor Security
Departments and Collective Contract Employees

Source: Ministry of Human Resources and Social Security: Statistical Bulletin on Human Resources and

Social Security (Calendar Year), http://www.mohrss.gov.cn/.

According to enterprise survey data of 2009 All-China Federation of Industry
and Commerce (ACFIC), 83% of enterprises have set up trade unions, 45.1%
of enterprises have established wage collective bargaining system, and 68.5%
of enterprises have established workers' congress system (See Table 11-3). By
region, the proportion of unionized enterprises implementing wage collective
bargaining system and workers' congress system is the highest in eastern region,
followed by central region with western region being the lowest.

Table 11-3   Enterprises with Trade Unions, Wage Collective Bargaining
System and Workers' Congress System (%)

	Trade Unions (%)	Wage Collective Bargaining System (%)	Workers' Congress System (%)
Eastern Region	88. 5	50. 8	72. 0
Central Region	83. 0	45. 3	68. 7
Western Region	79. 4	41. 2	66. 0
Total	83. 0	45. 1	68. 5

Source: calculated according to enterprise survey data of 2009 All-China Federation of Industry and
Commerce

Cities across China have endeavored to promote wage collective bargaining system. Hangzhou issued *Opinions on Further Promoting Wage Collective Bargaining System* which stipulates that enterprises with wage collective bargaining system will receive *Proposals for Rectification* in a timely manner if they refuse to discuss wage growth with their staff representatives. Those who refuse to rectify shall be ordered by labor security department to make rectification within a time limit. By the end of 2015, Hangzhou had signed 21,000 special wage collective contracts, covering 76,000 enterprises with over 90% of wage collective bargaining system rate.

The Three-Year Trade Union Plan for Wage Collective Bargaining System Promotion in Beijing was issued in December 2010. According to the plan, by 2013, Beijing will encourage above-scale enterprises to implement wage collective bargaining system on their own and below-scale enterprises to establish bargaining system by signing regional and special industrial wage agreements. Over 80% of unionized enterprises have established wage collective bargaining system with full coverage of all types of enterprises.

In recent years, Qingdao Federation of Trade Unions, with the goal of establishing wage collective bargaining and wage determination mechanism, has vigorously promoted wage collective bargaining system and continuously explored its forms, ways and methods so as to make wage collective bargaining system and collective contract an important means for trade unions to coordinate labor relations. A series of documents have been issued stipulating that enterprises should establish collective bargaining system and offer right and that enterprises should establish annual average wage growth mechanism through collective wage bargaining system. Wage bargaining system of Qingdao is characterized by its rich content including wage bargaining, wage distribution system, and wage adjustment bargaining and payment methods and by its varied form of wage bargaining ranging from internal bargaining to regional and industrial bargaining. Qingdao has also actively explored wage collective bargaining system for staff and workers not on the payroll of an institution. Human resources and social security departments shall order those enterprises refusing to sign wage collective agreement without proper reasons to rectify and order those enterprises refusing to rectify to be recorded in "Archives of 'Unscrupulous Credit Units'"to be made public.

In promoting wage bargaining system, Luohe City of Henan Province insists on "one enterprise one policy" in solving the problem of wage collective bargaining. Enterprises with better production and operation performance will bargain over wage, bonus distribution, subsidy and welfare. Enterprises with bad production and operation performance will bargain over wage payment and living expenses of workers leaving the post. Non-public enterprises will bargain over total wage growth of workers and staff with improvement of enterprise performance by taking into account local wage guidance line, consumption index and other factors.

Chapter XII

Income Distribution with International Experience and Lessons

ZHANG Juwei, CHENG Jie, ZHAO Wen[1]

I. Introduction

A better understanding of international experience of income distribution is to explore and summarize income distribution evolution with its economic development instead of being confined to a certain period or time, or being seen as a change in income gap or focusing solely on specific systems or policies. Income distribution in developed countries in modern sense came into being with the birth of capitalist production mode and experienced widening, narrowing and further widening income gap, each development stage of income distribution having

---

1   ZHANG Juwei, Director of the Institute of Population and Labor Economics of the Chinese Academy of Social Sciences, Research Fellow, Doctoral Advisor; CHENG Jie, Associate Research Fellow of the Institute of Population and Labor Economics of the Chinese Academy of Social Sciences; ZHAO Wen, Associate Research Fellow of the Institute of Population and Labor Economics of the Chinese Academy of Social Sciences.

its own inherent laws and characteristics and corresponding system and policy changes. As income distribution in developing countries have not experienced the same evolution as developed countries, international experience of income distribution here is mostly that of developed countries.

Early income distribution studies mainly focuses on functional distribution. Functional distribution refers to national income distribution among production factors (such as land, labor, capital, etc.), which can be used to observe contribution of different production factors to national income and corresponding return, such as labor share. Before the birth of modern capitalist production mode, there was no income distribution in modern sense mainly because production mode was relatively primitive back then so that contribution of production factors was difficult to distinguish clearly, making it impossible to discuss functional distribution in terms of production factors. With the emergence of capitalist production mode, early classical economists were most concerned about how to create national wealth and how to distribute it among different factors, thus income distribution in modern sense came into being. "Labor is the father of wealth; land is the mother of wealth", as Petty pointed out the importance of labor in value creation. Smith, Ricardo and so on have expanded "theory of labor value", believing that profit, interest, land, and rent is deductible part of value created by labor, based on which Marx put forward "surplus value theory" which holds that profit is surplus value created by exploitative labor. Labor played a unique role in early income distribution, denying contribution of other factors. However, Smith believes that production factors other than labor do contribute to production and wealth. Based on "three points" of political economy[1], Say put forward "trinity" distribution formula of labor-wage, capital-profit and land-rent, labor, capital and land being three indispensable factors of all social production.

---

1 After dividing political economy into three parts: wealth production, wealth distribution and wealth consumption, Say proposed "three production factors" theory of labor, capital and land and that factors create value so that a corresponding price must be paid for use of factors.

Each factor owner obtains his own income according to productive service he provides as compensation for his own consumption. It can be said that distribution of classical economics is related to production but independent of production and it is more of functional distribution, which tends to distribute according to labor or according to production factors.

After the rise of neoclassical economics, income distribution studies has become part of modern economics. Since results of functional distribution has theoretically made it clear that factor remuneration is determined by its marginal output, income distribution studies turn much of its attention to scale distribution, instead. Javens, Marshall and others open a chapter in neoclassical economics with "Marginal Revolution". Marginal utility principle has been applied to the whole field of production and distribution, as Schumpeter put it, "marginal principle naturally applies to income formation or distribution, as distribution is no longer a separate subject now".[1] Clark explicitly advocated studying production through studying distribution and developed "marginal productivity" theory applicable to all factors, which points out that in market economy, income distribution is always regulated by law of nature dividing total income of society into three parts of different nature: total wage, total interest and total profits, namely, labor income, capital income, and income from entrepreneurs reconciling production[2]. Under declining marginal effect, production factor remuneration is determined by its marginal product, and once pricing of such factors as labor, capital and land is settled, distribution is settled accordingly. According to Valla and Pareto, in general equilibrium, market allocation is welfare maximization. Neoclassical growth theory is more explicit (Solow, 1956) in that national income is also distributed according to factor marginal productivity. In equilibrium, factor marginal productivity is factor price, and long-term trend of factor income

---

1   Schumpeter, Joseph. *History of Economic Analysis* (Vol. 3). Trans. Zhu Yang et al. Commercial Press, 1994.

2   Clark, John Bates. *The Distribution of Wealth*. Trans. Peng Yilin et. al. People's Daily Press, 2010.

share depends on elasticity of factor output (share in its contribution to output). Therefore, mainstream view of economics tends to think that labor share in national income is stable or even invariable and that "Kaldor fact" (Kaldor, 1961) focuses on this typical feature. Therefore, functional distribution results under the framework of neoclassical economics are clear and less important so that many economists attach no more importance to it.

Scale distribution based on individuals and households has gradually become the focus of attention. Although factor remuneration is certain, there are great differences in factor endowments between individuals and households, which will inevitably lead to income inequality between society as a whole and groups, bringing uncertainty to economic growth and social stability. Kuznets (1955) proposed inverted "U" relationship hypothesis between income inequality and economic growth from perspective of scale income distribution, triggering extensive discussion and debate over scale income distribution. Up to now, income distribution study is still mainly based on scale distribution. But discussion of functional distribution has never stopped (Krueger, 1999) as in recent years, it has aroused heated discussion in China (Bai Zhong'en & Qian Zhenjie, 2009; Luo Changyuan & Zhang Jun, 2009; Zhang Juwei, 2012). Now, both scale distribution and functional distribution are regarded as two independent research areas, and connection between these two is an open question. However, internal relationship between them is gradually clear. In times of widening income gap, functional distribution becomes imbalanced and labor share decreases. When labor share increases, scale distribution will be more reasonable as income gap becomes stable or narrow.

Be it functional distribution or scale distribution, there is always contradiction between theory and practice. Although theoretically functional distribution results are certain in neoclassical framework, labor share will remain balanced and stable. However, this is not the case in real economy. Labor share in developed countries is not stable and it keeps going up with regularization of economy so that classic "Kaldor fact" has not become true (Harrison, 2002). In recent decades, labor share in many countries has fallen again. The same is true of scale distribution. Kuznets hypothesis, once considered classic, did not appear as expected in most countries. Many economies have never been able to find a turning point with narrowing income gap in economic growth. Instead, income gap continued to widen so that scholars' attempts to develop "hypothesis" into "theory" eventually became futile (Robinson, 1976).

Reality does not follow theory because theoretical assumptions are not consistent with changing reality and because of limited research perspective. It's necessary to find a better insight into income distribution evolution from the perspective of classical economy, dual economy, neoclassical economy to the whole economic development of modern new era. It is necessary to study income distribution from both functional distribution and scale distribution to grasp the inner logic and characteristics of income distribution evolution.

II. Reason for Widening Income Gap: Capital-dominated Distribution Pattern

Early distribution studies mainly focus on wealth distribution. Modern income distribution began to appear with capitalist production mode. The key reason why wealth distribution became the main aspect and even the whole of early distribution studies is its unique production mode and economic form. First of all, feudal society is dominated by agricultural economy and production mode is mainly self-sufficient with low productivity and stagnant economic growth. According to Madison (2003), GDP per capita growth rate of Western European countries between the first year and 1,000 AD was -0.01% and barely reached 0.14% between 1000 and 1820 with little wealth increment (national income) for distribution. Second, economic form of this period was dominated by mixed economy while traditional agricultural sector dominated in classical economic period. The proportion of agricultural employment in the Netherlands and United Kingdom, the most developed economy in early period, was also as high as 50%

around 1700 and the proportion of agricultural employment in the United States was still as high as 70% until 1820 with households as units of labor, land and a small amount of material capital without social labor division and distribution being naturally within households, difficult to distinguish contribution of factors so that there is no national accounting and no income distribution in modern sense. In early period, national income was inadequate and wealth was concentrated in feudal ruling class. Wealth distribution was dominated by political rights, social hierarchy so that gap between rich and poor was widening, leading to social contradictions and revolution.

With establishment of modern capitalist production mode, deepening of both social labor division and specialization promoted by industrial revolution, traditional mixed economy gradually giving way and economic growth accelerating, national income increased substantially and distribution mode changed because of production mode change and factor input and corresponding return can be distinguished so that national income can be calculated according to factors and distribution system is formed with land, labor and capital as main factors. As a result, modern income distribution began to be extensively studied. However, in the early stage of modern capitalistic development and industrialization, labor resources are abundant or even with a lot of surplus, but capital is very scarce, which will inevitably lead to low wage rate and high capital return rate. Factors determine capital-dominated national income distribution pattern with imbalanced functional distribution, small labor share and high capital share. As few people possess capital in the whole society, capital to labor tends to widen income gap, causing scale distribution to worsen.

(I) Rapidly Widening Income Gap

From classical economy to dual economy, labor and capital has become two core factors of economic growth and wealth creation. However, benefit pattern between them is obviously out of balance, which is basically "one-sided". Infinite labor supply and low marginal output and wage rate will cause small labor share in national income. Scarce capital and high marginal output and return rate will give rise to bigger national income share. Capital plays a vital role in national economy, naturally leading to its absolute right to speak in income distribution as capital is in the hands of minority groups, giving rise to ever-widening income gap and wealth concentration.

Despite limited historical data, concentration of income and wealth can be seen. According to research estimates (See Table 12-1), income share of top 5% and 20% of households with highest income in the UK was 35.6% and 58.1% in 1688 and rose to 39.2% and 63.2% around 1800 with Gini coefficient close to 0.6 so that there was increasing income inequality. Property inequality is even serious with net property share controlled by top 1% of Britain's wealthiest group accounting for 54.9% of all property in 1810, top 5% of Britain's wealthiest group controlling more than 85% of all property. The United States, a New World country, had characteristics in common, with 14.8% of total assets owned by 1% wealthiest group in early days of the founding of the U.S. rising to 32.7% in 1860, and Gini coefficient rising from 0.64 to 0.83. Centralization trend is obvious judging from distribution of residents' household income and property so that scale distribution has been seriously out of balance.

Functional distribution lies behind imbalanced scale distribution. In this development stage, capital is not only a "necessity" for growth but a "scarcity", dominating in wealth creation and distribution. According to three-point method of land rent, wage and profit, factor income share changes in the U.K. before and after Industrial Revolution is characterized by decline in land rent and labor share and rapid profit share growth. According to Allen (2005), profit share reflecting capital factor gradually rose from about 25% in 1770 to 30% in 1800, 40% around 1840, 50% around 1860 while labor share decreased from around 60% in 1770 to 40% in 1860, and land rent share decreased from 22% to less than 10% (See Chart 12-1). Between 1800 and 1855, average capital income share in the United States was only 34% and rose to 45% between 1855 and 1890, reflecting the fact that capital factor has created more new wealth in industrialization, more national income being shared. Japan had characteristics in common (Yujiro Hayami &

Yoshihisa Godo, 2005). Japan began its industrialization after Meiji Restoration with average capital income share rising from 33% to 39% and to 43% between 1888 and 1900, between 1900 and 1920 and between 1920 and 1937. Capital share growth in national income means labor share decline. Labor share decline, widening income gap and growing inequality is no coincidence but is inherently correlated.

Table 12-1   British Income Inequality during Early Industrialization

Income Inequality (pre-tax income share)			
Year	Top 5% Household Income	Top 20% Household Income	Gini coefficient
1688	35. 6	58. 1	0. 556
1759	35. 4	57. 5	0. 552
1801	39. 2	63. 2	0. 593
1867	41. 2	57. 3	0. 490
Property Inequality (Net Market Share)			
Year	Top 1% Share	Top 5% Share	
1670	48. 9	84. 6	
1700	39. 3	81. 9	
1740	43. 6	86. 9	
1810	54. 9	85. 3	
1875	61. 1	84. 0	

Source: Anthony B. Atkinson and Francois Bourguignon, *Handbook of Income Distribution*, Volume 1, Elsevier Science, 2000.

(II) Dual Economy: Factor Endowment Structure of Capital Scarcity and Labor Surplus

Establishment of capitalist production mode has led to rapid development of modern sector (or capitalist sector). Different from traditional agricultural sector in classical economic stage, modern sector operates in accordance with neoclassical economic mechanism with production and distribution determined by marginal productivity in accordance with marginal principle. However, in national economic structure, traditional sector (or non-capitalist sector) still accounts for a large proportion. The U.K. initiated industrialization in 1800, but its agriculture still accounted for 34% of its national economy. Agriculture of U.S. accounted for 45% of its national economy in 1840 (See Table 12-2). The traditional sector still works according to classical economic mechanism with real wage determined by subsistence level. The traditional sector mainly operates with land and labor while the modern sector operates with capital and labor with relatively fixed land, increasing capital and more prominent technological progress, so it is in urgent need of labor than the traditional sector, causing labor force to continue to shift from agricultural to non-agricultural sector. At the beginning of industrialization, the traditional sector is still dominant and economic society is characterized by dual economic structure of the traditional sector and the modern sector, classical economy and neoclassical economy.

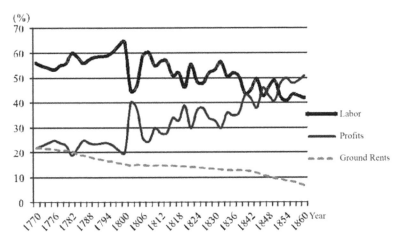

Chart 12-1   Factor Income Share in Early National Economy of the U. K.: 1770-1860

Source: calculation based on Robert C. Allen (2005).

In this stage, abundant labor supply, scarce capital factor and capital accumulation becomes main source of economic growth. Industrial revolution led to rapid expansion of the modern sector with significant improvement in productivity, enabling a large number of labor force from the traditional agricultural sector to enter urban and non-agricultural sectors. In addition, the agricultural sector benefits from industrialization with improved labor productivity resulting in abundant labor supply and even large surplus. Its wage rate is determined by marginal labor output in agricultural sector with laborers' wage being subsistence wage. Lewis (1954) describes such economic development under infinite labor supply as typical dual economic structure. Investment is a key source of economic growth at this stage, but there's very scarce capital for new equipment and new technologies to rely on and capital return rate is also very high as capital formation accelerates, which further stimulates capital accumulation and reproduction so that society as a whole tends to consume less, save more and invest more.

Savings of average household are small while investment comes mainly from savings of a few wealthy groups and profits of capitalists. In early industrialization, average worker's wage was very low for maintaining food and clothing with little savings. In 1875, total savings rate of urban worker household in the United States was only 3.3%. Household savings rate of less than $600 is even negative (See Table 12-3), which means household savings are not enough to make ends meet. Residents' savings mainly come from the wealthiest households while corporate savings come mainly from profits created by capitalists, main source of turning savings into capital. As Lewis (1954) put it, "very little savings from both workers and middle class are not conducive to productive investment. Main source of savings is enterprise profits. If savings share in national income has increased, enterprise profits share in national income has increased." According to early studies of consumption and savings share in national income, Kuznets (1955) also found that only high-income group can save as residents' total savings of the other nine income groups are almost zero, top 10% of households with highest income contributed to total savings, savings distribution being more unequal than property and capital.

Table 12-2 Economic Structure and Employment Structure of Major Countries during Industrialization

	Economic Structure (%)				Employment Structure (%)		
	Agriculture	Industry	Service		Agriculture	Industry	Service
the U.K.							
1800	34. 1	22.1	43. 8	1800	34. 4	30. 0	35.6
1860	19. 5	36.3	44. 2	1860	20. 2	43. 2	36.6
1924	4. 4	55.0	40. 6	1920	7. 2	56. 9	35.9
1955	4. 7	56.8	38. 5	1960	3. 7	55. 0	41.3
the U.S.							
1840	44. 6	24.2	31. 2	1840	63. 4	36. 3 *	
1890	25. 8	37.7	36. 5	1880	48. 6	29. 0	22.4
1930	11. 2	41.3	47. 5	1930	19. 9	38. 8	41.3
1955	5. 9	48.4	45. 7	1965	5. 7	38	56.3
Japan							
1880	62. 5	37.5		1870	85. 8	5. 6	8. 6
1910	40. 6	59.4		1900	71. 1	15. 7	13.2
1930	22. 4	77.6		1920	54. 6	25. 4	20
1960	13. 6	86.4		1960	27.6	37. 4	35.0

Note: * refers to total number of industry and service sectors. The time points of some data are similar years.

Table Source: Simon Kuznets(1973), *Economic Growth in Various Countries*, Transl. by Chang Xun, Commercial Press, 1973.

Table 12-3 Household Income and Urban Employees' Expenditure in the U. S. in 1875

	All Income Groups	$300-450	$450-600	$600-750	$750-1200	> $1200
Average Household Size (per person)	5.1	5.0	6.2	4.8	5.3	6.9
Average Income (US $)	763	395	549	679	871	1383
Average Expenditure (US $)	738	410	555	668	832	1212
Average Savings (US $)	25	-15	-6	11	39	171
Savings Rate (%)	3.3	-3.8	-1.1	1.6	4.5	12.4

Source: U. S. Bureau of the Census, *Historical Statistics of the United States: Colonial Times to 1970*, Washington, D. C., 1975.

(III) Capital-dominated Distribution Pattern

Since production mode determines distribution mode and economic growth is driven by capital factor, income distribution pattern must be capital-dominated: capital accumulation has become a requisite for industrial revolution and economic take-off; capital return rate and investment rate is relatively high, and capital deepening appears while average worker's wage grows slowly and is basically subsistence wage with serious urban poverty and unemployment. The government can only conform to factor relationship and distribution pattern of "strong capital but weak labor". Institutional policies tend to encourage and support capital accumulation, mistreat and even suppress average worker, unable to reverse widening income gap.

This development stage is characterized by high capital return rate and high investment rate, which fundamentally determines absolute dominance of capital in income distribution. Crafts (1985) estimated that productivity of capital factors in the British Industrial Revolution grew rapidly with annual average growth rate of 0.24% between 1700 and 1760, 0.35% between 1761 and 1800, 0.52% between 1801 and 1831 and 0.70% between 1831 and 1860, indicating that higher productivity is directly associated with higher return rate. Allen's (2005) estimates of capital profit rate clearly confirmed that around 1780 profit rate is around 10%, 14% in 1800, around 18% in 1820, and about 22% in 1840. Business owners was able to make easy money. Increasing capital return rate encourages the whole society to convert savings and profits into investment for reproduction so that investment rate has been on the rise. Allen (2005) estimates Briatin's investment rate rose from an average of 5.0% between 1700 and 1760 to 7.0% between 1760 and 1800 and reached 10.0% between 1801 and 1830, and 11.3% between 1831 and 1860. Feinstein (1981) estimates that total investment share in domestic total products grew from 8% in the 1760s to 14% in the 1780s. Moreover, capital accumulation tends to shift from working capital to fixed capital, that is, to improve organic capital composition. In the century after the 1760s, fixed capital rose from 30% of national wealth to 50%. The proportion of fixed capital in working capital rose from 0.83 to 2.56 between 1760 and 1830 mainly due to substantial increase in long-term fixed investment such as new technology and equipment, urban facilities and transportation, which is important for maintaining a steady increase in capital return rate. As Williamson (1985) concluded, although capital accumulation during the Industrial Revolution is yet to be known, two well-known hypotheses can be supported by evidence. One hypothesis is that Lewis and Rostow advocated that investment in the Industrial Revolution must be doubled. The other is, as is emphasized by Hicks, that the Industrial Revolution will lead to a shift in capital accumulation from working capital to fixed capital. It can be said that this period of capital deepening is economic acceleration. According to the revaluation of Crafts and Harley (1992), average annual capital growth rate in the U.K. between 1760 and 1800 was 1.0%, faster than 0.8% of labor growth rate over the same period, and rose to 1.7% between 1801 and 1831, faster than 1.4% of labor growth rate over the same period. Capital growth rate is always faster than labor growth rate, and the ratio of capital to labor tends to increase. In the same period, GDP growth rate also shows an increasing trend as average annual real growth rate of GDP between 1760 and 1780, between 1780 and 1800, between 1801 and 1831 was 0.64%, 1.38% and 1.90%. Piketty (2014) studies income distribution changes with ratio of capital to income. In the 19th and early 20th centuries, ratio of capital to income in Europe was 6 to 7, which means that more parts of national income were taken away and collected by capital and that income and wealth will tend to be more concentrated.

Average worker's wage growth is relatively slow, sharing less economic growth and productivity growth. According to estimates by Lindert and Williamson (1983), average British worker's real wage (mainly miners, cotton weavers, non-farm workers, etc.) barely grew significantly before 1820. Supposing 100 in 1851, real wage index was 47.5 in 1755. By 1781, it had dropped to 46.2 and slowly rose to 52.5 in 1797. But by 1805, it had dropped to 51.7. In these decades, average worker's wage income growth had been almost stagnant. Williamson (1985) revised and estimated all workers' wage and came to a similar conclusion that supposing 100 in 1851, real wage index was 42.5 for all workers in 1797 and dropped to 40.6 in 1805, fell further to 39.4 in 1810. During this period, labor supply was abundant and even a large amount of surplus resulted in severe unemployment. Although nominal wage grew, real wage fell and did not grow significantly until after 1820 (Wage index was 46.1 in 1820 and rose to 78.7 in 1835). If divided into three stages, real wage and living standard of working class between 1755 and 1797 basically did not change much. Between 1797 and 1820, wage decreased and living conditions deteriorated. Obvious improvement didn't appear until 1820. Between 1750 and 1850, real wage grew at average annual rate of less than 0.8%, lagging behind labor productivity growth of the same period and GDP growth rate as well. New wealth clearly did not favor average worker.

(IV) Capital-oriented Institutional Rules

Institutional policy of the government consistent with income distribution pattern tends to encourage capital and mistreat labor. The British government has established and improved protection system of private property rights, encouraged development of industry and commerce, and supported land annexation, free trade and overseas expansion, accelerating capital accumulation and creating new wealth and benefiting the government and its interest groups who did not intend to affect income distribution pattern by means of taxation which was only regarded as a wartime measure. It was not until in 1799 that the U.K. temporarily imposed income tax, which was abolished after the end of Napoleon War in 1816 and did not get restored until 1842. Tax system has always been single and non-progressive. Tax structure is dominated by indirect taxes (mainly tariffs, goods taxes) supplemented by direct taxes (income tax and property tax). The government does not care or expect to regulate income gap through tax system but tends to provide a good policy environment for the development of emerging bourgeoisie.

What happens to average worker is in quite sharp contrast. Unlimited labor supply makes it difficult for average worker to have a larger say. Primary point of departure of government policy is to provide stable cheap labor for industrial and commercial capital. Abolition of *British Residence Act* in 1795 was aimed to enhance free labor flow. However, the government tends to respond passively or even suppress the plea for working class' interest. In 1795, British Parliament proposed *Draft Wage Act*, seeking to set minimum wage for workers, but was strongly opposed by Prime Minister William Pitt. Trade unions were also severely restricted as *The Prohibition of Associations Act* was enacted in 1800 which was not abolished until 1824, but trade union activities was under strict restrictions, and the formal *Trade Union Act* was not promulgated until 1871. *The Poverty Alleviation Act* aimed to protect the poor has long been controversial, some calling for its abolition, main reason for which is to encourage lazy people to earn for nothing. Malthus accuses *The Poverty Alleviation Act* of being unnecessary government intervention in free market. *The Amendment of the Poverty Alleviation Act* of 1834 also succeeded in limiting workers' taking relief. In face of widening income gap, the government lacks either strong incentive to regulate or good means of regulation. Depending on "tangible hand" of the government to intervene in income distribution pattern by force may indeed distort efficiency of source allocation, affecting function of "intangible hand", and hindering the arrival of the Industrial Revolution and economic take-off.

III. Reason for the Narrowing Income Gap: Game between Labor and Capital

In middle and late stage of industrialization when capitalist mode of production and market economy system are maturing day by day, economic growth pattern and economic structure have changed greatly in that the proportion of agriculture in both economic and employment structure has been very low and that the traditional sector has given way to the modern sector so that dual economy has developed into neoclassical economy characterized by no more unlimited labor supply, declining marginal capital return, significant change between labor and capital, gradually elevated position of labor over capital, rapid wage growth, increased labor share with equalization tendency in national economy and decreasing capital share with concentrated tendency, bringing about narrowing income gap. Government system and policy attach more importance to interest of average worker and resident, laying and accelerating political and economic foundation for income redistribution system.

(I) The Narrowing Income Gap

Compared with previous period, income distribution has changed significantly with narrowing income gap and reverse trend of wealth concentration. By observing income distribution changes in the United States, the U.K., Europe and newly industrialized countries, there is on the whole an inverted "U" curve[1] similar to that of Kuznets (1955). Trajectory of income inequality change in middle and late stage of industrialization describes descending stage, the second half of inverted "U" curve.

Inequality in income and wealth in this period of the United States is now going downward. Kuznets (1955) observed that income share of top 1% and 5% of top earners began to decline after reaching its peak around 1930. Estimates of the Office of Business Economics (OBE) support this trend with income share of top 5% and top 20% of top earners decreasing rapidly from 30.0% in 1929 to 20.9% in 1947 and from 54.4% in 1929 to 45.4% in 1960 (See Chart 12-2). Results of Gini coefficient are similar to those of income share (See Chart 12-3). Gini coefficient estimated by OBE decreased from 0.49 in 1929 to 0.4 in 1962. CPS estimated that Gini coefficient decreased from 0.376 in 1947 to 0.364 in 1967. Wealth concentration has also declined, with wealth share of top 1% of top earners reaching a historic peak around 1930 at 44.2% and 30.7% measured by net worth and total assets respectively and hitting its lowest at 19.9% and 12.7% in 1976 by the mid-1970s.

---

1 Most European and American countries have completed industrialization before the 1970s. The early 20th century to the 1970s will be taken as observation stage of middle and late industrialization. For the newly industrialized countries, it is necessary to observe the situation after the 1970s.

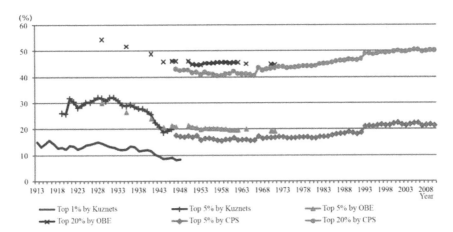

Chart 12-2   Income Inequality in the United States (1913-2008): Income Share (%)

Source: (1) The top 1% and 5% of Kuznets' income share was taken from Kuznets (1955), which involved pre-tax income and tax-paying units and was addressed to individuals between 1913 and 1948. (2) The top 5% and 20% of the income share estimated by the Office of Business Economics (OBE) was addressed to the consumer units between 1929 and 1971. (3) The current population survey (CPS) conducted by the Census Bureau was addressed to family between 1947 and 1967. After 1967, the results of both households and family as subjects are published at the same time.

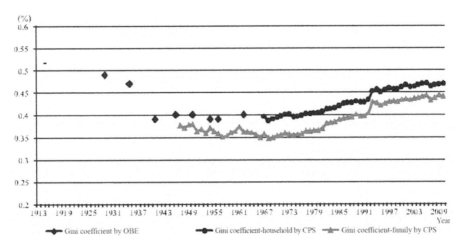

Chart 12-3   Income Inequality in the United States (1913-2009): Gini coefficient

Source: (1) Gini coefficient estimated by the Office of Business Economics (OBE) is addressed to consumers between 1929 and 1971. (2) Gini coefficient--household and Gini coefficient--family is taken from current population survey (CPS) conducted by the Census Bureau.

Inequality in income and wealth in the U.K. is also marked by a sharp decline. Early studies estimated that income share of top 5% and top 20% of top earners in 1911 was 38.7% and 55.2% respectively. Survey of personal income (SPI) began in 1938 when income share of top 5% and top 20% of top earners fell from 31.5% and 52.4% respectively at beginning of the 20th century to 19.7% and 42.1% respectively in 1954. Decline continued until the 1970s. Estimates from the Central Statistics Office (CSO) have come to a similar conclusion (See Chart 12-4). Estimates of Gini coefficient also show a downward trend in Britain's income inequality (See Chart 12-5), with Gini coefficient being 0.483 in 1911 in early studies. SPI estimates that Gini coefficient fell to 0.423 in 1938, 0.342 in 1954, and 0.322 in 1970. CSO estimates in terms of Gini-coefficient household is higher, but showed a downward trend, from 0.411 in 1949 to 0.385 in 1970. In terms of wealth share, in 1911 top 1% and top 5% of top earners reached 69.0% and 87.0% respectively, a historic peak and began to decline rapidly with wealth share of top 1% and top 5% of top earners in 1950 falling to 47.2% and 74.4% respectively and further to 30.1% and 54.3% in 1970. Decline in income inequality in the UK has continued throughout three quarters of the 20th century.

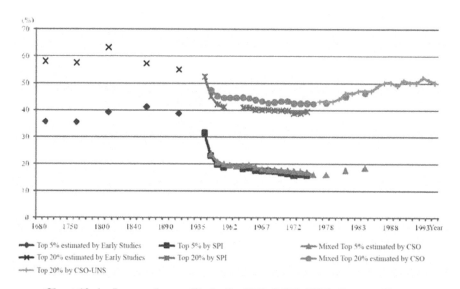

Chart 12-4   Income Inequality in the U.K. (1680-1995): Income Share

Source: (1) Early study estimates (1680-1867) were mainly taken from Lindert and Williamson (1983) and collation of Williamson (1985). The study is addressed at nominal pre-tax household income in England and Wales. After 1867 the study is addressed at the U.K., and Baxter and Bowley revised the data for 1867 and 1911 respectively. (2) Survey of personal income (SPI) originated from the Royal Special Commission of Inquiry (1977) which was targeted at income before income tax. (3) Mixed estimates of Central Statistics Office (CSO) is based on combined data of both Survey of Personal Income (SPI) and Family Expenditure Survey (FES) which takes family as personal tax unit between 1949 and 1984. (4) The CSO-UNS equalization income series of the Central Statistics Office comes from the article series "The Impact of Tax and Welfare on Household Income" published by Economic Trends. The subjects involve original household income and disposable household income. The "equalization" refers to the income distribution according to equalization of persons within household, that is, per capita income between 1977 and 1995.

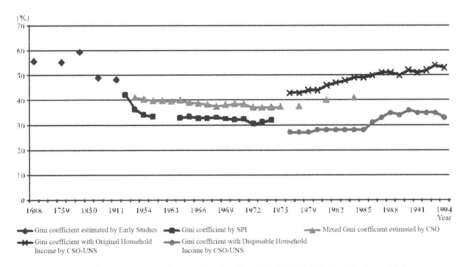

Chart 12-5   Income Inequality in the UK (1688-1994): Gini coefficient

Source: (1) Early study estimates (1680-1867) were mainly taken from Lindert and Williamson (1983) and collation of Williamson (1985). (2) Survey of Personal Income (SPI) originated from the Royal Special Commission of Inquiry (1977). (3) Mixed estimates of CSO is based on combined data of both Survey of Personal Income (SPI) and Family Expenditure Survey (FES). (4) CSO-UNS equalization income series of the Central Statistics Office comes from the article series "The Impact of Tax and Welfare on Household Income" published by Economic Trends, which estimates Gini coefficient of original household income and Gini coefficient of household disposable income respectively.

Income distribution of other European countries also changed significantly in middle and later stage of industrialization, with income gap generally getting narrow. Income share of top 10% of top earners in Europe decreased from 45.9% in 1900 to 38.7% in 1920 and further to 32.5% by the end of World War II, 1945 (See Chart 12-6). Income inequality fell even earlier in France [1], starting in the 1870s, with income share of top 10% of top earners being 49%, 46.5%, 41.1% and below 30% in 1864, 1905, 1930 and 1945. Germany's income share of top 10% of top earners decreased from 45.0% in 1900 to 38.5% in 1930 and further to 34.4% in 1950 after World War II. Denmark, the Netherlands, Switzerland and other European countries experienced a similar process over the same period with income gap getting narrow. Among them, Denmark's income share of top 1% of top earners decreased from around 16.2% in 1900 to 13.3% in 1930 and below 10% in 1950. In middle and late industrialization, income inequality of major European countries showed a decline to varying degrees, which basically coincided with declining stage of Kuznets' inverted "U" curve, difference being emergence of turning point of inequality decline, decline rate and war and political factor impact.

Intertwined with post-industrialization in Europe and the United States, newly industrialized countries quickly completed their industrialization after World War II, making it more difficult to define their middle and late stages of industrialization and Kuznets curve becoming more blurred. But it is also possible to find features of declining income inequality. Japan's defeat in World War II completely broke its social and wealth distribution pattern, with inequality falling sharply and with Gini coefficient at 0.31 in 1956 in early stage of economic recovery rising to 0.38 in 1962 with rapid economic growth and remaining steadily low since then. South Korea's income gap in industrialization also

---

1 Income inequality declined significantly after French Revolution, but the decline was mainly influenced by political rather than economic factor. Industrialization and urbanization at this stage were accompanied by wage stagnation, capital income inflation and wealth concentration, leading to increasing inequality.

remained narrow with Gini coefficient at 0.33 in 1970, rising to 0.36 in 1976 but falling to 0.31 in 1980. Gini coefficient in Taiwan, China was 0.33 in 1964 and fell to 0.31 in 1970 and 0.28 in 1980. Kuznets curve is blurred in these countries whose rising curve in early industrialization is compressed with declining curve in middle and late industrialization. Latin America's path to new industrialization is thought to be flawed with serious income inequality during economic take-off period, which continued to worsen between 1960s and 1980s, but has shown signs of decline in recent decade or so.

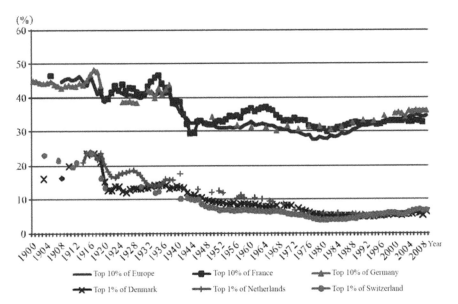

Chart 12-6   Income Inequality in Major European Countries (1900-2010): Income Share

Source: Piketty T., Capital in the Twenty-first Century, Belknap Press, 2014.

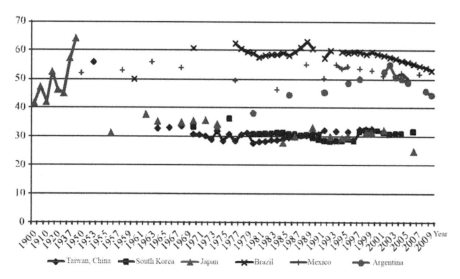

Chart 12-7   Income Inequality in Newly Industrialized Countries and Regions (1900-2010): Gini coefficient

Source: (1) Taiwan (China) data is from *The General Survey of Personal Income Distribution* (1987 Edition). (2) Korea's data is from survey of residents' income and expenditure of Korea National Bureau of Statistics. (3) Japanese data are from National Life Survey of Ministry of Health and Labor of Japan. Data prior to 1950 is taken from relevant studies. (4) Data of Brazil, Mexico and Argentina is from the World Bank database.

(II) Transformation of Development Stage: from Dual Economy to New Classical Economy

The Modern sector dominated by capitalist production mode gradually became dominant with gradual disappearance of dual economic structure. Driven by capital accumulation and technological progress, marginal labor productivity in the traditional sector will also rise. Once exceeding subsistence income, real wage in the traditional sector will be determined by marginal labor productivity. With agriculture becoming a component of the modern sector, the entire economy entered neoclassical stage whose growth is driven by labor, capital and technological progress. Kaldor (1957) divides economic development into two stages: classical stage with real wage fixed on subsistence, and the remainder being capitalists' profit; and Keynesian stage with profit determined according to Keynesian distribution theory, and wage being surplus. Turning point theory put forward by Lewis (1954) directly combines classical stage with neoclassical stage and explains formation and changes of dual economic structure. Japan, a backward country, is characterized by its rapid industrialization. Minami (1968) believes that before World War II, Japan's economy was of classical economy. By 1960, the proportion of agriculture in economic structure and employment structure had fallen to 13.6% and 27.6% respectively. Lewis' turning point theory can explain Japan's economic development in this period. With industrialization entering middle and late stage, economic development has realized fundamental transformation from classical economy to neoclassical economy, bringing about the end of dual economic and social structure in which the traditional sector and the modern sector coexist. The Proportion of British agriculture in national economy fell to 6.4% (in 1907) in early 20th century and the proportion of agricultural employment fell to 7.2% (1920). The proportion of American agriculture in economic structure and employment structure fell to 11.2% and 19.9% in 1930 respectively.

In neoclassical economy, economic growth pattern has changed significantly with rapid growth in labor productivity and declining marginal capital return. Economy grew at a faster pace during this period: average annual growth rate of Britain's output value was 1.93% between 1925 and 1963; average annual growth rate of output value in the United States was slower between 1929 and 1957 than in the previous period, but still close to 3%; average annual growth rate of output value in Canada was nearly 4% over the same period (See Table 12-4). However, economic growth source has changed with factor input growth rate significantly decreasing because on one hand labor input growth has decreased: average annual labor input growth rate in the United States has dropped to 0.53% between 1929 and 1957 or faster output growth meant a big increase in labor productivity and because on the other hand, capital input growth, although faster than labor input, was also slower than output growth, especially in the U.S., where average annual capital input growth rate fell to 1.01% between 1929 and 1957 while between 1889 and 1929, it reached 3.76%, a significant decline in capital output ratio.

Faster growth of total factor productivity (TFP) became the main economic growth source in this period: average annual growth rate of TFP in the United States between 1929 and 1957 reached 2.42%, higher than 1.96% in previous period with total factor productivity contributing 95% to economic growth. Thus, the contribution of total factor productivity to national output growth in this period has far exceeded factor input contribution. Economic growth depends more on technological progress while economic growth pattern in early stage of industrialization is mainly based on capital accumulation rather than technological progress (Abramovitz, 1993). Both changes in production mode and changes in economic growth mode have a profound influence on income distribution in this period.

Table 12-4   Economic Growth and Growth Source in Industrialization in Major Countries

	Average Annual Growth Rate (%)						TFP Contribution (%)
	Output Value (1)	Labor (2)	Capital (3)	Total Input(4)	Total Productivity (5)=(1)-(4)	TFP (6)= (1)-(2)	(7)=(5)/(6)
the U.K.							
Year1855-1913	1. 82	0. 74	1. 43	0.98	0. 84	1. 08	77.8
Year1925-1963	1. 93	0. 82	1. 77	1. 09	0. 84	1. 11	75.7
the U.S.							
Year1889-1929	3. 7	1. 74	3. 76	2. 43	1. 27	1. 96	64.8
Year1929-1957	2. 95	0. 53	1. 01	0. 64	2. 31	2. 42	95.5
Canada							
Year1891-1926	2. 96	1. 82	2. 74	2. 02	0. 94	1. 14	82.5
Year1926-1957	3. 89	0. 77	2. 86	1. 18	2. 71	3. 12	86.9

Note: Output value accounts of the U.K. is GDP-based (GDP) and Output value accounts of the United States and Canada are GNP-based.

Source: Simon Kuznets, *Economic Growth in Various Countries*, Transl. by Chang Xun, Commercial Press, 1973.Yujiro Hayami & Yoshihisa Godo, *Development Economics: From the Poverty to the Wealth of Nations*, Transl. by Li Zhou, Social Sciences Literature Press, 2009.

(III) Game between Labor and Capital

The deeper and more crucial factor of income distribution change caused by production mode change lies in game between capital and labor, two core factors. Fierce game in this period has obviously changed relative position of two factors. In terms of labor factor, according to Lewis' turning point theory, in entering neoclassical economy, there is no more infinite labor supply transferring from the traditional sector to the modern sector, resulting in labor scarcity and rising marginal productivity requiring higher wages. Average annual growth rate of labor productivity in the United States between 1929 and 1966 was 2.7%, higher than that of the previous period, and faster than capital-labor ratio growth (See Table 12-5).

In terms of capital factor, relative status of capital has declined significantly. First, compared with significant decline in labor scarcity, capital growth is faster than labor supply growth, and capital to labor ratio tends to increase so that each worker can have more capital. Average annual capital to labor ratio growth rate reached 1.7% and 11.6% in both the United States between 1929 and 1966 and in Japan between 1958 and 1970, higher than previous period. Higher capital to labor ratio also reflects pressure from diminishing marginal capital return, with capital price or capital return rising more slowly than labor price or labor return (even though the former is falling while the latter is rising). Second, in terms of contribution to overall economic growth, capital to output ratio has declined and contribution of capital accumulation has decreased significantly, far less than contribution of technological progress. Average annual capital contribution growth rate of US between 1929 and 1966 was 0.6%, well below total factor productivity growth rate (2.1%). Capital income share in the U.S. fell from 0.46 in previous period to 0.35 and capital income share in Japan also fell from 0.43 in previous period to 0.3 between 1958 and 1970. Third, capital in a broad sense includes material capital and human capital. In this stage, labor educational capital grows faster than material capital. According to estimates of Schultz (1962), educational capital growth rate of the United States between 1929 and 1957 was

2 to 3 times higher than net tangible assets growth rate, and education capital has a higher return rate with joint return rate of educational capital and male workers' on-the-job training in labor force being 4.8%. Tangible capital return was 3.9%. Therefore, labor factor status with relatively small difference in return rate increases while capital factor status with relatively large difference in return rate and uneven distribution decreases, determining income distribution change in this period.

Table 12-5　Factor Contribution to Economic Growth in Major Industrialized Countries

	Capital Income Share	Average Annual Growth Rate (%)				TFP Contribution (%)
	(1)	Productivity (2)	Capital against Labor (3)	Capital Contribution (4)=(1)*(3)	TFP (5)=(2)-(4)	(6)=(5)/(2)
the U.S.						
Year1800-1855	0. 34	0. 4	0. 6	0. 2	0. 2	50
Year1855-1890	0. 45	1. 1	1. 5	0. 7	0. 4	36
Year1890-1927	0. 46	2. 0	1. 3	0. 6	1. 4	70
Year1929-1966	0. 35	2. 7	1. 7	0. 6	2. 1	78
Year1966-1989	0. 35	1. 4	1. 8	0. 6	0. 8	57
Japan						
Year1888-1900	0. 33	2. 1	5. 7	1. 9	0. 2	10
Year1900-1920	0. 39	2. 7	6. 1	2. 4	0. 3	11
Year1920-1937	0. 43	2. 3	2. 8	1. 2	1. 1	48
Year1958-1970	0. 33	8. 2	11.6	3. 8	4. 4	54
Year1970-1990	0. 28	3. 8	7. 4	2. 1	1. 7	45

Note: Accounts of the U.S. are that of private GDP and accounts of Japan are that of non-agricultural private GDP.
Source: Yujiro Hayami & Yoshihisa Godo, *Development Economics: From the Poverty to the Wealth of Nations*, Transl. by Li Zhou, Social Sciences Literature Press, 2009.

Changes between labor and capital is directly reflected in income distribution pattern in which capital share in national income decreases while labor share in national income increases dramatically. In terms of structural relationship among labor, capital and proprietors (See Chart 12-8), labor share in the U.S. rose from about 55% in the early 20th century to 60.5% in the 1920s and rose to a staggered peak of 71.3% in 1933 during the Great Depression, accordingly capital share and proprietors' share fell to 15.9% and 12.8% respectively.[1] Labor share in the United Kingdom is also characterized by gradual stable increase.[2] Between 1860 and 1869, labor share in the United Kingdom was about 45%, and then gradually increased with industrialization, according to national income account statistics, it rose to 57.1% in 1948, and to 60.5% in 1962. During the first oil crisis[3], it reached its peak of 64.6% in 1975. In turn, corporate profits fell (See Chart 12-9). Studies show that France's capital share also fell from about 36% in 1853 to 18% between 1954 and 1960, and that Germany's capital share fell from about 35% in 1895 to about 25% between 1954 and 1960 (Kuznets, 1973)[4].

---

1 American national accounts statistics divide income into three main types: (1) Compensation of employees includes wage and salary disbursements, supplements to wages and salaries; (2) Asset income includes rental income of persons, corporate profits and net interest; (3) Proprietors' income includes non-corporate farm operator's income and non-farm operator's income and taxes, subsidies, transfer payments and so on.

2 According to the National Economic Accounts of the United Kingdom, gross domestic product at market prices is divided into: (1) Compensation of employees, (2) Total gross operating surplus, similar to corporate profits in the capital gains of the United States; (3) Net tax includes taxes on production and imports and other subsidies on products after taxation, similar to other items in the United States; (4) Mixed income, similar to U.S.'s proprietors' income excluding such property income as interest, and rent, etc.

3 External economic shocks can temporarily affect labor share, such as the Great Depression of the 1930s and the oil crisis of the 1970s where there was sudden temporary labor share growth with its weakening impact being gradually stable.

4 Kuznets (1973) summarized changes in capital share and labor share within a century of modern economic growth. Labor share of most countries rose from 55% to 75% while capital share fell from 45% to 25%. Asset share should be equal to total capital minus output ratio multiplied by capital return rate. If initial capital minus output ratio is 6-7 and capital return rate is 7%, then capital share should be between 42% and 49%. If total capital minus output ratio fell to 4 to 5 and capital return rate fell to 5%-6%, capital share would fall to 20% to 30%. This means that a fall in either total capital minus output ratio or capital return rate could lead to a decline in capital share.

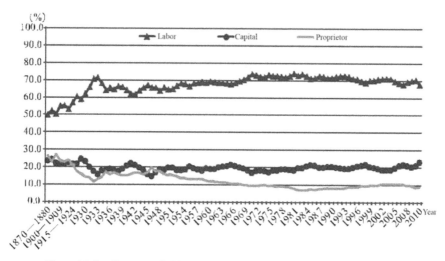

Chart 12-8   Structural Changes in U. S. National Income (1870-2010)

Note: (1) In addition to income from labor, capital and proprietors, national income includes other items such as taxation, subsidies, transfer payments, etc.. From the entire structure of national income, income including other items actually accounts for a very low proportion of national income. In 2010, for example, income from labor, capital and proprietors accounted for 62.1%, 21.1% and 9.1% of total national income respectively, and other items accounted for only 8.7%. (2) "Other items" include taxes on production and imports, subsidies, current surplus of government enterprises and business current transfer payments(net). Among them, subsidy is a minus item.

Source: (1) 1870-1928 data is from Kamil Dagmer, "*Factor Distribution in Canada, the United States and the United Kingdom*", ed. Asimacopoulos, ed. *The Theory of Income Distribution*, Trans. by Lai Desheng et al., (1995 edition) , The Commercial Press. (2) After 1929, the author calculated the data according to the data of Census Bureau and Bureau of Economic Analysis of the United States.

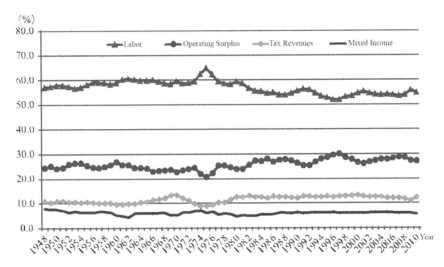

Chart 12-9   Structural Changes in British National Income (1948-2010)

Note: (1) Mixed income has been counted separately since 1997. Prior to 1997 mixed income was obtained by deducting compensation of employees, total gross operating surplus and net tax from total income. (2) Property income including interest, rent, enterprise income distribution and so on is not included here.

Source: calculated based on United Kingdom Economic Accounts from the Office for National Statistics (ONS).

(IV) Worker-oriented Institutional Systems

i. Income distribution pattern began to reverse with more importance attached to the establishment of institutional policies for average worker and resident, capital restraining mechanism being implemented and the government playing a greater role in regulating income distribution.

Kuznets (1955) observed a decline in inequality in the mid-late industrialization because of "double guarantees" of capitalist economic development and the government's redistribution system, although more importance is attached to the former. Adjustment of government's position and systems is not a sudden one, the logic behind which is still inseparable from the change in production mode and in labor factor and capital factor. During this period, contribution of capital accumulation to economic growth tends to decline and is giving way to technological progress with marginal capital return decreasing and powerful position of capital in early industrialization obviously weakening. While the government's top priority is still economic growth, it can no longer rely solely on capital accumulation.

ii. Working class' income and savings growth helps to achieve economic growth goals.

No more unlimited labor supply or even labor shortage and ever-increasing labor productivity has enabled average worker's income to grow rapidly and middle class to grow with more average resident' savings while only capitalists and a very small number of workers had saving in the previous period. In neoclassical economy, savings playing an important role can be transformed into investment to promote sustained economic growth. Between 1929 and 1960, private sector's savings has grown rapidly in the U. S., thus keeping total investment rate at 16% to 18%, of which residents' savings played a more important role, with private sector saving rate at 15.0% in 1929 and residents' savings rate reaching 7.8%, contributing more than half of total savings (52%), which further increased to about 60% by the mid-1950s (Denison, 1958). This means that economic growth the government cares about can also be realized through average worker's savings and residents' savings, which is more sustainable in the long run, laying an economic foundation for the establishment of a system that attaches importance to the interests of average worker.

iii. Adjust labor policies, support trade union development and establish minimum wage system to secure workers' political and economic rights.

The Clayton Act of 1914 in the U.S., called *The Charter of Labor Congress*, protects labor rights and restrict monopoly capital. In 1935, two thirds of the states made and enacted *The Wage Payments Act*[1]. *The National Industrial Relations Act of 1935* gave employees the right to join labor organizations so that union membership rate in the U. S. rose from 12% to 35% between 1935 and 1945.

---

1   Note: Since 1879, a number of state legislatures have passed *The Wage Payments Act* in favour of employees, with one state providing a monthly wage, 31 states paying wages every half a month and eight states providing a weekly wage.

The Fair Labor Act, introduced in 1938, began setting minimum wage, requiring enterprises to pay some workers no less than $0.25 per hour, after which minimum wage rose gradually[1].

iv. Establish and adjust such policies as taxation, social security, anti-poverty, education, etc. for average worker and resident in income redistribution.

During the Great Depression in the U. S. in the 1930s when Roosevelt's "New deal" and Johnson's "Great Society" came into being, redistribution system played an important role in narrowing income gap and promoting economic recovery and even long-term growth. ① Tax system has played an effective role in income regulation. The U. S. has established tax regulation system mainly based on personal income tax, supplemented by inheritance tax, gift tax, personal property tax, personal consumption tax and social security tax, among which personal income tax and inheritance tax (gift tax) carry out progressive tax rate, with the highest marginal tax rate of personal income tax as high as 50% and the highest marginal tax rate of inheritance tax as high as 70%[2]. British personal income tax adopts comprehensive tax system with eligible low-income people not paying tax; France's income tax system adopts high progressive tax system to ensure that low-income families do not pay or underpay income tax. ② Modern social security system has been established and has had its effect on income distribution. In 1935 the U.S. promulgated *The Social Security Act* which embodies social co-aid and redistribution. Replacement rate of low-income people in federal old-age insurance is 60% while that of high-income people is only 28%. A series of important social welfare acts, such as *The Old Age Maintenance Act* and *The National Insurance Act*, were enacted in the U.K. in 1908. In 1934, Beveridge submitted a report on *Social Security* and *Related Services* to the British Government in which social insurance, social assistance and voluntary insurance

---

1 In 1975, it was US$2.10 per hour. In 1995, it was US$4.25 per hour. In 2009, it was US$ 7.25 per hour.

2 Take 1974 for example, Gini coefficient of pre-tax cash income of American household unit was 0.395 and decreased to 0.318 after redistribution, down by 19.5%.

construction of a "welfare state" is recommended. Japan re-established its social security system after World War II and achieved its goal of "National annuity" in 1961. ③ Anti-poverty policy focusing on relief, subsidies or poverty alleviation for poor population or poor areas has a more direct effect of narrowing income gap. The U.S. began its regional aid policy focusing on the south after economic crisis of the 1930s. In 1933, the U. S. established The Tennessee River Basin Management Commission responsible for the Development in the Tennessee River Basin and in the mid-lower reaches of the Mississippi River. A national law that made unemployment and economic backwardness a national problem was enacted in 1961. ④ Education equalization has been playing an important role in solving long-term inequality. Both federal and state governments have increased their spending on compulsory education, the proportion of federal spending and state spending on public primary and secondary education with year 1940 as gauge dividing line, soaring from 0.4% and 16.9% before 1940 to 1.8% and 30.3% after 1940.

IV. Income Gap Widening again: Income Distribution in New Economic Era

In the 1970s, with their completion of industrialization in developed countries and arrival of new economic era pushed by new technological revolution, profound changes in economic growth mode with new knowledge and new technology as its key power, economic globalization has become an important feature and economic structure of developed countries has undergone significant changes. Although income redistribution system has played its positive role, the once narrowing income gap has widened again in new economic era and widening inequality has continued up to now and has not yet shown signs of narrowing. With production factor changes, new technological revolution has reversed the decreasing trend of marginal capital return and development of capital market and non-entity economy has enhanced capital. There has been labor division among workers as labor return of higher human capital has increased more rapidly. As a result, advantage position of capital in the game between capital and labor reappears. Capitalist free market economy has been unable to regulate income gap on its own as traditional redistribution has gradually failed with its negative effect on economic growth and employment, making it difficult to fundamentally solve income distribution problem.

(I) Widening Income Gap

New economy brought a new round of economic growth and the turning point of income gap as well. Kuznets (1955) observed that the effect of industrialization on narrowing income gap gradually disappeared, income gap reaching a stage low in the 1970s beginning to rise gradually. According to CPS, income share of top 5% and top 20% of households in the United States rose from 16.6% and 43.3% in 1970 to 18.5% and 46.6% in 1990 and to 21.3% and 50.2% in 2010. Gini coefficient rose from 0.39 in 1970 to 0.43 in 1990 and to 0.47 in 2010. Property inequality also took a turn in the 1970s with top 1% of household net worth rising from 29.1% in 1972 to 35.7% in 1990.

Other industrialized countries have also experienced widening income gap to varying degrees. According to CSO, income share of U.K.'s top 20% of households rose from 43% in mid-1970s to 50% in mid-1990s, and Gini coefficient of initial distribution rose from 0.34 in mid-1970s to 0.44 in early 1990s to the current 0.46. Gini coefficient of Denmark rose from 0.37 in mid-1980s to the current 0.42. During the same period, Gini coefficient of Germany rose from 0.44 to 0.50; Italy from 0.42 to 0.54; Japan from 0.35 to 0.46. Gini coefficient of initial distribution of OECD countries has now reached 0.46 (See Chart 12-10).

Redistribution reduces income inequality, but does not fundamentally reverse the widening income gap. Gini coefficient of initial distribution for the latest year of the United States is 0.49. and Gini coefficient after redistribution decreased to 0.38, down by about 22%; that of the U.K. decreased from 0.46 to 0.35, down by 24%. Redistribution regulation of Nordic countries is effective, whose Gini coefficient after regulation is reduced by about 40%. The overall Gini coefficient of initial distribution of OECD countries also decreased from 0.46 to 0.31 after redistribution with an average decrease of about 30% (See Chart 12-11). However, Gini coefficient after redistribution also tends to expand. For example, Gini coefficient after redistribution in the U. S. is still about 20% higher than that in the 1970s. That of the U. K. has increased by about 30% in the same period. Gini coefficient of such countries as Norway and Japan with narrow income gap and effective redistribution has also increased by 10% to 15%. Redistribution system can not be the fundamental means to regulate widening income gap, nor can Kuznets hypothesis be applied to income distribution pattern in post-industrialization.

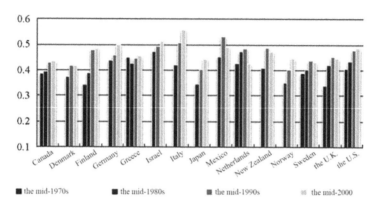

Chart 12-10   Gini coefficient in Major Countries since the 1970s: Initial Distribution

Source: OECD Bureau of Statistics. Note: There is a certain difference between countries in statistical data year. The mid-term refers to the year before and after 2005.

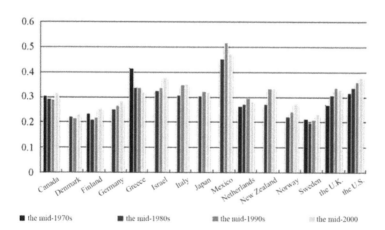

Chart 12-11   Gini coefficient in Major Countries since the 1970s: Redistribution

Source: OECD Bureau of Statistics.

(II) New Economic Era of Globalization

The third science and technology revolution represented by information technology, a new impetus to growth, has brought about a new round of rapid growth of global economy, causing economic structure of developed countries to continue to undergo profound changes. There has been further decline in the proportion of agriculture in national economy. In 2010, the proportion of agriculture in economic structure and employment structure of the U. S. has fallen to 1.2% and 1.5% respectively, a continuation of development trend of industrialization. However, major changes in economic structure have been rapid decline in industrial sector whose proportion kept rising in industrialization. The proportion of American industry in its economic structure fell from 35.2% in 1970 to 27.9% in 1990 and further to 20.4% in 2010. The proportion of British industry in its economic structure gradually decreased from 42.1% in 1970 to 21.8% in 2010. That of OECD countries decreased from 38.6% in 1970 to 23.7% in 2010 (See Table 12-6). Arrival of new economic era has fundamentally changed direction of economic growth in developed countries. Information technology has accelerated development of new service industries such as research and development, innovation, logistics, sales, and so on. Service industry share in U.S. economic structure rose from 61.2% in 1970 to 78.4% in 2010. Service industry share in U.K.'s economic structure rose from 55.0% in 1970 to 77.5% in 2010. Service industry share in OECD countries as a whole has reached 75%. Developed countries have taken service economy as their main development direction in post-industrialization.

Economic globalization, an important feature and necessary condition of new economic era, has expanded the boundary of neoclassical economic growth. Driven by information technology, industrial labor division and structural adjustment is under way on a global scale with capital and technology factors flowing around the world and economic ties across the world getting closer. Trade share in GDP in the U.S. rapidly rose from 11.3% in 1970 to 20.8% in 1980 and to 28.8% in 2010. Trade share in GDP in the U.K. rose from 43.6% in 1970 to 62.3%

in 2010. That of OECD countries rose from 25.5% in 1970 to 50.4% in 2010. Globalized economic growth has expanded boundary of neoclassical economic growth in a sense and factor allocation and marginal return are determined in a wider scope, which will have a deep impact on production mode, capital factor and labor factor, changing income distribution pattern.

Table 12-6 Economic Structure and Employment Structure of Major Countries in New Economic Era

		Year 1970	Year 1980	Year 1990	Year 2000	Year 2010
the U.S.						
Economic Structure (%)	Agriculture	3.5	2.9	2.1	1.2	1.2
	Industry	35.2	33.5	27.9	23.4	20.4
	Service	61.2	63.6	70.1	75.4	78.4
Employment Structure (%)	Agriculture		3.6	2.9	2.6	1.5
	Industry		30.8	26.4	23.2	19.9
	Service		65.7	70.7	74.3	78.6
Trade in GDP (%)		11.3	20.8	20.6	25.9	28.8
the U. K.						
Economic Structure (%)	Agriculture	2.9	2.1	1.8	1.0	0.7
	Industry	42.1	40.7	34.1	27.3	21.8
	Service	55.0	57.2	64.1	71.7	77.5
Employment Structure (%)	Agriculture		2.6	2.1	1.5	1.1
	Industry		37.2	32.3	25.1	19.5
	Service		58.9	64.8	73.0	78.6
Trade in GDP (%)		43.6	51.8	50.0	57.1	62.3
Japan						
Economic Structure (%)	Agriculture	6.0	3.6	2.5	1.8	1.4
	Industry	45.3	40.7	39.1	32.4	26.7
	Service	48.6	55.7	58.4	65.8	71.9
Employment Structure (%)	Agriculture		10.4	7.2	5.1	4.2
	Industry		35.3	34.1	31.2	27.3
	Service		54.0	58.2	63.1	67.3

contd.

		Year 1970	Year 1980	Year 1990	Year 2000	Year 2010
Trade in GDP (%)		20.1	27.9	19.8	20.5	29.3
OECD						
Economic Structure (%)	Agriculture	6.0	4.2	3.1	2.0	1.5
	Industry	38.6	36.2	32.2	27.5	23.7
	Service	55.3	59.6	64.7	70.5	74.8
Employment Structure (%)	Agriculture				7.0	5.1
	Industry				27.0	24.4
	Service				65.8	70.1
Trade in GDP (%)		25.5	36.3	35.3	45.3	50.4

Source: World Bank, World Development Indicators, 2011.

(III) More Capital Financialization

Capital financialization enhances capital and has been playing an increasingly prominent role in income distribution. Capital Financialization has enhanced the role capital factor plays in economic development, especially of non-entity economy. On the one hand, capital financialization has enabled capital to be effectively allocated globally and between industries. At the same time, capital enables new technologies to transfer and diffuse rapidly. Even developing countries with low saving capacity and scarce capital and technology can also achieve rapid growth with capital and technology inflow from developed countries. On the other hand, capital financialization has increasingly prominent effect on income and wealth. Capital concentrates and rapidly expands through leverage effect of capital market and accelerates accumulation and agglomeration of income and wealth without corresponding product or entity. Economic over-virtualization, the effect capital financialization has on income and wealth gradually deviate from its effect on resource allocation, thus creating greater inequality in income and wealth.

Impact of capital financialization on entity economy is immense. In global labor division, developed countries with capital advantage have transferred manufacturing-dominated real economy overseas, lower value-added intermediate end in industrial chain and low-end industries gradually flowing to developing countries. Two higher value-added ends of industrial chain, research & development and sales, stay inside developed countries. This global labor division, vividly portrayed as "smiling curve", enabled developed countries to take higher capital return rate through industrial restructuring and upgrading. But global labor division has also brought about industry "hollowing" of domestic economy with the proportion of manufacturing-dominated entity economy falling sharply, which has directly led to the declining proportion of industry in national economy (See Chart 12-12). Added value of manufacturing in GDP in the U.S. fell from 23% in 1980 to 13.4% in 2010. Over the same period, that of the U.K. decreased from 25.5% to 11.5%. Even that of manufacturing-dominated Germany fell from about 30% to 20% and that of the OECD countries has fallen to about 15%.

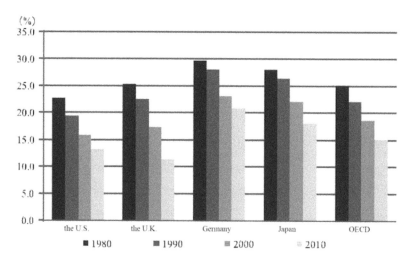

Chart 12-12   Industry Hollowing: Added Value of Manufacturing in GDP in Major Countries

Source: World Bank, World Development Indicators, 2011.

Industry "hollowing" directly leads to the following negative effect. First, industries and economies are more vulnerable to shocks. Financial crises and economic crises often hit the non-entity economic sector first, and then gradually spread to real economy. Service industry-dominated developed countries such as Europe and the U.S. have been involved in and affected by various financial crises and economic crises while real economy-dominated countries are relatively less hit by them. Second, there is no employment growth. Relatively higher capital labor ratio of non-entity economy and virtual economy, lower employment elasticity of industry and employment demand of high human capital have given rise to limited employment drive to economic growth and industrial expansion. High unemployment rate difficult to get rid of in Europe and America is definitely related to there being no employment growth. Third, middle class weakened. Non-entity economy expansion squeezed entity economy, the basis for middle class, leading to internal division of service industry, workers with higher human capital in industry enjoying more and low-end service industry developing slow.

(IV) Internal Division Among Working Class

More skill-dominated employment triggered by new technological revolution has led to internal division among working class. Both employment expansion and wage growth rate of high-skilled and high human capital employees is faster than that of less skilled and low human capital employees, especially internal division in service industry in particular. Middle class flourishing in industrialization is suffering the shock and even is on the verge of disintegration.

Technological progress is obviously an important factor in inducing skill-dominated employment (Goos et al., 2010). In addition, there are at least four main causes for internal division among working class. First, employees' human capital structure changes. The proportion of employees with higher education and higher human capital has gradually expanded, becoming main body of labor market with competitive advantage while employees with lower human capital are in a very unfavorable position and even solidified. In 2010, the proportion of employees with higher education rose to 61.1% in the U.S. dominated by employees with higher human capital while the proportion of middle-skilled jobs falling by about 15% over the past 30 years, leading to disappearance of middle-skilled employees and middle class (Tuzemen & Willis, 2012). The proportion of employees with higher education in the U.K., Japan and OECD countries has reached or even exceeded 1/3. However, employees with only primary education in the U. K. and OECD countries accounted for 21.5% and 28.7% (See Table 12-7).

Second, industrial structure and employment structure changes. Employment proportion of service industry in developed countries has increased significantly, but there has been a serious division in service industry with its high-end developing obviously faster than its low-end and accordingly there has been a serious division among employees of service industry as its high-end gathers high human capital employees whose wage, income and growth rate is faster than its low-end service employees, causing income gap between employees to continue to widen. According to IMF study (2007) , labor share of low-skilled sector has continued to decline while labor share of high-skilled sector has continued to rise. Labor share of low-skilled sector in the U. S. has gradually declined from 26% in 1980 to 18% around 2000. That of Europe and Japan fell from about 35% to 24%. In contrast, labor share of high-skilled sector in the U.S. rose from 38% to 44% over the same period.

Third, employment mode has changed. The decline in the proportion of self-employed workers means employment regularization consistent with general trend of labor market development and economic development and conducive to growth of the proportion of workers' remuneration in national economy. In recent years, self-employed employment rate in OECD countries has increased from 17.9% in 2000 to 19.7% in 2010. Higher self-employed employment rate is not conducive to narrowing income gap. Part-time employment rate growth, an important feature of employment mode change, is not conducive to employment security and income stability, causing income gap to widen. Part-time employment rate in the U.K. rose from 20.1% in 1990 to 23.9% in 2010. Part-time employment rate in the U.S. and OECD countries have risen in recent years, too.

Fourth, income structure has also changed. Labor remuneration generally comes from salary and supplementary pay. After 1970s, the proportion of supplementary pay increased obviously, for example, share of employees' wage in American national income in 1997 was 4.2% lower than that in 1959, but share of supplementary pay in national income was 6.7% higher than that in 1959 and share of supplementary pay in total employee remuneration rose from 7.6% in 1959 to 16.9% in 1997. With employees sharing "capital" rights with enterprise shares, ESOP plays a crucial role in widening income gap between workers and staff because management, managers and employees with higher human capital have more opportunities and capabilities to hold shares. In 1980, average annual income of general managers in large American enterprises was 42 times that of average worker, goes up to 85 times in 1990, 141 times in 1995 and 326 times in 1997.

Table 12-7   Human Capital Structure of Labor Force in Major Countries

		Year 1980	Year 1990	Year 2000	Year 2010
the U. S.					
Human Capital Structure of Labor Force (%)	Primary Education			13.7	9.5
	Secondary Education			51.5	29.4
	Higher Education			34.8	61.1
Proportion of Self-employed Workers (%)		9.4	8.8	7.4	7.0
Proportion of Part-time Workers (%)		14.4	14.1	12.6	14.1
the U. K.					
Human Capital Structure of Labor Force (%)	Primary Education			26.5	21.5
	Secondary Education			47.4	45.9
	Higher Education			26.1	31.9
Proportion of Self-employed Workers (%)		8.1	14.3	12.3	13.6
Proportion of Part-time Workers (%)			20.1	23.0	23.9
Japan					
Human Capital Structure of Labor Force (%)	Primary Education		31.6	17.2	
	Secondary Education		45.4	47. 7	
	Higher Education		21.2	35. 0	
Proportion of Self-employed Workers (%)		28.1	22.3	16.6	12.6
Proportion of Part-time Workers (%)				22.5	20.3

contd.

		Year 1980	Year 1990	Year 2000	Year 2010
OECD					
Human Capital Structure of Labor Force (%)	Primary Education			23.6	28.7
	Secondary Education			46.0	37.7
	Higher Education			27.7	36.8
Proportion of Self-employed Workers (%)				17.9	19.7
Proportion of Part-time Workers (%)				14.7	16.2

Note: Some countries' data of 2010 are not published and are replaced by data of 2008 or 2009.

Source: World Bank, World Development Indicators, 2011.

(V) Gradual Failure of Traditional Redistribution

In new economic era when technology and innovation have become the key driving force of economic growth, capital and labor has changed again in that fruits of economic growth are more shared by capital. As new technological revolution has prevented the decline of marginal capital return, the status of capital enhances again while there emerges internal division among employees. Unable to block mainstream trend, government systems and policies have been adjusted to adapt to changing situations as marginal capital tax rate declines, trade union is gradually weakening, and traditional redistribution which income gap regulation depends on has been unable to reverse the widening income gap trend. More severely, the negative effect of redistribution on labor market, employment and economic growth are becoming increasingly serious, triggering economic crisis.

Tax policy adjustment weakens regulatory function of income distribution. In the case of the U.S., highest tax rate during the Kennedy administration reached 70%. But by the mid-1970s, the enthusiasm for these efforts had waned so that in 1980 everything went back to normal. The Reagan and Bush administrations after 1980 implemented tax reduction and exemption favoring the rich and budget cuts in social services unfavorable to the poor. The 1981 tax code cut tax rate by 23% and introduced more favourable accelerated depreciation subsidies. The 1986 tax code cut maximum marginal tax rate from 50% to 20% and other tax rate to 15%. The Clinton administration pursued the policy of deficit reduction, in which some government spending for the poor was significantly reduced and maximum progressive tax rate for the rich continued to fall. The Bush Jr. administration abolished dividend tax and accelerated income tax cut with the core to cut tax burden of high-income taxpayers. All these policy adjustments have significantly weakened tax regulation on income gap, which in 1978 was able to reduce Gini coefficient of personal income by 8.5% while only by 5.8% in 1992.

Trade unions began to weaken markedly. During economic crisis and inflation in the 1970s, labor market also underwent institutional changes and trade unions began to weaken. From 1979 to 1988, union membership rate in the United States fell from 24% to 17% (from 31% to 22% among all male workers) and to 16% by the mid-1990s, with 11% in private enterprises. Trade unions weakened and collective wage bargaining contracts fell, affecting workers' real wages. The 1994 real hourly wage after tax fell by 10.4% from its peak in 1972 after World War II. Per capita output increased by 53% over that of 1967, but real wage after tax fell by 4%. Slow growth (or even decline) of real wage has widened income gap.

Redistribution system faces increasingly serious challenges of financial sustainability. Welfare tendency of redistribution system is becoming increasingly serious, which brings about increasingly heavy financial burden in European countries and the U.S., especially in economic crisis and slow growth period with heavy pressure of fiscal austerity when redistribution system adopted to regulate income gap is constrained so that this measure won't sustain. Much of the fund for high welfare comes from government borrowing. This kind of "robbing Jack to pay Jill" high welfare system is increasingly burgeoning country's debt burden as population ages and economic growth slows down, leading to a sovereign debt crisis. Europe is now in such trouble that average debt ratio--that is, public debt in GDP-- of the 17 EU countries has reached 93%, Italy and Portugal being more than 130% and Greece 170%, and the major developed countries that have long relied on redistribution have left themselves mired in debt.

Moreover, the negative effect of redistribution system on labor market and economic growth is becoming increasingly serious. High welfare redistribution system encourages workers to withdraw from labor market earlier or reduce labor supply, resulting in less mobility of jobs and occupations and less flexibility in labor market, which is not conducive to labor productivity growth and which leads to higher economic price and costs. For example, Beveridge social security model in the U. K., Denmark, the Netherlands and other countries provides a basic fixed pension scheme, attaching greater importance to social equity and civil rights instead of the link between income and contributions so that it has a relatively good income distribution effect. But this model encourages workers to retire earlier, causing higher unemployment rate and damaging economic growth. Traditional redistribution is gradually failing with heavy costs. How to adopt redistribution to regulate income gap needs to be examined and evaluated in a comprehensive way.

V. Conclusion and Implications

(I) General Logic of Income Distribution Evolution

By exploring and summarizing world history of various countries, income distribution changes with its stage characteristics and general laws of economic and social development. Production mode change is key determinant of income distribution pattern. Factor changes in land, labor, capital and technology runs through the increase and decrease in income inequality. There is inherent consistency between factor allocation share in national income (functional distribution) and individual or residents' income gap (scale distribution). Starting from classical economy, industrialization has ushered in brand new human civilization: this centuries-long history can be divided into four typical stages to show more clearly income distribution evolution (See Chart 12-13).

When capitalist production mode is yet to be established, classical economic growth has dominated pre-industrialization with petty peasant economy as its main body, very small national income, wealth distribution being main distribution, political rights and social hierarchy dominating distribution of highly concentrated wealth, and wide gap between rich and poor until bourgeois revolution and industrial revolution broke pre-industrialization pattern. In early industrialization when capitalist production mode was established, production factor of both capital and labor determined national income distribution but dual economic structure was characterized by capital scarcity, cheap labor, imbalanced capital-dominated income distribution pattern, capitalist-oriented government systems and policies, small labor share, and widening income gap. In the middle-late industrialization, capitalist production mode is maturing day by day with the end of dual economic structure and establishment of neoclassical economy which is characterized by declining marginal capital return, relative labor scarcity, and fierce game between labor and capital, government systems and policies attaching importance to workers, establishment of redistribution system, bigger labor share, and narrowing income gap. With the completion of industrialization and arrival of new economic era of globalization, economic growth pattern has changed again. Skilled-dominated development has broken the law of diminishing marginal capital return, capital finanicalization and virtualization has been quite obvious, and entity economy is hit so that capital plays an even more important role again. The working class is divided so that middle class is on the verge of disintegration. The income gap is widening again and there is no sign of narrowing so far. Traditional redistribution is almost out of order, making it difficult to solve income distribution problem fundamentally. Whether the income gap will continue to widen or narrow is not yet known.

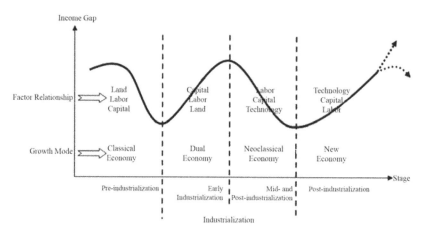

Chart 12-13   Stages and Characteristics of Income Distribution Evolution

(II) Main Characteristics of Income Distribution Changes

With international experience, grasping the following basic characteristics of income distribution evolution is of great significance to understand and solve income distribution problem.

First, income gap change show characteristics of economic development stage. In pre-industrialization dominated by feudal system, income and wealth was highly concentrated, With bourgeois revolution and collapse of feudal system, highly centralized distribution pattern was broken down with decline in inequality. With establishment of capitalist production mode, income inequality increased first and then decreased, entering inverted "U" type stage Kuznets (1955) described. In new economic era, income inequality increases again and has not stopped increasing. Over a longer period of time, inequality can be described as a "W" curve.   Second, rapid economic growth is usually accompanied by widening income gap. Economy tends to grow rapidly with greater capital and technological contribution and higher marginal return rate. When labor remuneration grows slow, when industrialization is promoted by industrial revolution and new economy is promoted by information technological revolution, and when capital and technology play their important role, income gap tends to widen rapidly. In rapid economic growth, it is necessary to balance both economic growth and income gap and attach importance to average worker condition improvement while income gap is widening.

Third, relatively speaking, capital factor tends to concentrate while labor factor tends to equalize. Factors in economic development change with income distribution pattern. When capital factor dominates, income inequality increases. When labor factor rises, income inequality decreases. Raising worker status and increasing labor share in national economy is conducive to decreasing income inequality in general, but an important premise is that there is no serious division among workers.

Fourth, wealth distribution and income distribution are interrelated as income accumulates wealth and wealth creates income. Before industrialization, economic growth is slow and income flow is relatively small so that wealth distribution is major income distribution problem. During industrialization, with rapid economic growth and increased income flow, income distribution problem in modern sense began to appear as wealth transforms into capital faster and wealth distribution and income distribution is closely related. To solve income distribution problem, importance should be attached to both wealth distribution and income distribution.

Fifth, there is an inherent consistency between functional distribution and scale distribution. Income inequality varies with labor share: bigger capital income share and smaller labor share means capital owner can get higher return but average worker, main body of residents, gets lower return, giving rise to widening income gap and vice versa. Functional distribution and scale distribution should not be studied separately as there is a close internal logical relationship between them.

Sixth, income distribution system and policy should conform to production mode and factors. The establishment or regulation of tax, trade union, social security and other redistribution systems and policies should basically conform to the trend and production mode and factors of a particular stage, key factor determining income distribution. In this sense, redistribution system is also endogenous not to be arbitrarily adjusted at any stage under any environment.

Promoting redistribution system while violating income distribution formation mechanism may have negative influence on economic development.

Seventh, redistribution system can not fundamentally solve income distribution problem. Although it can regulate income gap to a certain extent, redistribution system is not included in determination mechanism of income distribution change and cannot change the overall trend of income inequality. It is difficult to reverse changing direction of income gap by relying entirely on redistribution system. Initial distribution and redistribution needs to be balanced as initial distribution is determined by economic and social development and market mechanism and redistribution is more about social equity as an important means to improve income distribution. Moderate redistribution is needed to regulate income distribution without sacrificing economic growth.

Eighth, in new economy income distribution pattern is more complex. Technological innovation creating new economic growth opportunities have different effect on capital and labor by increasing marginal capital return, thus preventing or delaying its decline, and by rapidly increasing remuneration of workers with higher human capital and accelerating internal division of workers, thus widening income gap. As each technological revolution promotes economic growth and increases income inequality, dealing with income distribution in new economy has become a major issue.

(III) Implication of China's Income Distribution Reform

China is currently in the middle-late stage of industrialization from dual economy to neoclassical economy with visible turning point of income gap. Since reform and opening up, China has established socialist market economic system with economic growth mode and production mode undergoing fundamental changes. China's economy has grown at an average annual rate of nearly 10%. However, its investment-driven growth model determines the dominant position of capital as capital has made over 50% contribution to economic growth, inevitably leading to smaller labor share and widening income gap. China has currently entered a new development stage as, according to statistics, the proportion of agriculture in national economy has dropped to less than 10%, the proportion of industry has begun to decline after experiencing a rapid rise, urbanization exceeding 55% and GDP per capita in 2005 exceeding $8,000. All this shows China is now in the middle-late stage of industrialization and urbanization and income gap is expected to narrow. According to the National Bureau of Statistics, Gini coefficient has kept rising from 0.28 in early reform and opening up to about 0.49 in 2008 and fell to 0.462 in 2015 and urban-rural income gap gradually expanded from 2: 1 to its highest 3.3:1 and narrowed to 2.73: 1 in 2015.

Relationship between labor and capital is undergoing profound changes as basic conditions for improving income distribution have matured. Since the 21st century, urban-rural integration has accelerated, traditional dual economic structure has been broken and labor market has undergone profound changes as long-term unlimited labor supply has been replaced by labor shortage. There appeared "Lewis turning point" as average workers' wage has risen rapidly with wage convergence, marginal capital return diminishing law and new classical economic stage of urban-rural integration (Cai Fang, 2010). Entering this new stage, status of labor factor begins to rise which can be reflected in supply-demand relationship, wage growth and labor protection system of the government. Income distribution pattern is changing in favor of workers. In all, basic conditions for narrowing income gap were already in place.

However, China's industrialization and economic development has its own particularity. Under globalization, in a short period of several decades, China has quickly completed its industrialization which took traditional capitalist countries hundreds of years to complete. Although basic framework of market economy system has been established, institutions are not mature enough and institutional obstacles intertwine with market economy system, such as unfair income distribution in factor capitalization (Zhang Juwei, Cheng Jie, 2013). All these above affect China's economic growth mode and income distribution mechanism which enables China's income distribution evolution to be characterized not only by general law of economic development stage but by such institutional factors as system transition, incomplete reform, making it more difficult to understand and deal with China's income distribution.

China's current widening income gap mainly attributes to economic growth mode and market mechanism consistent with basic characteristics of economic development stage and conforming to basic law of income distribution evolution. However, income distribution can be solved. It is a feasible and optional path for China to regulate its income gap by perfecting institutional rules and relying on economic development and market mechanism. Therefore, income distribution reform should be part of overall economic system reform by focusing on initial distribution and giving top priority to elimination of unfair income distribution so as to remove institutional obstacles that hinder market mechanism and to optimize market economic system, factor market in particular, ensuring that factors can get their due return by maintaining balance between labor and capital so as to give full play to self-regulation of market mechanism. On this basis, redistribution system consistent with factors can be set up and perfected by avoiding distorting resource allocation and economic efficiency while properly playing its role of regulating income distribution.

Chapter XIII

Conclusion and Suggestions

ZHANG Juwei, CHENG Jie, ZHAO Wen[1]

I. Rethinking on China's Income Distribution

It is widely believed that there is serious income distribution in China and there is so-called "consensus" on some problems. But in-depth research will reveal that these "consensus" are only some popular views, there still lacks evidence. It's a must to re-examining some of the important issues.

(I) China's Current Income Gap

As the National Bureau of Statistics (NBS) has stopped publishing national Gini coefficient since 2000, judging China's current income gap has to rely on research results of different research teams. With different data sources and

---

1   ZHANG Juwei, Director of the Institute of Population and Labor Economics of the Chinese Academy of Social Sciences, Research Fellow, Doctoral Advisor; CHENG Jie, Associate Research Fellow of the Institute of Population and Labor Economics of the Chinese Academy of Social Sciences; ZHAO Wen, Associate Research Fellow of the Institute of Population and Labor Economics of the Chinese Academy of Social Sciences.

research methods, different research teams reach different conclusions. There are no consensus on China's current income gap.

It is widely believed that China's current income gap is still widening with worsening income distribution. According to a study, national Gini coefficient rose by 5% to 7% between 2002 and 2007, from 0.42 to 0.48 in 2007. Other studies even suggest that China's Gini coefficient rose from 0.327 in 1980 to 0.508 in 2008. However, some recent studies have concluded that China's widening income gap has stabilized and even showed signs of convergence. A study from OECD suggests that Gini coefficient in rural China has decreased from 0.44 in 2001 to 0.39 in 2010. Gini coefficient in urban China remained basically at 0.34 after 2005. National Gini coefficient remained stable at 0.46 after 2005 and widening trend of income gap has stopped.

Based on data from the National Bureau of Statistics, Gini coefficient declined from 0.45 in 2003 to 0.43 in 2009. Normative academic research results do not fully support the social consensus that there's widening income gap in China for lack of authoritative data, affecting the path choice and policy orientation in solving China's income distribution problem. Therefore, it is necessary to republish the official data on China's income gap so as to provide an objective basis for forming a social consensus on China's income gap. Otherwise, society and the public may be misled and have adverse consequences.

In view of this, the National Bureau of Statistics published Gini coefficient between 2003 and 2012 for the first time on January 18, 2013. According to official data, China's Gini coefficient rose from 0.479 in 2003 to a 10-year high of 0.491 in 2008 after some fluctuations. In 2015, it fell further to 0.462. So China's income gap has improved after 2008.

(II) China's Serious Income Gap in International Comparison

China's serious income gap is to be re-examined. It is generally believed that there's quite serious income gap in China, a country with the widest income gap in the world, threatening social stability. But if China's income gap is compared internationally, the conclusion will be quite objective.

When compared internationally, China's income gap is generally wider than that of most developed countries, but lower than that of some developing countries with serious income gap problem. At the same time, compared with developed countries, main reason for China's wide income gap is that redistribution does not play its role in narrowing income gap. From initial distribution, China's income gap is not that different from that of most developed countries. But after regulation of both tax and government transfer payments, income gap in developed countries is greatly narrowed by 10-15 Gini points. For example, Gini coefficient in Japan is narrowed from 0.43 after initial distribution to 0.28 after redistribution; Germany from 0.45 to 0.35; the U.K. from 0.41 to 0.26; China's redistribution doesn't work well with Gini coefficient hardly changing before and after redistribution. If China's redistribution works as well as that of developed countries, China's income gap will greatly narrow and there'll be no more widening income gap in China.

From income gap source, China's income gap is to a large extent caused by urban-rural gap and regional gap distinguishing China from other countries. Contribution of China's urban-rural and regional gap to Gini coefficient is 40% while that of the United States is only about 4%. Brazil's income gap, one of the world's widest with its Gini coefficient of more than 0.5, is exclusively caused by urban gap and rural gap rather than urban-rural gap. In this sense, Brazil's income gap is actually caused by its more serious income distribution. Urban-rural gap and regional gap can be resolved by rapid development as income gap relates to development. If urban-rural gap is completely eliminated, China's overall Gini coefficient will fall by 30% to 40% and widening income gap will be basically eliminated. Judging from its own characteristics, China's income gap should not be over-interpreted.

(III) Correct Understanding of China's Labor Share

There are currently some misunderstandings about China's labor share due to improper international comparison with different calibers. Sharp decline in China's labor share in recent years is more of the result of statistical caliber adjustment, not necessarily reflecting the real initial income distribution.

There are two statistical calibers for labor share internationally. The first is labor remuneration received by wage and salary recipients or employees' remuneration; the second includes both labor remuneration of wage and salary recipients and mixed income of self-employed workers. China adopts the second caliber for its labor remuneration data while internationally the first caliber for labor remuneration data is used. China's labor share is about 46% with the second caliber. Compared with labor share with the first caliber internationally, China's labor share is generally 50% to 60% of that of developed countries, not much of a difference but much higher than that of developing countries in general. However, such an incorrect comparison with different caliber leads to wrong conclusion.

With the first statistical caliber in line with international standard, China's labor share is only about 30%, much lower than that of developed countries and almost the same as that of many developing countries, typical of developing countries. Therefore, it is an indisputable fact that China's labor share is small.

Reason for China's small labor share is commonly believed to be too low wage which is not entirely true because when the first statistical caliber of employees' labor remuneration in GDP is used to measure labor share which is determined by both employees' wage and employees' number. Big labor share in developed countries lies in high employee employment rate. According to the latest data from International Labor Organization (ILO), average employee employment rate in developed countries and EU economies in 2008 was 86.2%, more than 90% in some countries, such as Japan, the U.K., and the U. S., 86.5%, 86.6%, and 93%. In developing countries, on the other hand, low employee employment rate is typical of Southeast Asia averaging 36.4%; Sub-Saharan Africa averaging 24.7%; South Asian countries averaging only 21.5%. According to calculation based on employment data released by the National Bureau of Statistics, China's employee employment rate has been stable at about 42% between 1995 and 2006. Despite its increase in recent years, it is only about 46% in 2009. Therefore, Low employee employment rate is major cause of China's small labor share. Keeping the current employees' wage unchanged, if China's employee employment rate can reach average level of developed countries, labor share will rise from 30% to 56%. Small labor share will no longer exist when it reaches higher level in developed countries.

These conclusions are of great significance to correct understanding of effective ways for China's labor share growth. Compared with self-employed employment, employee employment is characterized by its job stability, high income and great security. Therefore, employee employment rate can also be regarded as an index for employment regularization. The reason for high employee employment rate in developed countries is that they have completed industrialization, modernization, and employment regularization while China is still in this process. In view of this, fundamental measure for China's labor share growth is to expand employment, speed up rural labor transfer, and improve employee employment rate and regularization rate. Labor share not only relates to income distribution but to economic development and labor market.

(IV) Solution to Income Distribution: Initial Distribution or Redistribution

Developed countries are able to reasonably narrow their income gap determined by the market mainly because of redistribution. Lack of effective redistribution to regulate the income gap in developing countries is the major cause for widening income gap. Therefore, solution to China's income distribution should be mainly redistribution since initial distribution is entirely determined by the market.

China's current income distribution problem can not merely be solved through redistribution. On the contrary, many key problems in China are in initial distribution where extremely severe unfair distribution caused by institutional factors must be resolved through reform, institutional change being the cure. Although redistribution can help to improve the living conditions of low-income and poor groups, it does not help to strengthen social equity and eliminate social exclusion. In order to fundamentally reverse the widening income gap, institutional reform of initial distribution is the only way out. In fact, unreasonable institutional mechanisms make wealth accumulation inequality worse, main source of widening income gap and unfairness. The Gini coefficient of China's overall housing wealth is 0.6-0.7. Wealth possession inequality has become a new challenge to China's income distribution. It is far from enough to solve wealth imbalance through redistribution. Institutional mechanism reform is to stop the source of wealth accumulation inequality.

It must also be noted that with social security system construction and implementation of structural tax cuts in China in recent years, redistribution in China has been strengthening whose effect of narrowing income gap is expected to soon be seen from the statistics. However, too much emphasis on redistribution may bring about social welfare's "Great Leap Forward" and then bring about adverse economic and social consequences. Therefore, focus of solving current China's income distribution problem should not only be regulation of redistribution, more importantly, emphasize how to eliminate unfair distribution in initial distribution and stop source and loophole of unreasonable income and illegal income.

(V) Government's Role in Solving Income Distribution Problem

The government should take its responsibility to solve income distribution problem. Specifically, the government can play its role in solving the problem by taking the following measures: first, actively promote institutional reform in initial distribution with focus on unfair distribution so as to establish an institutional mechanism in which state-owned capitalized income is shared by all the people. Second, accelerate development, narrow urban-rural gap and regional gap by continuing to promote rural population migration to urban areas so as to realize equalization of public services between rural migrants and urban population. Third, enhance regulatory function of redistribution and improve social security system by adjusting government expenditure structure, especially expenditure increase in education, medical treatment and health care. Social security system construction should attach more importance to social equity by reducing social security payment burden and supporting middle-low income groups. Fourth, further improve tax system and form reasonable structure of direct and indirect taxation by implementing structural tax cuts and expanding value added tax reform and giving play to taxation function in regulating income distribution. Fifth, establish normal wage growth mechanism and further improve labor market by actively expanding formal employment, improving enterprise salary management system to enable wage growth to keep pace with labor productivity growth.

II. "Sticking Point" of China's Income Distribution Problem and its Solution

(I) Core of Current Income Distribution Problem: Unfair Distribution

China's current income distribution problem is characterized by widening income gap and increasing Gini coefficient at the micro level and by unreasonable income distribution pattern and low labor remuneration in initial distribution and low residents' income in national income at the macro level. In distribution rules, distribution disorder is characterized by private coffers, bonuses given out at will, and no equal pay for equal work. These problems are becoming so serious that growing public discontent has been threatening social and economic development.

These problems are caused by both the market itself and institutional rules, but the more important reason is China's unfair income distribution. The so-called unfair income distribution is the possession of wealth and income that they don't deserve. Particularity of China's unfair income distribution is closely related to stage characteristics of China's reform and development. With marketization acceleration, all kinds of China's economic components need to be capitalized. Capitalization reflects progress and depth of marketization reform and is also the inevitable requirement for various economic components to enter market competition and global labor division. However, in capitalization, by taking advantage of loopholes in institutional rules in social transformation, a small number of people take possession of social and state wealth through various hidden ways, leading to social wealth concentration and making majority of people feel deprived, middle and high income groups feel vulnerable, and beneficiaries feel uneasy with speculation from time to time. According to a survey, 27% of the rich people with 100 million yuan of investable assets have emigrated, and 47% are considering emigration, long-term investment, venture-oriented investment so as to evacuate overseas. This is clearly an extremely dangerous signal of China's economic development.

China has become the second largest country with overnight billionaires around the world. The increasing number of rich people is inevitable in economic development, but the problem in China is that the wealth accumulation of the "rich class" is closely related to unfair distribution. China's "super-rich class" is characterized by its limited industries and its limited wealth accumulation channels. According to *The Global Wealth Report* released by Boston Consulting in 2007, about 41% of China's wealth is controlled by 0.1% of "super-rich families." The main channels for wealth accumulation of Super-rich class are the acquisition or merger of wholly-owned enterprises at a low price, the listing of money and access to real estate, minerals and other industries.

Unfair income distribution often poses a serious threat to social stability. Unfair income distribution is not always characterized by widening income gap. Under China's planned economy system, income distribution fails to make some people get the income they deserve, typical unfair income distribution, leading to economic and social stagnation. Income distribution in North Africa, Middle East countries such as Tunisia, Egypt, Yemen and so on seems to be more "fair" with Gini coefficient below 0.4, but its unfair employment opportunities, corrupt government institutions, and extremely concentrated wealth greatly dampens economic vitality and leads to public discontent and social unrest. According to media reports, the Mubarak family wealth of $40 billion to $70 billion accounted for about a quarter of the country's GDP, and its unemployment rate always remained at 9.4%, youth unemployment rate at 15.8%. Thus, social harm caused by unfair distribution poses greater threat than that caused by widening income gap.

Unfair income distribution accompanied by widening income gap, principal cause of widening income gap, is the most dangerous income distribution. China is in such a state now. Therefore, it is urgent to solve unfair distribution problem, the core of China's current income distribution problem.

(II) China's Factor Capitalization: Main Cause of Unfair Income Distribution

The basic economic system of Chinese socialism is the side-by-side development of different ownership economy with public ownership playing a dominant role. In the marketization reform, means of production of public ownership priced through market transactions will become factor capital in order to accomplish the separation and transfer of ownership and right of use with various forms of market transactions and free flow such as property rights contracts, financial instruments and negotiable securities so that means of production will realize its optimal factor allocation and wealth re-creation. In planned economy, means of production of public ownership in China were not priced "wealth" with a large amount of land, mineral resources, state-owned enterprises, public facilities and so on being merely "dead", unable to create new wealth through market transactions without any attributes of capital. Factor capitalization has changed the situation that China has abundant wealth without capital, turning a "lack-of-money" China into a country with abundant capital.

Factor capitalization, a symbol of the development and progress of market economy, is required by the reform and development of China's socialist market economy. Well-developed market economy is characterized by its a more-than-a-century capitalization, well-developed rules, accumulated wealth, and competitive advantages of the world market. China's economic development has to go through factor capitalization. The achievements of China's reform and opening up, especially the rapid economic growth in the past decade, benefit from factor capitalization. Although China's early marketization reform, making possible the free trade of various products, has shortened the distance between "wealth" and "money", a large number of productive factors have not become capital that can create new wealth. Factor capitalization brought about by the deepening reform has transformed resource factor into capital, making resource allocation more efficient, faster and less costly, giving momentum to China's rapid economic growth.

China's factor capitalization, however, different from that of other market economies, is characterized by its peculiarity which is shown in the following two aspects. First, factor capitalization of average market economy is based on private property rights while China's is mainly based on public ownership requiring the separation of ownership and right of use, which is where the difficulty lies of theoretical innovation of socialist market economy with Chinese characteristics without any experience for reference. Second, any well-developed market economy is characterized by a hundred years' experience of capitalization, a well-developed market and perfect rules. China's newly-established market mechanism and imperfect market development with factor market lagging behind will add to the difficulty and complexity of factor capitalization. Developing side by side with marketization reform, China's factor capitalization of "exploring and pushing forward" will undoubtedly face more challenges.

The particularity of China's factor capitalization leads to unfair income distribution, the main source of income inequality in China. Although the capitalization of such factors as land, mineral resources, state-owned enterprises, public goods have created abundant new wealth, the state and all the people, owners of resource factor, were not able to enjoy the benefits of capitalization fairly as a great deal of wealth is held by a small number of people who have the right to use or have actual control in factor capitalization. The related fields of factor capitalization have become the target of public discontent and social conflict, which can be summed up in the following four aspects.

i. Income from land capitalization has been over-occupied by developers, local governments and interest groups, seriously eroding the interests of farmers and collectives.

Although land capitalization has provided an important source of capital for the construction of urbanization and accelerated the development of urbanization, the village collectives and villagers with land ownership who do not have enough control and income distribution right can not get their fair and reasonable income share. Collective land needs to be expropriated by local government to become state-owned before entering the market transactions, during which there emerges illegal, unreasonable expropriation and occupation of land, and even violent demolition, seriously infringing on the rights and interests of farmers. For instance, the compensation price is far lower than the market price and the land expropriation compensation is often only 30,000 to 50,000 yuan per mu, but the actual market value of the land can be as high as several million yuan, which has seriously eroded the interests of farmers. The income distribution of land capitalization has been seriously imbalanced and unfair. Some studies have shown that in the distribution of the value added income of collective land use transfer, the government, the village economic organizations and farmers gets 60%-70%, 25–30%, and 5–10% respectively. Land transfer funds have become an important source of local finance. In 2010, the total land transaction price (by statistical caliber of Ministry of Land and Resources) reached 2.9 trillion yuan, transfer funds of Anhui, Shaanxi, Chongqing and other provinces (cities) accounting for more than 40% of the local revenue. The unfair distribution of land capitalization has damaged the interests of the villagers and collective, has given rise to a group of overnight wealthy real estate owners and stimulated the "land finance", and is extremely likely to cause social conflict with frequent occurrences of such group incidents as petitions, self-immolation, explosions, attacks on local governments.

ii. Income from capitalization of mineral resource has been over-occupied by mining owners forming the super-rich group, damaging the interests of the state and the whole people.

Many mining rights of mineral resources are granted by way of administrative transfer and agreed pricing. However, the imperfect market trading system of "bidding and trading", low price transfer or even free plunder, low cost mining, extremely low tax on the use of mineral resources, local protection and rent seeking corruption, has enabled a small number of people to control mineral resources owned by the whole people, and to make high profits and even huge profits while the relevant management departments have also obtained grey income from it, seriously eroding the rights and interests of the owners of state-owned resources. Even in 2010, coal mines in Pinglu, Shanxi worth hundreds of millions was transferred for 10,000 yuan. The tax on mineral resources and the compensation for mineral resources are on the extremely low side. For example, the current coal resource tax is 0.3 to 5 yuan per ton, less than 2% of the market price; the natural gas resource tax is 7 to 15 yuan per thousand cubic meters, less than 3% of the price; the average oil resource tax is only 26 yuan per ton, less than 2% of the market price. Too low a resource use tax results in a too small proportion of the country's added value income and even less for its citizens. The unfair distribution of income from mineral resource capitalization has given rise to a group of super-rich coal boss, iron boss, copper boss and so on. According to the *Research Report on Private Capital Investment in China* released jointly by the Ministry of Housing and Construction and Goldman Sachs in 2011, there are no fewer than 7,000 billionaires of coal bosses in Yulin, Shaanxi, known as "China's Kuwait," boasting of 1 billion yuan of wealth per square kilometers. In 2010, 90% of China's Land Rover cars in mainland China were bought by coal owners in Ordos where there are at least 100,000 people with assets of tens of millions of yuan. The sharp contrast between the luxury life of these super-rich group and the difficult life of low-income group has become the source of social discontent.

iii. Income from capitalization of state-owned enterprises has been divided up by actual controllers, interest groups and internal workers instead of the state and the whole people who have to burden a large amount of subsidies.

Although the reform of and capitalization of state-owned enterprises have greatly promoted the efficiency of enterprises with valued state-owned assets and with transformation from "burden" to "wealth" due to the imperfect distribution mechanism, unfair income distribution has only benefited interest groups, damaging the interests of real owners of state-owned assets. The capitalization of state-owned enterprises, controlled by executives and insiders of enterprises, has resulted in embezzlement or sale of state-owned assets at a low price, and the fact that huge annual income of senior executives is inconsistent with their operating performance, and the fact that staff and workers of enterprises are well-paid with good welfare and monopoly income. In addition, state-owned enterprises enjoy resource factors, financing loans and other preferential treatments at the same time while the majority of corporate income is shared by only a small number of people. Between 2001 and 2009, the total profits of state-owned and state-owned holding industrial enterprises amounted to 5.8462 trillion yuan, only 6% of which is handed over to the state in 2009, and only 2.2% in 2010, with the rest of the profits distributed within the enterprises. As a result, the national dividend is also transferred mainly within the enterprise system, and the public finance basically does not get the income of the state-owned capital, let alone benefit the whole people. Moreover, state-owned enterprises also enjoy preferential treatment and financial subsidies from all citizens in terms of resource factors. Between 2001 and 2009, state-owned and state-owned holding industrial enterprises should have paid a total of 2.5787 trillion yuan in government rent accounting for 64% of the total nominal net profit of state-owned and state-owned holding enterprises; rents for natural resources, such as oil, gas and coal, were underpaid by about 497.7 billion yuan. Between 2007 and 2009, state-owned and state-controlled industrial enterprises received financial subsidies of about 194.3 billion yuan. In addition, some state-owned enterprises have been heavily involved in the real estate industry. In 2009, more than 70% of the 136 state-owned enterprises involved in real estate business, creating state-owned enterprise "land kings" one after another. Some state-owned companies have used their policy and credit advantages to pump billions of dollars into non-major businesses such as stocks, housing, derivatives and commodities, fuelling asset bubbles and worsening residents' income distribution. In all, the capitalization of state-owned enterprises lacks a perfect income distribution mechanism, leading to serious unfair distribution, and few interest groups have directly deprived the country or the whole people of their wealth, triggering increasingly intense public discontent.

iv. Capitalization of some public goods have enabled actual controlling organization and internal staff to get excess income while the public bears high cost, seriously infringing on the rights and interests of the public.

Although capitalization of some public goods has accelerated the construction of infrastructure in China, broken the bottleneck of economic growth and promoted the rapid economic development, its unfair distribution mainly lies in the fact that the public goods is controlled by a small number of people and interest groups, and the fact that the capitalized excess income is distributed only within the department. Moreover, as these public goods are often concerned with livelihood and security of the people, a few actual controllers with better bargaining chips are more likely to have monopoly power with the power sector, leading to high public service charges. Some expressways have become "income generating machines" controlled by interest groups with nominal expressways becoming de facto "private roads", changing the nature of public goods. In 2009, the tolls of The First Group were as high as 3.2 billion yuan while the daily maintenance expenditure was only 66.793 million yuan. The gross profit rate of listed Nanjing Shanghai Expressway in 2010 was as high as 74%. The operating profit margin of Chengdu-Chongqing and Wuzhou Development in Sichuan was 66% and 67% respectively. Expressway profiteering directly makes worker income super-high, seriously deviating from worker's human capital. For example, in 2010, per capita pre-tax annual income of Nanjing-Shanghai Expressway reached 105,000 yuan with only less than 10% of the staff having a bachelor's degree or above; per capita pre-tax annual income of Wuzhou Development reached 145,000 yuan with 80% of its front-line personnel and logistics personnel. The excess capitalized income of public goods is essentially the high cost borne by the public and occupied by a small number of actual controllers. This serious unfair distribution has intensified social conflict.

In addition, factor capitalization has given rise to "power capitalization". Due to the temptation of huge interest and imperfect supervision, there are rent-seeking corruption, power and money trading and opportunism in the market transactions of state-owned resource factors. For example, government departments or officials make use of land, mineral resources, enterprise listing, construction planning and other rights for rent-seeking. Government and business colluded to divide the income of factor capitalization. The destructive power capitalization bred in factor capitalization has become one of the main causes of unfair distribution of capitalized income. Moreover, it is more likely to cause public discontent and intensify social conflict.

(III) No reasonable distribution mechanism for income from factor capitalization resulting in private possession of public income

By summarizing unfair income distribution in factor capitalization in China, the essence of unfair income distribution is private possession of public income through two ways. First, unfair distribution of initial capitalized income. When state-owned resource factor is traded through the market for the first time, realizing the one-off capitalized income, that is, assets without price becoming valuable capital, resulting in a huge amount of new wealth, the government has not made it clear how to be reasonable and fair in its distribution so that a small number of people take too big a share of the income. Second, unfair distribution of capitalized income flow. In the capitalization of state-owned resource factors, new wealth or income flow can be generated every year, but as the right of its distribution is controlled by a few people, the income flows to some groups without being shared by the whole people, the biggest cause of unfair initial distribution.

In initial capitalization, unfair income distribution fails to reflect the market value of state-owned resource factor which reduces the wealth distributed to the state and the whole people. There are ownership transfer and right of use (right of management) transfer in factor capitalization, the former including collective land collection and occupation, private contracting of state-owned enterprises and the latter including mineral resource transfer and expressway transfer. No matter which property right is transferred, there will always be excessive possession of this one-time public income of initial capitalization by private individuals. One cause is direct erosion of state-owned assets without compensation. Without owners' authorization to deal with state-owned resources, actual controllers convert state-owned assets into private assets illegally through power abuse, and improper relations, causing the loss of state-owned assets. Capitalized income being wholly owned by private individuals who directly obtaining huge wealth will harm the interests of state-owned resource owners, causing the direct erosion and plunder of national wealth and the most evident unfair income distribution. The other cause is trading state assets at distorted prices. Due to serious information asymmetry, serious lack of supervision, and factor price manipulation in the non-standard market, state-owned resource factor is traded at distorted prices, resulting in under-pricing and cheap buying. The part below market price is rent-seeking space and most value-added income is divided up by minority interest groups, causing serious damage to national wealth.

Actual controllers have the say in distribution of capitalized income flow because for a long time, income distribution of state-owned resource factor lags behind without clear procedures and rules, leading to unfair income distribution. The first cause is absence of distribution system. If mineral resource management right is transferred to private individuals, the state receives very little income from this one-time transfer as capitalized income flow is handed over to the state only as low tax for mineral resource exploitation. For lack of reasonable income distribution system, huge profits are entirely taken by the operator. The second cause is unreasonable and imperfect distribution system. Although, according to current institutional arrangements, income distribution system requires state-owned enterprises to hand in a certain proportion of their profits, the state receives very low proportion of profits, most of which is still diverted within state-owned enterprises. Distribution mechanism of value-added income of collective land is unreasonable with village collective and villagers getting too little share of distribution. The third cause is improper and irregular distribution mechanism. State-owned enterprises or public sector transfer main business profits to non-main business through improper and irregular practice, resulting in a sharp decline in income distribution, or even asking for state financial subsidies, with real profits intercepted and divided up by a small number of people within the enterprise.

Therefore, in the unfair income distribution in China's factor capitalization, it is necessary to clearly define property rights so as to avoid excessive possession of public income by private individuals and to strengthen state-owned resources control so as to avoid being controlled by a small number of people or interest groups, and it's also necessary to establish reasonable income distribution mechanism so as to ensure that public income can be equitably shared by all the people.

(IV) Solution to China's Income Distribution Problem

As Confucius once says, "the problem lies not in scarcity of resources but in uneven distribution". China is currently faced with not only widening income gap but unfair income distribution caused by unfair distribution. Therefore, to solve China's income distribution problem is to eliminate unfair income distribution. To narrow the widening income gap is to speed up economic development and to improve redistribution system based on elimination of unfair income distribution .

To solve unfair income distribution, perfect institutional rules by establishing reasonable income distribution mechanism of land, mineral resources, state-owned enterprises, public goods so that all citizens can get their fair income.

In view of land capitalization, perfect land system by clarifying land property rights, reforming collective land collection and occupation system, increasing farmers' share in land value-added income and including land transfer fee in financial budget.

In view of mineral resources capitalization, establish a more stringent system for mineral resources exploitation by levying resource tax as soon as possible, raising tax on mineral resources exploitation and by establishing a profit-sharing system for mineral resources enterprises.

In view of capitalization of state-owned enterprises, improve management system of state-owned enterprises by strengthening supervision and control, turning in more profits and including state-owned enterprises profits in national budget, and by prudently listing industries of natural monopoly and strategic resources and public services concerning livelihood and security.

In view of public goods capitalization, further standardize it by cleaning up such enterprises as highways, municipal transportation and other enterprises having recovered their costs, supervising the entry of private sector into the field of public goods, and by reducing the cost of public goods and services.

In view of "power capitalization", strengthen supervision and administration of the government and society by cracking down on corruption and illegal practices such as power and money trading, insider trading, forced trading, illegal collection and occupation and by preventing state-owned resources from being eroded by interest groups.

III. A Correct Understanding of China's Labor Share

Labor share is an index to measure workers' share in initial distribution, one of the core issues of income distribution. However, there is still debate over China's labor share which is believed to be low with a downward trend, making it difficult to reach a solution, unfavorable to both economic and social development. Labor share changes relates not only to national income distribution pattern but to economic competitiveness and growth sustainability. Clarifying the problem is helpful for its solution.

(I) Misunderstanding of China's Labor Share mainly Resulting from International Comparison with Different Statistical Calibers

There are two statistical calibers for labor share internationally. The first is labor remuneration received by wage and salary recipients or employees' remuneration; the second includes both labor remuneration of wage and salary recipients and mixed income of self-employed workers. China adopts the second caliber for its labor remuneration data while other countries adopt the first caliber for labor remuneration data. Current misunderstanding about China's labor share is mainly caused by different calibers for international comparison.

There are currently three data sources for China's labor share, GDP accounting data of regional income method, funds flow table and input-output table. Labor share of these three sources is all based on the second caliber with different specific results but with the same basic trend: China's labor share has declined from 55% to 57% in the mid-1990s to the current 45%.

Since labor share with the second statistical caliber includes both employees' remuneration and mixed income of self-employed workers and the National Bureau of Statistics doesn't have a uniform standard for mixed income of self-employed workers, labor share often changes with statistical standards and calibers. Current studies show that considerable decline in China's labor share in recent years, mostly due to statistical caliber adjustment, does not necessarily reflect real situation of initial income distribution. Compared with labor share with the first caliber internationally, China's labor share is not that small at all.

According to the latest national income account statistics published by the United Nations, labor share of developed countries is generally stable at 50%-60% with 57% in the United States in 2007, 60% in the United Kingdom in 2005 and 54% in Germany in 2008. Labor share of developing countries are well below that of developed countries with 30% in India in 2008, 28% in the Philippines in 2008, and less than 10% in some developing countries. China's biggest annual labor share of 55%-57% is relatively big compared with that of developed countries, and even the current 45% is still similar to that of many developed countries and much bigger than that of typical developing countries.

That China's labor share is not small is mainly because the comparison is made between China's labor share with the second caliber and international labor share with the first caliber. This actually amounts to comparing two different things with wrong conclusion, main cause of confusion about China's labor share, which needs to be clarified.

Labor share with the first caliber is needed for international comparison to understand China's labor share. China's labor share with funds flow table is consistent with international labor share with the first caliber. The results show that China's labor share with the first calibre has been fluctuating at about 30% since 1992.

International comparison with the same statistical caliber shows that China's labor share is only about half the average labor share in developed countries, similar to that of some developing countries such as India and the Philippines, typical of developing countries. Therefore, it is an indisputable fact that China's labor share is low, one of the serious income distribution problems.

(II) Fundamental Cause for China's Low Labor Share: Low Employee Employment Rate and Low Regularization

When labor share is measured with the first caliber, factors determining labor share are not only employees' income but the number of employees. Given labor income, the larger number of employees, the higher employee employment rate, the bigger labor share will be. In this sense, labor share not only relates to income distribution but to economic development and labor market maturity to some extent.

Such is the case. Big labor share in developed countries is due to their high employee employment rate. Compared with self-employed employment, employee employment is characterized by job stability, high income and great security. Therefore, employee employment rate can also be regarded as an index to measure employment regularization. At present, developed countries have completed employment regularization with high employee employment rate. According to International Labor Organization (ILO), average employee employment rate of developed countries and EU economies in 2008 was 86.2% with more than 90% in some countries, Japan being 86.2%, the UK 86.6% and the United States 93%. On the other hand, developing countries is characterized by their low employee employment rate with Southeast Asian countries, Sub-Saharan Africa and South Asian countries averaging at 36.4%, 24.7%, and 21.5%.

According to the National Bureau of Statistics, China's employee employment rate has been stable at about 42% between 1995 and 2006. Despite its increase in recent years, it is still about 46% in 2009. Low employee employment rate is the major cause of China's low labor share.

Given the current employees' income, if employee employment rate reaches the average level of developed countries, China's labor share will rise from 30% to 56%, higher level of developed countries and there will be no more small labor share.

(III) Ways for China's Labor Share Growth

Labor share is not only an index of wealth distribution but of potential and ability of wealth creation. Small labor share is not conducive to economic and social harmony, stability and development. On the other hand, a too big labor share doesn't necessarily mean well.

Generally speaking, when economic growth truly reflects its development, employee employment rate and regularization will continue to improve with labor share growth. Economic development is, after all, regularizing employment and getting labor share bigger. In this sense, labor share growth is of a gradual process by taking correct measures. Otherwise, it will do harm to economic competitiveness and growth sustainability. Judging from causes of China's small labor share, China's labor share growth can be achieved by taking the following measures.

i. Improve Non-agricultural Employment Rate by Speeding up Rural Labor Transfer

Most agricultural employment in China is self-employed with poor employment stability, low income, and inability to share economic growth. Despite great achievement in China's rural labor transfer, agriculture is still a large employment sector, for example, in 2014, agricultural employment rate is still as high as 29.5% with 230 million people, the largest source of informal employment. If agricultural employment rate does not decrease, employee employment rate and regularization will not be able to improve and labor share will not be able to grow. Therefore, improve non-agricultural employment rate by speeding up rural labor transfer is an important prerequisite for China's labor share growth.

ii. Improve Employee Employment Rate and Regularization by Accelerating Economic Development and Structural Transformation

Unable to find suitable jobs, workers who have transferred to the non-agricultural sector have to engage in self-employed employment. Rural labor transfer of this kind does not contribute to employment regularization and labor share growth. China's rural labor transfer to urban area has brought about informal employment, the key cause hindering China's labor share growth. Therefore, speed up economic development and structural transformation and expand employment by creating more high-quality jobs to regularize labor market, the most critical measure for China's labor share growth.

iii. Make wage Growth Keep Pace with Labor Productivity Growth by Perfecting Wage Growth Mechanism

With rapid economic growth, if wage does not grow moderately, improvement in employment regularization will not necessarily lead to labor share growth. Only when wage growth keeps pace with labor productivity growth, employee employment growth rate will lead to labor share growth. Therefore, on the basis of realizing non-agricultural employment and regularization, it is necessary to ensure wage growth keeps pace with labor productivity growth for labor share growth. In this sense, important measures for China's labor share growth includes perfecting reasonable wage growth mechanism, carrying out wage collective bargaining system and strengthening workers' right to speak in wage determination.

IV. Curb China's Widening Income Gap through Redistribution

From international experience, countries adopt different attitude, methods and means to cope with widening income gap, a common phenomenon in rapid economic growth, with very different results.

(I) Whether widening income gap, a common phenomenon in rapid economic growth, can be regulated through redistribution, an important sign to show mature market economies are different from other countries

With rapid economic growth, income gap in many mature market economies has widened considerably once. For example, the Gini coefficient of the United States exceeded 0.5 in the 1920s; Gini coefficient of the U.K. reached 0.54 to 0.55 in 1867; Gini coefficient of Japan reached 0.57 in 1937. Middle-income Latin America's income gap widened even more during periods of rapid economic growth: between 1950 and 1975, Brazil's Gini coefficient rose from 0.36 to 0.64 and Mexico's Gini coefficient rose from 0.52 to 0.59; Argentina's Gini coefficient rose between 0.38 to 0.53 between 1970 and 2000; Chile's Gini coefficient rose from 0.45 to 0.55 between 1975 and 1995. China is now in a period of rapid economic growth with rapidly widening income gap, its Gini coefficient rising from 0.31 to 0.491 between 1978 and 2008, which reflects that China's widening income gap has the same or similar characteristics and laws as other market economies.

However, experience of mature market economies shows that narrowing the income gap is not a natural course, requiring establishment and improvement of various social systems and rules. For example, income gap of the United States began to narrow mainly because of the Roosevelt New Deal beginning in the 1930s, which greatly improved social welfare and income of low-income groups. The narrowing income gap of Japan after World War II is also mainly due to establishment of various redistribution systems conducive to income gap regulation. In general, income gap in developed countries can be narrowed because they generally establish fiscal and taxation policies and social security systems to regulate income distribution.

For lack of redistribution to regulate income gap, income gap in developing countries is either constantly widening or difficult to decline for a long time. For example, although many Latin American countries have begun their industrialization almost at the same time as the mature market economies, it is difficult to narrow their income gap for a long time for lack of redistribution mechanism to regulate their income gap, leading to economic and social difficulties or even stagnation or retrogression, falling into the so-called "middle-income trap".

(II) Redistribution regulating the income gap in developed market economies is to be initiated in China.

It is generally believed that income gap in developed market economies is reasonable. But few people know that it is mainly achieved through redistribution. In initial distribution, there has been a relatively wide income gap in developed market economies. For example, the Gini coefficient of the United States, the U.K. and Japan in initial distribution is 0.46, 0.46 and 0.44, respectively, so that the Gini coefficient in initial distribution in these mature market economies is no different from that of other countries. China's current Gini coefficient of 0.47 (0.462 in 2015) is even lower than that in Germany (0.51), Italy (0.56), Portugal (0.54), Poland (0.57) and many other OECD countries.

But after redistribution, income gap in developed market economies has narrowed considerably with Gini coefficient declining by an average of more than 10 Gini points. After year 2000, after redistribution, Gini coefficient in the United States, Japan, Germany, France, the U.K., and OECD countries fell from 0.46 to 0.38; from 0.44 to 0.32; from 0.51 to 0.3; from 0.48 to 0.28; from 0.46 to 0.34; and from 0.45 to 0.31 down by 14 Gini points.

For lack of redistribution mechanism to regulate the income gap in developing countries, the income gap basically does not change after initial distribution and redistribution. But after redistribution, China's income gap has widened, instead, indicating that redistribution has even adverse effect on income gap. According to a study, China's Gini coefficient may be 0.48-0.49 after taking into account regional cost of living, housing, social security and other redistribution factors, indicating wide income gap. Therefore, main reason why it's difficult to narrow China's income gap is that redistribution to regulate income gap has not yet been established.

(III) Initiating Redistribution to Regulate Income Distribution is the key to Narrowing China's Income Gap

If China could establish redistribution regulation mechanism as OECDs, its

Gini coefficient would decrease from the current 0.47 to 0.33 so that its income gap will be relatively equalized instead of serious inequality. Therefore, the key to narrowing China's current income gap is to establish redistribution mechanism to regulate income distribution compatible with mature market economy so that the following changes will have to be made.

First, optimize tax structure to enhance regulatory role of tax on income. China's tax system is dominated by indirect taxes with a small proportion of direct taxes with the function of regulating income distribution. Indirect tax (such as value-added tax, business tax, domestic consumption tax, and customs duties) which make up tax system make average worker bear a heavier tax burden with high-income groups bearing a relatively light tax burden. It is necessary to optimize tax structure by reducing indirect tax and increasing direct tax so that tax system can regulate income distribution. Optimization and change of tax structure can ensure that income gap is adjusted from the income procedure by playing its role of "cutting the peak" in income distribution. Therefore, with personal income tax reform by turning classified collection into comprehensive collection, inheritance tax, gift tax and other property possession tax (such as property tax) is to be levied.

Second, increase people's livelihood expenditure and enhance redistribution function of transfer payment. In China, grossly inadequate public expenditure on people's livelihood does not play its role in narrowing income gap. The large proportion of transfer payment of China's central government is mostly project expenditure without its redistribution effect of regulating income gap. In developed countries, the proportion of expenditure on people's livelihood is usually more than 50% with a large proportion directly, going to lower-middle income groups. Increase China's public expenditure in people's livelihood so as to enhance redistribution effect of transfer payment, enabling fiscal transfer expenditure to play its role of "filling the valley" in the regulation of income distribution.

Third, improve social security system and enhance its inclusiveness. Great achievements have been made in China's social security system in the past few years with its basic system framework. However, current social insurance system of urban workers fails to regulate income distribution. High contribution rate makes it difficult to expand the coverage of various social insurance systems for urban workers. Up to now, nearly half of urban employees have not been part of these systems which fails to regulate income distribution with even adverse regulation. Learning from general levy of social security tax in developed countries, improve China's urban worker social insurance system reform by integrating all social insurance contributions into social security tax and by thoroughly resolving social insurance coverage and transfer to enhance its inclusiveness and to play the regulatory role of social security system in income distribution.

References:

Introduction

Zhao Deqin (2000), *"Developing Ways, Stages, Experiences of Chinese Economy in 50 Years"*, Researches in Chinese Economic History, No.1.

Fan Gang, Yao Zhizhong (2002), *"Estimation of Asset Factors Allocation and Its Role in Income Distribution in China: Conceptual and Statistical Issues"*, Economic Research, No. 11.

Li Jiguang (2011), *"The Evaluation of the Property Ownership Structure Statistics in China at Present"*, Academic Journal of Zhongzhou, No. 4.

Chapter I

Gan Li et al (2012), *China Household Finance Survey*. Chengdu: Southwestern University of Finance and Economics Press.

Lu Yang, Cai Fang (2013), *"Relax the One-child Policy and the Long-term Potential Growth Rate in China"*, Journal of Labor Economy, No. 1.

Song Xiaowu et.al (ed.)(2013), *China Faces Inequality--studies in Income Distribution*. Beijing: Social Sciences Academic Press(China).

Sun Zhangwei (2013), *"Study On Japan's Gini Coefficient and Redistribution system"*, Contemporary Economy of Japan, No. 2.

Wang Xiaolu (2013), *Strategic Thinking on National Income Distribution*. Beijing & Haikou: Xuexi Press, Hainan Press.

Wang Xiaolu (2013), *"Grey income and Income Distribution in China"*, Comparative Studies, No. 5.

Dornbusch, Rudiger and Sebastian Edwards (1989), *"Macroeconomic Populism in Latin America"*, NBER Working Paper, No. 2986.

Eichengreen, Barry, Donghyun Park and Kwanho Shin (2011), *"When Fast Growing Economies Slow Down: International Evidence and Implications for China"*, NBER Working Paper, No.16919.

Palma, Jose Gabriel (2011), *"Homogeneous Middles vs. Heterogeneous Tails, and the End of the 'Inverted-U': the Share of the Rich is What It's All About"*, Cambridge Working Papers in Economics, No.1111.

Chapter II

Cai Fang, Du Yang (2011), *"Wage Growth, Wage Convergence and Lewis Turning Point"*, Economic Perspectives, No. 9.

Chen Guangjin (2010), *"Market or Non-Market? An Empirical Analysis of the Main Causes of Income Inequalities in China Today"*, Sociological Studies, No. 6.

Chen Zhiwu (2009), *The Logic of Finance*. Beijing: International Culture Publishing Company.

Chen Zongsheng, Ma Caoyuan (2012), *"Theoretical and Empirical Research on Echelon Changes in Income Gap among Urban Residents in China"*, Journal of Finance and Economics, No. 6.

Cheng Yonghong (2007), *"China's Overall Gini Coefficient and Its Decomposition by Rural and Urban Area Since Reform and Opening up"*, Social Science in China, No. 4.

Fan Gang, Yao Zhizhong (2002), *"Estimation of Asset Factors Allocation and Its Role in Income Distribution in China: Conceptual and Statistical Issues"*, Economic Research. No. 11

Gao Wenshu, Zhao Wen, Cheng Jie (2011), *"The Impact of Rural Labor's Migration on Income Gap statistics of Rural and Urban Residents"*, (ed.) in

Reports on China's Population and Labor (No. 12). Beijing: Social Sciences Academic Press(China).

He Lixin, Sato Hiroshi (2008), *"Social Security and Income Redistribution in Urban China: An Empirical Analysis Based on Annual and Lifetime Income"*, World Economic Papers, No. 5.

Hu Zhijun, Liu Zongming, Gong Zhimin (2011), *"Estimation of the Gini Coefficient in China: 1985--2008"*, China Economic Quarterly, No. 4.

Jia Kang, Liang Jiwei (2012), *"Five Features of International Personal Taxation"*, Contemporary Bankers, No. 1.

Lai Desheng, Chen Jianwei (2012), *"The Emergence of the Turning point of Narrowing of China's Income Gap"*, Policy Research and Exploration, No. 5.

Li Jiguang (2011), *"The Evaluation of the Property Ownership Structure Statistics in China at Present"*, Academic Journal of Zhongzhou, No. 4.

Li Shi, Luo Chuliang (2011), *"How Unequal is China?"*, Economic Research, No. 4.

Li Zhuo (2009), *"Review of the Tax System Construction since the Founding of People's Republic of China in 1949"*, Taxation Research Journal, No. 10.

The Unirule Institute of Economics (2011), *"The Nature, Performance and Reform of the State-owned Enterprises"*, Working Paper.

Xu Bing, Zhang Shangfeng (2010), *"Inverted U-curve with Multi-inflexions for Economic Growth and Inequality of Income Distribution"*, The Journal of Quantitative and Technical Economics, No. 2.

Zhao Renwei (2007), *"An Analysis of the Income Allocation and Property Distribution of Residents in China"*, Contemporary Finance and Economics, No. 7.

Zhou Yunbo (2009), *"Urbanization, Urban-Rural Income Gap and Overall Income Inequality in China: An Empirical Test of the Inverse-U Hypothesis"*, China Economic Quarterly, No. 4.

Atkinson A.B., Bourguignon F. (2000), *Handbook of Income Distribution(Volume 1)*. Amsterdam: North Holland.

Gustafsson, B., Li, S., Sicular, T. (2007), *Inequality and Public Policy in China.*

New York and Cambridge: Cambridge University Press.

John Knight, Deng Quheng, Li Shi (2011), *"The Shortage of China's Peasant-workers, and the Surplus of the Rural Labor Force in China"*, Management World, No. 11.

Li S., Zhao R. (2011), *"Market Reform and the Widening of the Income Gap"*, Social Science in China, No.2.

Nagel, J. (1974), *"Inequality and Discontent: A Nonlinear Hypothesis"*. World Politics, Vol.26.

Ravallion, M., Chen, S. (2007), *"China's Uneven Progress Against Poverty"*, Journal of Development Economics, Vol.82.

Richard H. (2011), *"China's Emergence as a Market Economy: Achievements and Challenges"*, OECD Economics Department, Working Paper, March.

Chapter III

Chong-En Bai, Zhenjie Qian (2009), *"Who has Eroded Residents' Incomes? An Analysis of China's National Income Distribution Patterns"*, Social Science in China, No. 5.

Chang Jinxiong, Wang Danfeng (2010), *"Wage Differentials between Formal and Informal Employment of China's Urban"*, The Journal of Quantitative and Technical Economics, No. 9.

Dai Yuanchen, E. Hon-ming Li (1988), *"Wage Swallowing up Profit--A Hidden Danger in the Reform of China's Economic System"*, Economic Research, No. 6.

Hua Sheng (2010), *"The Serious Misunderstanding of the Low Labor Share in GDP--The Second Working Paper on China's Income Distribution"*, China Securities Journal, A21 of Oct. 14.

Jia Kang, Han Xiaoming, Liu Wei (2010), *"Upper Middle Level of China's Labor Share"*, China Securities Journal, May 11.

Tang Zongkun (1992), *"Drain and Redistribution of Profits and Reproduction Capacity of State Enterprises"*, Economic Research, No. 7.

Zhang Juwei, Zhang Shibin (2011), *"A Study on Labor Share in GDP in China"*, Labor Economy Review, Vol. 4, No.1.

Deane, hyllis, W.A.Cole (1962), *British Economic Growth 1688-1959.* Cambridge: Cambridge University Press.

Johnson, D.Gale (1954), *"The Functional Distribution of Income in the United States: 1850-1952"*, The Review of Economics and Statistics, Vol.36, No.2, pp.175-182.

Gollin, D. (2002), *"Getting Income Shares Right"*, Journal of Political Economy, Vol.110, No.2, pp.458-475.

ILO, *The Key Indicators of the Labor Market*, the sixth edition.

Kaldor, Nicholas (1961), *"Capital Accumulation and Economic Growth"*. In The Theory of Capital, edited by Friedrich A. Lutz and Douglas C. Hague. New York: St. Martin's Press.

Kravis. I. B. (1959), *"Relative Income Shams in Fact and Theory"*, American Economic Review, Vol.49, No.5, pp.917-949.

Solow, R.M. (1958), *"A Skeptical Note on the Constancy of Relative Shares"*, American Economic Review, Vol.48, No.4, pp.618-631.

Chapter IV

Cai Fang (2011), *"Middle Income Trap: Theory, Experience and Pertinence"*, Economic Perspectives, No. 12.

Chen Yuyu, Wang Zhigang, Wei Zhong (2004), *"The Unequal Wages and Their Change of Residents in Town of China during 1990's"*, Science of Economy, No. 6.

Cheng Chengping, Zhang Xu, Cheng Li (2012), *"Study on the Effects of Rising Wages on Chinese International Competitiveness of Manufacturing: An Empirical Analysis Based on the 1980-2008 Data"*, China Soft Science, No. 4.

Dai Yuanchen, E. Hon-ming Li (1988), *"Wage Swallowing up Profit–A Hidden Danger in the Reform of China's Economic System"*, Economic Research, No. 6.

Du Yang, Qu Yue (2009), *"Labor Reward, Labor Productivity and the*

Advantages of Labor Cost--An Empirical Analysis Based on the Data of Manufacturing Enterprises", China Industrial Economics, No. 5.

Du Yang, Qu Yue (2012), "*Trends of Unit Labor Force Cost in China's Manufacturing Industries and its Influences*", in Reports on China's Population and Labor (No. 13). Beijing: Social Sciences Academic Press (China).

Feng Yi, Li Shi (2013), "*Wage Differential of Chinese Migrant and its Dynamic Change*", China Economic Studies, No. 2.

Li Wenpu, Zheng Jianqing, Lin Jinxia (2011), "*Research on Change Trend of Labor Remuneration in Manufacturing Industry and Industrial Competitiveness*", Economic Perspectives, No. 8.

Liu Wei, Li Shaorong (2001), "*The Ownership Change and the Economic Growth and Upgrading of Factors Efficiency*", Economic Research, No. 1.

Lu Zhengfei, Wang Xiongyuan, Zhang Peng (2012), "*Do Chinese Sate-owned Enterprises Pay Higher Wage?*", Economic Research, No. 3.

Luo Rundong, Fu Guangxin, Li Yuxin (2014), "*Wage Determinants and Wage Differentials between State-owned Sector and Non State-owned Sector*", China Economic Studies, No. 2.

Ma Xiaohe (2010), "*Transforming of Demand Structure and the Restructuring of the Industrial Structure to Pass the 'Pitfall of Medium-Income'*", Macroeconomics, No. 11.

Park Bokyeong, Huang Yanghua (2013), "*Economic Transformation to Avoid the Middle Income Trap: Lesson from Korea's Experience*", Comparative Economic and Social Systems, No. 1.

Tang Zongkun (1992), "*Drain and Redistribution of Profits and Reproduction Capacity of State Enterprises*", Economic Research, No. 7.

Harry X. Wu (2013), "*Measuring and Interpreting Total Factor Productivity in Chinese Industry*", Wu Jinglian (edi). Comparative Studies, No. 6. Beijing: China Citic Press.

Ye Linxiang, Lishi, Luo Chuliang (2011), "*Industrial Monopoly, Ownership and Enterprises Wage Inequality–an Empirical Research Based on the First*

National Economic Census of Enterprises Data", Management World, No. 4.

Zhang Juwei (2012), *"The Changes in the Share of Chinese Labor Compensation and Estimation and Analysis of the Overall level of Wages"*, Economic Perspectives, No. 9.

Zhang Juwei (2012), *"The Changes and Implications of China's Labor Share"*, Journal of Shandong University (Philosophy and Social Sciences), No. 5.

Zhao Wen, Zhang Zhanxin (2013), *"The Effect of Statistical Methods on the Estimation of Urban-Rural Income Gap and Its Recalculation"*, Journal of Labor Economy, No. 1.

Indermit Gill and Homi Kharas (2007), *An East Asian Renaissance: Ideas for Economic Growth*, Washington, D.C.: World Bank Publications.

Song, Zheng, Kjetil Storesletten, and Fabrizio Zilibotti (2011), *"Growing Like China"*, American Economic Review, Vol.101, No.1, pp.196-233.

Chapter V

An Tifu, Jiang Zhen (2009), *"On the Adjustment of China's National Income Distribution Pattern to Improve Residents' Distribution Share"*, Review of Economic Research, No. 25.

Chong-En Bai, Zhenjie Qian (2009), *"Who has Eroded Residents' Incomes? An Analysis of China's National Income Distribution Patterns"*, Social Science in China, No. 5.

Fu Guangjun (ed.)(2009), *Taxation and Distribution of National Income.* Beijing: China Market Press.

Gao Lingjiang (2011), *"The Empirical Study of Reasonable Tax Structure in China"*, Finance and Trade Economics, No. 10.

Gu Cheng (2010), *"Taxation and Income Distribution: A Reflection on Individual Income Tax of Developing Countries"*, Business Management Journal, No. 7.

Guo Qingwang (2012), *"Distributional Effects of Tax: Further Research"*,

Finance and Trade Economics, No. 8.

National Taxation Bureau(ed.) (2014), *Tax Laws and Regulations of the People's Republic of China (2014 Edition)*. Beijing: China Tax Press.

Jia Kang (2010), *"Reform of Financial System and Adjustment of Income Distribution Structure"*, Capital Shanghai, No. 12.

Liu Yi, Nie Haifeng (2009), *"The Different Impacts of Value Added Tax and Business Tax on Income Distribution"*, Finance and Trade Economics, No. 6.

Ouyang Cao (2010), *"A Study on the Impact of Income Distribution of Urban Residents from Turnover Tax in China"*, Master Dissertation of Jiangxi University of Finance and Economy.

Sun Jing, Wang Yali (2013), *"The Impact of Tax on Income Redistribution Effect of Urban and Rural Residents in China"*, Journal of Zhongnan University of Economics and Law, No. 5.

Tang Yun (2010), *"Can the Third Distribution Narrow the Gap between Rich and Poor"*, Xiaoxiang Morning, June 12.

Wan Ying (2011), *"The Impact of Personal Income Tax on Income Distribution: Observing from Tax Progressivity and Average Tax Rate"*, Reform, No. 3.

Yang Zhiyong (2009), *"Income Distribution and Individual Income Tax Reform in China"*, International Taxation in China, No. 10.

Yue Shumin, Li Jin (2011), *"Comparison and Analysis of Tax Treatment for Labor, Capital and Consumption in China"*, International Taxation in China, No. 6.

National Bureau of Statistics of China, *China's System of National Accounts*(2002). Beijing: China Statistics Press.

Chapter VI

He Fan, Zhang Yuyan (1996), *"Nature of the State-owned Enterprises"*, Management World, No. 5.

Li Daokui, Liu Linlin, Wang Hongling (2009), *"The U Curve of Labor Share in*

GDP during Economic Development", Economic Research Journal, No. 1.

Li Rongrong (2008), "*Grand Project Invaluable Experience–on the 30-year Reform and Development of State-owned Enterprises*", Qiushi Journal, No. 6.

Liu Shijin (1995), "*The Nature and the Reform Logic of the State-owned Enterprises in China*", Economic Research Journal, No. 4.

Liu Yongji (2002), *Owners' Reflections on the State-owned Enterprise Reform.* Beijing: China Economy Press.

Luo Deming, Li Ye, Shi Jinchuan (2012), "*Factor Distortion, Resource Misallocation and Productivity*", Economic Research Journal, No. 3.

Wang Yanmei (2012), "*A Legal Analysis of the Concept and Status of Enterprise*", Social Science Front, No. 1.

Komiya Ryūtarō (1993), *Modern Economy of China*, Trans. by Zhu Shaowen. Beijing: The Commercial Press.

Janos Kornai (1986), *Economics of Shortage*, Trans. By Zhang Xiaoguang et al. Beijing: Economic Science Press.

Yao Xian'guo, Guo Dongjie (2004), "*A Case Study of Labor Relations in System-transformed Enterprises*", Management World, No. 5.

Yuan Tangjun (2009), "*Total Factor Productivity Performance of Chinese Enterprises*", Economic Research Journal. No. 6.

Yuan Zhigang, Shao Ting (2010), "*The Historic Position, Function and Further Reform of SOE*", Academic Monthly, No. 1.

Zhang Juwei, Zhang Shibin (2010), "*Changes in Primary Income Distribution and Resulting Problems: A View of Labor Share in GDP*", Chinese Journal of Population Science, No. 5.

Zhang Juwei, Zhang Shibin (2012), "*The Change of China's Labor Share: Non-stylized Fact and an Explanation*", Population and Development, No. 4.

Acemoglu, Daron (2003), "*Labor–and Capital–Augmenting Technical Change*", Journal of the European Economic Association, Vol.1, No.3, pp.1-37.

Bentolina, S., and G.Saint-Paul (2003), "*Explaining Movements in Labor Share*", The B.E.Journal of Macroeconomics, Vol.3, No.1, pp.9-30.

Coase, R.H. (1937), *"The Nature of the Firm"*, Economica, Vol.4, No.16, pp.386-405.

Harrison, A.E. (2002), *"Has Globalization Eroded Labor's Share Some Cross-Country Evidence"*, UC-Berkeley and NBER Working Paper, October.

Jensen, M.C. &W.H. Meckling (1976), *"Theory of the Firm: Managerial Behavior, Agency Costs and Ownership Structure"*, Journal of Financial Economics, Vol.14, No.3, pp.305-360.

Chapter VII

Gan Li (2013), *"Income Gap from Chinese Household Financial Survey"*, Journal of Translation from Foreign Literature of Economics, No. 4.

Li Shi (2004), *"A Review of Income Inequality in China"*, The Research Institute of Economics of CASS Working Paper.

Liu Shangxi (2012), *"Major Vein of Doubling per Capita Income for Urban and Rural Residents: Reconstruct the Relationship among State, Enterprises, and Residents"*, Reform, No. 11.

Liu Shucheng (2011), *"The Analysis of China's Economic Growth and Fluctuation in 2011 and the Twelfth Five-year Plan Period"*, Economic Perspectives, No. 7.

Meng Xin (2004), *"China's Economic Reform and Urban Income Gap"*, in *The Price of Economic Transformation* (ed.) Li Shi, Hiroshi Sato. Beijing: China Financial and Economic Press.

Su Hainan (2012), *" Not Far From Income Doubling"*, Human Resources, No. 12.

Tian Weimin (2008), *"A Study on the Optimal Share of Residents' Income Based on China's Economic Growth during 1978-2006"*, Contemporary Finance and Economics, No. 6.

Zhang Juwei (2012), *"The Changes in the Share of Chinese Labor Compensation and Estimation and Analysis of the Overall Level of Wages"*,

Economic Perspectives, No. 9.

Zhang Juwei, Zhao Wen (2014), *"Should Wage be Increased?--Observation on Changes of Employee's Compensation in China"*, in Analysis on the Prospect of China's Economy (2014). Beijing: Social Sciences Academic Press (China).

Chapter VIII

Cai Fang, Wang Meiyan (2009), *"Why Labor Mobility has not Narrowed the Income Gap between City and the Countryside"*, Economic Perspectives, No. 8.

Bourgignon, Francois, M. Fournier, and M. Gurgrand (1998), *"Distribution, Development, and Education: Taiwan, 1979-1994"*, Paper presented at LACEA Conference, Buenos Aires.

Cai Fang, Du Yang, Zhao Changbao (2007), *"Regional Labour Market Integration since China's World Trade Organization Entry: Evidence from Household-level Data"*, in Garnaut, Ross and Song Ligang (eds) China-Linking Markets for Growth, Canberra: Asia Pacific Press, pp.133-150.

Du Yang, Wang Meiyan (2010), *"Discussion on Potential Bias and Implications of Lewis Turning Point"*, China Economic Journal, Vol.3, No.3.

Fields, Gary S. (1998), *"Accounting for Income Inequality and its Change"*, Mimeo, Cornell University.

Morduch, Jonathan and Terry Sicular (2002), *"Rethinking Inequality Decomposition, with Evidence from Rural China"*, Economic Journal, Vol.112, No.476, pp.93-106.

Park, Albert (2007), *"Rural-Urban Inequality in China"*, in Shahid Yusuf and Tony Saich(eds) China Urbanizes: Consequences, Strategies, and Policies, the World Bank,Washington.D.C..

Ravallion, Martin and Shaohua Chen (1999), *"When Economic Reform is Faster than Statistical Reform: Measuring and Explaining Income Inequality in Rural China"*, Oxford Bulletin of Economics and Statistics, Vol.61, No.1, pp.33-56.

Shorrocks, Anthony F. (1982) *"Inequality Decomposition by Factor Components"*, Econometrica, Vol.50 , No.1, pp.193-211.

Chapter IX

Yang Fei, Liu Pengfei (2008), *"An Analysis of Economics on Informal employment of Migrant Workers in Urban"*, Economic Research Guide, No. 14.

ILO (1972), *Employment, Income and Equity: A Strategy for Increasing Productive Employment in Kenya, Geneva*.

ILO (1993), *Resolution Concerning Statistics of Employment* in *the Informal Sector*, http://www.ilo.org/global/statistics-and-databases/standards-and-guidelines/resolutions-adopted-by-international-conferences-of-labour-statisticians/WCMS_087484/lang—en/index.htm.

ILO (2003), Guideline Concerning a Statistical Definition of Informal Employment, http://www.ilo.org/global/statistics-and-databases/standards-and-guidelines/guidelines-adopted-by-international-conferences-of-labour-statisticians/WCMS_087622/lang—en/index.htm.

Mincer, J. (1974) , *Schooling, Experience and Earning*, New York: Columbia University Press for the National Bureau of Economic Research.

OECD (2004), *Employment Outlook*, http: //www.oecd.org/dataoecd/36/19/43244453.

Oaxaca (Ronald (1973), *"Male-Female Wage Differentials in Urban Labor Market"*, International Economic Review, Vol.14, No.3, pp.693-709.

Chapter X

Cai Fang (2010), *"The Lewis Turning Point and the Reorientation of Public Policies: Some Stylized Facts of Social Protection in China"*, Social Science in China, No. 6.

Li shi, Luo Chuliang (2007), *"Re-estimating the Income Gap between Urban and Rural Households in China*", Journal of Philosophy and Social Sciences, Peking University, No. 2.

Li Zhi (2011), *"The Impact of Social Security Expenditure on the Urban-Rural Residents' Income Gap"*, Contemporary Economics, No. 5.

Tao Jikun (2008), *"Social Security System and Urban-Rural Income Gap"*, Lanzhou Xuekan, No. 12.

Tao Jikun (2010), *"A Comparative Analysis of Income Disparity Adjustment Systems of Western Countries"*, Contemporary Economic Research, No. 9.

Wang Shaoguang (2012), *The Income Inequality in Hongkong*, in Jinjun Xue (ed.) Economic Growth and Income Distribution. Beijing: Social Sciences Academic Press (China).

Wang Xiaolu, Fan Gang (2005), *"Income Inequality in China and Its Influential Factors"*, Economic Research Journal. No. 10.

Xiang Ling (2002), *"Social Security and Income Distribution"*, Journal of Hunan Business College, No. 5.

Yang Cuiying (2004), *"On the Difference and Coordination of the Social Security System in the Urban and Rural Areas of China"*, Journal of Zhejiang University, Humanities and Social Sciences, No. 3.

Zhang Jihai (2008), *"China's Social Security System and Residents' Income Distribution"*, Journal of Educational Institute of Jilin Province, No. 4.

Zhao Guizhi, Wang Yanping (2010), *"The Role of China's Social Security System in Adjusting the Secondary Distribution of Income: the Theoretical and Practical Analysis"*, China Business and Market, No. 5.

Zhao Haoran (2010), *"The Interactive Mechanism between Social Security and Income Distribution"*, Knowledge Economy, No. 5.

Zheng Gong-cheng (2010), *"On Income Distribution and Social Security"*, Heilongjiang Social Sciences, No. 5.

Ervik, R. (1998), *"The Redistributive Aim of Social Policy: A Comparative Analysis of Taxes, Tax Expenditure Transfers and Direct Transfers in Eight Countries"*, Luxembourg Income Study Working Paper, No.184.

Jesuit, D. and V. Mahler (2004), *"State Redistribution in Comparative Perspective: A Cross-National Analysis of the Developed Countries"*, Luxembourg Income Study Working Paper, No.392.

Chapter XI

Cai Fang (2008), *Lewis Turning Point: A Coming New Stage of China's Economic Development*. Beijing: Social Sciences Academic Press (China).

Cai Fang, Du Yang (2003), *"Destructive Effects of 'Cultural Revolution' on Physical and Human Capital"*, China Economic Quarterly, No. 4.

Xie Zengyi (2008), *"The Minimum Wage Law in the UK: What China can Learn"*, Journal of Graduate School of Chinese Academy of Social Sciences, No. 6.

Abowd, John M., Francis Kramarz, Thomas Lemieux and David N. Margolis (2000), *"Minimum Wages and Youth Employment in France and the United States"*, in David G.Blanchflower and Richard B.Freeman (ed.), *Youth Employment and Joblessness in Advanced Countries*. Chicago, University of Chicago Press.

Bernard Gernigon, Alberto Odero and Horacio Guido （2000）, *"ILO Principles Concerning, ILO Principles Concerning Collective Bargaining"*, International Labour Review, 139 (1), pp.33-55.

Keune, Maarten (2008), *"Introduction: Wage Moderation, Decentralization of Collective Bargaining and Low Pay"*, in Maarten Keune and BélaGalgóczi (ed.), Wages and Wage Bargaining in Europe. Brussels: ETUI-REHS.

The World Bank (2011), *"Productivity Linked Wage System"*, Progress Report, Washington, D.C., The World Bank.

Toke S. Aidt and Zafiris Tzannatos (2002), *"Trade Unions, Collective Bargaining and Macroeconomic Performance: A Review"*, Industrial Relations Journal, 39 (4): pp.258-295.

Zenglein, Max (2007), *"US Wage Determination System"*, Working Paper of the Institute of Management Berlin at the Berlin School of Economics (FHW Berlin),

No.32.

Chapter XII

Angus Maddison (2003), *The World Economy: A Millennial Perspective*, Trans. by Harry X. Wu et. al. Beijing: Peking University Press.

Chong'En Bai, Zhenjie Qian (2009), *"Factor Income Share in China: The Story behind the Statistics"*, Economic Research Journal, No. 3.

Cai Fang (2010), *"Demographic Transition, Demographic Dividend, and Lewis Turning Point in China"*, Economic Research, No. 4.

Luo Changyuan, Zhang Jun (2009), *"Labor Income Share and Economic Development: An Empirical Study Based on Chinese Industry-level Data"*, Social Sciences in China, No. 4.

Yujiro Hayami, Yoshihisa Godo (2009), *Development Economics: From the Poverty to the Wealth of Nations*, Transl. by Li Zhou. Beijing: Social Sciences Academic Press(China).

Simon Kuznets (1973), *Economic Growth of Nations*, Transl. by Chang Xun. Beijing: The Commercial Press.

Zhang Juwei, Cheng Jie (2013), *"Problems of Income Distribution and Capitalization of Productive Factors--where is the Key to Income Distribution problems in China?"*, Economic Perspectives, No. 3.

Zhang Juwei (2012), *"The Changes in the Share of Chinese Labor Compensation and Estimation and Analysis of the Overall Level of Wages"*, Economic Perspectives, No. 9.

Abramovitz, M. (1993), *"The Search for the Sources of Growth: Area of Ignorance, Old and New"*, Journal of Economic History, Vol.53.

Allen, R.C. (2005), *"Capital Accumulation, Technological Change, and the Distribution of Income during the British Industrial Revolution"*, Department of Economics, Oxford University, Working Paper.

Crafts, N.F.R. and C.K.Harley (1992), *"Output Growth and the British*

Industrial Revolution: A Restatement of the Crafts-Harley View", The Economic History Review, Vol.45, No.4.

Crafts, N.F.R. (1985), *British Economic Growth during the Industrial Revolution*. New York: Oxford University Press.

Denison, E.F. (1958), "*A Note on Private Saving*", The Review of Economics and Statistics, Vol.40, No.3.

Feinstein, C.H. (1981), "*Capital Accumulation and the Industrial Revolution*", The Industrial Revolution in Britain II , edited by Julian Hoppit and E.A.Wrigley. Oxford: Blackwell Publisher.

Goos, M., M.Alan, S.Anna (2010), "*Explaining Job Polarization in Europe: The Roles of Technology, Globalization and Institutions*", The London School of Economics and Political Science, CEP Working Paper, No. 1026.

Harrison, A. E. (2002), "*Has Globalization Eroded Labor's Share? Some Cross-Country Evidence*", UC- Berkeley and NBER Working Paper.

International Monetary Fund (2007), *World Economic Outlook: Globalization and Inequality*, October.

Kaldor, N. (1957), "*A Model of Economic Growth*", Economic Journal, Vol.57.

Kaldor, N. (1961), "*Capital Accumulation and Economic Growth.*", In The Theory of Capital, edited by Friedrich A.Lutz and Douglas C.Hague. New York: St.Martin's Press.

Krueger, A. (1999), "*Measuring Labor's Share*", The American Economic Review, Vol.89, No.2.

Kuznets,S. (1955), "*Economic Growth and Income Inequality*", The American Economic Review, Vol. 45, No.1.

Kuznets,S. (1973), "*Modern Economic Growth: Findings and Reflections*", The American Economic Review, Vol.63.

Lewis, A. (1954), "*Economic Development with Unlimited Supply of Labor*", The Manchester School, Vol.22.

Lindert, P.H.and J.G.Williamson (1983), "*English Workers' Living Standards during the Industrial Revolution: A New Look*", The Economic History Review,

Vol.36.

Minami, R. (1968), *"The Turning Point in the Japanese Economy"*, Quarterly Journal of Economics, Vol.82.

Piketty, T. (2014), *Capital in the Twenty-first Century*. Cambridge, MA: Belknap Press.

Robinson, S. (1976), *"A Note on the U Hypothesis Relating Income Inequality and Economic Development"*, American Economic Review, Vol.66.

Solow, R.M. (1956), *"A Contribution to the Theory of Economic Growth"*, Quarterly Journal of Economics, Vol.70, No.1.

Schultz, T.W. (1962), *"Reflections on Investment in Man"*, Journal of Political Economy, Vol.70.

Tuzemen, D.and J. Willis (2012), *"The Vanishing Middle: Job Polarization and Workers' Response to the Decline in Middle-Skill Jobs"*, Federal Reserve Bank of Kansas City, Economic Review, First Quarter.

Williamson, J. (1985), *Did British Capitalism Breed Inequality?* London: Allen & Unwin.

This book is the result of a co-publication agreement between China Social Sciences Press (China) and Paths International Ltd (UK)

This book is published with financial support from the Chinese Fund for the Humanities and Social Sciences.

Title: A Study of Income Distribution in China
Authors: Cai Fang, Zhang Juwei et al.
Translated by Wen Yayun
ISBN: 978-1-84464-670-8
Ebook ISBN: 978-1-84464-671-5

Paths International Ltd
www.pathsinternational.com
Published in the United Kingdom

CPSIA information can be obtained
at www.ICGtesting.com
Printed in the USA
LVHW061254280522
719864LV00002B/3

9 781844 646708